P9-DTC-306

THE NECESSITY FOR CHOICE

THIS BOOK WAS WRITTEN UNDER THE AUSPICES OF THE
CENTER FOR INTERNATIONAL AFFAIRS, HARVARD UNIVERSITY

BY THE SAME AUTHOR:

NUCLEAR WEAPONS AND FOREIGN POLICY

A WORLD RESTORED: Castlereagh, Metternich
and the Restoration of Peace, 1812-1822.

THE
NECESSITY
FOR
CHOICE

★ ★ ★

Prospects of American Foreign Policy

by

HENRY A. KISSINGER

HARPER & BROTHERS, PUBLISHERS   NEW YORK

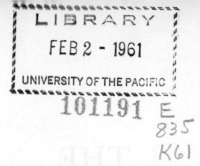

LIBRARY

FEB 2 - 1961

UNIVERSITY OF THE PACIFIC

101191 E
835
K61

THE NECESSITY FOR CHOICE

Copyright © 1960, 1961 by Henry A. Kissinger

Printed in the United States of America

All rights in this book are reserved.
No part of the book may be used or reproduced
in any manner whatsoever without written per-
mission except in the case of brief quotations
embodied in critical articles and reviews. For
information address Harper & Brothers
49 East 33rd Street, New York 16, N. Y.

FIRST EDITION

M-K

Library of Congress catalog card number: 61-6187

2-5-61

To My Parents

CONTENTS

PREFACE

This book is my attempt to point out some of the major issues which confront American foreign policy in one of the most critical periods of American history. I have tried to state the alternatives and my own conclusions. Inevitably, this involves disagreeing with the views of some men I greatly respect. I have sought to sum up these views fairly—though it is possible that my own convictions have caused me to overlook aspects which they would have liked to see included. In some instances—especially with respect to the political development of the emergent nations—I have confined myself to describing what I take to be a serious problem even though no comprehensive solution has occurred to me. It is unfortunately easier to think of problems than of remedies. But equally, a difficulty must be recognized before it can be dealt with.

Though the book is published under the auspices of the Center for International Affairs of Harvard University, I alone am responsible for its content or conclusions. At the same time, I am grateful for the opportunity afforded to me by the Center for International Affairs. Its program combines to an extraordinary degree a stimulus for research and a forum for testing ideas. Each year a group of carefully selected senior civil servants from all over the world spends a year at the Center participating in its seminars and conducting research of its own. I have profited enormously from the opportunity to exchange ideas with those experienced and thoughtful men. In addition, the research programs at the Center have stimulated many a train of thought. Finally, I have had the benefit of frequent conversations with my colleagues, Robert Bowie, the Director of the Center, Edward Mason, and Thomas Schelling. Mr. Bowie also read the chapters on strategy and made many incisive comments.

The Center for International Affairs, in addition to its formal program, acts on occasion as a focal point for the discussion of contemporary issues through a series of informal seminars composed of members of the faculty of Harvard University and the Massachusetts Institute of Technology, as well as of other interested persons in the Boston area. I have had the advantage of participating in the discussion of a group on arms control composed of the following members: Robert Bowie, Saville Davis, Max F. Millikan, Thomas Schelling, Arthur Schlesinger, Jr., Marshall Shulman, Jerome Wiesner, Jerrold Zacharias. I am grateful to my colleagues in this group for many challenging ideas. I am unhappy about the fact that some of my conclusions, especially with respect to nuclear testing, may pain them.

I have profited not only from the program of the Center for International Affairs, but also from the assistance which it gives its faculty members by easing their research and administrative burdens. George Kelly has been a most thoughtful research assistant. The chapters on Negotiations and Arms Control in particular owe much to his collection of materials and to his sharp insights. He has also made innumerable helpful comments on the other chapters.

Elissa Norris has been a devoted and enormously efficient secretary, research assistant, and copy editor. Without her cheerful help this book would have been delayed for months.

Max Hall, Editor for Publications for the Center, has struggled heroically with my involved syntax. His assistance has been invaluable.

Maury Feld, the librarian of the Center, has been most helpful in collecting materials and checking references.

I must say a word about two other institutions which have given me encouragement and support: the Carnegie Corporation of New York and the Council on Foreign Relations.

It is customary to express gratitude to a foundation for investing financial resources. I would like to take this opportunity to thank the Carnegie Corporation for a subtler, more difficult, and even more helpful contribution: a heavy investment of intellectual resources. John Gardner, the President of the Carnegie Corporation, and James Perkins, the Vice President, have been constant sources of inspiration and intellectual support. Their interest, advice and unfailing kindness have meant a great deal to me.

Five years ago, the Council on Foreign Relations gave me my first opportunity to work systematically on problems of foreign policy. My relations with it have remained close and my admiration for it has, if anything, increased. The combination of practical experience and scholarly standards supplied by its study groups is, in my opinion, unique. In 1958-59 I had the privilege of acting as research secretary for a discussion group on Political and Strategic Problems of Deterrence which was chaired by James Perkins. Its members were: Frank Altschul, Robert Amory, Major General Charles H. Bonesteel, John Fischer, James B. Fisk, Hon. William C. Foster, H. Rowan Gaither, Jr., Lt. General John K. Gerhart, Roswell Gilpatric, Caryl Haskins, Townsend Hoopes, Klaus Knorr, Rear Admiral William Miller, Hans Morgenthau, Courtland Perkins, Hon. Dean Rusk, and Albert Wohlstetter. The chapters on strategy in this book owe a great deal to the work of this group. In fairness to the members I must point out that they are not responsible for my conclusions. No memoranda of mine were circulated and no chapters were actually shown to them.

A number of others have contributed to my thinking or have offered valuable assistance:

Caryl Haskins' friendship and his penetrating criticism have been perhaps the greatest single influence on me. Dr. Haskins has read the entire manuscript and has made many extraordinarily wise comments.

Philip Quigg has read the entire manuscript. Whatever coherence or force it may have is due largely to his precise criticism and his fine editorial hand.

Donald Brennan has made very useful comments on portions of the arms control chapter.

Stephen Graubard has read portions of the manuscript and allowed me to discuss many of my ideas with him.

My wife, Ann, was patient and cheerful through the difficult months of writing. Her support and encouragement have made this book possible.

Portions of this book have appeared in *Foreign Affairs, The Reporter, Harper's Magazine,* and *Daedalus,* the journal of the American Academy of Arts and Sciences.

Of course, the inadequacies of this book are my own.

HENRY A. KISSINGER

I

THE NECESSITY FOR CHOICE

As THE twentieth century enters its seventh decade, America has reached a turning point in its relations with the rest of the world. The patterns of action of a secure past no longer work. We have come to the end of the policies and of the men that dominated the immediate post-war period. Whatever aspect of American foreign policy we consider, the need for new departures is apparent. The issues which have gone unresolved for a decade no longer permit delay. At every turn America confronts directly and urgently the necessity for choice.

The nature of the challenge can be stated as follows: the United States cannot afford another decline like that which has characterized the past decade and a half. Fifteen years more of a deterioration of our position in the world such as we have experienced since World War II would find us reduced to Fortress America in a world in which we had become largely irrelevant.

It is futile now to debate the causes of this state of affairs. Many of the misconceptions of the immediate post-war period were no doubt inevitable. Without them, we could not have endured psychologically the pressures and tensions of the Cold War. We would never have known whether a more trusting policy might not have succeeded. Nor has the period under discussion been without great achievements. The Marshall Plan, NATO, Point Four, the decision to enter the Korean war, were major acts of statesmanship. Measured against our historical experience, we can even be said to have done rather well.

But our performance will not be judged ultimately by such standards. Relative achievements are small comfort in the present

1

world. Our period offers no prizes for having done rather well. Nothing is more difficult for Americans to understand than the possibility of tragedy. And yet nothing should concern us more. For all the good will, for all the effort, we can go the way of other nations which to their citizens probably seemed just as invulnerable and eternal.

Our margin of survival has narrowed dangerously. But we still do have a margin. The possibility of choice remains thus. We can still shape our future. The prerequisite, however, is that we give up our illusions. We are not omnipotent. We are no longer invulnerable. The easy remedies have all been thought of. We must be prepared to face complexity. Above all, we must not delude ourselves about the gravity of our position.

To grasp the measure of our decline we need only compare the world in which we find ourselves with that which existed at the end of World War II. We were then the strongest nation in the world, in possession of an atomic monopoly, secure, confident, victorious. Communism ruled in but one country, which was desolated by war. The East European nations were in the process of being strangled, but even there the outcome did not seem foreordained. As colonialism began to crumble, a surge of hope went through parts of the world which had been dormant for centuries. And almost everywhere, the new nations looked towards the West—and particularly to the United States—for inspiration and assistance.

The rapidity with which these conditions have passed marks our period as an age of revolution. Our atomic monopoly has ended. We have to live with the consciousness that our survival and that of mankind can be jeopardized by a single attack lasting perhaps an hour. Eastern Europe is enslaved. China is lost to the cause of freedom. Everywhere Communism presses aggressively on its peripheries. The new nations, unsure of their own proper direction, uneasily seek to balance the two power centers against one another. The early enthusiasm of independence has all too often been replaced by frustration and doubt. Our leadership is being questioned even by our allies. Our actions lack assurance.

The very shape of the debate defines the crisis: Is there or is there not a missile gap? Is Communism gaining ground in the underdeveloped nations? Is there any hope for democracy in the new nations? Is NATO still meaningful a decade after its inception? Whatever the answers, the questions are a testimony to the deterioration of our position. When our ability to survive is being doubted, when Communist penetration has become a major concern even in the Western Hemisphere, when we enter negotiations with an agenda almost every item of which was placed there by Communist pressure or initiative, only self-delusion can keep us from admitting our decline to ourselves.

Of course, much of the deterioration was inevitable. We could not expect to perpetuate indefinitely the fortunate accident of the security conferred by two great oceans. It was one of history's cruel jokes that the atomic age, which was to make us totally vulnerable, was ushered in by a brief period which seemed to demonstrate that we were forever totally secure. But though we could not have maintained our traditional invulnerability, it was not foreordained that we should become so defensive and so insecure. It was not inevitable that all over the world peoples would find less and less in America with which to identify themselves. They may admire our achievements, but we have not succeeded in making either our values or our accomplishments seem applicable to their tasks.

Our dilemma is made more intractable because our foreign policy has been bi-partisan in the deepest sense. Over the decade of the 1950's one looks in vain for any fundamental criticism of the main trends in American policy. No Churchill or De Gaulle has hurled warnings or offered alternatives. It is difficult to remember even what some of the so-called great debates were about. Such criticism as has been offered was frequently tactical or *ex post facto*. The fatuous diplomacy which preceded the abortive summit meeting of 1960 in Paris went largely unchallenged until its failure became apparent. But the test of statesmanship is the adequacy of its evaluation *before* the event. A democracy, to be vital, requires leaders willing to stand alone.

For all innovation spells loneliness. Creativity invariably involves doing the unfamiliar. It requires a willingness to leave behind what is generally understood. When rapid change is occurring, in technology, in political structures, in human aspirations, creativity presupposes a willingness to alter even the seemingly successful. Rarely before—and never in our history—has every accomplishment so much contained the seeds of its own failure or every advance so threatened to turn into a roadblock.

Whatever aspect of policy is considered, the need for new departures is apparent. It is not so much that we confront unsolved problems—in a world of revolutionary change this could hardly be otherwise. It is rather that in many areas of policy we lack yardsticks by which to judge our alternatives or the "progress" which is being so insistently demanded.

In the field of national security, we have rigidly pursued patterns which may have been adequate when they were developed but which have become dangerously dated in the interval. Militarily, we are best prepared for the kind of war most inconsistent with our values, our tradition, and indeed our national policy: a surprise attack against the Soviet Union. We are not nearly as ready to withstand a surprise attack ourselves, even less to resist local aggression. Fifteen years after the advent of the nuclear age we still cling to the strategy of World War II: the bombardment of enemy centers of population. We have not yet settled the relative emphasis to be given to nuclear or conventional weapons, all-out or limited war. As a result, each crisis forces us to improvise a response under the pressure of events. Temptations for Communist pressure multiply.

Because we lack a strategic doctrine and a coherent military policy, it is inevitable that our proposals on arms control are fitful. We are in no position to know whether a given plan enhances security, detracts from it, or is simply irrelevant. As a consequence, proposals are developed as a compromise between competing groups and without an over-all sense of purpose. Instead of urging disarmament conferences because we wish to advance a scheme in which we have confidence, we have reversed the process: typically we have been forced to assemble a set of hasty proposals because we have agreed to go to a conference under the pressure of world opinion or Soviet diplomacy. The confusion is demonstrated by the fact that, though our military establishment is built around nuclear weapons, our arms control negotiations have stigmatized the strategy on which we have been relying. To conduct both policies simultaneously is clearly disastrous.

NATO, the cornerstone of our foreign policy, has not been adapted to changed strategic and political relationships. The role of the military forces in Europe, the future of Germany, the nature of Atlantic relationships, have all gone largely undefined. Formal declarations of unity cannot obscure the confusion within the alliance. The diplomacy prior to the abortive summit conference of 1960 was characterized by indecision and squabbling among the principal partners, each of which made a separate approach to the Soviet dictator. Mr. Khrushchev's intransigence at Paris caused these fissures to be papered over. Yet the malaise is deep-seated. Unless NATO overcomes its evasions, the confusion and disarray which followed Mr. Khrushchev's Berlin ultimatum will surely be repeated.

The situation is no more reassuring in the diplomatic field. Instead of debating the goals of diplomacy, attention has been focused for several years on a fruitless controversy over whether we should be "conciliatory" or "tough," "flexible" or "rigid." The fact is, however, that the periods of so-called flexibility have been as barren as those of "rigidity." The reluctance to confront the Communists diplomatically had the consequence of eroding the cohesion of the free world and of enabling the Communists to appear as the advocates of peace. But the excursion into a flexibility identified with personal diplomacy ended with American prestige at an unprecedented low and with Soviet negotiators treating their opposite numbers from the West with brutal contempt. No middle ground has been discovered between a frozen attitude seemingly fearful of diplomatic contact and a kind of diplomacy which becomes a means of evading all difficult choices.

And our response to the anti-colonial upheaval has been similarly inadequate. True, we have extended economic and military assistance on a fairly substantial scale. But much of our foreign aid program has been characterized by a kind of nostalgia for the Marshall Plan and the New Deal. We have never faced up to the fundamental difference between the needs of the West—for example the need for economic assistance in Europe or for enlightened social policies in the United States—and the problems of the emerging nations. In the West, the political and social framework was basically stable. The chief danger was the economic dislocation caused by war or depression. Economic and social programs by removing discontent also permitted the political and social order to be stabilized. But in the new nations the gap between expectations and reality is coupled with the absence of a political structure. Economic programs by themselves are empty if they do not involve also an act of political construction. Indeed, economic assistance, to the extent that it is effective, must subvert the existing largely feudal or tribal order. Many of the new nations lack the institutions or the traditions identified with democracy in the West. Their forms of government all too frequently place a premium on demagoguery and encourage the emergence of some form of Caesarism. Our responsibility is not simply to raise the standard of living of the new nations but to make our belief in freedom and human dignity relevant to their special conditions.

Equally worrisome is our interpretation of the process in which we find ourselves engaged. Throughout a decade of almost continuous decline the notion that time was on our side has been at the basis of much of our policy. Our attitudes therefore have tended to remain passive. When history contains a guarantee of eventual success, survival can easily become the primary goal. Creativity, innovation, sacrifice pale before tactical considerations of dealing with day-to-day concerns. A powerful incentive exists for deferring difficult choices. It is not surprising, then, that our policies have lacked vitality and that public discussion has focused on symptoms, not causes. But it is equally clear that such attitudes doom us to sterility in a revolutionary period.

If these trends continue, the future of freedom will be dim indeed. It is difficult for Americans to visualize national disaster. Yet the outlines of what may be ahead are not too difficult to discern. Tempted by the growing disparity in power the Soviet Union will bring pressure on all surrounding areas. The loss in ideological dynamism will be more than compensated by the increasing opportunities presented by our weakness. Communist policy will alternate between protestations of peaceful intentions and spasms of intransigence designed to demoralize the West. Negotiations will turn into a kind of psychological warfare. If the West can be humiliated over a period of time, the new nations, whatever their moral preference, will consider Communism the wave of the future. The success of Moscow and Peiping will have the same kind of attraction as the accomplishments of Europe in the nineteenth century. No amount of economic assistance will avail against the conviction that the West is doomed. Considerations of national interest, of wishing to be "progressive," will bring about an accommodation to Communist wishes.

The worst need not happen, however. We can still reverse these trends if we move boldly and with conviction and if we overcome our penchant for choosing the interpretation of current trends which implies least effort. We still have the opportunity to remedy the weakness which must increasingly invite Communist pressures as the missile age develops. NATO can still be revitalized and extended. The North Atlantic group of nations is in a position to take a new initiative leading to some form of confederation. We are still able to contribute a sense of direction to the new nations and to help bring about a political framework that gives meaning to independence and content to our belief in freedom and human dignity.

As the free world gains in purpose, cohesion and safety, the Communist approach to negotiations may alter. Instead of using arms control negotiations to tempt or blackmail the West into unilateral disarmament, the Communist leaders may address themselves seriously to the problem of how to reduce the tensions inherent in an unchecked arms race. Then coexistence may become something other than a slogan. But whatever Communist purposes may be, our task is essentially the same: to define for ourselves the nature of a peace consistent with our values and adequate for our security.

To be sure, in the 1960's the goals we can set ourselves are different from those open to us a decade ago. Then we still possessed a wide margin of safety and, therefore, considerable scope for constructive action. In many areas of national policy only foresight was required to shape the future. But in the 1960's many choices which were available earlier have been foreclosed. Many relatively minor problems have become full-fledged crises. And this process will accelerate unless we change our approach to policy. The price

we will have to pay for deferring choices will go up with each passing year.

Nothing is more important for America than to give up its illusions. Too much of our domestic debate gives the impression that
we are working towards a static condition called peace. We sometimes argue as if only a single new initiative or one brilliant move
stands between us and normalcy. Many of us seem to believe that we
can dramatically sweep all before us in an atmosphere of universal
approbation.

But even with the wisest policies we can expect nothing of the
sort. Our generation will live in the midst of change. Our norm
is the fact of upheaval. The success of our actions is not measured
by short-term tranquillity. It is defined by whether we can shape
the currents of our time in the light of our values. What is needed
even more than different policies is a different style and a more
dynamic attitude.

The decade of the 1960's will require heroic effort and we will
not always have the solace of popular acclaim. Almost all the essential measures are long-term in their effect and require detailed,
patient labors. Neither in the field of military policy, nor in our
alliance policy, nor in arms control, nor in relations with the new
states can we expect dramatic results.

There is an inevitable difference in time scale between our efforts
and those of Communism. The main interest of Communism is to
prevent stability by fanning all resentments. Chaos can be produced
rapidly. Those seeking to exploit dissatisfaction need not concern
themselves with long-term effects. We, on the other hand, have a
duty to seek to construct a new set of international relationships—
a task where the rewards cannot be immediate. We must strive to
counteract the temptation to conduct policy by striking poses. We
must strive to convince those in need of assistance of our concern
but also of the need for patience and for the willingness to go
through a painful period of construction—qualities likely to be
in direct conflict with their image of themselves. And we must carry
out these measures while our security, indeed our survival, is directly and immediately menaced.

All this will make demands on us unprecedented in our history and perhaps in the history of any nation. It would be idle to pretend that all our problems are soluble or that all errors can be avoided. We can, however, attempt to clarify our choices. In our domestic debate two groups have tended to inhibit understanding even though each pays lip service to the other. While making a bow to the need for an imaginative diplomacy, one segment of opinion identifies foreign policy with the development of military power. While making obeisance to the need for security, another segment in effect equates diplomacy with negotiating skill and ascribes all our difficulties to an overconcern with military factors.

As a nation of specialists we like to believe that a problem is either political, or spiritual, or economic, or military. And we are tempted to assume that among all our challenges we must concentrate on one to the exclusion of the others. One of the most anguished students of American policy has written:

To my own countrymen who have often asked me where best to apply the hand to counter the Soviet threat, I have accordingly had to reply: to our American failings—to the things we are ashamed of in our own eyes: to the racial problem, to the conditions in our big cities, to the education and environment of our young people, to the growing gap between specialized knowledge and popular understanding. I imagine that similar answers could be found for other Western countries. I would like to add that these are problems which are not going to be solved by anything we or anyone else does in the stratosphere. If solutions are to be found for them it will be right here on this familiar earth, in the dealings among men and in the moral struggles of the individual.[1]

But the times do not permit such an order of priorities. We do not have the choice between improving ourselves and dealing with the menaces to our security. We must be willing to face the paradox that we must be dedicated both to military strength and to arms control, to security as well as to negotiation, to assisting the new nations towards freedom and self-respect without accepting their interpretation of all issues. If we cannot do *all* these things, we will not be able to do *any* of them. Our ability to master the seeming paradoxes will test even more than our ability to survive; it will be the measure of our worthiness to survive.

[1] George F. Kennan, *Russia, the Atom and the West* (New York, 1957), p. 13.

II

THE DILEMMAS OF DETERRENCE

1. The Psychology of Deterrence

In order to act with assurance in international affairs, a country must understand the requirements of its survival. Though such knowledge does not guarantee a constructive policy, no constructive policy is possible without it. A nation unsure about the circumstances that impair its safety can hardly be expected to address itself with confidence to its positive tasks. It will be torn between complacency and premonitions of catastrophe, between obsession with military security and dismissal of it. When it thinks itself in jeopardy it will act as if military security were its only problem. When the danger does not materalize immediately it will lapse into euphoria. Its measures are likely to be fitful. Its national mood will alternate between hysteria and smugness.

Such has been the experience of the United States since the end of World War II. Although we entered the nuclear age fifteen years ago, its implications for our security have remained elusive. Does the undoubted power of our nuclear arsenal prevent aggression? Or does our increasing vulnerability to Soviet attack tempt blackmail? Is the peace best preserved by threatening an aggressor with the direst retribution of which we are capable? Or should we rather seek to deter aggression by more limited means? Even more elementary questions have gone unanswered: What is the meaning of vulnerability? What are the elements of security? Lacking a clear sense of direction, we have repeated familiar shibboleths while a volatile technology has changed the very framework of strategy. As a result, with each passing year our peril has been growing even though our weapons arsenal has become more potent.

This is illustrated by the debate over our military policy during recent years. Critics of our military establishment insist that our very existence is in jeopardy. The reply is made that we have never been stronger. It is charged that we are becoming increasingly vulnerable to surprise attack. But it is also maintained that we have the capacity to destroy the Soviet Union several times over. Some argue that there is both a missile and a deterrent gap. This is refuted with the contention that, since no Communist military aggression has occurred for nearly a decade, our strategic concepts must be valid. Concern is expressed about our inferiority in missiles. The reply is that it is foolish to invest in weapons which will be obsolescent in a few years. Since our danger is permanent, so the argument goes, our military program must have "balance" over a period of time. We cannot afford peaks and valleys. Our procurement must be orderly; our replacement rate well phased.

When experts differ so completely and so violently, the attitude of the average citizen is likely to be one of resignation. How can he resolve, indeed understand, issues which seemingly require so much technical information? It is therefore difficult to mobilize public pressures for a change in military policy, particularly one that seems successful. The temptation is overwhelming to rely on the superior judgment of those in positions of responsbility.

Understanding becomes even more difficult because almost all the assertions listed above are correct. We *are* stronger than ever, but we have also never been more vulnerable. We *can* destroy the Soviet Union several times over, and yet there is serious doubt about the efficacy of deterrence. There is no question that the next family of missiles will be a drastic improvement over our current arsenal. The issue, however, is what risks we can justify until they are ready.

How can the statements of our strength and our vulnerability be simultaneously true? How is it possible that our survival is threatened at a moment when we have the capacity to destroy any aggressor several times over? The seeming contradictions are due to the nature of deterrence, the volatility of technology, and the character of the existing strategy.

The problem of deterrence is novel in the history of military policy. In the past, the military establishment was asked to prepare for war. Its test was combat; its vindication, victory. In the nuclear age, however, victory has lost its traditional significance. The *outbreak* of war is increasingly considered the worst catastrophe. Henceforth, the adequacy of any military establishment will be tested by its ability to preserve the peace.

The paradoxical consequence is that the success of military policy depends on essentially psychological criteria. Deterrence seeks to prevent a given course by making it seem less attractive than all possible alternatives. It therefore ultimately depends on an intangible quality: the state of mind of the potential aggressor. From the point of view of deterrence a seeming weakness will have the same consequences as an actual one. A gesture intended as a bluff but taken seriously is more useful as a deterrent than a bona fide threat interpreted as bluff. Deterrence requires a combination of power, the will to use it, and the assessment of these by the potential aggressor. Moreover, deterrence is a product of those factors and not a sum. If any one of them is zero, deterrence fails. Strength, no matter how overwhelming, is useless without the willingness to resort to it. Power combined with willingness will be ineffective if the aggressor does not believe in it or if the risks of war do not appear sufficiently unattractive to him.

Similar considerations affect not only the major protagonists—the United States and the U.S.S.R.—but also all other countries whose survival is threatened. If a victim of Soviet pressure comes to believe—rightly or wrongly—that the aggressor is militarily superior to the United States, it will seek an accommodation regardless of our resolve to resist. If an irresponsible smaller country believes itself protected by Communist preponderance, it may taunt or challenge the United States regardless of the "real" power relationship.

In any given situation a country may be inferior militarily but superior psychologically. It may be able to deter not because it is militarily stronger but because it values an objective highly enough —or can make its opponent believe this—so that it can make plausible a threat to exact a price its opponent is unprepared to pay. We were deterred from intervening in Hungary even though we were still militarily vastly superior because the Soviet Union convinced us—and probably without bluffing—that it would run all risks to maintain its rule. We were deterred not by the threat of defeat but because of our unwillingness to pay the price of victory.

This suggests that the debate about whether there is a deterrent gap is inherently misleading. There can be no gap in deterrence. Deterrence is either effective or it is not. There is no margin for error. Mistakes are likely to be irremediable. If the gains of aggression appear to outweigh the penalties even once, deterrence will fail.

The psychological aspect of deterrence becomes especially acute when technology is volatile. For then the truths of one year become the perils of another. Policies which were adequate at the time of their conception become obstacles to clear understanding when new conditions arise.

Thus, at the same time that the absence of aggression will create powerful pressures in favor of the prevailing military policy, a rapidly changing technology will inevitably transform the conditions which accounted for the apparent success. What makes matters worse is that there is no experience to guide those charged with the final responsibility. In the nuclear age, deterrence is importantly based on conjecture regarding the significance of unprecedented technological developments. Deterrence may then fail simply because the opponents interpret available data differently. In the absence of conclusive experience the assessment becomes more significant than the reality. Or rather, the assessment becomes the only reality.

A changing technology has brought about transformations in the strategic situation more rapidly than they could be assimilated into doctrine and policy. There have been four phases since World War II: (1) the period when the United States possessed an atomic monopoly and a monopoly on the means of delivery; (2) the period when our monopoly of weapons ended but when we still possessed an overwhelming advantage in the means of delivery; (3) the period when the Soviet Union began to develop a substantial delivery system but we still retained a decided advantage because of our superiority in numbers and the strategic location of our base system; (4) the period when both in number of weapons and in the means of delivery the capabilities of the two sides began to approach each other—indeed when in some categories the Soviet Union pulled ahead.

When defenders of the strategic doctrine of the past decade speak of our overwhelming retaliatory power, they use the categories of the first three phases of the nuclear age—the period of our strategic preponderance. As long as our strategic striking power was preponderant, we could indeed think of deterrence primarily in terms of destructive ability. Then any increase in the power of our weapons arsenal could be considered as increasing the aggressor's inhibitions. The doctrine of massive retaliation was an expression of these views. By threatening retaliation "at times and places of our choosing" it sought to prevent aggression all around the Soviet periphery. As long as we were immune to direct attack, our retaliatory power was a positive deterrent in the sense that we did not have to make our response dependent on the magnitude of the threat. Rather our primary concern was to decide that some response was called for. A strategy of devastation could be reasonably effective as long as we were so invulnerable that no doubts could arise about the willingness to resort to it.

But those who question the adequacy of our military establishment do not doubt our destructive capability. They *are* concerned that our increasing vulnerability may paralyze our will to use our power or make an aggressor believe so. Hence deterrence may fail despite our strength—and, in a curious way, perhaps because of it. No matter how vast the destructiveness of our weapons arsenal, the inhibitions against resorting to it must grow with every increase in Soviet retaliatory power—or so the aggressor may calculate. In the age of nuclear plenty and of multiplying retaliatory forces on both sides, destructiveness may be vitiated by paralysis of will or by the low credibility of the deterrent threat. A gap inevitably opens up between deterrence and the strategy we are prepared to implement should deterrence fail. The mere fact that the West constantly feels constrained to emphasize that a nuclear conflict is unthinkable may raise serious questions about its resolve to resort to the chief strategy at its disposal. Similarly none of the Western countries, though relying on the threat of nuclear retaliation to deter aggression, have taken even the most elementary steps to protect their populations against nuclear attacks—an omission hardly calculated to enhance the credibility of their deterrent threat.

This doubt will be reinforced by the experience of the period of our strategic preponderance. Long before the Soviet Union developed a nuclear capability and the means to deliver it, we had failed to resort to the doctrine of massive retaliation in the face of a considerable number of challenges. The reason was psychological, not strategic. The very enormity of our destructive capability had the paradoxical consequence of creating a threshold below which we were reluctant to commit our forces. We had in a sense deterred ourselves by the power of our deterrent arsenal. Even during our atomic monopoly we usually took great pains to insist that the particular issue then confronting us was not the one for which our nuclear arsenal was designed. This gap between our deterrent policy and the strategy for fighting a war has been accentuated with every passing year. A threat is effective only if it is believed, and a threat which cannot be brought to bear on the issues at stake loses its credibility.

Thus the phrase "we have never been stronger" is irrelevant to the concern about our ability to deter. The issue cannot be settled by comparing our present strength with that of previous years. Deterrence depends on our strength in relation to that of possible aggressors. Since what has been called *the* Deterrent—the retaliatory power—proved inadequate to deter a vast range of challenges even during the period of our nuclear preponderance, there is a serious cause for worry when the missile gap approaches. What, then, of the missile gap and the strategic problem of deterrence?

2. The Strategic Problem of Deterrence

For all the heat of the controversy, it is important to note that there is no dispute about the missile gap as such. It is generally admitted that from 1961 until at least the end of 1964 the Soviet Union will possess more missiles than the United States. The disagreement concerns the significance of this state of affairs. There are three schools of thought: (1) The Eisenhower Administration held that the diversity of our retaliatory force compensated for our inferiority in long-range missiles. The combination of airplanes, Polaris submarines and long-range missiles would continue to make the risks of aggression prohibitive for the Communist states. Hence deterrence would remain unimpaired. (2) Some critics believe that the missile gap may enable the Soviet Union to launch a surprise attack on the United States. In their view the missile gap turns into a deterrent gap. (3) A third group is of the opinion that even if the disparity in strategic striking power does not reach the point at which a Soviet surprise attack on the United States becomes possible, it will nevertheless enable the Communist states to blackmail all contiguous areas. Even after the missile gap ends, so this argument goes, our retaliatory force will no longer be able to protect major portions of the free world. The issue then turns (1) on our ability to deter all-out war and (2), assuming this problem to be solved, the ability of the threat of all-out war to deter other forms of aggression.

Turning first to the problem of deterrence, it is important to understand what considerations are involved in the decision to launch all-out war. For if a strategy of deterrence is to be effective, it must seek to overcome these motives. A country may launch an all-out war for offensive or defensive reasons. It can set out deliberately to destroy an opponent. Or it may strike in order to forestall what it believes to be an imminent attack: in other words, to destroy the opponent before being destroyed. The former is called a surprise attack; the latter a pre-emptive attack. A surprise attack is a deliberate attempt to eliminate the opposing retaliatory force—regardless of the intentions of the other side. Its motivation is aggressive. The timing is set by the attacker for the moment he considers most propitious. The motive for a pre-emptive war, by contrast, is defensive. An attack is made only as a last resort and because it is considered the only means of avoiding disaster. The timing of pre-emptive war thus depends on the opponent's measures.

In order to launch a surprise attack an aggressor requires preponderant strength and a high degree of assurance of success. No country will run the risk of annihilation if there is only a slight probability of victory. Surprise attack is thus deterred when the aggressor must calculate that, regardless of the scale of his attack, he will suffer unacceptable damage in retaliation. It is important to remember, however, that the criterion of unacceptability is the aggressor's and not the defender's. A level of damage which may seem unacceptable to us may prove bearable to the Soviet Union and even more so to Communist China. Deterrence can fail simply because the two sides have different notions of what constitutes intolerable damage. Or, put another way, deterrence will fail if the aggressor is prepared to pay a price for victory which the defender had thought too high. This alone indicates that to deter surprise attack we may have to make a bigger effort than the Communists, for probably our level of "acceptable" damage is lower than theirs.

Pre-emptive war, on the other hand, can come about even when the two sides are fairly evenly balanced. It is a result of two inter-acting factors: fear of an imminent attack and the vulnerability of the retaliatory force. If a nation's retaliatory force is highly exposed, it must live with the nightmare that a successful attack would place it at the aggressor's mercy. Hence, the less vulnerable a country's re-taliatory force the less incentive that country will have for a pre-emptive blow. The motive for a pre-emptive blow is reduced to a minimum if the retaliatory force is so well protected that it can afford to ride out an attack and still retain the capacity to inflict unacceptable damage. By the same token, such a degree of readiness will eliminate the aggressor's incentive to launch a surprise attack in the first place.

Deterrence of pre-emptive war is psychologically more compli-cated than deterrence of surprise attack. Ten million casualties may be unacceptable when a country can avoid any by maintaining the peace. But they may seem to be the lesser of two evils when the country concerned believes it must either launch an attack or receive a blow that may eliminate its striking force and produce a hundred million casualties. The level of unacceptable damage required to deter a pre-emptive attack is thus higher than that required to deter a surprise blow.

A pre-emptive attack can be deterred only by meeting two re-quirements: (1) by avoiding measures which, whatever their intent, lend themselves to being interpreted as a prelude to surprise attack and (2) by protecting the retaliatory force so well that the opponent, even if he should feel threatened, cannot substantially improve his position by striking first. In short, the greater the gap between a country's capability to inflict damage before and after suffering a sudden blow, the greater the danger of a sudden attack. The smaller the gap between a country's first- and second-strike capability, the lower will be the opponent's incentive to launch a pre-emptive blow.

The requirement of invulnerability is not easy to meet in the missile age—even with the best efforts. Indeed, the structure of the retaliatory forces may bring about an inherently pre-emptive situation. As long as these forces are composed of airplanes and stationary, liquid-fuel missiles, they will be extremely vulnerable. They represent a tremendously powerful first strike capability. Their ability to strike back is much more problematical. A very great advantage, therefore, goes to the side that launches the first blow.

When the age of nuclear plenty came into view, many commentators, including this author, considered that it ushered in a period of nuclear stalemate. It was thought then that superiority in the capacity for destruction might prove strategically insignificant because in a war between major powers the two sides would probably have destroyed each other long before the nuclear stockpiles were exhausted. All-out war would be deterred because, regardless of what damage the victim of a surprise attack might suffer, it would always be able to guarantee the destruction of the opponent. A stalemate would come about because, while all-out war could still exact a fearful toll—indeed an ever increasing one—it could no longer be used to impose a nation's will upon another.

While it remains true that a surprise attack will be deterred if the retaliatory blow threatens unacceptable damage, it has become apparent that, for an interim period at least, the strategic advantage of the offensive in missile warfare was not adequately foreseen. Given the speed and power of modern weapons and the unexpected improvements in accuracy, a missile attack may well be overwhelming. As long as the retaliatory forces were composed of airplanes, many factors had to combine for a successful attack. Airplanes would be in transit for several hours. Weather conditions might interfere. Bombing and navigational accuracy could not be fully tested under battle conditions. The defender might detect the attack and launch his force, or he might destroy a high percentage of the aggressor's planes, or both. In short, in considering whether to launch a surprise attack there would always remain a residue of uncertainty to which the cautious element in the aggressor's leadership group could appeal even in the face of seemingly foolproof staff plans.

With missiles, on the other hand, surprise attack can be prepared with a degree of certainty approaching that of an artillery barrage. Tests will have revealed the reliability and the accuracy of the missile involved. Once launched, its flight cannot be impeded except by internal malfunctions whose frequency is statistically known—at least in the absence of anti-missile defense whose feasibility many doubt and which because of the budgetary restrictions of the Eisenhower Administration cannot now come into existence until 1966. If the targets are reasonably well known—as United States stationary bases are—it becomes almost a mathematical problem to determine the number of missiles required to destroy them. Of course, this level may not be attainable in the immediate future. The fact remains that for any given force level the factor of uncertainty is likely to be less and the advantage of surprise greater with missiles than with airplanes.

Pronouncements which seek to relate deterrence to the total numbers of missiles and airplanes are highly misleading. For the side on the defensive the numbers prior to attack are essentially irrelevant. The only figure that matters is the number which can survive a sudden blow. From the point of view of deterrence, the size of our retaliatory force is less important than the number of aiming points it presents to the aggressor. Fewer airplanes and missiles which are widely dispersed may be strategically more useful than a larger force which is concentrated and highly vulnerable and whose very size may provoke a pre-emptive strike. For a very large and very vulnerable force makes sense only if a surprise attack is planned. At least, whatever the real intentions, it may be so interpreted by the opponent. It is therefore beside the point to invoke the by now well-worn cliché that one thermonuclear bomb exceeds in destructive power all the bombs dropped on Germany in five years of war. Over-all strength will deter only if enough of it can survive attack to threaten an unacceptable level of damage in retaliation *and* if it is of such a nature that an opponent does not construe it as inherently threatening.

In short, the security of our retaliatory force provides a reason for serious concern. The inferiority in missiles is not as worrisome as the vulnerability of the entire retaliatory force. By 1961 we will still have less than 75 SAC bases and these will be supplemented by perhaps 50 Atlas intercontinental missiles. These missiles will be in "soft" sites; a miss of several miles could destroy either their launching or their guidance mechanism. Moreover, the early emplacements are in clusters so that one Soviet hit will be able to destroy three of our missiles. Even when dispersal reaches the point where no more than one of our missiles can be destroyed by a Soviet missile—a condition which is not in prospect until the end of 1962—it is not too difficult to calculate the extent of our peril.

If the Soviets require four missiles to destroy one of ours or one airbase—an assumption which favors us—the total Soviet missile force required to have a high degree of probability of success of wiping out our retaliatory force would have to number around 500. General Power, commander of our retaliatory force, has estimated that 300 Soviet missiles would suffice. It would be rash to maintain that this figure is unattainable. Many serious observers argue that it is well within Soviet reach. The intelligence estimate that the Soviet Union does not possess this number may be accepted. It is nevertheless a measure of our peril if our survival has come to depend on a hundred Communist missiles more or less which can be produced reasonably rapidly and perhaps before we learn of them or are able to take countermeasures.

The peril of the defender is magnified by the nature of surprise in the missile age. The speed of missiles and the decreasing time required to launch them will soon make it possible to start an attack with almost no warning. It is unfortunate therefore that so much of our strategic thinking is still geared to the expectation of obtaining tactical warning. In the debate about the proposal to protect the Strategic Air Command by means of an airborne alert —keeping a substantial proportion of our heavy bombers constantly in the air—the Eisenhower Administration claimed that it was time enough to take such a step *after* the international situation grew tense. In short, they believed that we would always receive sufficient warning to alert our retaliatory force.

Such a view misses the essence of missile warfare. By their very nature, missiles can be launched without extensive preparation. In a few years, when solid fuel missiles become operational, they will require a count-down of less than ten minutes. In such circumstances, we can be certain that, whatever else may happen, a surprise attack will *not* be preceded by a tense situation. The last thing an aggressor would do is to alert our retaliatory force by disquieting us. There are many technical and political arguments against an airborne alert. But the possibility of obtaining warning is not one of them.

Even if warning were obtained, it is far from clear to what use it could be put as the missile age develops. When solid-fuel missiles become operational, the maximum warning available is likely to be less than fifteen minutes—during which time information must be obtained, transmitted, evaluated and acted upon. This is hardly an interval making for sober calculation. And in the missile age the penalty of acting on the basis of incorrect information is enormous. Airplanes can be launched as a defensive measure, for they can be recalled if the information turns out to be faulty. The decision to launch a missile is, however, irrevocable. The danger of accident is therefore high.

Yet the effort to reduce this risk may increase vulnerability. The more carefully and strictly warning is interpreted the less useful it may be. A country whose retaliatory force depends for its security on the ability to obtain warning will be torn between the Scylla of being too cautious and the Charybdis of being too trigger-happy. In short, in the missile age a retaliatory force cannot gear its security to the expectation of warning. It must be sufficiently invulnerable so that it can ride out an attack and still inflict unacceptable losses on the aggressor.

This has been well expressed by General Power, the Commanding General of the Strategic Air Command:

> The radars have picked up 1,000 objects. The computer says they are ballistic missiles, and they will impact in the United States.
> I have about 12 minutes left because it took him at least 3 minutes to do that.
> What am I going to do?

I can launch the alert force.

. . . I will do that without any hesitancy because I know that, if this turns out to be a spurious signal, no harm is done. . . . But in this time period we will also have a button whereby I can send the ICBM's on their way. I can press that button and send the missiles on their way.

Do I want to do it, assuming I had authority to do so? Because sure as shooting, in another 2 or 3 minutes, this lad will say, "I am sorry, but those blips have disappeared off the scope." They were sputniks, interference, or something like that. Therefore, I say the missile will have to ride out the attack.[1]

All of this suggests that for an interim period until the middle of the 1960's the design of our retaliatory force involves major risks. Its size may appear an overpowering threat to the Soviets while its vulnerability creates constant temptations to remove the source of the danger once and for all. The large gap between our first- and second-strike capability represents a powerful incentive for a sudden Soviet blow. Indeed it erodes the dividing line between surprise attack and pre-emptive war. It is quite possible that the present design of our retaliatory force may bring about a Soviet attack for reasons which the Communist leaders take to be defensive: to eliminate a retaliatory force whose dispositions make sense only as a preparation for attack.

The discussion of the strategic requirement of deterrence has led to three conclusions:

(1) *The precondition of deterrence is an invulnerable retaliatory force.* Invulnerability exists when regardless of the scale and timing of his attack an aggressor must expect unacceptable damage in retaliation. An invulnerable retaliatory force reduces the risk of accidental war. If it is able, in General Power's words, to "ride out an attack," its dependence on warning will be greatly diminished. The possibility of error is thereby greatly lessened. The strategic posture will be less tense and hair-trigger.

At the same time, the retaliatory force should be so designed that (2) *if the goal is stability, invulnerability should be sought through measures which, in so far as possible, convey a defensive*

---

[1] Hearings before the Subcommittee on Appropriations, House of Representatives, 86th Congress, 1st Session, "Department of Defense Appropriations for 1960," Part 2, Financial Statements, Field Commanders, pp. 378 and 379, 1959.

intent.[2] Invulnerability is not an absolute term. It depends on numbers, dispersal, hardening of bases and mobility of the defending retaliatory force, and similar characteristics on the part of the aggressor's striking power. Increasing the numbers of the defending force reduces vulnerability even if each individual weapon is highly vulnerable—provided dispersal enables each attacking vehicle to destroy only one defending vehicle. In that case, it may be possible simply to out-produce the opponent and to impose impossible force requirements on him.

On the other hand, the attempt to achieve invulnerability through numbers alone would lead to a highly unstable situation. For a retaliatory force of such size would represent a perhaps overwhelming first-strike capability. It may therefore be interpreted as designed for a surprise blow and tempt a pre-emptive attack. Hence whenever a choice exists, invulnerability should be sought by such measures as dispersal, hardening and, above all, mobility. These steps increase the ability to strike back. They do not improve the ability to strike first. They improve the defensive, not the offensive capacity. They enhance stability because they reduce the incentive for surprise attack without furnishing an additional motive for pre-emptive strike. Each of these measures has advantages and disadvantages.

Dispersal complicates the aggressor's task by multiplying his targets. Hardening means protecting the target against explosion by placing it in some form of shelter. Its effectiveness depends on the attacker's accuracy. Given the power of modern weapons, hardening is not a protection against an attack of sufficient precision. Nevertheless, it complicates the calculations of the aggressor and imposes additional requirements of strength and accuracy on him— thus adding to deterrence.

Perhaps the single most fruitful approach to invulnerability lies in creating a mobile deterrent system. The proposed airborne alert of the Strategic Air Command is a step in this direction. Similarly missiles should be so designed that part of our missile force is constantly shifting position. Some—such as the projected Minuteman— could be moved by rail; others by barges on rivers; still others on

[2] For further discussion see pp. 210 ff.: "The Problems of Arms Control."

coastal ships; still others in submarines. Submarines are more difficult to detect than small coastal ships, but this advantage must be weighed against the lower expense and better communications of the latter. From this point of view, the best use of airplanes is not so much to penetrate enemy territory as to provide a mobile missile launching platform. This implies a need for an airplane of moderate speed but great endurance capable of cruising perhaps for days just out of range of detection.

The function of a mobile system would be to produce the maximum degree of uncertainty in the mind of a potential aggressor about the chances of a successful attack. To the degree that the retaliatory force cannot be located it cannot be destroyed. To the extent that a potential aggressor cannot calculate with high probability that our counterblow will be reduced to "safe" limits, he will be deterred. At the same time, mobility, while adding to our ability to survive attack, does not furnish a motive for a pre-emptive blow. It improves our second-strike, not our first-strike, capability.

In describing the advantages mobility will add to our retaliatory force we must take care, however, not to identify a future prospect with present reality. Mobile land-based intercontinental missiles will not exist until 1964 at the earliest. The Polaris submarines will not join the fleet until 1961 and by the end of that year only five will be operational. For an interim period until well into 1964 the backbone of our retaliatory force must consist of airplanes and stationary missiles. In this time period, dispersal and hardening will be our primary protection. And the effort to attain both is totally inadequate at present.

Invulnerability should not be conceived as a task which, once achieved, can then be neglected. Constant effort will be required to maintain it. And it should be sought with full awareness that each method has its advantages and disadvantages. A price must be paid for each form of protection. Mobility complicates the aggressor's calculations but it also makes more difficult the defender's problem of communication and control. A sea-based system probably will be sufficiently secure so that it does not have to react to warning and can gear its response to the actuality of an attack. This reduces the risk of accidental war. On the other hand, the same factor may make it more vulnerable to attrition—the reduction of the retaliatory force through a gradual whittling away.[3] An attack on a submarine at sea is less likely to evoke all-out retaliation than a blow against a missile within the continental United States.

Hardening and dispersal avoid the problem of attrition to some extent while adding others. Dispersal, for example, raises problems of control. The larger the number of individual decision points, the greater is the chance of an act based on misinformation or overeagerness—that is, the greater is the risk of accidental war. In short, no single method should be adopted as a "cure-all." Reliance on any one approach increases the vulnerability to a technological breakthrough. Invulnerability is best assured by a "mixed" force relying on various methods of protection and control. Such a force makes it most difficult for an aggressor to calculate his chances of success. To determine the proper "mix" becomes one of the chief goals of strategy.

(3) *To maintain deterrence two dangers must be avoided. One is to consider any given strategic relationship as static. The other is to subordinate present readiness to long-term balance in procurement.*

The rapid rate of technological change would threaten to upset any apparent equilibrium. Even highly mobile and well-dispersed retaliatory forces could be overcome by new developments. Improved anti-submarine measures could make the sea-based retaliatory force vulnerable to attrition. Advances in guidance or in the warheads of missiles could overcome almost any conceivable hardening. Successful defense against missiles could give one side a decisive advantage. Any balance will be precarious. In the absence of comprehensive, inspected arms control—and perhaps even with it—the most stable strategic relationship may prove ephemeral.

The difficulty of keeping up in the technological race is magnified by our adoption of the strategic defensive—a position dictated by our value system. For the side which is on the defensive must *constantly* be prepared. Any weakness, however temporary, may tempt attack. Homilies such as "Be not the first by which the new is tried nor yet the last to lay the old aside"[4] totally misinterpret

---

[3] See p. 43.
[4] Pres. Eisenhower, Press Conference, Dec. 4, 1959, quoted in the *New York Times*, Dec. 5, 1959.

the requirements imposed on us by the decision to concede the first blow. The aggressor can afford to build towards a target date. He may skip a family of weapons and concentrate on a new development—as the Soviet Union did when it decided not to build up its long-range bomber fleet and to emphasize missiles instead. The defender, by contrast, can deter only if he is ready at every moment of time. Here long-range planning is meaningful only if it also produces *instant* readiness. The aggressor can risk a temporary weakness, for the choice of opening hostilities depends on him. For the defender any unbalance, however temporary in design, may prove fatal. A stress on balance, on stretching out procurement, on awaiting new technological developments at the cost of present readiness, can be disastrous.

Under the best of circumstances, then, the missile age will pose grave tasks and serious perils. The missile gap in the period 1961-1965 is now unavoidable. Lead-times of modern equipment are so long that even should we change course immediately we could narrow the gap but not close it. If our retaliatory force remains highly vulnerable or if the Soviet Union produces more missiles than now appears likely, the Soviet Union could be tempted to launch a surprise attack. Even if surprise attack were avoided, we could provoke a pre-emptive attack by the design of our retaliatory force. We could be subjected to a pre-emptive attack also if we continue to rely on the threat of all-out war to deter all forms of Soviet blackmail. For then in a crisis—perhaps one not even directly provoked by the U.S.S.R. such as the revolution in Iraq—our threat, if taken seriously, might cause the Soviet leaders to believe that they have no recourse other than to strike first.

These problems should not be ascribed entirely or even largely to the missile gap. The missile gap does not so much change strategic relationships as make them explicit. It speeds up what technology would have made inevitable in any case: the decreasing utility of the threat of all-out war as deterrence for an ever wider range of challenges. Even if the Eisenhower Administration were correct in its assumption that the missile gap will not lead to a Soviet surprise attack—and no Administration would deliberately stake the fate of the country—fundamental security problems would remain.

Overcoming the vulnerability of our retaliatory force is the condition of security policy. It cannot be its sole aim. For an invulnerable retaliatory force will bring us face to face with the issue we have avoided for nearly a decade: the relation between deterrence and strategy should deterrence fail. Nothing could be more dis-astrous for a new Administration than to patch up present flaws while continuing to beg all principal questions.

3. The Design of the Deterrent Force

A. Counterforce or Finite Deterrence

The most fundamental problem concerns the purpose of our retaliatory force; specifically, what actions is it supposed to deter and by what methods? The attempt to answer this question has produced a debate between adherents of what has been termed *counterforce strategy* and proponents of what has come to be known as *finite deterrence*. The issue turns on the nature of the threat which produces deterrence: whether the primary goal of the deterrent force should be the elimination of the opposing military establishment or whether the proper target is the aggressor's war-making potential and civilian population.

Proponents of a counterforce strategy argue that deterrence requires not only the prospect of damage to industry and civilian population but also of military defeat. Consequently, the primary target must be the opponent's striking force. Once this is crushed, victory is assured. A counterforce strategy therefore requires a retaliatory force so large and so well protected that it can guarantee the destruction of the opponent's offensive power. As the opposing missile force grows, ours has to multiply correspondingly and at a ratio which maintains the possibility of victory. In the age of nuclear plenty and of mobile missiles, the force requirements of a counterforce strategy are likely to become astronomical.

The major difficulty with the notion of a counterforce strategy is that it is almost impossible to reconcile with the adoption of the strategic defensive. If we concede the first blow, an all-out war will start with what under the best of circumstances must amount to catastrophic damage. In that case, the destruction of the opposing striking force may become impossible, because part of our retaliatory force will be destroyed and because the aggressor's missiles will no longer be at their launching sites. In these circumstances, the best possible outcome will probably be a stalemate through a deliberate effort to destroy the aggressor's national substance. Short of an extraordinary technological breakthrough, victory in an all-out war can be achieved only through surprise attack.

Arguments such as these have led many thoughtful individuals to the conclusion that our retaliatory force should be designed not so much to destroy the strategic power of the opponent as to threaten his social substance. Our only options, it is said, are to deter by threatening the aggressor with catastrophe or to inflict devastation if deterrence fails. By conceding the first blow, so the argument goes, we have also conceded the possibility of achieving victory. Against the background of limited military budgets, many have come to the conclusion that the resources devoted to developing a capability to win an all-out war would be better expended on other forms of preparedness. Instead of embarking on the elusive effort to achieve a counterforce capability, it is said, we should develop a well-protected striking force which is able to exact whatever level of damage is likely to be considered unacceptable according to the Soviet value system. The proponents of finite deterrence hold that the retaliatory force need not be very large, nor should a heavy investment be made in bombing accuracy. The basic requirement is the ability to survive a surprise attack and still devastate the Soviet Union. And accuracy need be adequate only to the mission of maximum destructiveness. The cruder versions of the finite deterrence theory relate the size of the retaliatory force to the number of large Soviet population centers.

The dispute between adherents of the counterforce and finite deterrence strategies repeats essentially the arguments of the B-36 controversy of 1949 with the roles reversed.[5] As in a stately minuet, the services have exchanged positions and only the old acrimony has remained. In 1949, the Air Force insisted that deterrence de-

---

[5] For a description of this controversy see the author's *Nuclear Weapons and Foreign Policy* (New York, 1957), p. 35.

pended on the threat of devastating centers of population and industrial complexes. The Navy described such a strategy as unethical and ineffective and called attention to the moral and strategic imperative to destroy military targets. Today the same arguments are repeated, though the Air Force is following the Navy script of 1949 and vice versa. The irony of this situation should not obscure the deadly seriousness of the issue. For on it depends the shape of our military establishment and the nature of our diplomacy.

The difficulty with the dispute is that our options are often vastly oversimplified. The choice is not between a complete counterforce capability or none at all nor between a strategy of pure devastation or a strategy which guarantees victory in all circumstances. Between these limiting conditions many other possibilities exist, each with its own implications for deterrence and for strategy should deterrence fail. Moreover, we have to consider not only the design of our retaliatory force but that of the opponent as well. The impact of the vulnerability and target systems of the opposing retaliatory forces on each other determines the types of deterrent threats which are possible, their credibility and their suitability for given objectives.

Finally, the utility of the retaliatory force has to be considered in relation to two kinds of dangers: the threat of general war and that of limited war. General war for these purposes can be defined as aggression which, if not resisted, will lead immediately to the collapse of the victim. The victim is reduced to impotence; he can survive only at the aggressor's pleasure. A successful attack on the retaliatory force would enable the aggressor to impose his terms.

Limited aggression, by contrast, is a threat which jeopardizes survival *ultimately*. Victory for an aggressor will lead to a deterioration of our international position but it will not jeopardize our existence immediately. A successful attack on, for example, Burma would undermine the other free countries of Asia. But our own survival would not be threatened except indirectly. Resistance would have to be justified with the argument that the defeat of Burma would set in motion a chain of events which might lead to our eventual downfall. Obviously the case of Burma presents a different deterrent problem from an attack on our retaliatory force both from the point of view of the risks which we may be willing to run and the kinds of threats which may prove credible.

As between the retaliatory forces of the United States and those of the Soviet Union four different relationships are possible.

TABLE 1:   Possible Interrelationship of U.S.–Soviet Retaliatory Forces[6]

U.S.	U.S.S.R.	
1. Vulnerable	Vulnerable	
2. Invulnerable	Vulnerable	This was the situation during our atomic monopoly.
3. Vulnerable	Invulnerable	One interpretation of missile gap.
4. Invulnerable	Invulnerable	Minimum result of missile gap.

Turning first to the problem of mutual vulnerability, this exists when neither side is able to protect its retaliatory force against surprise attack. Either side can win by striking first or lose by striking second. The gap between the first- and the second-strike capability is complete. Even though both sides may be equally vulnerable, the relationship is not symmetrical. Whoever strikes first wins; the side which waits loses. Under conditions of mutual vulnerability, the intentions of a country matter less than its opponent's interpretation of those intentions, for neither side can afford to wait. Where an attack *must* be disastrous, safety consists in forestalling it.

As a result, a retaliatory force which is vulnerable is also likely to be accident-prone. It can survive only if it receives adequate warning—in itself a difficult technical feat. With intercontinental missiles in transit for less than thirty minutes, the reaction to warning must be made as nearly automatic as possible. The fateful decision to go to war may thereby be removed from any meaningful political and perhaps even military control. And the information acted upon may be faulty since there is simply not enough time to determine its accuracy.

[6] It must be understood that these relationships do not exhaust all possibilities. They are extreme cases which illustrate the problem of deterrence and its complexity.

Mutual vulnerability thus produces almost the classic condition for pre-emptive war. When two vulnerable retaliatory forces confront each other, the offense is not the best, it is the *only* defense. In these circumstances the retaliatory force loses all utility as a diplomatic instrument. It cannot be used for making a retaliatory threat. The only safe method of employing it is in a sudden strike. A threat, if believed, will trigger a pre-emptive blow by the opponent, particularly if the opponent is vulnerable as well. Deterrence of all-out war will be highly ineffective.

Paradoxically, limited aggression may be discouraged to some extent. When the deterrent equation is so unstable, it is foolhardy to risk general war by engaging in peripheral moves and safer to attack the opposing retaliatory force directly. But this relative safety from local aggression is a heavy price to pay for the general instability when both sides are vulnerable. Any crisis—even when not sought by the major nuclear powers—may set off a holocaust. No matter what the intentions of the two sides may be, mutual vulnerability is the most dangerous of all strategic relationships. It makes all-out war almost inevitable.

The situation is different when an invulnerable retaliatory force confronts a vulnerable one. Invulnerability can take two forms: It can mean the ability to win even *after* suffering a surprise attack. We were in this position until the Soviet Union developed a substantial stockpile of nuclear weapons and the means to deliver them. It is unattainable now, short of totally unexpected breakthroughs on the part of the defense. Invulnerability can also mean a retaliatory force capable of guaranteeing an unacceptable level of damage even after an attack. This is the sense in which the term "invulnerable" will be used in the subsequent discussion.

When an invulnerable retaliatory force confronts a vulnerable one the strategic relationship is as follows: the side which is invulnerable can protect itself by other means than pre-emptive war because—by the definition of invulnerability—it will not lose its retaliatory force even by conceding the first blow. It will therefore be less tense and less prone to accidents. At the same time, pressure and blackmail can be deterred to some extent by threatening nuclear retaliation. In such conditions, the threat of all-out war will deter limited aggression up to a certain point. For the vulnerable side will always be constrained by the fear that an aggressive act may be used as a pretext for a showdown.

As for the vulnerable side, where under conditions of mutual vulnerability it would win by striking first, this action can now only guarantee mutual suicide. The vulnerable country will have no motive whatever for surprise attack and a greatly reduced incentive for a pre-emptive strike—for no reasonable purpose will be served by it. As a result, the credibility of its threat of all-out war is likely to diminish to the vanishing point. Indeed, apart from its low credibility, the act of threatening is extremely risky for it may provoke an attack which—by the definition of vulnerability—could not fail to be decisive. Vulnerability of the retaliatory force may thus turn into an irremediable weakness, and even the attempt to achieve invulnerability may furnish the incentive for a showdown.

This indicates that it makes a great deal of difference which side possesses the invulnerable force, whether it is the potential aggressor or the potential defender. If the defender is invulnerable and the potential aggressor vulnerable, stability will be enhanced. A *status quo* power, by definition, will not take advantage of its superiority to attack and the aggressor will be deterred by his vulnerability from pressing military moves too far. This essentially was the situation during our atomic monopoly and the subsequent period, when our dispersed base system guaranteed our strategic superiority. This era has now ended, and unless we make major efforts immediately it could even be reversed.

If the potential aggressor is invulnerable and confronts a vulnerable opponent, his position will be overwhelming. He will be able to choose between blackmail and military action. If he blackmails, the victim will be under great pressure to surrender, for its vulnerability makes it reckless to test whether the aggressor is bluffing. If aggression actually takes place, there exists a wide latitude between limited and all-out means. The defender cannot threaten all-out war for fear of being destroyed. And he must be very cautious about resisting limited aggression lest he furnish an excuse for a showdown. As will be seen below, this may be one consequence of the missile gap. If so, the early 1960's will be a period of mortal danger.

What, then, when two invulnerable retaliatory forces confront each other? Under conditions of mutual invulnerability a stalemate would come about regardless of which side struck first. Or, put another way, each side is capable of inflicting unacceptable losses on the other even if it should be the victim of surprise attack. With no advantage to be gained by striking first and no disadvantage to be suffered by striking second, there will be no motive for either surprise or pre-emptive attack. Mutual invulnerability means mutual deterrence. It is the most stable situation from the point of view of preventing all-out war.

At the same time, it is the least stable situation with respect to using the retaliatory force to deter limited aggression. Since, under conditions of mutual invulnerability, all-out war can result only in mutual suicide, it is extremely unlikely that an aggressor could believe that an American President would deliberately favor this resort in resisting *any* attack which is explicitly less than all-out. And a threat which is incredible will cause deterrence to fail no matter how resolute we "really" are. Moreover, such a policy would be reckless in the extreme even were we prepared to carry it out. It would mean that the consequence of any failure of deterrence would be probably catastrophic damage.

The foregoing analysis enables us to sum up the deterrent equation as seen in the chart on the following page.

B. The Debate Reconsidered: The Missile Gap and Finite Deterrence

The table below permits a reconsideration of the missile gap as well as of the controversy between the adherents of a counterforce strategy and of finite deterrence. When the doctrine of massive retaliation was first developed, deterrence was thought to depend on the destructive potential of our Strategic Air Command. Hence, it has been natural for us to assume that our deterrent position improved with every increase in the power of our weapons arsenal. Our military policy has remained essentially unaltered for a decade because of the conviction that no technological change has so far reduced our ability to inflict widespread devastation on the U.S.S.R.

State of Retaliatory Force		Outcome of All-Out War		Ability of the U.S. Retaliatory Force to Deter:	
U.S.	U.S.S.R.	U.S.	U.S.S.R.	All-Out War	Limited Aggression
1. Vulnerable	Vulnerable	1st strike wins 2nd strike loses	1st strike wins 2nd strike loses	Highly Unstable	* Uncertain— but unstable
2. Vulnerable	Invulnerable	1st strike— stalemate 2nd strike loses	1st strike wins 2nd strike— stalemate	Very low against deliberate surprise attack	Almost useless
3. Invulnerable	Vulnerable	1st strike wins 2nd strike— stalemate	1st strike— stalemate 2nd strike loses	Deterrence against all-out war high	All-out capability can discourage limited aggression
4. Invulnerable	Invulnerable	1st strike— stalemate 2nd strike— stalemate	1st strike— stalemate 2nd strike— stalemate	Mutual deterrence	All-out war threat almost useless

* See next chapter: It is dangerous to engage in limited aggression with a vulnerable retaliatory force but equally dangerous to resist. The side with stronger nerves tends to prevail in this situation.

—if anything, the advances in science have enhanced our ability to do so.

In fact, deterrence has always been more subtle and complex. The Soviet Union has been deterred from aggression, particularly local aggression, not only by the power of our strategic striking force but also by its own inability to retaliate. During our atomic monopoly we were completely invulnerable in the sense described above; the U.S.S.R. was completely vulnerable. Afterwards our dispersed base system and superior experience with long-range aircraft gave us a strategic advantage which the Soviet Union could not eliminate through surprise attack. Under these conditions, a certain constraint existed against exploitation by the Soviet Union of its local preponderance, for it could not be certain that we would not use a crisis for a showdown. Even then, our strategic superiority did not prevent the Berlin Blockade, the Korean war, the repression of the Hungarian revolt, and the threat of missile attacks against Britain and France during the Suez episode.

Whatever the strategic significance of massive retaliation in those conditions, it will be reckless to rely on it in the years just ahead. There is no dispute that the "missile gap" will materialize in the period 1960-1964. The only controversy concerns its significance. It may mean that we could lose if the Soviet Union struck first. In that case we would be fortunate if we escaped a surprise attack. It would be foolhardy in the extreme to invite a pre-emptive blow by threatening all-out retaliation to limited aggression.

But even if the worst is avoided, the missile gap guarantees Soviet invulnerability in the sense that we will be unable to destroy the Soviet retaliatory force *even by striking first*. As long as our missile force is significantly smaller than that of the U.S.S.R., the U.S.S.R. can engage in local aggression with greatly reduced fear of American all-out retaliation. During the missile gap we do not have—by definition—enough missiles to destroy the Soviet retaliatory force. Even if each of our missiles destroys one of the Soviet's —an extremely unlikely possibility—a substantial number will remain. And our heavy bombers, because of their relatively slow speed, are relatively ineffective in defeating missiles. If we launch a bomber attack, the Soviet Union will have at least three to four hours' warning—the flying time from the Soviet radar screen to most missile installations. This is more than enough time to launch Soviet missiles, particularly in crisis situations when they will be in a high state of readiness.

Thus the Soviet Union will be able to inflict intolerable damage in retaliation, regardless of the scale of our blow. The missile gap will therefore reduce substantially, perhaps completely, the threat of our retaliatory force against any challenge to our survival, except the most direct. Even if the missile gap is never sufficient to enable the Soviet Union to attack the United States, it should provide increasing opportunities for the kind of blackmail of which the crisis over Berlin is but an augury.

These considerations bear importantly on the debate between the adherents of a counterforce strategy and those of finite deterrence. For in a sense the most favorable result of the missile gap will be precisely the condition envisaged by the exponents of finite deterrence: we may be able to inflict catastrophic damage on the aggressor's social fabric but only at the price of a similar devastation of the United States. This may deter a direct attack on the United States but, by the same token, there is a range of local pressures against which the threat of all-out war will become less and less effective. The version of finite deterrence according to which we are said to require only a small retaliatory force capable primarily of destroying cities or other area targets in fact amounts to a deliberate United States effort to guarantee the invulnerability of the Soviet retaliatory force. If our deterrent force is designed primarily for a mission of punishment, an aggressor will know that short of the most overriding threat to our existence—and perhaps not even then—the threat of massive retaliation *must* be bluff. And there is a wide psychological difference between the assessment that we probably will not wish to retaliate and the knowledge that we are unable to do so.

This dilemma cannot be avoided by returning to a counterforce strategy. Whatever our preferences, technology will prevent this. A counterforce strategy can imply one of two situations:

1. A superiority such that we could win an all-out war even if we conceded the first blow.

2. A strategy in which we could win an all-out war but only if we struck first.

No doubt the most desirable situation is one where we could win even after suffering a surprise attack. Under these circumstances, an attack on our retaliatory force would be senseless because, by hypothesis, the aggressor would lose whether he struck first or second. Hence, he would have no incentive for attacking at all. At the same time, he would have to be cautious about limited aggression because this might unleash our retaliatory force. And the aggressor could not improve his position by a pre-emptive attack, because by hypothesis he would still lose. This is the *only* situation in which the threat of all-out war can reliably deter local aggression.

Such a degree of superiority is almost certainly unattainable today. Given the growing missile forces and nuclear stockpiles, a Soviet surprise attack is bound to inflict enormous damage. Only on the assumption of an almost 100 per cent effective air defense can we even conceive of victory in a *defensive* all-out war. Such a defense is not now in prospect and if it came into being we still could not stake our entire strategy on it. For during the period of our atomic monopoly, when we in fact enjoyed a position of absolute invulnerability, our strategic preponderance was not sufficient to deter Soviet blackmail and aggression.

The effort to develop such a counterforce capability would involve us in a *tour de force*. It would impose staggering force requirements on us, draining off all other military capabilities. The mere effort to develop such a force could not fail to lead to a spiraling arms race and perhaps provoke a pre-emptive attack. Even if we succeeded in building our retaliatory force to the necessary levels, it might still fail to deter for two reasons: (1) we might not be confident enough of our superiority to risk all-out war to resist local aggression; (2) the aggressor might not credit our superiority and might assume that his retaliatory force was really invulnerable. In either case deterrence would fail. A counterforce strategy designed to win a victory *after* we concede the first blow is an illusion.

It *is* conceivable that we could develop a retaliatory force capable of winning a war *provided* we struck first—though the technical difficulty of even this task in the age of mobile missile systems should not be underrated. But its utility as a threat in crisis situations is limited by the Soviet capability for a devastating pre-emptive blow. The *best* foreseeable strategic relationship will be *less* favorable than it was in the period of our strategic preponderance—and even that period demonstrated the limitations of the threat of massive retaliation.

We should therefore have no illusions about what is ahead of us. Though the most desirable situation is one where our retaliatory force is invulnerable while the opponent's is vulnerable, this is also the most unlikely situation in the long run. If invulnerability is possible for us, it would be only sensible to assume that it is attainable for the Soviet Union as well. A condition of mutual invulnerability is likely regardless of our preferences. When this condition comes about, the threat of all-out war will lose its credibility and its strategic meaning—particularly against aggressions which are explicitly less than all-out.

Massive retaliation could deter local aggression as long as there existed a reasonable prospect of victory in an all-out war and as long as a potential aggressor understood this. But victory in an all-out war has lost much of its meaning. It is out of the question if we suffer the first blow. And even if, in response to limited aggression, we should attack pre-emptively, victory will become technically increasingly difficult, if not impossible. The first family of Soviet missiles is stationary and therefore vulnerable. But they are protected by the missile gap. After our missile force increases and the gap is closed, mobility, dispersal, numbers and hardening will make a "win strategy" a will-o'-the-wisp, imposing ever spiraling force requirements for marginal benefits. Only a very foolish Soviet policy would make victory possible at all. And it is reckless to gear our strategy to the expectation of Soviet inadequacy. The only safe basis for planning strategy is on the assumption of the mutual invulnerability of the retaliatory forces.

The dilemma posed by the reliance on all-out war, then, is as follows: A counterforce strategy is nearly impossible technically and equally complex psychologically. On the other hand, finite deterrence as a deliberate national policy may be an invitation to local pressures. If not coupled with a drastic build-up of local forces, it will expose the free world to constant pressure and blackmail. Thus, the threat of all-out war will deter an ever smaller range of challenges.

This suggests that we confront two seemingly contradictory strategic problems. For an interim period, perhaps until the middle sixties, the vulnerability of our retaliatory force will create major opportunities for Soviet nuclear blackmail—even to the extent of threatening direct attacks on the United States. With massive efforts this period can be shortened. But having achieved a secure retaliatory force, we will have dealt only with our most overwhelming danger, not the most likely one. Mutual invulnerability—the inability to rely on a counterforce strategy—will confront us in the most dire fashion with the problem of how to protect the free world from Communist blackmail and local aggression.

Of course, there is a big difference between having *some* counterforce capability and none at all. In the latter case—the extreme position of finite deterrence—the aggressor knows that retaliation turns into a completely irrational act. An American President ordering it would sign the death warrant of tens of millions and he would do so with the knowledge that this sacrifice would have served no military purpose. In these circumstances, local aggression will be encouraged; an aggressor may even feel safe in waging a campaign of attrition against our retaliatory force. If we have no counterforce capability whatever, an aggressor may attack our submarines and perhaps even individual missile bases in the United States while sparing our civilian population. For he may calculate that an American President would be loath to initiate a campaign against cities which could not fail to have appalling consequences. To avoid these dilemmas, our retaliatory force must retain *some* counterforce capability—at least sufficient to deter a campaign of attrition against our retaliatory force.

But even with *some* counterforce capability, the threat of all-out war will lose its effectiveness as a deterrent to most challenges short of a direct attack on the United States. To the degree that mutual deterrence of all-out war is achieved, the perils of limited aggression *must* multiply. The preposterous aspect of the U.S. military policy is that even in the face of first the missile gap and then the approaching mutual invulnerability, we continue to rely on the threat of all-out war as our primary deterrent. The argument is advanced that *any* aggression by the Soviet Union and Communist China is general war by definition. It is said that deterrence is achieved not so much by the certainty that we *will* strike but by the uncertainty that we *might*. No Communist leader will stake his hard-won industrial complex on the chance that we do not mean our threats. But if an overwhelming counterforce capability was insufficient to prevent Communist pressure during the period of our strategic preponderance, reliance on it will be sheer irresponsibility in the age of invulnerable retaliatory forces. This is not to speak of the possibility that for a few years we may be even inferior in the equation of all-out war.

4. The Political Implications of Mutual Invulnerability

It would be a mistake to believe that the problem of the aggressor's invulnerability, having come upon us as the result of the missile gap, can be eliminated by closing that gap. On the contrary, the missile gap has hastened what volatile technology would have made inevitable in any case. An overwhelming first-strike capability—the prerequisite for the effectiveness of the threat of all-out war—will become more and more difficult to achieve as the missile age develops. Though we must close the missile gap, we could make no worse mistake than to assume that we can return to the period of our preponderance in strategic striking power. Some form of mutual invulnerability is the most likely result of the period after the missile gap ends, and the attainment of even this will require major efforts which we have so far been reluctant to make.

Under conditions of mutual invulnerability, the structure of deterrence will change fundamentally. Deterrence, to be effective, has four requirements:

1. The implementation of the deterrent threat must be sufficiently credible to preclude its being taken as a bluff.

2. The potential aggressor must understand the decision to resist attack or pressure.

3. The opponent must be rational, i.e., he must respond to his self-interest in a manner which is predictable.

4. In weighing his self-interest, the potential aggressor must reach the conclusions the "deterrer" is seeking to induce. In other words, the *penalties* of aggression must outweigh its *benefits.*

Under conditions of mutual invulnerability, these conditions will become increasingly difficult to fulfill by the threat of all-out war.

When the theory of deterrence was first developed, it was assumed that an aggressor had basically two options: to attack or to fail to do so. Deterrence was thought to depend on the aggressor's knowledge that the penalty for aggression—on any scale—was an overwhelming retaliatory blow by the United States. Later on, as the psychological inhibitions produced by the doctrine of massive retaliation multiplied, it was argued that deterrence would be effective as long as the aggressor could not be sure that we would *not* retaliate.

However, it has become apparent that the aggressor has other choices than to attack or fail to do so. He can attack on a scale which makes the threatened retaliation appear to involve disproportionate risks. More importantly, he has the opportunity to engage in blackmail. And the effect of blackmail is to force the threatened side to make the next move. Henceforth, the potential victim faces the dilemma of interpreting the opponent's intentions. He must determine whether the aggressor "means" his threat. Although the aggressor cannot be certain that the defender will not retaliate, the defender cannot be certain that the aggressor does not mean *his* threat. Blackmail tilts the psychological balance against the defender if the only recourse is all-out war. For the distinctive qualities of a *status quo* power will cause it to be reluctant to stake its survival on the assumption that the aggressor is bluffing. Soviet tactics in a whole series of crises from Berlin to the Congo to Cuba seem primarily designed to bring home to the West the full implications of its alternatives: to make an accommodation or to run the risk, however slight, that the Soviets are prepared to fight a major war to vindicate their demands.

The distinction between issues that threaten survival directly and those that menace it only over a period of time becomes crucial in such a test of nerves. In the past, nations would often resist seemingly minor aggressions in order to prevent an ultimate disaster. When Great Britain declared war in 1939, the major objective was not safeguarding the Polish Corridor as such. Rather it was the conviction that to yield on this issue must sooner or later have catastrophic consequences, and cause the inevitable showdown to take place under even worse conditions. *Eventual* national catastrophe was believed to be the penalty for failure to resist the immediate challenge. The worst consequence would be the *loss* of a war. But when the *outbreak* of all-out war comes increasingly to be considered the worst catastrophe, this reasoning will no longer apply. It does not make sense to threaten suicide in order to prevent eventual death.

If all-out war is our only possible response to aggression of any type, more and more challenges will begin to appear as indirect threats only. Under conditions of mutual invulnerability, aggression that does not threaten the retaliatory capability may be inherently ambiguous. The very fact that the aggressor has foregone the advantages of surprise attack may be taken as a proof of limited objectives and of the futility of all-out war.

This becomes apparent if we ask just what a "rational" response would be if the Soviet Union engaged in some limited operation in West Germany ostensibly to disarm the Federal Republic. If this move were coupled with a guarantee of immunity of our territory and that of our allies, and if the Soviet Union offered to begin immediate peace negotiations, is it clear that all-out war would be a rational course? Even if it is "clear" to us, can we count on the Soviet leaders to assess our situation similarly? We could, of course, devastate the Soviet Union, but only at the price of suffering catastrophic damage in return. What would the Chairman of the Joint Chiefs of Staff advise the President regarding the purpose of a war that could have no victory and could only guarantee mutual suicide?

Or let us take an even more extreme example. For the entire nuclear age it has been considered axiomatic that an attack on our retaliatory force must unleash an all-out counterblow. We have sought to design our retaliatory force to combine a rapid reaction with tight control over the decision to retaliate. The former, we thought, was necessary in order to deter aggression; the latter in order to avoid the risks of accidental war. From a strictly rational point of view, however, a rapid counterblow is by no means a foregone conclusion. And effective deterrence even of an attack on our retaliatory force may depend on the belief by the Communists that in certain circumstances the President may *lose* control over events.

This becomes clear if we consider a "rational" United States reaction to a blow against our retaliatory force. Suppose that such an attack reduced our retaliatory force by 50 per cent but held civilian casualties to a minimum. Assume also that coincident with the attack the Soviet ambassador presented an ultimatum to the President somewhat to this effect: "We have just destroyed x per cent of your retaliatory force while sparing your cities. If you retaliate against our civilian population, we will respond in kind and our ability to inflict damage is superior to yours at least by the factor of destruction inflicted on your retaliatory force. We offer peace negotiations on certain specified conditions."

Considered purely rationally, there would be little sense in American retaliation. If our retaliatory force were designed according to the maxims of finite deterrence—as a small countercity force —there would be no point in retaliation whatsoever. A blow against Soviet cities would devastate the Communist homeland. At the same time it would guarantee even more appalling destruction in the United States, because our population is more concentrated and because—by hypothesis—our retaliatory force will have been considerably disrupted by the initial Soviet attack. In these circumstances, the harrowing possibility exists that the Communist leaders might come to believe that if they could induce *any* delay in our response they might escape unscathed from even a nuclear attack. Conversely, if they refrain from such a course it will be because they are convinced that an attack on the United States would elicit reactions transcending any rational calculations. In short, deterrence would result from the impression not that the President would order a counterblow but that he would not be able to prevent it.

Indeed, if our retaliatory force were designed exclusively for an attack against the aggressor's civilian population—and so understood by the opponent—we might be able to prevent a war of attrition only by making our response nearly automatic. The aggressor would have to believe that our retaliatory force was so designed that an attack of a certain scale would trigger a counterblow almost mechanically. In that eventuality, blackmail could not be effective because once a surprise attack were launched the President would no longer *control* the decision to react. By launching a surprise attack, the Soviet leaders would guarantee their own destruction. Such a mechanical trigger is, of course, politically intolerable. It indicates, however, the dilemmas of seeking to make credible the threat of all-out war—even in cases where previously it was considered a matter of course.

As the gap between the threat on which we rely for deterrence and the strategy we are prepared to implement widens, the threat of massive retaliation becomes increasingly irresponsible and ineffective. An aggressor may calculate that if he can force us to pause for even twenty-four hours before committing our retaliatory force, sober calculation will reveal to us the suicidal nature of our strategy. A premium is thereby placed on *faits accomplis*. However drastic our retaliatory threat, the inability to assign any military purpose to it may deprive it of credibility. And it does not matter how resolute we "really" are. A threat which is disbelieved causes deterrence to fail.

Under conditions of mutual invulnerability, a country relying for deterrence primarily on the threat of all-out war faces a perhaps insurmountable task in meeting the second criterion for an effective deterrent: convincing an aggressor of the decision to resist. As has been seen, the threat of mutual destruction can be made plausible only by convincing the aggressor that the response to aggression will be nearly automatic; that at some point we will lose control over events. A country relying on the doctrine of massive retaliation can resist blackmail only by maneuvering deliberately to demonstrate that on some issues the question of whether they are worth a cataclysm will not be asked. A rational policy designed to make the threat of all-out war credible in these circumstances would have to convey our capacity for acts which normally would be considered irrational.

Yet the very qualities that make us a *status quo* power will also prevent us from adopting so daring a diplomacy. No American President can run the risk of all-out war without having convinced the American people that he has exhausted all alternatives. He can justify the decision to go to war only by having conclusively proved his devotion to peace. In any crisis, rather than show our "nervousness"—which would be a wise course from the point of view of deterrence—we are much more likely to seek to demonstrate that we are "calm," "rational," "calculating," "accommodating"— all qualities which, if taken seriously by the aggressor, may cause him to doubt our resolve to resort to all-out war. When President Eisenhower said with respect to Berlin that "only a madman would start a nuclear war," he may have intended to warn the Soviet leaders. In fact, he was merely illustrating our dilemma. For the Soviets would not need to start a nuclear war to menace Berlin, while we would have to be willing to start an all-out war to defend it. We, not the Soviets, would have to be ready to act like madmen.

Given the values of our society, the feat of convincing the Soviet leaders of our capacity for irrationality and our own people of our devotion to peace is probably insuperable. A President acting in this manner would lose all domestic support. Similar constraints are produced by the requirements of coalition diplomacy. We can hold our alliances together only if our partners are convinced that we represent an added security against attack, not an invitation to it. And each of our allies is likely to be faced with a public opinion much like our own. In any given crisis, the need to obtain domestic support *and* the agreement of our allies is almost certain to inhibit the only diplomacy which could be effective given the options provided by our military policy. As long as we rely on the threat of all-out war as the chief deterrent, we will condemn ourselves to the dilemma that in order to avoid blackmail we must be able to act irrationally with conviction while we can hold the free world together only if we lead it with steadiness and calmness.

Indeed, reliance on all-out war is inconsistent with the third requirement of deterrence: the assumption of the opponent's rationality. The more "rational" the Soviet Union is, the less likely is it to credit our threat of retaliation; the more it may be tempted by the opportunities confronting it. Moreover, if international relations turn into a series of threats and counterthreats of the direst type, a premium will be placed on irresponsibility. The aggressor will have an incentive to stake his prestige deliberately and in the most extreme fashion in order to give credence to the claim that he is prepared to run the risks of nuclear retaliation. Mr. Khrushchev's behavior over Berlin illustrates this. Almost every move had the result of so committing him to his course that it soon seemed an intolerable provocation to ask him to withdraw an unprovoked threat. Similarly, a great deal of Mr. Khrushchev's violence during the General Assembly of 1960 may have been designed as a warning of his capacity for irrationality if thwarted.

This tactic is a familiar Soviet device, of course. It would be employed no matter what our strategy was. But against a doctrine of all-out war, it is particularly effective. Reliance on deterrence by the threat of all-out war will lead to a diplomacy of irresponsibility. Rational calculation is likely to produce irrational behavior on both sides. As for the West, it is difficult to see how it can avoid demoralization when confronted by a series of decisions, each posing the alternative of suicide or at least partial surrender. If both sides conduct a policy which depends for its impact on convincing the opponent of the capacity for irrationality, a showdown is almost inevitable. Such a course will erode all restraints and all hope for ultimate stability.

Similar difficulties apply to the fourth prerequisite for effective deterrence, that the penalties of a given course must seem to outweigh the benefits. If the threat of all-out war is to deter, it must produce the following calculations on the part of a potential aggressor: (1) that the United States would prefer to strike an all-out blow rather than acquiesce in a Soviet gain, however small; (2) that it is willing to suffer a Soviet retaliatory blow; (3) that despite its readiness to launch all-out war in retaliation and despite the certainty that this would produce vast devastation, the United States is unlikely to launch a pre-emptive blow or to be so trigger-happy as to start an accidental war; (4) that consequently the Soviet Union runs no risks if it does not launch a pre-emptive blow itself.

These requirements imply a combination of readiness and

subtlety almost impossible for a peaceful *status quo* country to achieve—much less for a coalition of such countries. We will either be disbelieved and thereby encourage aggression, or we may be thought too bellicose and thus tempt a Soviet pre-emptive attack. Moreover, the consequences of the threat of all-out war are largely out of our control. They depend to a considerable extent on Soviet vulnerability. If the Soviet Union believes its retaliatory force to be invulnerable, our threat may be ineffective in deterring. If it is highly vulnerable, the Soviets may see no other option except that of anticipating our attack. The problem of using the all-out deterrent in a situation of mutual bluff is that it is either too convincing or not convincing enough.

Complex as the strategic problem is, the psychological difficulty of balancing penalties and benefits is more complicated still. For if the benefits of aggression seem to outweigh the penalties only once, deterrence will fail. And this could come about simply because the two sides interpret the nature of benefits and penalties differently. In any given situation a number of psychological asymmetries are likely to prevail as between us and the Communist countries. These are only indirectly related to the strategic balance. They involve such factors as the importance of the objective, the willingness of the contenders to run risks, their reputation and their political relationship to the threatened territory. These asymmetries will be discussed in turn.

1. *Importance of the Objective.* Only on the most fundamental questions of national survival will both sides feel equally committed. In almost every conceivable crisis, one side or the other is likely to have a psychological advantage. Hungary seemed more important to the Soviet Union than to us. Though we were still significantly stronger, the Soviets, in repressing the Hungarian revolution, substituted the importance they attached to maintaining their position in the satellite orbit for real strength. Though we could still have won an all-out war at tolerable cost, we were deterred from intervening by the fear that the Soviet leaders were prepared to run all risks in order to prevail. In some circumstances, an area may be protected by the importance that it has or which it is thought to have. Our threat of all-out war is more effective in

protecting Europe than in protecting countries like Laos or Burma or Iran because it is more credible: Europe "matters" more to us— it is therefore credible that we may pay a higher price in its defense.

Theoretically, the psychological balance should favor the defender. The aggressor can gain only what he has never possessed; the defender stands to lose something heretofore identified with his world position. That the Communist bloc has managed to press on all peripheral areas nonetheless is due to two factors: (a) the Communist ability to bring to bear forces graduated to the nature of the issue. This has shifted the onus and the risk of initiating all-out war on us. In effect, we have paralyzed ourselves by the alternatives which our own doctrine and military establishment have presented; (b) superior Communist will power or at least the reputation for it. The Soviet leaders have managed to convince many in the West that their desire to prevail is stronger than the West's interest in the *status quo*.

The side which is willing to run greater risks—or which can make its opponent believe that it is prepared to do so—gains a psychological advantage. During the Suez crisis, the Soviet Union threatened obliquely to launch rocket attacks against London and Paris—despite the fact that it would almost certainly have lost an all-out war. During the Hungarian revolution the West, though it was far stronger, was not willing to make similar threats against the U.S.S.R. This trend has continued at an accelerated pace. In every crisis, from Berlin to the Congo to Cuba, the Soviet Union has threatened missile attacks often in a fashion which has made subsequent actions seem to have been the result of Soviet missile blackmail. The diplomatic position of the Soviet Union has been greatly enhanced by its ability to shift to its opponents the risks and uncertainties of countermoves.

2. *Reputation.* Since deterrence depends not only on the magnitude but also on the credibility of a threat, the side which has a greater reputation for ruthlessness or for a greater willingness to run risks gains a diplomatic advantage. This reputation is importantly affected by what may perhaps be called *the experience of the last use of force.* The Communist leaders have used force to maintain their sphere, as in Hungary and Tibet. They have threatened the use of

force to expand their influence, as in the Middle East, Berlin and Cuba. The brutality of the repression in Hungary and Tibet may reflect the conviction that as long as the opprobrium of using force had to be shouldered it may as well be coupled with a reputation for ruthlessness and overwhelming power. By contrast, our last experience in resisting aggression, that of Korea, produced a bitter domestic debate and a seeming resolve never again to engage in what many have described an "unproductive" war. The decision of a threatened country, allied or neutral, to resist and its resolution in the face of a menace may importantly depend on its assessment of the past actions of the West and the Communist countries.

3. *Political Alignment.* A final asymmetry derives from the political context in which deterrence takes place. The threat of all-out war is more credible as a counter to a direct threat to a nation's survival than to a challenge to an ally. A challenge to an ally will call forth a greater willingness to run risks than pressure on a neutral. A psychological imbalance is created by the structure of the free world as against the Communist empire. The Soviet Union or Communist China can threaten all peripheral areas from their own territory. No country around the Communist periphery is capable of resisting alone. The Soviet Union can threaten our allies or neutrals. In order to deter by the threat of all-out war, we must menace metropolitan Russia or China. This alone creates a psychological problem in making the threat of all-out war credible and will do so increasingly as the Soviet nuclear and missile arsenal grows. For however firm allied unity may be, the threat of all-out war in defense of a foreign territory is less plausible than in defense of one's own. At least an aggressor may believe this, and such a conviction, however unjustified, would cause deterrence to fail.

The imbalance is emphasized also by the structure of alliances in the free world as compared to the Communist bloc. The free-world alliances are composed of *status quo* powers. The Communist world is composed of revolutionary states of varying degrees of fanaticism. To hold the free world alliances together it is necessary to demonstrate calmness, reasonableness and willingness to settle differences. By contrast within the Communist bloc, whatever the personal convictions of individual leaders, it is necessary to engage in periodic acts of intransigence to prove ideological purity. The pressures within the free world are in the direction of a lowest common denominator. Within the Communist bloc the requirements of alliance policy tend to produce a kind of addition of the different goals.

These asymmetries explain why our undoubted strategic superiority did not deter a whole range of Soviet challenges even during the period of our atomic monopoly. Our strategic superiority was more than outweighed by the fact that the alternatives posed by our military policy gave the Soviet Union a psychological advantage. From the Berlin blockade to Korea, to Indo-China, to Suez, to Hungary, to the Congo and Cuba, the combination of reputation for ruthlessness, willingness to run risks, and the difficulties of alliance policy enabled the Soviet Union to blackmail the free world. The dilemma of our post-war strategy has been that the power which was available to us has also produced the greatest inhibitions, while we have had no confidence in the kind of forces which might have redressed the psychological balance.

If deterrence by the threat of all-out war is difficult for us, it is nearly insurmountable for our allies. The retaliatory force on which we rely for deterrence is at least within our own control. We have the possibility of increasing its credibility by a daring diplomacy. But daring, even recklessness, will avail our allies little unless it is backed up by the United States. If the threat of all-out war is the chief counter to Soviet aggression, none of our allies will be able to pose an effective retaliatory threat should they create strategic forces of their own.[7] The result will be either a sense of impotence or irresponsibility, either resignation or a futile attempt to achieve an independent deterrent position.

Such a situation will expose our allies to the most intractable form of blackmail. Their leaders can be told that unless they accede to Soviet demands it will make little difference whether or not we retaliate against the Soviet Union. Resistance would mean certain devastation, so the Soviet argument may go, even if the United States made good on its promise to retaliate. Indeed, it would give

[7] This problem will be discussed in greater detail in "The United States and Europe," Chapter IV, pp. 99 f.

the Soviet Union an added incentive to create a *fait accompli*. The destruction of their country can be prevented only by accommodating themselves to the Soviet Union. This indeed was the theme of Premier Khrushchev's press conference after the collapse of the summit conference:

It is said that the United States would discharge their [*sic*] duties to their allies. By doing so they tell those countries where the bases are located, don't be afraid, if the Soviet Union smashes you, strikes a retaliatory blow with rockets, we shall attend your funeral when you have been smashed.[8]

If deterrence by the threat of all-out war was difficult when we were strategically superior, it will grow intolerable in the age of mutual invulnerability. It will put a premium on recklessness and thus undermine the psychological basis for our foreign policy. It will lead to a diplomacy of bluff where even success makes for instability. If over a period of years the contenders become convinced that the situations of threat and counterthreat will always be resolved by *somebody* backing down, a showdown may be produced by this very sense of security. After all, the crisis which led to World War I seemed at first no different from innumerable others which had been resolved by the threat of going to the brink of war. And when war finally came, it was fought as a total war over a relatively trivial issue because no other alternative had been considered. It would be tragic if our generation allowed itself to repeat the errors of its grandfathers. The penalty now would be incomparably more severe.

5. Deterrence through Uncertainty

The above reasoning is criticized by many proponents of a strategy of all-out war as taking too abstract an approach to the problem of deterrence. The threat of all-out war will continue to deter *all* forms of aggression however small, it is argued, even though the notion of victory in general war has become meaningless and perhaps because of it. Deterrence, it is claimed, is produced not so

[8] *New York Times*, June 4, 1960.

much by the certainty of retaliation as by the uncertainty in the aggressor's mind that we *may* devastate his country. In any given situation, the potential aggressor must weigh the value of the objective against the probability of all-out retaliation. To be sure, if the objective is relatively insignificant, the credibility of the threat of all-out war may be low. By the same token, from the point of view of the aggressor, the marginal gain may not be worth even that degree of risk. To deter a surprise attack on the United States the retaliatory threat must seem certain. To deter an attack on Azerbaijan the probability of retaliation need be much less. The Soviet Union, so the argument goes, will not risk aggression in Iran if the chance of losing all the achievements of a generation is even 10 per cent. Thus, though the credibility of the threat of all-out war is declining, it is to some extent compensated for by its increasing horror. According to this school of thought, there will always remain a residue of uncertainty sufficient to make the Soviet leaders recoil before aggression on any scale.

One difficulty with this theory is that the "uncertainty effect" obviously has not prevented many forms of Communist military pressure ranging from blackmail to outright aggression. The Berlin blockade and Korea, the repression of the Hungarian revolution, the constant threat of missile and nuclear attacks, and the renewed pressure on Berlin were not deterred even by our strategic preponderance. More fundamentally, a statesman relying on the uncertainty effect leaves himself no margin for miscalculation. If it fails, even in the case of minor aggression, he is either committed to the most cataclysmic form of warfare or he must yield, reducing the credibility of the deterrent threat still further in the future. In practice, the "uncertainty effect" removes control over events entirely from our hands. In most situations it works *against* not *for* the free world, because in the case of blackmail it could never be sufficiently certain that our opponent did not mean his threat.

Criminal blackmail operates essentially on the principle that uncertainty can be made to work for the criminal, if the alternatives confronted by the victim are dire enough. From a rational point of view, a kidnapper has no motive for killing his hostage if ransom is not paid. Murder will not improve the possibility of obtaining ransom and it will increase the penalty if he is caught. Nevertheless, the threat is often effective because the family of the victim can run no risk, however slight, that the criminal is bluffing. His mere determination to have his way coupled with the enormity of the victim's risk gives him an overwhelming bargaining position. Similarly, peaceful countries, which are such, after all, because the *status quo* seems preferable to any change, impose an impossible psychological burden on themselves if they can be defended only by the threat of suicide.

Moreover, the question arises what, precisely, the "uncertainty effect" involves. It may be interpreted as inherent in the threat of all-out war, even when we make every effort to convince the aggressor of our intention to retaliate. Or it could mean, as is often argued, that there is a positive advantage in deliberately magnifying the uncertainty in the aggressor's mind. Both interpretations demonstrate the risk of relying on the threat of all-out war as a deterrent to all forms of aggression. If the threat of all-out war has an inherent element of implausibility, the result must be demoralizing for the other countries of the free world whose security is made to depend on it.

This will be magnified if we set about to produce uncertainty deliberately. Such a course is capable of being interpreted both by the Communist and by the free world as an attempt to keep open the option of *not* retaliating at all. For, so the reasoning may go, if we had decided to resist by the primary strategy available to us, the obvious course would be to say so. Given the inherent incredibility of the threat of all-out war, even our most solemn declarations may be discounted to some extent. Regardless of what we say, there always exists the possibility that we might recoil at the last moment before the prospects of a cataclysm. To strive for ambiguity deliberately must magnify these fears. Our all-out deterrent may work for a while longer *despite* its increasing lack of credibility. But we should consider this a fortunate bonus. To make of ambiguity a principle of conduct is to court disaster.

It is sometimes argued that deliberate ambiguity is desirable because to be too specific about our response eases the aggressor's task: it tells him in effect the "price tag" for each action and enables him to plan accordingly. It is not obvious, of course, why knowledge of the consequences of aggression should encourage aggression, *so long as the price tag is unacceptably high.* More importantly, this argument fails to distinguish between two kinds of uncertainty: (1) uncertainty about whether we plan to resist at all and (2) uncertainty about the range or the method of our resistance. The former uncertainty *must* weaken deterrence because it leaves open the possibility of non-resistance. Uncertainty with respect to the range or method of our resistance has a certain utility. It makes the calculations of the aggressor more difficult. It can be a device for committing ourselves to *some* form of resistance. Uncertainty about the *nature* of our retaliation may be the best means of producing certainty that *some* retaliation will occur.

The dangers as well as the uses of deliberate ambiguity were well illustrated by the Quemoy crisis of 1958. At the beginning we sought to leave the Chinese Communists in doubt as to whether we would resist an attack on the off-shore islands. Both the President and the Secretary of State made statements that we would resist only if the Communist attack seemed a prelude to an assault on Formosa and the Pescadores. Since this implied that there were *some* attacks to which we would *not* respond, the impression was created that we might want to leave a loophole for yielding. When Communist pressure continued, we were therefore forced step by step to depart from our original stand. Every succeeding statement made the American commitment to defend Quemoy more explicit. We went further and engaged in a series of actions whose only purpose could be to remove any doubt about whether there would be American resistance: the transfer of United States tactical aircraft to Formosa, the convoying of Nationalist supply ships to within three miles of Quemoy, the strengthening of United States naval forces in the Far East. The crisis was thus ended, not by Communist uncertainty as to our decision to resist but by the strong likelihood that a full-scale assault would meet with United States opposition.

And so it has been in every area considered vital. In each case we have been at pains to remove any doubt about our resolve. One purpose of the stationing of United States troops in Europe is to warn the Soviet leaders that any hostile act must inevitably involve us. Our forces are, in a sense, hostages which guarantee that we will not make our response depend on circumstance. Stationing troops in the direct line of a possible Communist advance thus has a significance transcending their immediate military utility. It is a reminder to the Communist leaders that in case of a Soviet attack we have to some extent resigned control over our actions. The rationality of resistance will no longer be the issue. There will not be time for fine calculations. Our deployment ensures a measure of automatism in our response which no verbal commitment could achieve.

It is essential, then, to be clear about the range of uncertainty which is acceptable. The lower limit must *not* include the possibility of yielding or of a resistance so feeble that aggression is encouraged. The upper limit must not pose a threat which is either incredible or which would provoke a pre-emptive attack if believed. The lower limit of uncertainty should set the minimum price unacceptably high and, while keeping the maximum price open, avoid the impression of an automatism which is out of control once force is used.

These requirements will soon be impossible to meet by the threat of all-out war. In most foreseeable contingencies such a threat will either start an automatic chain reaction or it will be incredible— i.e., fail to satisfy the lower limit of uncertainty. If both retaliatory forces are vulnerable, to threaten all-out war is to invite pre-emptive attack. If our retaliatory force is invulnerable while the Soviet force is exposed, we can threaten to resort to all-out war with some degree of credibility—though even then the Soviet capability for a pre-emptive attack would make our position more precarious and our threat less credible than it was during the period of strategic preponderance. If conditions are reversed, of course, to threaten all-out war is to commit suicide—and we are more likely to find ourselves in this position than in any other if the "missile gap" becomes more serious. If both sides develop invulnerable retaliatory forces, a threat of all-out war would lack all purpose, for it could have no military meaning. The same factors which would make a threat of all-out war militarily feasible would then operate to reduce its plausibility. In short, the side which has to make the ultimate decision to vindicate its interests and its values by all-out war imposes an impossible handicap on itself, all the more so if it is a *status quo* power. It simply does not make sense to seek to defend one's way of life with a strategy which guarantees its destruction.

For these reasons, the notion that there is only *one* form of deterrence—the threat of nuclear retaliation—must be abandoned. It found expression in the very term we have applied to our retaliatory force: *the* Deterrent. This implied that all other forms of power were a dispensable luxury and essentially irrelevant to the problem of security. Current military policy still holds the view that any aggression involving the Soviet Union or Communist China is general war, by definition, which will bring our retaliatory force into play at the outset. Graduated responses fit only police-type actions like Lebanon. The military program for 1960-61 was again justified by the proposition that the increasing range and power of our weapons permitted us to consider redeployment of our local forces.

But the dilemmas described in this chapter cannot be dealt with by definition. We no longer have the choice between an all-out strategy and other forms and we should stop debating as if we did. Our choice is to adapt to new conditions or face paralysis and disaster. What used to be called *the* Deterrent will still be needed to prevent a direct challenge to our survival. Major efforts are required—far beyond those being made—to make these forces invulnerable. To achieve this must be the first goal of any military policy. The difficulty arises that this effort, massive, complex and subtle as it is, will provide only the condition for stability. It will not enable us to achieve the entire spectrum of deterrence. The flexibility so often demanded of our diplomacy is impossible without a spectrum of military capabilities. The relationship of the various forms of deterrence is perhaps the central problem of American strategy. It is to this relationship that we shall now turn.

III
LIMITED WAR—A REAPPRAISAL

1. THE NATURE OF LIMITED WAR

As THE consequences of all-out war grow more horrible, reliance on it also becomes more absurd. The gap between the threat made for purposes of deterrence and the strategy which we are prepared to implement will widen. Every increase in destructiveness is purchased at the price of reduced credibility of the retaliatory threat. In this vicious circle, deterrence may fail. If it does, the reliance on massive retaliation will guarantee the direct outcome. It will lead either to surrender or to the most catastrophic form of war.

Nothing is more urgent than to harmonize our deterrent policy with a strategy we are prepared to implement. The wider the gap, the greater the scope for Soviet blackmail. The more we rely for deterrence on nuclear retaliation against the Soviet homeland, the more exposed the other countries of the free world will be to Communist pressures threatening *faits accomplis*. In the missile age, the side which can add another increment of power without resorting to all-out war—or which can threaten to do so—will gain a perhaps decisive advantage over an opponent who does not have this ability. Flexibility in both diplomacy and strategy requires that a maximum number of stages be created between surrender and Armageddon.

The argument is frequently heard that the purpose of the West's military establishment is to deter war, not to wage it. Duncan Sandys has said, for example:[1]

. . . we believe that the British people will agree that the available resources of the nation should be concentrated not upon preparations to wage war so much, as upon trying to prevent that catastrophe from ever happening.

[1] Hansard 568, p. 1759, April 16, 1957.

Any inquiry into a tolerable strategy, it is alleged, is therefore beside the point. It will weaken deterrence by reducing the risk in the aggressor's mind. To the degree that the consequences of war appear tolerable to us, they may grow acceptable to the aggressor as well. Aggression will thereby be encouraged. And once war starts, on whatever scale, it may become all-out.

However, this argument avoids the principal problem: that deterrence cannot be separated from strategy. Deterrence depends not only on the extent of the retaliation to aggression but also on its likelihood. These two factors are related to each other in an inverse ratio. If either is very low, deterrence fails. If the side seeking to deter emphasizes the destructiveness of its response at the expense of the likelihood of retaliation, aggression may be encouraged. If too much stress is placed on a strategy of minimum cost, the penalties against aggression may be too low for effective deterrence. Deterrence is at a maximum when the product of these two factors is greatest. The challenge before our military policy is to strike the best balance between deterrence and the strategy we are prepared to implement should deterrence fail.

These considerations bear importantly on the problem of limited war. Limited war has been much debated over the past few years. Many refined theories have been developed. But the basic concept is simple. It maintains that the threat of massive retaliation has lost both credibility and utility. Since a retaliatory strategy would have to be carried out with the knowledge that a counterblow would inflict perhaps catastrophic damage, we must seek to deter Communist aggression by developing military forces capable of checking this aggression at whatever scale of violence it may be initiated. Deterrence would be complete if the aggressor could not defeat the military forces of the free world whatever form aggression took. If adequate limited war forces are coupled with an invulnerable retaliatory force, the aggressor would be unable to benefit from either limited or all-out conflict. In that case, military actions would be foreclosed to him.

Theorists of limited war do not deny that the risk which this strategy poses to the aggressor is less than that of massive retaliation. But they argue that this is more than made up for by the increase in the certainty of the response. Moreover, the notion that deterrence requires the threat of total devastation is a vestigial argument from our period of invulnerability. It is reckless in the age of nuclear plenty. Aggression would seem to be senseless if the aggressor knew in advance that he could not achieve any gain regardless of the nature or the scale of his attack. Limited war forces, properly designed, should ensure this. If the Communist countries were certain that they could not win a limited war, their opportunities for blackmail would be sharply reduced. A strategy of limited war would seek to achieve deterrence not so much through the threat of devastation but through depriving the aggressor of the possibility of gaining his objective.

Many object that a strategy of limited war is meaningless. Neither side, they say, would be willing to accept defeat without first employing all weapons at its disposal as long as it still had available uncommitted resources. Hence there is a danger of "escalation": the adding of increments of power until limited war insensibly merges into all-out war. By seeking to avoid the ultimate risk, so the argument goes, a strategy of limited war makes it inevitable.

It is true that the possibility of all-out war is inherent in a limited war among major powers. Since limited war by definition does not involve *all* the resources of the opponents, it is easy to "prove" how a war *could* expand. No one can know whether either side would accept defeat. But we must be clear about what is involved in pressing the argument about escalation too far. A country prepared to risk mutual destruction rather than forego the possibility of gaining its objectives can be deterred only by surrender. While it is true that war can be kept limited only if the two sides wish to keep it limited, it is equally true that an aggressor convinced that its intended victim is unwilling to run *any* risk may be positively encouraged to resort to the direst threats. A country not willing to risk limited war because it fears that resistance to aggression on *any* scale may lead to all-out war will have no choice in a showdown but to surrender.

The purpose of a strategy of limited war, then, is first to strengthen deterrence and, second, if deterrence should fail, to provide an opportunity for settlement before the automatism of the retaliatory forces takes over. The *worst* that could happen if we resisted aggression by means of limited war is what is *certain* to happen if we continue to rely on the strategy of the past decade.

Limited war is based on a kind of tacit bargain not to exceed certain restraints. One side's desire to keep the war limited is of no avail unless the other co-operates: it takes two to keep a limited war limited or a local defense local. In a limited war between major powers both sides, by definition, have the technical ability to expand the war. It is easy, therefore, to "prove" the unreasonableness of any restraints. As long as either side has uncommitted resources at its disposal, any limitation can be made to appear arbitrary or ridiculous.

However paradoxical it may seem, the danger of escalation is one of the chief reasons why a strategy of limited war contributes to deterrence and also why, if deterrence fails, there is a chance of keeping a conflict limited. A strategy of limited war adds to deterrence for the very reason usually invoked against it. The danger that a limited war may expand after all works both ways. An aggressor may not credit our threat of massive retaliation because it would force us to *initiate* a course of action which will inevitably involve enormous devastation. He may calculate, however, that once engaged in war on any scale neither he nor we would know how to limit it, whatever the intentions of the two sides. The stronger the limited war forces of the free world, the larger will have to be the Communist effort designed to overcome them. The more the scale of conflict required for victory approaches that of all-out war the greater will be the inhibitions against initiating hostilities. In this sense a capability of limited war is necessary in order to enhance the deterrent power of the retaliatory force.

The risk that war could become general places constraints on both its extent and its duration. If either side *wanted* an all-out war, it would be foolish to alert the retaliatory force of the opponent by engaging in local conflict. The mere fact that a limited war is taking place is a signal of the desire to avoid a showdown. Experience has shown that each side generally leans over backwards to convey its limited aims and methods to the other.

Those who deride specific limitations as illogical miss the central point: an illogical limitation is often particularly effective in conveying self-restraint to the other side. During the Korean war we did not attack the bases in Manchuria from which air attacks against our forces were being mounted. The Communists in turn did not bomb the only two ports through which we could obtain supplies. Similar restrictions were observed in the conflict over Quemoy. Despite the fact that Communist China has always claimed that its territorial waters extend twelve miles, our ships were permitted to approach within three miles of Quemoy without being fired on. We then loaded supplies on small Nationalist landing vessels. These were shelled as soon as they crossed the three-mile limit which had been tacitly agreed upon. We in turn did not use planes against Chinese shore batteries. Neither of these limitations came about through explicit agreement. Neither would have been thought very sensible had it been proposed as a model at military staff colleges.

Though limitations must be to some extent arbitrary, not every limitation is equally useful. Self-restraint, illogical or otherwise, will be effective only if each side understands the intentions of the other and co-operates. Otherwise, what is intended as limited resistance may be construed as the prelude to all-out war and dealt with accordingly. However intense the desire to limit a conflict, it could expand because of a failure of communication.[2] For these reasons, the limitations which inspire greatest confidence are those which might most "naturally" occur to *both* parties—assuming they wish to establish limitations—and without this desire no limitation of any kind is feasible.

For example, any limited war must have some sanctuary areas— if only because a global war cannot be considered limited. There is no particular reason for establishing the boundaries of these sanctuaries in any particular place. In practice, however, the danger of misunderstanding is least if the sanctuary follows national boundaries. This is not because other demarcation lines are technically unfeasible. It is rather that it will prove more difficult to agree on a line chosen entirely at random. The more "unfamiliar"

[2] For a brilliant discussion see Thomas Schelling, "Bargaining, Communication and Limited War," *Journal of Conflict Resolution*, Vol. 1, No. 1, March, 1957.

the limitations, the more difficult it will be to make them stick. This consideration will be of importance in discussing the relative emphasis to be given to conventional or nuclear weapons in limited war.

Nevertheless, it would be irresponsible to minimize the risk of escalation. It will be great in proportion as limited war is conceived entirely as a strategic problem rather than an opportunity for a pause to permit negotiations. Limited war should not be considered a cheaper method of imposing unconditional surrender but an opportunity for another attempt to prevent a final showdown. We must enter it prepared to negotiate and to settle for something less than our traditional notion of complete victory. To be sure, the most likely outcome of a conflict fought in this manner is a stalemate. But the high likelihood of a stalemate would seem to deprive aggression of its object. Hence deterrence would be achieved.

It is often argued that, if both sides could agree on anything as complicated as limited war, they could probably agree on keeping the peace in the first place. But this is essentially a debating point. The problem of limited war obviously will not arise if there is agreement on outstanding issues or if the Communists do not resort to pressure, blackmail or aggression. But at the end of a decade marked by the Korean war, the Indo-Chinese war, the Hungarian rebellion, Suez, Lebanon, Quemoy, the pressure on Berlin, the threats over Cuba and the Congo, it should no longer be necessary to argue about the possibility of conflict. Limited war is not a solution for all contemporary problems. It is not a substitute for constructive policy. It does offer the possibility—not the certainty—of avoiding catastrophe. A strategy based on it enhances deterrence. If deterrence fails, it provides another opportunity for both sides to prevent a catastrophe.

The claim is made that the functions of obtaining a breathing space for negotiations and of bringing home to the opponents the risk of all-out war do not require a very substantial limited-war establishment. As a token of our determination, so the argument goes, a regiment may be as useful as a division. Indeed, its deterrent effect may be greater. Even if a limited-war establishment is necessary to make plausible the threat of massive retaliation, we must not leave the impression that we would be prepared to rely *entirely* on limited-war forces. According to this school of thought, the sooner the point is reached at which we could escape a setback only by resorting to all-out war, the stronger our deterrent position will be. A substantial limited-war establishment might raise doubts about our ultimate resolve and thereby bring on aggression.

But as the missile age develops, an inadequate limited-war establishment may combine the worst features of every strategic choice. If we place only a *little step* between surrender and all-out war, the Soviet opportunity to blackmail the free world will substantially remain. The dread alternative of surrender or suicide will even be compounded by the risk of a series of "small" defeats, none of which seems "worth" an all-out war. The consequences may be positive Communist incentive to defeat small American limited-war forces—if only to demonstrate our impotence. In the approaching period of mutual invulnerability, the United States cannot impose on itself the burden of having to respond to every challenge with the threat of self-destruction. And it only fudges the issue to look at the limited-war establishment primarily as a trigger for the retaliatory force. The free world will not be really safe until it can shift on to the aggressor the risk of initiating all-out war.

There are two categories of criticism of the concept of limited war, then. Some question it because they believe limitation will be *too* effective and this, they assert, violates traditional notions of warfare. Others object because they do not believe limitation can be effective enough.

The fact of our vulnerability has not been easy to accept by those who but ten years ago conceived the retaliatory strategy as the most "modern" utilization of our industrial potential and who now find themselves in the conservative position. Many of them construe any attempt to develop an alternative to a strategy of devastation in the age of nuclear plenty as foregoing a unilateral advantage. General Power has argued: "I think if we get into a war which is not a little tiny police action, I do not want to see us use conventional bombs, because I have a deep moral sense as it applies to Americans. I get a little indignant with people who become very lofty in their thinking and do not want to kill a few of the enemy but would gladly risk additional American lives. My crews are more important to me than the enemy. If I can send only one airplane over and do the job of a thousand, that is what I want to do."[3]

The problem of nuclear as against conventional warfare will be discussed later in this chapter. For present purposes, it is enough to point out that even by General Power's yardstick the problem is not nearly so simple. The choice is not between airplane crews and enemy targets. An attack on the aggressor's civilian population may cost *more* American lives than any other strategy because of the certainty of retaliation. Deterrence is the art of posing the maximum *credible* risk. In the age of nuclear plenty and growing missile forces this is more likely to be provided by a strategy of limited war than by a retaliatory threat always in danger of becoming an empty pose.

It is easy to understand the objection of the traditionalists to the concept of limited war. But the violence of the criticism of some of the other groups is puzzling. They pretend that those who urge a greater reliance on limited war wish to bring it about. They give the impression that the choice before us is peace or limited war and they then proceed to demonstrate the easy proposition that peace is preferable.

However, our alternatives are quite different. No responsible person advocates *initiating* limited war. The problem of limited war will arise only in case of Communist aggression or blackmail. In these circumstances, if we reject the concept of limited war, our only options will be surrender or all-out war. And it does not make sense to ridicule the notion of limited war because it *might* lead to general war and then to rely on a military policy which gives us no other choice but all-out war. The conclusion is almost inescapable that in case of Soviet aggression—the only contingency worth discussing in this context—many of those ridiculing the concept of limited war would prefer surrender to resistance.

Since surrender will not be our national policy, it is important

[3] General Power in Hearings before the Subcommittee of the Committee on Appropriations, House of Representatives, 86th Congress, 1st Session, Part 2, p. 388, Feb. 13, 1959.

to get our choices straight. Limited war is palatable only when compared with other even starker alternatives. It is preferable not to peace, but to surrender or all-out war. It is, to be sure, a subtle and complex task, and it presupposes a rare blend of psychological, political and military skill. Yet facts cannot be evaded by refusing to admit their existence. We do not have the time to lament our condition. Our best thought is required for adjusting to new conditions in a world where the truths of one decade become the obstacles to the understanding of another.

2. SOME FORMS OF LIMITATION

A. *The Prerequisites of Limitation*

There are three prerequisites for a strategy of limited war: (1) the limited war forces must be able to prevent the potential aggressor from creating a *fait accompli;* (2) they must be of a nature to convince the aggressor that their use, while involving an increased risk of all-out war, is not an inevitable prelude to it; (3) they must be coupled with a diplomacy which succeeds in conveying that all-out war is not the sole response to aggression and that there exists a willingness to negotiate a settlement short of unconditional surrender.

If the limited war forces of the free world can be overrun easily, aggression or blackmail will be encouraged and the dilemmas of massive retaliation will then confront us in even sharper form. The danger of a *fait accompli* must demoralize our allies, whose major concern is not eventual liberation but protection of their territories from Communist occupation. If we resist by measures which we intend to be limited but which an opponent interprets as the prelude to an all-out war, he may launch a pre-emptive attack. If our diplomacy cannot take advantage of pauses in military operations to negotiate a settlement, if we make the issue depend on "purely" military considerations, any conflict is likely to expand by stages into a conflagration.

Considered in the abstract, these requirements can be met in a number of ways. Some argue that the retaliatory force is also suitable for limited war because of its ability to engage in graduated retaliation or limited strategic warfare. Others advocate a strategy of indirect retaliation designed to punish an aggressor, though not necessarily at the place where aggression occurs. Still others would rely on guerrilla activity. Finally, there is a school of thought which stresses the importance of local defense.

All of these measures afford opportunities for resisting aggression short of all-out war. Each of them has uses in deterring aggression and in furnishing alternatives to general war. Yet their consequences for diplomacy, deterrence and strategy vary. They will be discussed in turn.

B. Limited Strategic War and Graduated Retaliation

The concepts of "limited" strategic war and graduated retaliation are based on the premise that the retaliatory force can be used for objectives other than general war. Limited strategic war seeks to resist aggression by measures which are normally a prelude to all-out war without making an irrevocable commitment to a showdown. It strives for a military advantage but stops short of launching an all-out blow. For example, in response to Soviet occupation of West Berlin we could destroy part of the Soviet radar warning net or part of the Soviet retaliatory force. This would serve as a warning of the consequences of persisting in the aggressive course by increasing Soviet vulnerability to an all-out attack. If taken seriously and if the Soviet Union were unwilling to risk all-out war, such a course might lead to a restoration of the *status quo ante*.

Graduated retaliation would not strive for a military advantage as such. Rather an attempt would be made to inflict sufficient damage on the aggressor to cause him to desist without impairing his retaliatory capability. In case of an attack on Iran, for example, we might announce that we would destroy certain specified Soviet installations or cities each week until the Soviet army had again withdrawn behind its borders. According to the theory of limited retaliation, the aggressor will settle when the cost of retaliation exceeds the value of the objective.

There are major difficulties, however, with using the retaliatory force in this manner. From the point of view of deterrence, it is not easy to imagine how a country would convey its determination to resist aggression by using its retaliatory force while at the same time convincing the opponent that such measures are *not* a prelude to an all-out blow. All the difficulties of making the threat of all-out war plausible would seem to apply with even greater force in this case. If we convey our desire to establish *some* limitation to our retaliation, the threat of all-out war may lose the last vestiges of credibility. On the other hand, if we do not make the attempt to communicate our intention to limit the employment of our retaliatory force, a Soviet pre-emptive strike would seem inevitable. In short, the threat of limited strategic war or graduated retaliation is either too convincing or not convincing enough.

Reliance on either limited strategic war or graduated retaliation would in fact confront us with an almost hopeless dilemma. In case of Communist aggression, an American President would be faced with the decision of initiating a type of conflict which could not protect the victim of the aggression and which might expose the United States to fearful devastation. This becomes clear if one imagines a Communist note to the United States delivered concurrently with an attack on an ally somewhat along the following lines: "We are very eager to avoid all-out war. Moreover, it is pointless to retaliate against us since our retaliatory force is invulnerable. To show our good intentions we will overlook attacks you make in the first few hours after this communication. From then on, we will devastate the United States in precise proportion to your attack but no more." Is it a foregone conclusion that a President would use our retaliatory force in that case? Or that he would be wise to do so?

Even if we resorted to a retaliatory strategy—however limited—we would still be at a fundamental psychological disadvantage. We would be forced to engage in actions each of which would almost guarantee similar destruction in the free world, and we would run the constant risk of all-out war while the issue which produced the conflict had already been settled in the aggressor's favor. Every passing day would strengthen the Soviet hold on its prize and bring home to us the futility of our course. The Communist leaders may well calculate that skillful peace offensives would cause us to weary of so unrewarding a strategy, unless complete frustration were to induce us to launch an all-out war.

From the strictly military point of view, a strategy of "limited" strategic war is equally risky. If the aggressor's retaliatory force is vulnerable, he will have no choice but to launch a pre-emptive attack. For his vulnerability prevents him from waiting to determine the extent of the blow. If his force is invulnerable, however, the result may be a strategy of tit for tat leading to devastation approaching the scale of all-out war. In short, we may find that we have to choose between ineffectualness or all-out war.

Graduated retaliation might supply less of a military incentive to retaliate than limited strategic war. As long as his retaliatory force remains intact, the aggressor may be prepared to endure a measure of damage without retaliation, if only to demonstrate the futility of our military effort. On the other hand, it would be reckless to count on this. While the military compulsion on the aggressor to retaliate may be weaker than in the case of limited strategic war, the psychological compulsion will be greater. It will be difficult not to react when one's own civilian population is under attack. Moreover, the aggressor may mistake what we intend as graduated retaliation for the prelude to an all-out attack—unless we behave with a self-defeating circumspection. Thus, whatever eventuality is considered, the most likely outcome of the limited employment of the retaliatory force is either defeat or all-out war.

To be effective, the limited employment of retaliatory forces must meet two requirements which in practice cancel each other out: The aggressor must be convinced (1) that a strategy of limited strategic war or graduated retaliation, while it increases the risk of all-out war, is not an inevitable prelude to it and (2) that we *are* prepared to resort to all-out war rather than accept defeat. If we fail to meet the first condition, the opponent will probably strike pre-emptively. If we fail to meet the second condition, the aggressor may be encouraged to outwait us or to engage in a test of nerves with a built-in escalator to all-out war.

Of course, the very riskiness of such a course may make the aggressor recoil. The ease with which matters *could* get out of hand may add to deterrence. But as long as the aggressor is in possession of his prize he may have an incentive to outlast us. A strategy of tit for tat would still amount to a victory for him. In most circumstances, limited strategic war will probably combine the disadvantages of limited and of all-out war.

The problem is even more serious for other countries of the free world. Communist blackmail against them is based importantly on the ability to overrun them and to expose them to all the problems of Communist occupation and social upheaval. This danger is not reduced by using our retaliatory force in a limited manner. The Communist leaders would still be able to menace the Prime Minister of a free country somewhat as follows: "If you do not disarm completely, our forces will move in to dismantle your military establishment. To be sure, in that case the Americans *may* retaliate against us. But this will only give us an added incentive to remain and to restore our economy from your country. Whether the American retaliation is limited or all-out we will respond in kind. We shall see whose nerves snap first. Whatever the outcome of a Soviet-United States war, your country as you now know it will cease to exist."

In the face of such a threat resistance may well seem quixotic. For whether we retaliate or not, the threatened country will be overrun. In these circumstances, many nations of the free world may seek to obtain the most favorable terms possible. Thus the limited employment of retaliatory forces confronts the free world with most complex psychological and political problems, while at the same time committing us to a strategy peculiarly unsuitable to limitation.

C. Indirect Retaliation

Advocates of a strategy of indirect retaliation address themselves to what they consider the basic dilemma of our defense policy: attacks on the Communist homeland and particularly on its retaliatory force are too risky, while it is impractical to defend the entire Communist perimeter locally. Accordingly they argue that resistance need not occur at the spot where aggression takes place. Rather we should utilize the special advantages of our strategic position, particularly our superior seapower. Aggression against, say, Iran could be resisted, so the argument goes, by such measures as closing the Dardanelles or a blockade of the Soviet Union. Pressure against Berlin could be countered by economic sanctions against Eastern

Europe or perhaps closing the Straits of Denmark.

Such a strategy would avoid many of the risks of the limited use of our retaliatory force. It might enhance deterrence by emphasizing a threat which is plausible. The gap between deterrence and the strategy we are willing to implement would be smaller. At the same time a strategy of indirect retaliation raises serious problems of its own. From the point of view of deterrence it may reduce the risk to the aggressor to the point where blackmail or military pressure becomes tempting. Where the limited use of the retaliatory force involves an undue danger of all-out war, most measures of indirect retaliation are too circumscribed and long-term in their effect to influence the immediate situation. Closing the Dardanelles could not save Iran any more than a naval blockade could save Berlin. And the impact of these measures on the U.S.S.R. would be long delayed.

As a result, we would be forced to maintain over an indefinite period measures whose utility every passing day would cast in doubt. They might in fact supply an incentive to the Communists to demonstrate their immunity to American pressure and the impotence of our response. And, after a sufficient lapse of time, it would be difficult to resist Soviet suggestions urging us to adjust to facts. The increasing pressure to accept the Soviet domination over Eastern Europe is a good case in point.

If such a strategy presents great complexities for the United States, it is perhaps the least desirable course of action for our allies. The blackmail situation described earlier will be even more poignant when the American response is so indirect. With Soviet occupation unavoidable in case of resistance, wide scope exists for the gradual erosion of morale through steady Soviet pressure. A strategy based entirely on indirect retaliation must lead eventually to a disintegration of the free world.

D. Guerrilla Warfare

Many thoughtful people, horrified by the risks of nuclear war, have come to the conclusion that any conflict involving the great powers would carry with it an intolerable risk of expanding into a nuclear holocaust. They therefore urge that the aggression be deterred by organizing the civilian population into guerrilla groups and confronting the Communists with the prospect of a long drawn-out campaign of pacification.

One difficulty with this view is that it oversimplifies the task. There is no known instance of large-scale sustained partisan activity in any Communist-controlled territory. Those uprisings which have occurred were suppressed ruthlessly and quickly. Little in their experience would cause the Communist leaders to be overly impressed by the threat of popular resistance, and Communist theory would make them doubt even its possibility. Popular resistance in Hungary and Tibet did not prove an extended obstacle to Communist rule.

Moreover, whatever the effectiveness of guerrilla warfare as a strategy, its utility as a threat for purposes of deterrence is highly questionable. A country relying on partisan warfare for deterrence would have to convince the potential aggressor that, while it would offer no organized resistance, it would be able to train guerrilla groups and would persevere in using them until the aggressor withdrew. These two requirements are to a large extent inconsistent with each other. The decision not to resist with organized forces can only be interpreted by the aggressor as lack of will. The threat to resort to partisan warfare is most likely to be construed as bluster. It is not easy to see what concrete steps could be taken to demonstrate the readiness for guerrilla warfare or how a leadership group could be certain of its ability to carry out its threat.

To make such a deterrent effective, a government would have to convince an aggressor that, while unable to protect its people against invasion, it has sufficient prestige to ask for the most difficult and, for those involved, most costly form of resistance. The more highly organized a society and the greater its discipline, the more an aggressor is likely to regard the threat of guerrilla warfare as bluff. In highly integrated Western societies, moreover, the measures required to prove a serious intention to conduct partisan warfare are also likely to inspire a feeling of hopelessness. The specialization of function on which Western societies depend requires an efficient administrative group and a cohesive governmental apparatus. The occupying power has, therefore, many foci for pressure. It can appeal to the sense of order and discipline of the administrators. It can use terror. And if it fails, the breakdown of the subtle interrelationships of modern society is almost certain to have more direct consequences for the indigenous population than for the occupying power.

Partisan activity has generally been most effective in primitive societies and precisely because of the absence of identifiable control. In these societies there exists no group with sufficient authority against which effective pressure can be brought. To propose such a strategy for Europe reveals a deep misunderstanding of the requirements of deterrence and of the psychology of Western societies.

Guerrilla warfare almost invariably requires special conditions to be possible at all: conditions of terrain, as in Yugoslavia or Algeria, or of overwhelming numbers, as in China, or of vast expanse, such as in Russia. Even then it could be conducted generally only when there was outside support, both military and moral, giving some prospect of eventual victory. Partisan warfare can make a contribution to other forms of resistance. It cannot be substituted for them.

E. The Requirement of Local Defense

If the free world is to avoid gradual erosion, it must be able to avoid the *fait accompli* of Communist occupation. A capacity for local defense is essential to bring our deterrent policy in line with the strategy for fighting a war and the requirements of our security with those of our allies.

A *fait accompli* changes the attempt to *prevent* a given event, which is the basis of deterrence, to an effort to *compel* a certain course of action. Once a *fait accompli* exists, the purpose of strategy is no longer to induce a potential aggressor to refrain from attacking. It must force him to withdraw. In deciding to attack, the psychological burden is on the aggressor: he must take an affirmative step and his hesitation will be great in proportion as the objective seems unattainable. Once the aggressor is in possession of his prize, however, the psychological burden shifts in his favor. The defender must now assume the risk of the first move. The aggressor can confine himself to outwaiting his opponent. The aggressor becomes more committed to his prize the longer he is in possession of it, while his opponent's incentive to persevere is diminished with every day that the *fait accompli* endures. When resisting occupation, the defender has the option of persevering in self-defense or surrendering. When the aggressor has already gained his objective, the defender can have peace by settling for the new *status quo*. In all limited-war strategies save that of local defense, the psychological balance is in favor of the aggressor and will become so increasingly the longer the conflict lasts. This is because only local defense can prevent a *fait accompli*.

If threatened areas cannot be protected against occupation, the scope of Communist blackmail will constantly expand. The disparity in forces suitable for local defense must be remedied or the crisis over Berlin will prove but an augury of ever-increasing pressure. A measure of this security can no doubt be achieved by some of the schemes for arms control discussed below. But unless the present disparity in local power is remedied, the Soviet leaders will see little incentive for serious negotiations. The Soviet Union will feel better protected by its local preponderance than by an arms control scheme that might be negotiated.

In building up these forces, the West faces many obstacles, not the least of which are its own preconceptions. For over a decade and a half, the axiom that the West could not possibly match Communist manpower, interior lines of communication, and more centralized command arrangements has been essentially unchallenged. The conviction is general that technology must substitute for manpower. A strategy of punishment has been seen as the best counter to the Communist "hordes." These notions have been reinforced by budgetary considerations. No Western government has been willing to ask of its people the sacrifices required to develop a capability for local defense. "More bang for the buck" thus emerged as an axiom not only of strategic but also of fiscal wisdom.

But whatever the merit of these views when they were first developed, the simple choices of our period of invulnerability are no longer open to us. Continued reliance on the military policy of the past decade will produce not deterrence but paralysis. Far from holding our alliances together, it will undermine them. Building up a greater capacity for local defense is no longer a question of choice. It has been imposed on the free world by the technological revolution of the past decade and a half.

Many of the assumptions regarding the impossibility of local defense are either fallacious or exaggerated. In total available manpower the free world still is superior, and its industrial potential exceeds that of the Communist bloc by a factor of three. There is no reason except lack of will why Western Europe and the United States cannot create local forces capable of arresting almost any scale of Soviet aggression.[4] To be sure, in other areas the problem is more complicated. In the so-called "gray areas" of the Middle East and South-East Asia, the Communist bloc can concentrate its manpower and material against countries weaker, less closely allied, and less well situated to support each other than those of the North Atlantic Community. On the other hand, these are also the areas where the political penalties for aggression would be greatest. An attack on a new nation would antagonize all the other uncommitted nations and it would lead to an increased mobilization of Western resources. Moreover, difficulties of terrain and communications place a ceiling on the number of troops an aggressor could utilize effectively even there.

The inability to protect every area locally is no excuse for failing to secure those where it is possible. The minimum goal of local defense must be to prevent the possibility of cheap victories. The optimum situation is where aggression can be defeated locally. The latter situation is attainable in Europe. And the position of other areas can be improved through their own forces and increases in the American limited-war capability.

Perhaps, as is often alleged, public opinion in the West would not support such an effort. But no one can know, for the issue has never been presented to it. If the democracies cannot muster a leadership willing to stake its political future on a program essential to survival, its political future is dim indeed. In that case, at least lack of courage should not be compounded by self-delusion. No technical gadget can substitute for sacrifice. No refinements or adaptations of retaliatory strategy can change the fact that opportunities for Com-

---

[4] See "The United States and Europe," Chap. IV, pp. 101 ff.

munist blackmail will constantly increase. Not to build up a capacity for local defense in the name of maintaining living standards is to purchase a brief period of comfort at the risk of losing everything.

Building up a capability for local defense is a complex but not insoluble task, made all the more necessary by the starkness of the alternatives. The rewards are high. To a considerable extent, a strategy of local defense will lift from the West the impossible choices of current military policy. It will increase the flexibility of Western diplomacy. It is the prerequisite of effective arms control negotiations. For as long as there is a wide disparity in local power, the Soviet Union will not have an incentive for serious arms control. In devising a strategy of local defense, however, we come up squarely against one of the great unresolved issues of Western military policy: the relative significance of nuclear and conventional weapons.

3. LIMITED WAR: NUCLEAR OR CONVENTIONAL?

A. *The Nature of the Debate*

Few issues have aroused more controversy than the relative roles of conventional and nuclear weapons in Western strategy. Its resolution is of vital significance for our strategy, our alliance policy, and the future of arms control negotiations.

Two facts need to be understood at the outset. The first is that no war in the nuclear age can ever be completely free of the specter of nuclear weapons—at least until arms control measures are much further advanced and much more reliable. In a war between nuclear powers, even if no nuclear weapons are used, both sides would have to take account of the possibility that they *might* be. The tactics would necessarily differ from those of World War II; deployment would have to guard against the sudden introduction of nuclear weapons. Diplomats would have to negotiate with the knowledge that any prolonged conventional war might turn into a nuclear conflict, if not a final showdown. Every war henceforth will be nuclear to a greater or lesser extent, whether or not nuclear weapons are used.

A second fact is equally important: the choice between using conventional or nuclear weapons is no longer entirely up to us. The Soviet nuclear arsenal is growing. Soviet military journals report tactical exercises with nuclear weapons. We cannot gear our strategy or stake our survival on the assumption that nuclear weapons will *not* be used against us. Even if we prefer to resist with conventional weapons, we have to be prepared for nuclear war as well. Only being ready for limited nuclear war will give us the option of a conventional strategy.

With this background, we can summarize the arguments for both sides. Advocates of a nuclear strategy emphasize the disparity in mobilizable manpower between the Communist bloc and the free world, a disparity made even more acute by the Communist ability to concentrate their whole weight against states much smaller and much less well equipped. Nuclear weapons, it is claimed, can serve as a substitute for manpower. At the very least they will force an aggressor to disperse his forces. This will prevent breakthroughs of established defensive positions and the consolidation of occupied territory.

The proponents of a nuclear strategy admit that if nuclear weapons were simply added to the tactics of World War II the result would probably be the complete devastation of the combat zone. They point out that such a course would be senseless. The cost of a nuclear strategy must be judged in terms of the tactics appropriate to nuclear weapons. Since nuclear weapons are so destructive and at the same time so easy to transport, large military formations cannot be maintained in the field. And they are unnecessary because firepower is no longer dependent on massed armies. To concentrate is to court disaster. Safety resides in mobility. Logistics must be simple. The traditional supply system is too cumbersome and too vulnerable. Accordingly, a great premium will be placed on small, self-contained units of high mobility. In such circumstances, it is argued, damage would not be excessive; indeed, it might be less than that of a conventional war of the World War II variety with a flankless front line rolling over the countryside.

A nuclear strategy according to its proponents would have these advantages: (a) The dispersal of troops would separate the requirements of victory from those of controlling territory. To prevail in a nuclear war, it is necessary to have small, highly mobile units. To control territory, larger concentrations are required, particularly in the key centers of administration. For example, the Soviet army required some twenty divisions to crush the Hungarian rebellion. Such a concentration, it is argued, would have been impossible if the Soviets had had to face nuclear weapons. (b) Nuclear war would complicate the aggressor's calculations—if only because it is an unfamiliar mode of warfare. The Soviet Union and Communist China possess many "experts" in conventional warfare, but with respect to nuclear war their calculations are of necessity theoretical. There would always remain the inevitable uncertainty of embarking on a course in which no experience is available. (c) Nuclear war would be an effective device to weaken Communist control over the satellite areas. The small detachments which are appropriate for nuclear war will be extremely vulnerable to guerrilla activity and can be handicapped severely by a hostile population. Since the population on the Western side of the Iron Curtain is more loyal to its governments than those under Communist rule, a nuclear war is thought to be the best means of exploiting Soviet political difficulties—at least in Europe—and therefore the most effective means of deterring Soviet aggression. (d) Nuclear weapons are our "best weapons," the result of our most advanced technology. To forego using them is to deprive ourselves of the advantages of a superior industrial potential. (e) Any other course would impose impossible force requirements. It is admittedly impossible to fight a conventional war against a nuclear enemy without having a nuclear establishment in the field—otherwise, the temptation for the aggressor to use nuclear weapons and sweep all before him might become overwhelming. This means that we would need a well-protected retaliatory force, a capable limited-war force, and increasing conventional strength. Since the expense of maintaining each category even at present levels is multiplying, any attempt to build up conventional forces must result in a fundamental, perhaps fatal, weakness in each category.[5]

[5] For a fuller discussion of limited nuclear war, see the author's *Nuclear Weapons and Foreign Policy* (New York, 1957), Chap. VI: "Problems of Limited Nuclear War," pp. 191 ff.

The advocates of a conventional strategy reply that the decision to use nuclear weapons is inconsistent with the very concept of limitation. Pointing to such military exercises with nuclear weapons as *Carte Blanche* in Europe and *Sagebrush* in the United States, they stress that the inevitable consequence of nuclear war will be the desolation of the combat zone and the decimation of the population. No country would wish to be defended at that price. Even a "successful" nuclear war would provide a conclusive argument for future Soviet blackmail.

Moreover, once nuclear weapons are used, so this school of thought reasons, all restraints may disappear. It will be difficult enough to establish the limits of a conventional war. Because of their very unfamiliarity, nuclear weapons would make the task nearly impossible. The fact that there exists a continuous spectrum of destructiveness in nuclear weapons, so often invoked by advocates of a nuclear strategy in defense of their thesis, is used by their critics against them. If the distinction between the low-yield and high-yield weapons is so difficult, if so much depends on the manner of employing them, any effort to set limits based on explosive equivalent will be meaningless. The temptation to resort to ever more destructive weapons will be overwhelming.

Proponents of a conventional strategy question not only the possibility of limitation but also the efficacy of the tactics thought to be appropriate for nuclear war. Small detachments, they contend, whatever their nuclear firepower, would be extremely vulnerable to harassment and defeat by conventional forces. When confronted by an opponent possessing both a nuclear and a conventional capability, they are almost certain to lose, for they would be largely defenseless against small conventional raiding parties. Nuclear weapons, it is argued, are not a substitute for manpower. On the contrary, nuclear war, because of its high rate of attrition, would probably require more troops, not less.

Finally, so the argument goes, our industrial potential will be less significant in a nuclear war than in a conventional one. Since nuclear weapons provide greater destructiveness per unit cost than conventional explosives, reliance on them enables economically weaker nations to redress the strategic balance much more easily than they could with conventional forces. A point is likely to be reached for any given objective or area at which additional increments of explosive power are no longer strategically significant. When this "saturation point" is reached, superiority in nuclear weapons may be meaningless. Nuclear weapons place a premium on surprise attack and sudden thrusts to which the defender is much more vulnerable than the attacker. To rely on a nuclear strategy, it is urged, would thus be adopting a course of conduct which rewards the qualities in which potential aggressors excel.

A conventional strategy according to its advocates would have these four advantages: (1) It would provide the best chance to limit any conflict that might break out. (2) It would use our industrial potential to best advantage. Since the destructive power of individual conventional weapons is relatively low, victory can be achieved only through a substantial production effort which puts a premium on our special skills. At the same time, the relatively slow pace of military operations—at least compared to nuclear war—and the need to build up supplies before each new engagement give the maximum opportunity for attempting a political settlement. (3) Conventional defense provides the best means of preventing the occupation of threatened countries. The concept of a flankless line which advocates of a nuclear strategy wish to abandon is likely to be considered by threatened countries the best guarantee of their safety. Liberation will always be a less attractive prospect than protection. (4) If nuclear weapons were used, after all, the onus of initiating such a war would be shifted to the Communist states.

One of the difficulties in resolving these arguments is that the moral fervor of the debaters sometimes obscures the nature of the issues and often causes them to claim too much: those who think that to forego nuclear weapons is an offense against progress have as their counterpart those who are passionately convinced that even to consider modalities of nuclear warfare is to insult morality. As a result, arguments that closer examination would reveal as imprecise and sometimes as erroneous have been elevated into dogma.

For example, it is often said that a nuclear war cannot be limited because neither side would accept defeat without resorting to ever larger weapons. Now, there are many good reasons for concern about the possibility of limiting nuclear war. But the argument that neither side will be prepared to accept a setback without expanding the conflict implies that it is somehow politically more unbearable to be defeated in a limited nuclear war than in a limited conventional one. In this form, it is a criticism of *every* form of limited war and not simply of the nuclear conflict. It is not clear why a country should be more willing to acquiesce in a conventional than in a nuclear defeat. On the contrary, the decision as to whether a war is to be expanded is likely to depend more on the value attached to the objective than on the weapons used to attain it. Whatever the technical difficulties of limiting nuclear war, the political argument that it makes defeat unacceptable does not bear scrutiny.

On the other side of the debate, a nuclear strategy is often justified by the spectrum of available weapons. The smallest nuclear weapons, it is said, are less destructive than the most powerful conventional devices. There is therefore no technical reason for recoiling before nuclear warfare and every reason to use our most "advanced" technology. However, the effort to base a nuclear strategy on the discrimination of nuclear weapons surely goes too far. The chief motive for using nuclear weapons is, after all, their greater destructive power and their lower weight per explosive equivalent. Nuclear weapons no more destructive than conventional ones would probably not be worth the increased risk of escalation inherent in an unfamiliar mode of warfare.

The controversy has produced frustration rather than clarity because, in so many respects, both the proponents and the opponents of a nuclear strategy are right: their disagreements arise from the perspective from which they consider the issue. Looking at the problem from the point of view of deterrence, the advocates of a nuclear strategy argue that nuclear weapons are the most effective sanction against the outbreak of a war. Considering the actual conduct of a war, the opponents of a nuclear strategy are above all concerned with reducing the impact of military operations and increasing their predictability. The destructiveness of individual weapons and the uncertainties of an unfamiliar mode of warfare which are correctly adduced as contributing to deterrence can, with equal justification, be cited as working against effective limitation.

The issue therefore turns on the question of what should be stressed: deterrence or the strategy for fighting a war. Obviously an overemphasis on destructiveness may paralyze the will. But an overconcern with developing a tolerable strategy for the conduct of war may reduce the risks of aggression to such a degree that it will be encouraged. While the deterrent threat must be credible, the quest for credibility must not lower the penalties to a point where they are no longer unacceptable. A course of action that increases the opponent's uncertainties about the nature of the conflict will generally discourage aggression. If war should break out, however, through accident or miscalculation, it may make limitation extremely difficult.

B. A Direction for U.S. Strategy

Some years ago this author advocated a nuclear strategy.[6] It seemed then that the most effective deterrent to any substantial Communist aggression was the knowledge that the United States would employ nuclear weapons from the very outset. A nuclear strategy appeared to offer the best prospect of offsetting Sino-Soviet manpower and of using our superior industrial capacity to best advantage.

The need for forces capable of fighting limited nuclear war remains. However, several developments have caused a shift in the view about the relative emphasis to be given conventional forces as against nuclear forces. These are: (1) the disagreement within our military establishment and within the alliance about the nature of limited nuclear war; (2) the growth of the Soviet nuclear stockpile and the increased significance of long-range missiles; (3) the impact of arms control negotiations. The first of these considerations raises doubts as to whether we would know how to limit nuclear war. The second alters the strategic significance of nuclear war. The third influences the framework in which any strategy will have to be conducted and determines the political cost.

While it is feasible to design a theoretical model for limited nuclear war, the fact remains that fifteen years after the beginning of the nuclear age no such model has ever won general agreement. It

[6] See the author's *Nuclear Weapons*, pp. 174 ff.

would be next to impossible to obtain a coherent description of what is understood by "limited nuclear war" from our military establishment. The Air Force thinks of it as control over a defined air space. The Army considers it vital to destroy tactical targets which can affect ground operations, including centers of communications. The Navy is primarily concerned with eliminating port installations. Even within a given service, a detailed, coherent doctrine is often lacking. The Strategic Air Command and the Tactical Air Force almost surely interpret the nature of limited nuclear war differently. Since disputes about targets are usually settled by addition—by permitting each service to destroy what it considers essential to its mission—a limited nuclear war fought in this manner may well become indistinguishable from all-out war. At least it would diminish our self-assurance and subtlety in an operation in which everything would depend on the ability to remain in control of events.

The disagreements between our services are repeated in relations with our allies. Few of our allies possess nuclear weapons. Those that do have emphasized the retaliatory and not the tactical aspect of nuclear warfare. Public opinion in most allied countries has been mobilized against nuclear weapons by a variety of sources. And these attitudes are reinforced by current trends in arms control negotiations. In these circumstances, it will become increasingly difficult to construct a strategic and tactical doctrine which is accepted by the alliance and maintained with conviction in the face of Soviet pressure. This leads one to doubt whether the West will possess either the knowledge or the daring to impose limitations. If it relies *entirely* on a nuclear strategy, its vulnerability to nuclear blackmail both before and during hostilities will be considerable.

To be sure, any limitation of war is to some extent arbitrary. There is probably some disagreement even as to the nature of limited conventional war. The problem of communicating intentions to an opponent will be difficult regardless of the mode of warfare. But this makes it all the more important that the limitations which are attempted should be reasonably familiar.

Even with the best intentions on both sides, a nuclear war will be more difficult to limit than a conventional one. Since no country has had any experience with the tactical use of nuclear weapons, the possibility of miscalculation is considerable. The temptation to use the same target system as for conventional war and thereby produce vast casualties will be overwhelming. The pace of operations may outstrip the possibilities of negotiation. Both sides would be operating in the dark with no precedents to guide them and a necessarily inadequate understanding of the purposes of the opponent, if not their own. The dividing line between conventional and nuclear weapons is more familiar and therefore easier to maintain—assuming the will to do so—than any distinction within the spectrum of nuclear weapons. This uncertainty may increase deterrence. It will also magnify the risks of conflict should deterrence fail.

These considerations are reinforced by the strategic changes wrought by the advent of the age of nuclear plenty and of the long-range missile. When nuclear material was relatively scarce, it was possible to believe that tactical nuclear weapons might give the West an advantage in limited war. Under conditions of nuclear scarcity, the Soviet Union would have had to make a choice: it could not simultaneously push the development of its retaliatory force and also equip its ground forces for nuclear war. Whatever alternative was chosen would produce a weakness in *some* category. Since the logical decision for the Soviets seemed to be to give priority to the retaliatory force, it was then held that tactical nuclear weapons could be used to offset Soviet conventional preponderance.

In the meantime, the Soviet nuclear stockpile has multiplied. A nuclear strategy will now have to be conducted against an equally well-equipped opponent. In these circumstances, numbers become again important. Because of the destructiveness of nuclear weapons, the casualty rate among combat units is likely to be high. The side which has the more replacements available therefore stands to gain the upper hand. The notion that nuclear weapons can substitute for numerical inferiority has lost a great deal of its validity.

The development of missiles has accentuated the strategic problems of limited nuclear war. As long as delivery systems were composed of airplanes, air domination over the battle area on the model of our experience in the Korean war was conceivable. And tactical skill in handling the weapons *within* the combat zone might have led to victory on the nuclear battlefield. However, as missile forces grow on both sides, as even airplanes are equipped with medium-range missiles, this possibility steadily diminishes. For one thing, since nuclear weapons can be delivered accurately at considerable distances, it seems unnecessary to introduce major nuclear forces into the combat zone. More importantly, the only way of achieving what used to be considered air superiority is to destroy most of the opponent's medium- and intermediate-range missiles. Such an operation is difficult to reconcile with an attempt to limit hostilities. If, however, the areas where these missiles are located become sanctuaries, it would appear that a stalemate will almost inevitably be the outcome of a limited nuclear war.

Of course, such a result must not be minimized. An aggressor, certain that his attack would be checked, would presumably be deterred. The difficulty is the devastation of the combat zone, which would be the price of a stalemate. In some situations, it may be to the Communist advantage to settle for the *status quo ante* in a war that obliterates the disputed area. If a Soviet attack on West Germany should lead to the desolation of the Federal Republic, the Soviet Union would score a major gain even if it offered at some point to withdraw to its starting point. The devastation of Germany could be a means of convincing all other threatened areas of the futility of resistance. An "unsuccessful" attack of this nature might ensure the success of all future Soviet blackmail.

Finally, it would be idle to discount the impact on strategy of the pattern of arms control negotiations. At each conference, nuclear weapons have been placed in a separate category and stigmatized as weapons of mass destruction without any distinction as to type or device. The goal of eventual nuclear disarmament has been avowed by all states. A moratorium on nuclear testing has been in existence for two years and it is probable that a formal agreement will be signed. Future negotiations will almost inevitably reinforce this trend. The consequence will be that the inhibitions against using the weapons around which the West has built its whole military policy will multiply. Whatever the other consequences of a nuclear test ban, it will reinforce the already strong reluctance to use nuclear weapons in limited war.

In any given crisis, the possibility that resort to nuclear weapons would probably abrogate a test ban would probably be considered as one of the factors against using them. Similarly, we would have to weigh the tactical advantage of nuclear weapons against the political cost. Once nuclear weapons were used in limited war, it is possible that the pressure of other countries to acquire nuclear weapons of their own would grow irresistible. Or else world opinion would impel a renunciation of a strategy which might appear to have brought humanity to the brink of catastrophe. Whatever the likely result, the concern that use of nuclear weapons may have incalculable political effects could outweigh all military considerations.

These factors will create an extremely precarious situation if the free world continues to rely primarily on a nuclear strategy. The more the pressures against *any* use of nuclear weapons build up, the greater will be the gap between our deterrent policy, our military capability, and our psychological readiness—a gap which must tempt aggression. The years ahead must therefore see a substantial strengthening of the conventional forces of the free world. If strong enough to halt Soviet conventional attacks—as in areas such as Europe they could be—conventional forces would shift the onus and risk of initiating nuclear war to the other side. Even where they cannot resist every scale of attack, they should force the aggressor into military operations on a major scale. They would thereby make ultimate recourse to nuclear weapons politically and psychologically simpler, while affording an opportunity for a settlement before this step is taken.

Many of the assumptions regarding the impossibility of conventional defense and of "hordes" of Communist manpower are either fallacious or exaggerated. Both in available manpower and in industrial potential the free world still is superior. And conventional warfare favors the defense. It has been truly remarked that, but for the development of nuclear weapons, the defense would long since have achieved ascendancy over the offense. Even in World War II, the attacker generally required a superiority of three to one. And with improvements in conventional weapons technology— far simpler than many of those already accomplished in other fields

—this ratio could be increased further still.

At a minimum, the conventional capability of the free world should be sufficiently powerful so that a nuclear defense becomes the *last* and not the *only* recourse. The best situation is one in which the conventional forces of the free world can be overcome *only* by nuclear weapons. There is no technical reason why this should not be possible in Western Europe at least. Such forces would remove many opportunities for Soviet blackmail. They would increase the flexibility of our diplomacy. They would enable us to negotiate about the control of nuclear weapons with confidence.

C. Some Consequences

While a substantial build-up of conventional forces and a greater reliance on a conventional strategy are essential, it is equally vital not to press the conclusions too far. In their attempt to prove their case, many of the proponents of a conventional strategy have thought it necessary so to deride *any* reliance on nuclear weapons or to paint so awful a picture of atomic war that they defeat their own object. For against an opponent known to consider nuclear war as the worst evil, nuclear blackmail is an almost foolproof strategy. Conventional forces will be of no avail if an aggressor is convinced that he can probably force surrender by threatening to use nuclear weapons. A greater emphasis on conventional defense presupposes that the aggressor cannot promise himself an advantage from either the threat or the actuality of nuclear war. However much conventional war may be preferred to the use of nuclear weapons, limited nuclear war is preferable to all-out war.

Conventional forces should not be considered a substitute for a limited nuclear war capability but as a complement to it. For against an opponent equipped with nuclear weapons, it would be suicidal to rely entirely on conventional arms. Such a course would provide the precise incentive an aggressor needs to employ nuclear weapons and to sweep all before him. A conventional war can be kept within limits only if nuclear war seems more unattractive.

This becomes apparent when we analyze what options we have if, despite our best efforts in the conventional field, nuclear weapons are actually used against us. Three choices would then seem available: to accept defeat; to resort to general war; or to seek to conduct limited nuclear war. If we are unwilling to accept defeat—and to accept it under such circumstances would make us forever subject to nuclear blackmail—our choice resolves itself into all-out war or limited nuclear war. All-out war will become increasingly senseless as the missile age develops. Hence, conventional war can be kept conventional only if we maintain, together with our retaliatory force, an adequate capability for limited nuclear war. The aggressor must understand that we are in a position to match any increment of force, nuclear or conventional, that he may add. This would reduce the incentive to engage in aggression and, should deterrence fail, would provide the best chance of limiting hostilities.

It may be argued that this line of reasoning demonstrates the absurdity of placing greater reliance on conventional weapons. Nuclear weapons must favor one side or the other. If they favor us, so the argument runs, we should use them. If they give an advantage to the Communists, they will use them. In either case, nuclear war is inevitable. But the logical syllogism does not necessarily hold. Unless the superiority of one side grows overwhelming, the increased risks of an unfamiliar mode of warfare may outweigh the purely military benefits.

It is sometimes argued that a conventional strategy does not necessarily require an increase in conventional forces. Our national history reminds us of many wars where we prevailed, despite initial defeats, because of the might of our industrial potential. An aggressor, so the argument goes, would be more deterred by the possibility that we would build up our strength during a conflict than by the forces-in-being available to us at the beginning. The Korean war is only the latest demonstration of our ability to build up fairly quickly, provided only that we are able to hold the initial thrust of the aggressor for some time.

This view has great merit. Conventional weapons have a relatively low order of destructiveness and yet require a fairly substantial production effort. They therefore do place a premium on the West's industrial potential. At the same time, care must be taken not to draw the extreme conclusions from this fact. In both World Wars our side not only had a superior industrial potential but also a vast preponderance of manpower. Nevertheless, victory required a build-up of nearly two years and protracted campaigns whose bloodiness must not be obscured by the horror of nuclear warfare.

Whatever the significance of prolonged mobilization in the era of what is now called conventional technology, it becomes an extremely risky course in the nuclear age. When both sides possess nuclear weapons, there is always the danger that they will be used regardless of declarations and perhaps even intentions. The risk of escalation is a product of two factors: the nature of the limitations and the duration of the conflict. A limited nuclear war lasting one day may involve a smaller danger of escalation than a conventional war lasting a year. Aggression may be tempted by the prospect of dramatic initial victories and the possibility that the free world may not be willing to run the risks of nuclear war inherent in a prolonged mobilization.

Forces-in-being are therefore more important than at any previous time in our history. This does not mean that they must be able to hold every square inch of every threatened area. It does indicate that enough of an area must be protected so that the governments concerned consider resistance not simply a quixotic gesture. And the prospect of restoring the situation must be sufficiently imminent so that the aggressor sees no prospect in creating a *fait accompli* and then "out-enduring" his opponents. In short, greater reliance on a conventional strategy implies that we are prepared to maintain conventional forces and mobilizable reserves in a higher state of readiness than ever before. It is as dangerous to think of a conventional strategy in which nuclear weapons could somehow be eliminated from our calculations as it is to continue to consider nuclear weapons from the perspective of our now-ended invulnerability.

These considerations bear importantly on the question of how the decision to place greater reliance on conventional weapons is to be made manifest. Many thoughtful persons have proposed that we should strive to bring about a mutual renunciation of the first use of nuclear weapons. We should, it is urged, resist Communist aggression with conventional forces and resort to nuclear weapons only against nuclear attack. Nothing less, so the argument goes, will induce us to develop the necessary conventional forces and doctrine.

There is no doubt that such a course has many tempting aspects. It would be a stunning initiative if we proposed a formal agreement to renounce the use of nuclear weapons and perhaps a serious Soviet political setback if it were rejected. It would force us to come to grips with the problems of conventional strategy more urgently than seems otherwise possible. Indeed, *if* a renunciation should be thought desirable, it may well be that a unilateral Western step would be the wisest course. A formal agreement has the advantage that the Soviet Union would have to violate a solemn treaty if it resorted to nuclear weapons or to nuclear blackmail. But this inhibition would hardly be greater than one produced by a unilateral renunciation by the United States. Nuclear blackmail would lead to a renunciation of our renunciation and, *a fortiori,* so would the use by the Soviets of nuclear weapons. In both cases, the onus for returning to a reliance on nuclear weapons would be placed on the Soviet Union—within the limits of certainty produced by what will almost surely be a highly ambiguous situation. The slight additional advantage of a formal agreement would be more than made up for by the clarity and initiative achieved by a unilateral declaration.

However, the propagandistic gain does not outweigh the political and strategic disadvantages. A really effective renunciation would imply that either side—or at least the side renouncing nuclear weapons—would prefer to be defeated by conventional weapons rather than employ its nuclear arms. This in itself would be a hard and probably impossible decision to make. Are we prepared to lose Europe to a conventional attack? If we are not—and we cannot be—a formal renunciation may be meaningless. On the other hand, if the aggressor accepts a renunciation of nuclear weapons at face value, as indicating a decision to accept a defeat by conventional forces, aggression may actually be encouraged.

Assuming that it were possible to return to a *pure* conventional strategy—with either side preferring a defeat by conventional weapons to a nuclear war—what would be the consequences? It seems inevitable that deterrence would be weakened. The history of warfare in the conventional era indicates that it is not easy to convince an aggressor of the risks of embarking on war. Because of the relatively low destructiveness of individual weapons, the side which can suddenly mass its forces can usually achieve a breakthrough. The key to success is the ability to concentrate more forces *at any given point* than the opponent. In both World Wars, Germany began the war even though it was numerically inferior, relying on tactical skill and mobility. The Allies' victory was ultimately achieved only after prolonged and ruinous conflict, which indicated that the certainty of defeat required for deterrence is not easy to obtain with conventional weapons. Arms control can ameliorate this situation, but not eliminate it. Even if the forces on both sides are stabilized, it will not be easy to stabilize tactical skill and mobility.

On the historical record, then, conventional weapons are not very effective for deterrence. The frequency of warfare in the "conventional era" proves it beyond any doubt. This situation may even be magnified in the nuclear age. An aggressor may seek to achieve a victory by conventional means and then protect it by nuclear arms. We will then face the dilemma of either accepting the defeat or engaging in a kind of warfare which our renunciation of nuclear weapons was designed to avoid and which would seem incapable of depriving the aggressor of his prize. If the Soviet Union should succeed in overrunning Europe or even Iran with conventional forces, it could then offer peace while threatening to resist the restoration of the *status quo ante* with nuclear weapons. It would appear extremely difficult to land on a hostile shoreline or to fight our way across the Continent, say from Spain, against an opponent prepared to use nuclear weapons. In short, the combination of a conventional strategy for an overwhelming initial victory and a nuclear strategy to prevent a recapture of lost territories may be the most effective form of Communist aggression.

These risks, moreover, would be run for a gesture which might be meaningless. For, regardless of what we tell the aggressor or even ourselves, we could not guarantee that if pressed too hard we would not use nuclear weapons after all. This uncertainy about whether we "meant" our renunciation or knew our own mind would add to deterrence. It indicates, however, that at best a formal renunciation of the use of nuclear weapons would not weaken deterrence. At worst it might open new scope for Communist blackmail. The nuclear age has not repealed the principle that actions speak louder than words. We should make immediate and energetic efforts to restore the conventional forces of the free world. We must adjust our doctrine accordingly. But it would be extremely risky to create the impression that we would acquiesce in a conventional defeat in vital areas. Once the conventional balance of forces were restored, we could then responsibly announce that we would employ nuclear weapons only as a last resort and even then in a manner to minimize damage. To the extent that the Communists are unable to defeat the conventional forces of the free world without resorting to nuclear weapons, the practical effect will be our renunciation of the first use of nuclear weapons. Even where this is not the case, strengthened conventional forces would pose an increased risk for the aggressor and provide opportunities either for the mobilization of additional conventional forces or for negotiations before we take the decision to use nuclear weapons. The inability to defend every area with conventional forces should not be used as an excuse for failing to build up our strength. The free world must not become a victim of asserting that if it cannot do *everything* it will not do *anything*.

The relation between our conventional and nuclear capabilities is subtle and complex. If we are serious about placing a greater reliance on conventional forces, we must reassess a notion which has become almost axiomatic in our military establishment: that our military forces can be equipped and trained as dual-purpose units capable of fighting both nuclear and conventional war. This concept has merit as regards the Navy and the Air Force—or any other unit not in constant contact with the opponent and therefore subject to more or less continuous control from higher levels. But it is fallacious with respect to ground operations. To be sure, troops can be trained to use both nuclear and conventional weapons. They should be aware of the elementary forms of protection against nuclear attack. But once committed to combat, the units actually engaged in military operations must choose one mode of warfare or another. For one thing, it is probably impossible to shift from conventional to nuclear war at the opponent's initiative. The side using nuclear weapons first can disperse, while the side relying on conventional weapons must remain concentrated in order to have the firepower necessary for defense. The front-line units of the side conceding the first nuclear blow will almost certainly suffer heavily should the war turn nuclear. Their protection is not so much in having nuclear weapons of their own as in having available within striking distance *other* units capable of conducting nuclear operations.

If nuclear weapons become an integral part of the equipment of *every* unit, it will be next to impossible to keep a war conventional regardless of the intentions of both sides. Even if the plan is to employ nuclear weapons only as a last resort, this becomes empty when the responsibility of defining a last resort becomes too decentralized. A regimental or even a divisional commander should not be the judge. Lacking the over-all picture, he will always be tempted to utilize all weapons available to him. When he is hard pressed, it would require superhuman discipline not to employ arms which he believes may solve his difficulties. And the further down a unit is in the chain of command, the less can its experience be taken as a guide to the general situation. Regiments or divisions have been destroyed even in the midst of an over-all victory.

While a great deal of attention has been given to the diffusion of nuclear weapons to new countries, the diffusion downward of nuclear weapons *within* our military establishment is also a cause for concern. The more foci of control, the greater the possibility that these weapons will be used—not so much through the action of the "mad" major of the horror stories of accidental war as through the best judgment of a hard-pressed officer in the confusion of combat.

An action which would bespeak our increased emphasis on conventional weapons more convincingly than any declaration would be the creation of nuclear and conventional commands for purposes of combat. The units could be trained interchangeably. But, once committed, the conventional forces would not have nuclear weapons at their direct disposal. Deterrence as well as the conduct of nuclear war would be in the hands of separate commands whose weapons would be made available to the conventional forces only on the basis of an explicit decision at the highest level.

The need for separate commands indicates that a conventional capability cannot possibly be accommodated within present force levels. In the absence of reliable arms control, larger military budgets will surely be necessary. This is a price worth paying. But we should not imagine that the shift to a greater reliance on conventional weapons is as simple as the decision to do so. It will require substantial efforts, intellectual and material, and it will be neither cheap nor easy.

The course we adopt with respect to the relation between conventional and nuclear strategy will determine the future direction of both our strategy and our diplomacy. This is particularly evident with respect to arms control negotiations. In this respect, the present state of our military establishment places us at a severe disadvantage. Given the disparity in Sino-Soviet and Western conventional forces, many measures, such as a percentage reduction of forces or a troop freeze, may be a means of perpetuating an inequality which will be an increasing source of danger as all-out war becomes more and more senseless. The same effect will be produced by concentrating on nuclear disarmament without addressing ourselves to the gap in conventional forces.

We can escape this vicious circle only if we realize that the price of flexibility is sacrifice and effort. If our military establishment continues to be built around nuclear weapons and if we refuse to make the sacrifices involved in greater reliance on conventional weapons, the current emphasis of arms control negotiations must be shifted. In such circumstances it will not be wise to lump all nuclear weapons into a separate category of special horror. Rather we should then elaborate as many distinctions between various types of uses and explosive power as possible in order to mitigate the consequences of nuclear war. On the other hand, if we really believe in the need for a greater emphasis on conventional weapons, we must be prepared to accept the paradox that the best road to nuclear arms control may be conventional rearmament.

This is not to say that arms control should be reserved for the nuclear field. On the contrary, the balance in conventional forces should be based on a combination of increase of our conventional strength and control schemes to stabilize an agreed level of forces. But we cannot rely on arms control as a *substitute* for an effort in the conventional field. For, if the disparity in local power becomes too great, the Soviet Union will lose any incentive for responsible negotiations. No scheme of arms control will then seem to enhance its security as much as its existing superiority. And the requirements of inspection become excessive when the strategic position of one or both sides is so precarious that it can be overthrown by even a minor violation.[7]

This is the measure of the task ahead. At the same time that we build up our capability for limited war and our conventional forces, we will be embarked on arms control negotiations of crucial import. Our leadership must convince public opinion that we have to increase our military expenditures even while making earnest efforts to negotiate on arms control. The danger of slighting one or the other effort is enormous.

Yet history will not excuse our failure simply because the task is complex. The divorce between diplomacy and strategy will produce paralysis. If we want limited-war forces, we will get them only by a major effort. If we are serious about disarmament, we must restore the balance of our military establishment. To continue to combine incompatible policies must lead to disaster.

4. Conclusion

IN THE present state of our domestic discussion, it sounds hopelessly abstract to advocate an expanded United States military effort. In terms of our present force levels and those of our allies, an analysis of the nature of limited war must remain a theoretical exercise. The dispute between the advocates of an all-out and a limited-war strategy is unreal in a situation where the free world's forces are not only grossly inadequate for limited war but are also growing dangerously vulnerable to all-out war. The debate about the

[7] For an expansion of this point see, "The Problem of Arms Control," p. 214.

relative merits of a nuclear or a conventional strategy will remain beside the point as long as our forces are insufficient for either.

With fourteen divisions, some of them understrength and most of them less well equipped than their Soviet counterparts, we are in no position to fight a limited war against a first-class opponent. And if we consider the interaction of conventional and nuclear forces, the problem becomes more complicated still. Our tactical airpower is the lowest priority item in the Air Force. The Marine Corps is at the very bottom of its statutory requirements. Our airlift is inadequate. These shortcomings are not the fault of the services— though the inadequate organization of the Defense Department does not help matters. The basic difficulty is that recent budgetary levels have caused *every* mission to be neglected. Adjustment within the military budgets of the past eight years can do no more than alleviate our growing weakness somewhat. We have to admit to ourselves that we cannot finance our necessities by eliminating Pentagon "waste." The times are too serious for such evasions. To be sure, waste should be eliminated. But the basic requirement is a dedication to a major national effort.

One of the symptoms of our difficulties is the self-delusion to which we have become subject. It is maintained that we have never been stronger. The experience of Lebanon is invoked as a proof of the efficiency of our limited-war forces. We argue that there is no limited-war problem, for every war in which the U.S.S.R. and China are involved is general by definition and because our limited-war capability is adequate to deal with any other opponent. According to this definition, even our present limited-war forces are excessive, for they are clearly larger than what is required for police actions like Lebanon.

Unfortunately, the dilemmas described in this chapter cannot be solved so easily. To define every war with the Soviet Union or Communist China as all-out is to deal with a national crisis through verbal legerdemain. No more urgent task confronts the free world than to separate itself from nostalgia for the period of its invulnerability and to face the stark realities of a revolutionary period. Our problem is precisely that over-all strength does not guarantee strength relevant to particular situations. This is because of the increasing vulnerability of our retaliatory force and also because of our inability to bring our undoubted power to bear against various local pressures.

As for the experience of Lebanon, so widely hailed as a demonstration of our limited-war capability, it in reality exhibited its futility. In order to intervene in the Middle East, we were forced to pull two divisions out of Germany and tie up most of our strategic airlift. In other words, we weakened the most sensitive area, Europe, at the precise moment when international tensions were highest and the threat to it was therefore potentially greatest. And we had to reduce the mobility of our Strategic Air Command while it was most needed to perform its deterrent function.

As worrisome as the imbalance of our military establishment is the inadequacy of our doctrine and the erratic nature of our diplomacy. We not only lack the forces for limited war. There is also no agreement about what forces we would need provided that we were willing to make the effort and what diplomacy might most effectively convey our notion of limitation to an opponent. Our three services operate on the basis of partially overlapping, partially competing concepts. It is not necessary to decide which view is correct. It is sufficient to point out that we are hardly in a position to communicate what we understand by limitations to an opponent as long as we do not know it ourselves.

Our confusions will make it more difficult to limit any war that does break out. They will force us to improvise under the pressure of military operations and they will complicate the already difficult task of establishing limits. The price we may have to pay for our confusion is that an aggressor will misunderstand our intentions and that he will launch a pre-emptive blow in response to what we intended as limited resistance. The penalty for combining a nuclear military establishment with a diplomacy striving for nuclear disarmament may be that an aggressor will underrate our willingness to resist with the sole weapon we have available and that deterrence may fail.

The task of restoring cohesion and responsibility to our security is not eased by the tendency of too many to criticize concern with questions of military security as a preoccupation with the Cold War.

Some fear that to debate issues of preparedness may deflect attention from the urgency of the quest for peace. Others insist that an obsession with Communist military capabilities blinds us to our real challenges in the field of economic competition and in the development of our own society. Military expansion, they claim, is contrary to the image that inspires the Communist leaders and the least likely form of the Soviet menace. The obsession with military security is alleged to be at the root of many of our difficulties. Many of the most virulent attacks on the concept of limited war come from individuals who rebel against the very notion of strategy, such as the advocates of universal or even unilateral disarmament.

Such attitudes—if they became generally accepted—would doom us as a nation. Far from reducing tensions, they reward Soviet intransigence. Against an opponent known to recoil before the risk of *any* war, the most brutal threat is the most effective. It is well to remember that Mr. Khrushchev has justified the need for peaceful coexistence primarily by one argument: the disastrous nature of modern war for *both* sides. Should the strategic balance shift so that this condition is no longer met, the reason for even the formal defense of peaceful coexistence will fall away.

A responsible leader does not have the right to stake the survival of his society merely on the assessment that a country which has subjugated tens of millions of people in a decade is not concerned with military expansion. Many of the other arguments against an effort to build up our limited-war forces are based on a curious distrust of the American people. They assume that we must be motivated by either fear or euphoria, that we cannot be both strong and conciliatory.

The impression is sometimes created that America is bound to behave irresponsibly unless it is deprived of all alternatives to peace save suicide—and occasionally this proposition is made explicit. If this is true, no constructive policy of any kind will be possible. A nation which cannot be trusted when strong will hardly be able to deal with the much more difficult task of living in dignity when impotent. Rather than deliberately paralyzing our society by posing impossible alternatives, many of the proponents of the above views would do better to address themselves to the question of how we can become worthy of our responsibilities.

There is no doubt that the Western world is in deep trouble. It has not been able to articulate either a philosophy or a program adequate to our time. It has failed to identify itself with the revolutionary period through which we are living. It has not had the vision or the willingness to carry through a sustained program to bring a sense of direction to a world in turmoil.

But granting all these criticisms, the fact remains that even in the military field we are inadequately prepared. We are falling behind in the equation for all-out war. We have insufficient strength for limited war. Our conventional forces are constantly shrinking. The answer to our political problems is not to be found in reducing our defenses—for even here more effort and imagination are required—but in injecting a greater sense of purpose into our over-all performance.

IV

THE UNITED STATES
AND EUROPE

1. The Problem

In no other area of policy is the integral relationship between diplomacy and strategy more evident than in the relations of the United States with Europe. Whether the issue is the defense of Europe or arms control, German unification or the diffusion of nuclear weapons, invariably the solution depends on the ability of the West to harmonize its need for security with its positive goals. Nowhere else are the stakes so high. If the states bordering the North Atlantic were to split up into a congeries of squabbling sovereignties, it would be a final proof to all the uncommitted nations of the bankruptcy of the liberal values of the West. The United States would find itself isolated not only physically but also spiritually. Sooner or later, these states on the fringe of the Eurasian land mass would be drawn into the Communist orbit. The source of our culture and our values would then be alienated. Americans, for the first time in our history, would live in a world where we were foreign in the deepest sense, where people would share neither our values nor our aspirations, where we might meet hostility everywhere outside of North America.

An even stronger reason for North Atlantic cohesion is that it is a prerequisite for realizing opportunities for constructive action. It is beyond the capacity of either the United States or our European allies to deal individually with all the concurrent revolutions of our time. No one nation has sufficient intellectual or material resources to assist the development of the new nations, keep up in the technological race, help work out a new set of international relationships, and realize its own opportunities. If our hopes for a world based on the values of freedom and human dignity are to be realized, the closest co-operation between North America—indeed, the entire Western Hemisphere—and Europe is essential.

If these countries, industrially highly developed, efficiently administered, sharing similar values and institutions, cannot meet their challenge, the future of freedom is dim. Conversely, the courage, dynamism and convictions of the North Atlantic group of nations can become a symbol to the entire world of the vitality of an association of free peoples.

It might have been thought that the enormity of the danger and the vastness of the opportunity would evoke a creative, dynamic Western response. Unfortunately, this has not been the case. Since the creation of the Marshall Plan and of NATO, we have been in effect barren of ideas, evading difficult choices, drawing on capital. Europe is prosperous as never before. But its economic well-being is the result of a policy conceived over a decade ago, vigorously pursued in the interval. As the economic goals of the Marshall Plan have been achieved, the need for a comparable political vision has become ever more apparent. At the end of a decade of unparalleled economic growth, the West appears uncertain and confused. Even in the economic field deep fissures have developed.

All the evasions of the past decade were brought to a head by the Soviet pressure which began with a proposal to turn Berlin into a free city. A clear Soviet menace to the very vitals of the Western alliance did not elicit a closing of ranks as in the past. Rather it produced an often acrimonious debate about all the issues that should have been settled long before. What is worse, these issues were taken up in an atmosphere of confusion that threatened to deprive any resulting actions of their full impact. The recurring protestations of formal unity, followed by haggling over details, emphasized the inability of the alliance to agree on its program or its future. NATO strategy, the significance of nuclear weapons, arms control, German unification, European security, all evoked discordant opinions barely obscured by general declarations of amity. Though Soviet intransigence after the abortive summit conference at least outwardly produced a closing of ranks, we could make no worse mistake than to pretend that the underlying difficulties have been solved. Unless the North Atlantic group of nations develops a clearer purpose it will be doomed.

2. NATO STRATEGY

MANY of the problems of the Western alliance are traceable directly or indirectly to the inability to develop a common strategy. A welter of disputes fills the air. Is Europe more secure because our nuclear arsenal is more powerful than ever, or less secure because we are vulnerable as never before? Does the increase in the range of missiles and airplanes make a substantial military establishment on the Continent more important or less? Should NATO forces be designed to defeat Soviet aggression in Europe or does their function remain to hold only until the effects of the nuclear retaliatory blow have made themselves felt? Almost all the outstanding issues in Europe depend on a resolution of the basic issue: the significance of all-out war for the defense of Europe in the missile age.

During the first decade of its existence, NATO relied on a retaliatory strategy. The strategic striking forces, however, remained under the exclusive control of the two extra-continental allies, the United States and Great Britain. With its primary weapon outside the NATO structure and not subject to NATO control, the Western alliance inevitably took on something of the character of a unilateral guarantee. The demand by our European allies for a substantial commitment of United States and British troops on the Continent did not mean that Europe was to be defended locally. On the contrary, the role of these forces was conceived almost as that of hostages —to ensure that the American and British retaliatory power would in fact be employed against a Soviet attack. The military establishment on the Continent came to be thought of as a trip-wire designed to unleash the United States and British retaliatory force.

Because of the reliance on an all-out strategy, our Continental allies have been reluctant to make a defense contribution which would give military value to the commitment of the United States and British troops. They have resisted the effort to achieve an adequate local defense, partly for economic reasons, but above all because they feared that it might reduce the American and British willingness to resort to all-out war in the defense of Europe. This strategy has now reached an impasse.

The threat of all-out war can ensure the security of Europe only if we are able to meet two conditions: (1) our retaliatory force must be strong enough to *win* an all-out war if we strike first and (2) it must be so invulnerable that even if we should be the victim of a surprise attack it can inflict damage considered intolerable by the Soviet Union. In these circumstances, the Soviet Union would not dare to attack Europe for fear of triggering a pre-emptive strike which would destroy its means of retaliation. It could not launch a simultaneous attack on Europe and the United States for our retaliation would, by hypothesis, still produce unacceptable losses. Under these conditions, the local forces in Europe would, in fact, perform the role of a trip-wire. Their purpose would be to deal with minor incursions. The Soviet Union could not risk major aggression, however. If it attacked Europe alone, the penalty for a Soviet miscalculation would be complete defeat. If it launched a simultaneous attack on the United States, the result would be mutual devastation. This in effect was the situation during the period of our strategic preponderance.

However, in the period of the missile gap, that is, between 1961 and at least 1964, it will be technically impossible for us to win an all-out war. During that time we will do well to protect our retaliatory force against surprise attack. It will be reckless to rely on it to deter aggression elsewhere. A strategic striking force which is numerically inferior in missiles and relies to a considerable extent on airplanes cannot hope to win an all-out war, even by striking first. With the possibility of a pre-emptive strike ended beyond any doubt, the threat of massive retaliation will lose much of its significance even for the defense of Europe.

After the missile gap ends, it is theoretically conceivable that we could again achieve strategic superiority through either offensive or defensive breakthroughs. But this is extremely unlikely, if only because of the increase in the total number of missiles and their growing mobility. In any case, we cannot gear our policy to such an expectation. The only responsible course is to base strategy on the

assumption of the mutual invulnerablity of the retaliatory forces—
and to admit that to attain even this goal requires efforts we have
heretofore refused to make.

Under conditions of mutual invulnerability it will become increasingly futile to rely on the strategy of the past decade. The
defense of Europe can, then, no longer rest on the threat of all-out
war alone, for this threat might not be believed and thus tempt
aggression. Or it might encourage a pre-emptive attack. Even if we
made good our threat, this would only ensure our destruction without protecting our allies. Western Europe could not be saved from
Soviet occupation and social upheaval. We could achieve no more
than mutual devastation. If the only recourse against aggression in
Europe is to devastate Soviet centers of population, deterrence
may fail. The Soviet leaders, in view of their own capability to
retaliate, may come to believe that our threat of all-out war is bluff.

If NATO can be defended *only* by all-out war, it will face a hopeless dilemma: to yield to pressure will set up a pattern of Soviet
blackmail, while to resist will involve catastrophic devastation. The
Berlin crisis is probably but an augury of things to come. As
the strategic choices of NATO grow more stark, Soviet policy
is likely to become increasingly bold.

These difficulties became explicit at the time of Sputnik. For
the first time, Soviet advances in the missile field—heretofore
attributed to the imaginings of overwrought pessimists—became
manifest. The result was a conviction in the West that the Soviet
earth satellite heralded an immediate United States inferiority,
from which was drawn the strange conclusion that Ameria's panicky
reply—the offer of intermediate-range missiles to Europe—was for
our exclusive benefit. "The Gaither report," wrote a British journal,
"has revealed that, irrespective of any efforts which America may
now make, the Soviet preponderance in advanced weapons has
reached such an absolute stage that America's national survival will
depend, until 1961 at least, on 'Russian benevolence.' "[1] And a
speaker in the House of Commons said: "Hitherto I have always
thought that the principle of an alliance was that it gave greater
protection to ourselves. On this occasion with these rockets we are

[1] *New Statesman*, editorial, Jan. 4, 1958.

clearly inviting the risk of attack in some way and we are giving a one-sided protection to the United States."[2]

Against the background of the strategy on which the prevailing military policy of the alliance was based, these arguments were remarkable. For *if* the United States had, in fact, become vulnerable as a result of Sputnik, and *if* the bases in Europe were a means to remedy that vulnerability, it would appear that our European allies should have had a positive interest in obtaining intermediate-range missiles. Though it should have been obvious that the security of our allies depended on the security of the United States, many of our critics in Europe implied that it was not to Europe's interest to make a contribution to our defense. They questioned not the strategy which had been developed but the wisdom of participating in it.

Nothing could have revealed better the futility of continuing to rely on all-out war for the defense of Europe. Many people in Europe, after Sputnik confronted them with the implications of NATO strategy, seemed above all concerned with banishing war from their territory. In the process, they neglected to ask themselves this crucial question: If so many Europeans recoiled before the consequences of the only strategy available, even in the defense of Europe, how could the United States be expected for an indefinite period of time to assume even more cataclysmic risks on behalf of foreign countries however closely allied?

A strengthening of the forces for the local defense of Europe is therefore essential for the very reasons usually invoked against it. It is argued by many that since European bases are no longer required for all-out war the need for a substantial military establishment on the Continent has disappeared.[3]

Quite the reverse is true. It is surely inconsistent to argue that the United States must be prepared to run greater risks than ever for an area whose strategic significance is constantly declining. It is true that European bases are not essential for the event of all-out war. But precisely because they are an advantage of steadily

---

[2] Viscount Hinchingbrooke, *Hansard* 580, p. 806, Dec. 20, 1957.
[3] Speech by the Italian Ambassador to Germany, Signor Quaroni, at the University of Frankfurt, *Frankfurter Allgemeine Zeitung*, Apr. 1, 1959.

diminishing importance, a substantial military establishment on the Continent is necessary to give Europe a defense other than massive retaliation. The increasing speed, range and destructiveness of weapons have added new dimensions to the problem of deterring an attack on Europe and of resisting it should it take place. We have been loath to make this proposition explicit lest we alarm our allies and because we have been unwilling to accept the fact of our vulnerability. Our allies in turn have not wished to believe in the changed situation. They have looked the other way in order to avoid the necessity of making a greater effort and for fear that a realization of the inconsistencies of present NATO strategy might lead to the withdrawal of the United States from Europe. In all European countries, the contribution to NATO has become almost the first item to be reduced when budgetary retrenchment takes place— thus implying a strange set of priorities: present comfort takes precedence over ultimate survival.

Such evasions must be demoralizing in the long run. Europe need only recall its own hesitation over the offer of United States missile bases to understand the difficulty soon to be imposed on NATO by its present strategy. If Europe proved reluctant to participate in an all-out war for the defense of the United States—the only meaningful rationale for the doubts about establishing missile bases—so might the United States be reluctant to risk total destruction for the defense of Europe, particularly if the Soviet leaders with their customary skill in confusing the issues make the challenge appear local. NATO should have every incentive to develop a strategy which does not force the United States to have to choose between all-out-war and inaction in the defense of Europe.

The security problem of Europe may be summed up as follows: (a) The Soviet Union can threaten all of Europe from its own territories. Consequently, alliances are not essential for its safety. (b) No European country alone is capable of withstanding Soviet pressure. Security is therefore inseparable from unity. (c) The threat of all-out war is losing its credibility and its strategic meaning. (d) The defense of Europe, therefore, cannot be conducted solely from North America, because the aggressor can pose threats which will not seem to warrant total retaliation and because, however firm allied unity may be, a nation cannot be counted on to commit suicide in defense of a foreign territory.

It may be objected that the Soviet Union would not be so foolhardy as to bring pressure on the most sensitive area. The more weakly defended region on its southern periphery would seem to be be much more tempting. An attack on, say, Iran would have a high probability of military success and the obstacles to American retaliation would be even greater than in the case of Europe. But the risk of an attack on Iran is only apparently smaller. Overt aggression against Iran would demonstrate to other countries the crucial importance of a local defense force. A Soviet adventure in the so-called "gray areas" would inevitably lead to a rapid build-up of strength in Europe. Whatever the U.S.S.R. would gain in the Middle East would be made up by an accretion in the power of Europe and perhaps of the uncommitted regions. In this sense, the areas along the southern periphery of the Soviet Union are protected less by the military arrangements in which they participate than by the fear that pressure on them would cost more than it is worth in the form of a rapid mobilization of the resources of Europe and the rest of the free world.

On the other hand, were the impotence of NATO to be demonstrated, all other areas would fall to the Soviet Union almost by default. Whatever their moral preferences, considerations of national interest would impel them to seek the best terms available. If Europe should prove unable to resist Soviet pressure and if United States support should appear unavailing or unsuited to the nature of the threat, it would be futile to challenge any further demonstrations of Soviet power. Soviet pressure against Berlin is therefore significant not only in terms of Europe. It will importantly influence the actions of governments on the periphery of Eurasia. In the new strategic situation, Europe is a logical focus for Soviet pressure.

By the same token, NATO will be able to resist Soviet blackmail only to the extent that the military establishment in Europe is capable of withstanding a wide range of challenges. The stronger the local forces, the less the likelihood that certain kinds of threats will be made at all. The willingness to resist Soviet encroachments will be increased if a maximum number of alternatives is created between surrender and a war which may appear suicidal. Since the object of deterrence is to pose a risk to the aggressor out of proportion to the objective to be obtained, local forces in Europe would perform a vital function even if they could not withstand *every* scale of Soviet attack. Sweden and Switzerland maintain substantial armies. Their purpose is not primarily to defeat a major power which might attack—for this they are quite inadequate—but to exact a price a potential aggressor is unwilling to pay. Similarly a substantial military establishment on the Continent would do much to deter rash Soviet adventures. At the very least it could force the Soviet Union into a scale of military effort which would remove any doubt about its ultimate intention and thus make a Western threat of all-out war more convincing. Even if one argues that any Soviet attack on Europe would ultimately lead to all-out war, it does not necessarily follow that a defense of Europe should *begin* with such a strategy. Since an all-out war would threaten the survival of mankind, it should be invoked only as the last resort. We must have other means for countering Soviet moves.

The line of demarcation between local defense of Europe and all-out war need not be determined in the abstract. The more effective the military establishment on the Continent, the larger must be the Soviet attack designed to overcome it. The more the required effort approaches the scale of all-out war, the clearer will be the challenge, and the more plausible the threat of all-out war becomes. The most favorable situation would exist if the military establishment in Europe could not be overcome locally. Then the risk of initiating all-out war would be shifted to the Soviet Union. At the very least, the forces in Europe should be sufficient so that the scale of effort required to overcome them raises the risk of all-out war to an intolerable level for the U.S.S.R.

Some opponents of a greater military effort on the Continent argue that the building up of local forces will invite the dangers it seeks to avoid. It may be interpreted by the Soviet Union as an additional indication of the reluctance to engage in all-out war and thus furnish an incentive to exploit the Soviet local superiority while it still exists. This argument calls attention to the delicate nature of our task. But it is absurd to maintain that the West must perpetuate a weakness which represents a *permanent* danger because the effort to remedy it involves a *temporary* risk. Nor is the attempt to build up a greater capability for local defense the basic reason for the declining utility of the threat of all-out war. The appalling consequences of all-out war are the real cause for the lack of credibility of current strategy, and to ignore this fact will only increase our peril.

To attempt to maintain the doctrine of massive retaliation in the face of these developments by deliberately leaving a vital area inadequately defended is to conduct a policy of reckless bluff. It simply does not make sense for the United States and Western Europe, whose combined manpower and industrial resources still far exceed those of the Soviet Union, to continue to claim that they cannot afford what is needed for their defense or to cite "hordes" of Soviet manpower as a justification for what is basically a lack of will.

Present NATO deployment, in fact, probably combines the worst features of massive retaliation and of local defense. Too strong for a trip-wire, too weak to resist a major Soviet advance, it represents an uneasy compromise which tempts Soviet blackmail and must lead to irresolution in the face of pressure. The reliance on all-out war paralyzes the will in times of crisis and furnishes a rationale for a reduction of local defense forces in periods of calm. In terms of a strategy of all-out war, the American forces on the Continent are much too large. The function often ascribed to them—to serve as a symbol of our commitment to defend Europe—could be carried out as well by much smaller, indeed by token, contingents. If we continue to rely on our present strategy, disengagement of our forces may become inevitable. If it occurs as a gesture of frustration, we will not even have the benefit of seeking Soviet concessions by negotiating about it.

Of course, some of the resistance by our European allies to building up more effective local defense forces stems from the fear that a greater effort by them will be used as an excuse to enable us to withdraw. It must be admitted that this argument is not without foundation, either in American utterances or in American behavior.

Too many statements, both by officials of the Executive Branch and in Congress, have used the build-up of European, particularly of German, divisions as a justification for a reduction of U.S. forces. This lends support to the belief that the United States advocates a European build-up in order to relieve itself of some of its burdens.

However, if the United States understands its own interests, it will not pursue so irresponsible a course. For one thing, present forces of NATO are too low. The planned minimum goals have never been achieved and in the light of changing technology they are almost certainly inadequate. Replacement of American by European divisions would therefore not change the basic problem. More importantly, the defense of Europe must always involve American participation from the outset. The certainty of this adds to deterrence. A commitment of U.S. forces raises the risks to an aggressor. A limited war over Europe involving the United States may represent an intolerably high risk of all-out war—if only because the Soviet leaders could not be confident that either they or we would know how to keep such a war limited. And if deterrence failed, only American participation could keep a conflict localized or ensure a favorable outcome. For only the United States possesses adequate means of retaliation against a Soviet strategy of nuclear devastation. If Europe attempts independent action, it may only tempt a demonstration of Soviet ruthlessness. An effort by either Europe or the United States to leave the defense of Europe entirely in European hands would prove disastrous to all partners.

Of course, it is always possible that the United States will *not* understand its own interests. But in that case, little hope exists. If the United States is indeed so blind, it will not be possible to base a long-range policy even on present NATO strategy. If such a condition exists, no subterfuge will be able to commit us in the long run. However, Europe, with which we have been associated in the Marshall Plan and to which we are tied by history, culture, and many common endeavors, should not have to seek to "trick" us into a commitment for a common effort by what will turn into an increasingly irrational policy.

While our allies have a right to insist on American participation in their defense and must be able to count on it, they should not be permitted to prescribe a course of action which involves the most catastrophic risks, the more so if this strategy reduces the willingness of *all* partners to resist the most likely challenge. A local deterrent in Europe is required to increase the range of our options and to bring the deterrent policy of NATO into line with the strategy it is prepared to implement. A strategy of local defense is essential not as a device to save the alliance, though it will serve this purpose. Rather, the alliance alone offers the possibility of a strategy which does not inevitably involve catastrophe.

3. NATO and Nuclear Weapons

To recognize the need for a stronger military establishment in Europe is to raise questions about its nature, about the relation of nuclear weapons to NATO strategy, and, above all, about the diffusion of nuclear weapons to our European allies. The declining credibility of the threat of massive retaliation has not only produced the need for an increase in the conventional forces in Europe, it has also raised in acute form the problem of control over what has heretofore been called *the* Deterrent. The growing Soviet capability to menace the United States has magnified doubts which first appeared during the Suez crisis: whether the United States can be relied upon to respond by all-out war to every challenge which our allies may consider vital and, if we do, whether we will use our power in a manner they deem necessary to protect their interests.

The fear that the United States might not be prepared to risk devastation on behalf of its allies, or else that it might use its power in a manner likely to destroy a partner's national substance, has given rise to the attempt to develop independent retaliatory forces within NATO. President de Gaulle has insisted that France requires a nuclear arsenal of its own because the United States might make a separate arrangement with the U.S.S.R. He has also argued that the major nuclear powers might make a tacit agreement not to devastate each other and to confine their violence to other parts of the world. In either case, nuclear weapons under French control would be a means of keeping France from being a victim of nuclear war:

No doubt the sort of equilibrium that exists between the atomic powers of the two camps is for the moment a factor of world peace. But who can say what will happen tomorrow? Who can say that, for example, some sudden advances in development, especially for space rockets, will not provide one of the camps with so great an advantage that its peaceful inclinations will not be able to resist it?

Who can say that if in the future, the political background having changed completely—that is something that has already happened on earth—the two powers having the nuclear monopoly will not agree to divide the world?

Who can say that if the occasion arises the two, while each deciding not to launch its missiles at the main enemy so that it should itself be spared, will not crush the others? . . . In truth, France in equipping herself with a nuclear weapon, will render a service to world equilibrium.[4]

These views, though much criticized, differ from similar arguments in Great Britain only in their bluntness. In 1957 Aneurin Bevan said:

What this conference [Labor party conference], ought not to do—and I beg them not to do it now—is to decide upon the dismantling of the whole fabric of British international relationships without putting anything in its place. . . . If they carried the resolution [to eliminate nuclear armament], with all its implications . . . they would send a British Foreign Secretary, whoever he was, naked into the conference chamber.[5]

Both British and French deterrents have been justified with the argument that possession of nuclear weapons would enable our allies to exert a greater influence over our actions. The question then arises just what this influence consists of. A nuclear capability, however small, obviously admits a country to certain negotiations. France, for example, has been excluded from the test ban conference even though its survival depends as much on our decisions with respect to controlling nuclear weapons as with respect to deploying them. Not the least paradoxical aspect of the nuclear age is that in some circumstances arms control negotiations can supply a motive for nuclear diffusion.

Another influence thought to be conferred by nuclear weapons is of course in the field of strategy. Our allies have sought to create an independent deterrent, at least in part, to remove any doubt in

[4] Press conference, Nov. 10, 1959, quoted in *New York Times,* Nov. 11, 1959.
[5] Speech at Brighton, Oct. 3, 1957, quoted in the *Times* (London), Oct. 4, 1957.

the mind of a potential aggressor about the likelihood of retaliation when their security is at stake—regardless of what the United
States might decide to do. And the same reasoning has been applied
to the actual conduct of a war: the British deterrent was justified as
a means of guaranteeing that targets considered vital in Britain
would be attacked whatever their role in an over-all strategy as seen
from the United States. "There are . . . big administrative and industrial targets behind the Iron Curtain," said Sir Winston Churchill in 1955, "and any effective deterrent policy must have the power
to paralyze them all at the outset or shortly after. . . . Unless we make
a contribution of our own . . . we cannot be sure that in an emer-
gency the resources of other powers would be planned exactly as we
would wish."[6]

The reliance by NATO on a retaliatory strategy has thus had
one of two consequences: either our European allies have considered
themselves protected by our retaliatory force and have therefore
seen no point in a military effort of their own. Or else they have
concentrated on developing a separate retaliatory capability, dupli-
cating the strategic category in which we were already strongest.
Unilateral disarmament—tacit or avowed—and the quest for independent retaliatory forces are two sides of the same coin.

Either course is disastrous for NATO. The inadequacy of forces
for local defense weakens Europe in the face of the most likely
dangers. At the same time, the attempt to develop independent
retaliatory forces has faced our European allies with all the dilemmas
of our doctrine of massive retaliation without our resources and at a
moment when it has become incongruous even for us. Great Britain
and France have paid as little attention as we did some years ago to
the problem of protecting the retaliatory force. They have no more
taken into account the paradox that a force which can inflict vast
damage in an offensive war may be useless if it is the victim of
surprise attack.

Independent retaliatory forces in Europe stand in danger of
producing an illusory feeling of security which in some respects
magnifies the danger. None of our European allies is capable of
creating from its own resources a retaliatory force capable of defeat-

[6] *Hansard* 315, p. 1901, March 1, 1955.

ing the U.S.S.R., *even* by striking first. For all practical purposes, then, the strategic striking power of the Soviet Union is invulnerable in relation to the retaliatory force of any single European nation. Thus it is extremely unlikely that any European country would retaliate by initiating nuclear war, even in the face of considerable provocation. For such an attack could not achieve victory, but would only guarantee the devastation of the country concerned. Europe is more densely populated than the U.S.S.R. The distance to targets in Western Europe from Soviet missile bases is relatively short. Compared with an attack on the United States, a retaliatory blow by the Soviet Union would therefore be more accurate and, because each missile would be able to carry a heavier payload, more destructive. Indeed, the Soviet Union might have a positive interest in ravaging the first European country which attempted independent retaliation against it. Reduced to rubble, that country could become a symbol, warning all others of the perils of opposing Soviet designs by means of nuclear retaliation.

Will retaliatory forces under national control at least be able to prevent nuclear attack against the country possessing them? Some people argue that the deterrent effect of an independent national retaliatory force does not depend on its ability to win. In order to deter, it need only be able to inflict damage out of proportion to any gain an aggressor might achieve. Yet if the Soviet Union could be reasonably sure that the United States would not intervene in case of a challenge to individual European allies—which is, after all, the chief motive of our allies for building up independent striking forces—the national retaliatory strength in Europe would be likely to be overwhelmed by the Soviet blow. No European country seems capable of developing a retaliatory force strong enough to survive a determined Soviet attack. None of them has a sufficient area in which to disperse its forces or adequate resources to "harden" them by placing them in concrete shelters—and hardening will be relatively ineffective or extremely costly against the accuracy possible in a Soviet missile attack on Europe.

Indeed, until the retaliatory forces of our allies become mobile and preferably seaborne, they may constitute an invitation to Soviet preemptive attack. For any of our allies to attempt independent retaliation is almost certain suicide. The major utility of separate retaliatory forces in Europe would thus seem to be that they increase the aggressor's risk of American, not European, retaliation. They can deter only if the Soviet Union is convinced that conflict on a certain scale will unleash the United States strategic forces. Far from making us dispensable, the effectiveness of separate retaliatory forces depends on the likelihood of United States intervention. Their function would not be substantially different from that of the tripwire forces on the ground.

This is not apparent, however, in the early stages of nuclear weapons development. The first reaction to the possession of nuclear weapons and the means to deliver them has generally proved to be an excess of confidence. The realization of vulnerability comes only later with the study of the strategic implications of the new-found strength; it may then produce a feeling of impotence. Great Britain, for example, does not seem to have derived particular firmness and resolution from its reliance on nuclear weapons.

Whether the reaction is overconfidence or a sense of futility, the growth of individual retaliatory forces is almost certain to weaken the cohesion of the Western alliance. The very act of creating an independent retaliatory force springs from a lack of confidence in either American understanding of the common interest or American willingness to run risks on behalf of its allies. Moreover, unless a country's retaliatory force is directly threatened, a powerful incentive exists not to run major risks on behalf of allies. Each European country will face in relation to its partners the inhibitions against resorting to all-out war which they have ascribed to the United States and which induced them to develop an independent retaliatory force in the first place. They will reserve nuclear retaliation for direct and overwhelming attacks on their national existence. In relation to all other issues, their relative weakness and greater proximity to the U.S.S.R. will probably produce hesitations exceeding our own. By the same token each ally that may be fearful of being involved in a nuclear war against his will may take drastic steps to dissociate himself from his partners in tense periods. The result of a multiplication of national retaliatory forces must be the weakening, if not the disintegration, of NATO. Such a course will diffuse the risks while detracting from over-all strength.

At the same time, we must understand the dilemma that has led to the effort by Great Britain and France to develop retaliatory forces of their own. Present NATO doctrine confronts our allies with a very real and serious problem: the alliance relies for its primary weapon on the United States Strategic Air Command and, to a lesser extent, the British Bomber Command—forces which are outside NATO control, indeed, whose deployment for purposes of deterrence and dispositions in case of war are unknown to our allies. While our partners are urged to integrate their conventional forces—which are adjuncts in terms of prevailing strategy—they have no effective voice in controlling the weapons on which, by our own assertions, their security primarily rests. In this situation our allies may come to feel that as long as the United States assumes the almost exclusive responsibility for the defense of Europe, it may subordinate their vital interests to its conception of the requirements of the over-all strategic situation. As the United States grows more vulnerable, our allies may fear that ever fewer objectives may seem "worth" an all-out war. Even Europe may not appear important enough, particularly in the case of ambiguous challenges.

Such fears may appear to us unfair. Yet, would we react differently if the defense of Alaska depended on Britain's willingness to employ her retaliatory force on our behalf and if we knew that the decision to retaliate would mean the destruction of the British islands? Our European allies have every reason to be realistic: within this generation they have abandoned allies themselves.

It may be argued that the distinction between our interests and those of our European allies is mistaken, that there can be no proper conflict if all parties understand the need for unity. Yet this view, however correct in the abstract, does not meet the central concern of the Western European nations. Little in the recent behavior of NATO suggests that it considers itself a unit militarily, economically or politically. The United States and Great Britain have retained exclusive control over their strategic striking forces—the key weapon in their arsenal. There was the British and French adventure in Suez, in which we in turn opposed our closest allies. There was the American landing in Lebanon, about which our NATO allies were not consulted in advance, even though it involved the redeployment of NATO divisions and clearly increased the risk of Soviet pressure on Europe. The disagreements among the Allies over the future of Berlin and Germany, which extended over a year in the face of Soviet pressure, hardly inspire conviction about the periodic declarations of formal unity. The diplomacy initiated by Mr. Macmillan's sortie to Moscow and by Khrushchev's visit to the United States saw each ally dealing separately with the Soviet Union and did little to create faith in the cohesion of the West. Though these conferences were formally described as "conversations," this distinction is hardly significant. Heads of state by definition cannot simply converse. Whatever the protestations to the contrary, separate dealings raised the possibility of separate arrangements. This must have been their chief attraction in Khrushchev's eyes. The correctness of these various measures is not at issue. They symbolize the fact that on a whole range of problems the Allies either took independent action or were in open opposition to each other.

In any alliance, the danger is always present that there exist as many foci for pressure as there are sovereign states. After all, the very essence of sovereignty is the ability to take independent action. We do not have to station nuclear weapons in Alaska under state control in order to make credible our determination to resist an attack on it, even if only a single nuclear weapon were exploded there. It is "self-evident" that in the case of an attack on any part of the United States the question of whether the particular objective is "worth" the risk of nuclear retaliation will not be asked, even though its value may actually be less than that of an objective in Europe. But, whether we like it or not, our allies' quest for independent retaliatory forces is based on a doubt about our reliability. And such a state of mind tends to be self-confirming. It raises the possibility that the Soviet Union will be able to blackmail our allies one by one—a course of action which the Soviets would not attempt vis-à-vis a state of our Union.

The logical solution to NATO's strategic problem would be a specialization of functions, by which we concentrate on nuclear forces and our allies on conventional arms. But this is inhibited by two factors: the predominance of fiscal considerations in recent American policy and the trends inherent in nuclear weapons technology. Many pronouncements of high American officials have given rise to the impression that we consider every increase in European military strength a substitute for our own forces. This has fortified the already powerful reluctance of our allies to make greater efforts. To be sure, some of their objections were based on the same fiscal thinking as that of the Eisenhower Administration. But they have also been inhibited by their conviction that the practical effect of the course being urged on them would be to substitute forces with inferior equipment—at least to the extent that they do not possess nuclear weapons—for the present United States commitment.

As for the strategic factors inhibiting the specialization of functions, the situation would seem to be as follows: If our European allies created stronger conventional forces—as they should—these would still be at the mercy of the Soviet tactical nuclear arsenal, which is being developed apace.[7] Against a nuclear opponent only the threat of nuclear retaliation can keep a conventional war conventional.[8] By the same token, the inability of the victim to retaliate with nuclear weapons can serve as a powerful incentive for the aggressor to resort to them or at least to threaten with them. For even a small number of low-yield nuclear weapons could overwhelm a defense force which is equipped only with conventional weapons.

As long as the control over nuclear weapons remains exclusively in United States and British hands, even substantially larger conventional defense forces would not solve the security problem of our European allies. Whenever the United States was reluctant to invoke nuclear retaliation, European conventional forces would be useless. And it is idle for us to protest that such contingencies could not arise. Within the space of a decade too many divergent policies have been pursued within NATO to take refuge in such assertions. If the divergences between the various military establishments in NATO become too great and if our allies do not share in the control over nuclear weapons, a situation made to order for Soviet atomic blackmail may arise. The Soviet Union may strive to paralyze our partners through their sense of impotence and us through the fear of all-out nuclear war.

[7] See Khrushchev's speech, *New York Times,* Jan. 15, 1960.
[8] See p. 86.

The United States has sought to deal with this problem in two ways: by stationing intermediate range missiles in Europe and by creating stockpiles of nuclear weapons in Europe under the so-called "double-veto" system, which requires the approval of the host country before the missiles can be launched. Neither really goes to the heart of the problem.

The stationing of 1,500-mile missiles in Europe was a reaction to the Soviet launching of Sputnik. In its precipitateness and manner of justification this action gave the impression of panic rather than of sober thought. The immediate explanation for the offer of intermediate-range missiles to NATO was that, whatever the advances in Soviet rocket development, they could be more than overcome by increasing the retaliatory threat from Europe. Intermediate-range missiles would add to the West's destructive potential and therefore to its deterrent ability. Their greater accuracy might make them even more potent than the Soviet intercontinental missile they were designed to counter. The only adaptation made necessary by Sputnik, we seemed to say, was to transform air into missile bases.

Overlooked was the problem of vulnerability, of the difference between a retaliatory force designed for offensive, as compared with one designed for defensive, war and of the suitability of these particular missiles for the tasks assigned to them. Intermediate-range missiles in Europe would have been essential from the point of view of over-all NATO strategy only if there had been a long interval between the development of intermediate-range and intercontinental missiles and then only if in that period our Strategic Air Command had become useless. Neither assumption was correct. The development of 1,500-mile and intercontinental missiles proceeded at approximately the same rate. Since the launching of Sputnik, the Soviet Union has not possessed enough missiles to risk an attack against our Strategic Air Command. When and if they do, little additional safety will be provided by the IRBM's in Europe.

Intermediate-range missiles in Europe under United States control would be significant for the deterrence of all-out war only if an attack on them would detract from the Soviet capability to menace the United States or if they could be protected so that they would add to our ability to retaliate. Neither contingency is likely to occur. The attacking vehicles required for a surprise attack against the United States do not compete with those necessary to destroy European bases except perhaps for nuclear materials—a deficiency which, if it still exists, will soon be overcome. An attack on the United States would be carried out by intercontinental missiles and long-range bombers. A blow against Europe would require medium- and intermediate-range missiles and similar types of airplanes. The U.S.S.R. possesses the latter in quantity. It therefore will soon have the capability to attack both Europe and the United States simultaneously.

Moreover, the present family of intermediate-range missiles in Europe will be even more difficult to protect against surprise attack than weapons stationed in the United States. An intermediate-range missile based above ground—as most of our European missiles are—could not survive a nuclear blast even at a distance of several miles. At the same time, whatever the significance of "hardening" for missiles based far from the Soviet launching sites, it will offer little protection to weapons stationed in Europe. Hardening can always be overcome by more explosive power, greater accuracy or more weapons on the target—all of which are relatively easy to achieve against European bases.[9]

This is not to say that missiles stationed in Europe are without any utility. But their primary significance is less for a retaliatory strategy than for local defense, and they should be designed accordingly. Accuracy and, above all, mobility are prime requisites. Accuracy is necessary to permit a discriminating application of power. Mobility is needed to reduce the vulnerability to surprise attack. NATO should therefore strive to create a missile system which can be moved by motor, a major part of which is continually shifting position. Submarines and surface ships provide another form of mobile launching site. Even coastal steamers or barges could supply considerable protection against surprise attack. Missiles of ranges up to 800 or 1,000 miles would prove highly useful for local defense. The fact that the missile force in Europe could not be decisive in a general war would remove a motive for a Soviet pre-emptive attack.

[9] Similar and more detailed arguments have been made by Albert Wohlstetter in "The Delicate Balance of Terror," *Foreign Affairs*, January, 1959, p. 222.

The inability of the missile force in Europe to destroy the entire Soviet retaliatory power would be a guarantee of its defensive intent.

Mobility will deal with only one horn of Europe's dilemma, however. It would facilitate the protection of European-based missiles, but it does not solve an even more serious problem of our allies: whether retaliation will in fact take place in situations where the European countries believe their vital interest to be at stake and we differ. The double-veto system under which the intermediate-range missiles are based in Europe gives our allies only a negative control. According to it, missiles cannot be launched except with the approval of the United States and the host country. And the nuclear warheads remain in exclusive United States custody. Thus our allies can *prevent* us from retaliating. They cannot *compel* us to do so. Nor is the double-veto system symmetrical. While we can veto retaliation from Europe by the simple device of withholding warheads, our allies cannot veto retaliation from the United States.

This system has serious drawbacks. It is difficult to visualize how it would operate in a defensive war. The warning time available to European-based missiles is not likely to exceed ten minutes. As a practical matter it will be next to impossible to obtain the consent of the governments concerned—or even of their military staffs—in this interval.

The double-veto system—far from being sensitive to the individual allies' conception of their interests—guarantees that the response will be of the lowest common denominator obtainable within the alliance. Intermediate-range missiles in Europe under the present system of control, therefore, hardly reduce the scope of Soviet blackmail. In any concrete case, NATO will still be entirely dependent on our willingness to run the risks of nuclear war. This state of affairs may be desirable from our point of view, since it ensures that our allies cannot force us into a nuclear war against our will. But we should not be surprised that some of our allies are restless with an arrangement which gives them so little influence over their own destiny.

The double-veto system also affects the utility of European-based missiles for deterrence of limited aggression. These missiles would provide an additional element of deterrence only if they increased the likelihood of nuclear retaliation in case of a local Soviet attack that *spared* the missile sites. But it is difficult to see why the mere fact of stationing missiles in Europe would increase our willingness to initiate a nuclear war in response to conventional aggression, and the double-veto system, coupled with our control over the nuclear stockpiles, makes *our* willingness the determining factor.

How, then, to reconcile the dilemma that Europe requires stronger local forces to prevent Soviet pressure but that these forces are unlikely to be created as long as our allies remain vulnerable to Soviet nuclear blackmail? Can a capability for local defense be brought about as long as we retain exclusive control over the weapons that alone can enforce the limit of any war? If national control of nuclear weapons does not enhance security and the double-veto system is essentially a device for preventing unilateral United States action from European bases, how can we fashion a deterrent that is both effective and certain?

Two general solutions present themselves: one based on the North Atlantic Community as a whole, the other on a more closely integrated Europe. If the North Atlantic Community can increase its political cohesion so that it begins to approach a federal system, the control of nuclear weapons and their location will become much less urgent problems. The deployment of NATO forces will then become an essentially *technical* issue. The only meaningful debate will concern the best dispositions of *common* weapons for the *common* welfare. Once it becomes clear that even a minor threat against Europe will engage the United States as fully as a minor threat against Alaska, temptations for Soviet pressure will be substantially reduced. Once our allies are convinced that a threat against what they consider their vital interests will be treated in fact like an attack on the United States, one of the prime motives for developing independent retaliatory forces will disappear. Great Britain and the United States do not have a moral right to deplore the acquisition of nuclear weapons by their allies unless they are prepared to take drastic steps in the direction of greater political integration. The minimum condition is to move in the direction of a North Atlantic confederation.[10]

[10] See pp. 165 ff.

Some steps towards confederation can be taken even within the existing NATO framework by negotiating an agreement along these lines:

(a) The level of the nuclear stockpile available to NATO should be fixed periodically by agreement among the NATO powers.

(b) Once the stockpile is determined, the United States would agree not to withdraw weapons without the agreement of all allies, or, to prevent capricious veto, by a two-thirds majority.

(c) The NATO countries should specify certain conditions under which nuclear weapons would be automatically released to SHAPE (the military command).

(d) The United States would earmark a portion of the Strategic Air Command for NATO and place it under NATO command.

(e) The British and French retaliatory forces, except perhaps for token units, would be placed under NATO command.

(f) The Allies would build up their conventional forces to the levels agreed upon under joint plans and would not reduce their forces assigned to NATO except with the agreement of the number of allies required to reduce nuclear stockpiles.

The first two provisions—setting the level of the stockpile by agreement among the Allies and undertaking not to withdraw weapons from it by unilateral action—are designed to meet the concern of our allies that they have neither control over the most essential weapons nor certainty about the availability of *any* weapons. For without an agreement specifying the nuclear stockpiles, our allies may fear that we may withdraw our weapons by unilateral action.

A treaty specifying some of the circumstances in which nuclear weapons would be released to NATO commanders would reassure each ally of the support on which it could rely in case of crises which are now foreseeable. Of course, not all conceivable Soviet pressures can be specified. But if NATO planning is not to be a mockery, the Allies must surely be able to agree on some threats which they consider serious enough for nuclear retaliation. Specifying at least some of these would be a major step towards overcoming the fear that in times of crisis our allies will be placed at the mercy of Soviet nuclear threats. With at least some of what our allies consider "vital interests" protected by solemn and detailed obligations, the Soviet capacity for blackmailing each ally separately will be sharply reduced. The conditions for the release of nuclear weapons to the military command would, of course, have to be negotiated at periodic intervals.

Once NATO has agreed on the goal of its nuclear establishment, the Allies can place part of their retaliatory forces under NATO command. Such a step would reflect the realities of the strategic situation. National nuclear establishments designed for independent retaliation are quixotic. None of our NATO allies can rationally engage in nuclear war without the support of the alliance and especially of the United States. A NATO nuclear establishment composed of British, French and United States contingents would give formal expression to this realization. And it would improve the Western negotiating position in arms control negotiations seeking to prevent the diffusion of nuclear weapons to other countries: the so-called Nth country problem.[11]

The proposal to place part of the Strategic Air Command under NATO control will undoubtedly meet strong opposition in the United States—perhaps from the same quarters which are impatient with France for resisting the further integration of its forces into NATO. But it should be obvious that as long as we retain exclusive control over what official declarations call the "sword" of NATO, our allies will attempt to achieve the same mastery over their affairs which we claim over our own.

It will be argued that to give up control over part of our strategic forces would weaken us in conducting a global strategy. But all difficult policy decisions involve choices: if we want to arrest the spread of independent nuclear forces within NATO and the fragmentation of the alliance, we must do our share to give NATO a framework of common purpose. Moreover, placing a portion of SAC under NATO command should not in practice prevent us from carrying out our responsibilities ouside Europe. There are three contingencies in which we may wish to use our retaliatory forces: (1) for all-out war; (2) for limited war in the NATO area; (3) for limited war outside the NATO area.

[11] See pp. 240 ff.

In the case of all-out war, our NATO allies would be bound to support us, both by the NATO treaty and, no doubt, by the formal agreement specifying the circumstances for nuclear retaliation described above. If our allies should seek to evade their responsibilities we would thereby be freed of all obligations and the part of our retaliatory force assigned to NATO would revert to U.S. control. If NATO is involved, however—as by treaty and self-interest it must be—*all* forces assigned to it should be part of an over-all plan. Placing a part of SAC under NATO control would thus present no handicap in the eventuality of all-out war.

In case of limited war in the NATO area, the assignment of a portion of SAC to NATO would unify command arrangements. It would formally put at the disposal of NATO what by solemn treaty obligations we are bound to supply in any case. Such command arrangements would make limitations somewhat easier by making a distinction, however tenuous and formal, between our over-all strategic forces and those assigned to NATO. (Though these distinctions may not mean much in practice, they can serve as a useful signal of limited intention; as, e.g., the Chinese term "volunteer" for their forces in Korea and our use of the phrase "police action" for the same conflict.)

In a limited war outside the NATO area, we would not require the strategic forces assigned to NATO, since a limited war is one which does not make claims on *all* available forces. Assignment of part of SAC to NATO, though a radical departure, would be one of the simplest means for increasing the cohesion of the alliance.

There are many who look with horror upon the diffusion of even this degree of control over nuclear weapons. Some thoughtful people would like us to guard not only our technology but the disposition of our forces. They recoil before the prospect of a world in which nuclear weapons become an integral part of the strategic planning of more and more regions.

It is not difficult to share this concern. Few problems confronting mankind are more urgent than that of dealing with the diffusion of nuclear weapons.[12] The fact remains that we cannot act as if all

[12] See pp. 240 ff.

choices were equally open: Great Britain has nuclear weapons and so does France. We are hardly in a position to press them to surrender their nuclear arsenal and, if we did, France at least would surely refuse. The best means of preventing the multiplication of national retaliatory forces is the NATO system described here. If we agree to share control over our weapons with our European allies, we may gain some influence over the manner of the diffusion and the direction of future nuclear policy. Standing aloof and refusing to share control of the strategic forces with the NATO alliance may supply the precise motive for a proliferation of national nuclear establishments. Refusal to share control over our weapons has the practical consequence not of preventing the diffusion of nuclear weapons but of forcing our allies into a wasteful duplication of a scientific effort already carried out by us as well as by the potential aggressor—thus further reducing the effectiveness of the over-all performance.

If a NATO nuclear establishment proves unfeasible and if national possession by our European allies is politically dangerous and militarily useless, what alternative presents itself? In default of the NATO solution described above, the most hopeful approach would seem to be a European Atomic Force into which the British and soon-to-be French retaliatory forces would be merged. If they pool their resources, the European powers including Great Britain will possess sufficient resources to create a substantial nuclear establishment. To be sure, Europe could not win an all-out war with the U.S.S.R. even by striking first. But it might deter, through the ability to extract an exorbitant price in case of aggression. The price would be exorbitant when even a successful nuclear war with Europe might weaken the Soviet Union to the point where it would become inferior to the United States and thus vulnerable to a preemptive attack. As a result, there would be no incentive to use nuclear weapons against Europe alone. And an attack against Europe and the United States simultaneously should lead to unacceptable damage from a retaliatory blow. A European Atomic Force—provided it was well protected—might not only deter a nuclear attack, it could also furnish an umbrella for a conventional defense.

Politically, the advantage of a European Atomic Force is that it would not expand the number of nuclear powers, European control replacing the British and French deterrent forces. And it would enable Europe to participate in arms control negotiations as an equal partner. Such a force would also enable NATO to negotiate much more flexibly about the stationing of its nuclear weapons.

Nevertheless, a European Atomic Force involves great complexities. An adequate force would be extremely costly and technically difficult. Resources devoted to it would be at the expense of the local defense forces, particularly those in the conventional field. Then again, a European Atomic Force would be politically or strategically significant only if it reflected a greater willingness to resist Soviet pressures than would be the case under the present NATO arrangement. If, however, a European Atomic Force is subject to the same inhibitions as the United States Strategic Air Command and on the same issues, it would represent a wasteful duplication of resources, adding little effective strength and creating another focus for Soviet pressure.

A European Atomic force would make sense only if European political cohesion were strengthened—though its contribution to that end should not be underrated. But it would be idle to pretend that the necessary cohesion is now in sight. Great Britain is politically no closer to the Continent than the United States; if anything, it appears less prepared than we are to run risks for what seem to it Continental issues.

Even should Europe strengthen its political unity, an independent European Atomic Force would be less desirable for both political and military reasons than the NATO solution described earlier. As long as the defense of Europe depends ultimately on United States participation—as it must—it is best not to leave any doubt in the mind of a potential aggressor about America's willingness to engage itself.

This consideration applies with particular force to a scheme advanced by the influential French strategic thinker, General Gallois.[13]

---

[13] P.-M. Gallois, "L'Europe et la défense de l'Occident," in Hersch, Frenay (et al.), *L'Europe au défi* (Paris, 1959); also, his "New Teeth for NATO," *Foreign Affairs*, October, 1960, p. 67.

He urges the retention of the present double-veto system for the control of nuclear weapons. But he proposes that it be supplemented by an understanding that in certain specified circumstances the United States would turn over nuclear weapons to its allies under national control. In case of a threat to a vital French interest, France could then count on being able to retaliate. This plan combines the worst features of unilateral national control and the present NATO system. Either the double-veto system reduces the response to Soviet pressure to the lowest common denominator or else turning over nuclear weapons to individual nations during a crisis will be interpreted as clear proof of America's disinterest in the dispute. For the presumption will be strong that if we thought our own interests intimately involved there would be no point in shifting nuclear weapons into the possession of allies. As for the recipient nation, this implication of United States disinterest would deprive these weapons of most of their utility for no European country would be able to conduct by itself a nuclear war against the U.S.S.R. In short, whatever system of control is finally adopted, care must be taken that it permits no doubts to arise in the mind of an aggressor about the United States commitment to the defense of Europe.

A generous and understanding U.S. policy which takes into account the concern of our European allies to see their special interests protected would be a wiser course than the multiplication of separate nuclear forces. Placing part of our deterrent under NATO command is a more imaginative solution than forcing our European allies into a wasteful duplication of effort. But either the NATO military establishment or the European Atomic Force is preferable to the present system, which is too weak for local defense and too divided for joint resistance to nuclear blackmail.

A modification of the system of control over nuclear forces will remain empty, however, unless NATO is prepared to make greater efforts to strengthen its local defenses, particularly in the conventional field. As long as NATO relies on a modified version of massive retaliation, no arrangement for control of nuclear weapons can overcome the inherent weakness and lack of credibility of such a course. If NATO is not willing to increase its forces so that nuclear retaliation becomes the last recourse instead of the sole strategy, it must accept the practical consequence that the United States will reserve the right for itself to define the *casus belli*. The decision to resist aggression cannot in such circumstances be a European one. In time this state of affairs must produce increasing opportunities for Soviet pressure and even greater demoralization of NATO. Without an increased capability for local defense, any effort to strengthen the nuclear deterrent will prove ineffective. The declining credibility of the threat of massive retaliation can only be ameliorated, not overcome, by a new system of control over NATO's nuclear arsenal.

Whatever course is adopted in the military field, however, the test of Western policy is its response to the political challenge. Security against aggression is the condition of policy—it is not in itself a policy. Whenever Europe is considered, one comes up inevitably against the problem of the future of Germany.

4. THE PROBLEM OF GERMANY

THE "German problem," so dramatically apparent today, has a long history. Arrangements in Germany have been the key to the stability of Europe for at least three centuries. The notion that the peace of Europe is jeopardized by a powerful, unified Germany is really based on the experience of the twentieth century only. Until the unification of Germany in 1871, stability had been as frequently threatened by Germany's weakness and its divisions. When Germany was composed of a congeries of competing states, it was the arena of conflict for the other European powers, which sought to perpetuate its divisions by balancing the rivalries of the German sovereigns. This involved them in a struggle not only to thwart German national aspirations, but also to prevent one another from gaining a preponderant influence.

A unified and strong Germany has had an even more upsetting impact on the European equilibrium. Unification came to mean the construction of a state capable of protecting itself against simultaneous invasion from east and west, which had been the bane of Germany for centuries. But a Germany powerful enough to defend itself against *all* its neighbors simultaneously was also strong enough to defeat each of them singly. Moreover, the effort to develop this capability required a mobilization of resources, a sense of discipline, and an exaltation of national feelings that were bound to disquiet all of Europe. Even when Germany's intentions were basically defensive—as they were throughout the major portion of the German Empire—to other countries they were indistinguishable from aggressive designs. Germany's effort to achieve security against the possibility of hostile coalitions made these coalitions inevitable. Germany for centuries has seemed either a temptation for the ambitions of its neighbors or a menace to their safety.

The ideal situation would be a Germany strong enough to defend itself but not strong enough to attack, united so that its frustrations do not erupt into conflict and its divisions do not encourage the rivalry of its neighbors, but not so centralized that its discipline and capacity for rapid action evoke countermeasures in self-defense. Such a Germany has existed only at rare periods. To help establish it must be a major task of Western policy.

But can one talk realistically of the unification of Germany? Is this not one of the issues which seem to be ignored by tacit agreement? It is often maintained that acceptance by the West of the *status quo* in Eastern Europe and especially in Germany is the key to stability in Europe. We are urged to recognize facts we are powerless to change in any case. We are told that once Soviet rule in Eastern Europe is formally accepted, the Soviet Union will be a "satisfied" power no longer interested in expansion.

The notion that wisdom consists of adjustment to facts is, of course, hardly a heroic one. Pressed to its extreme, it implies a policy without goal and measures without conception. It places the direction of events in the hands of those strong enough and ruthless enough to bring about a "fact." Nothing in the world would ever have been changed were adjustment the sole rule of conduct. It is an odd doctrine for the United States, which originated during a revolution and which now seeks to deal with a world in upheaval. Nor is the idea particularly novel. Stalin regularly offered the West a division of the world into spheres of influence, and he failed largely because the West was not yet prepared to adjust to a reality which involved surrendering other peoples' rights.

No doubt the division of Germany is likely to persist whatever the Western policy. No brilliant plan is likely to produce unification. The issue, however, is not only whether unification can be achieved but what attitude the West should take toward this "fact." Should it in effect co-operate with Soviet repression of freedom in Eastern Germany by formally accepting the division of Germany? Or should it strive to force the Soviets to accept the onus for thwarting Germany's national aspirations? True, Western policy has often ignored the issue of German unification. The memory of two World Wars and the tendency to stick with what is not intolerable have combined to bring about what comes close to a *de facto* acceptance of the *status quo.* Western policy with respect to German reunification has seemed to be conducted largely in response to Soviet initiatives. Between 1955 and 1959 no negotiations took place, nor did the West raise the issue of Germany. When Khrushchev in 1958 delivered his ultimatum on Berlin, a proposal was hastily manufactured under the pressure of a Soviet deadline. As soon as the Soviet threat was deferred, the West refrained from urging its plan. The question remains whether we should cap the omissions of the past with a formal recognition of the East German regime. It does not make too much sense to use the errors of the past to justify new mistakes.

In assessing the proposition that we should accept the *status quo* in East Germany, it is important to distinguish the problem of Germany from that of the other satellite countries. In Eastern Europe the West has long since recognized the existing governments. Diplomatic relations have been established. Commercial agreements have been concluded. Even economic aid has been extended, as in the case of Poland. The Hungarian upheaval proved that the West is not prepared to support anti-Communist revolutions with force. It is therefore difficult to assign any concrete meaning to the term "recognition of the *status quo*" or to imagine anything more the West could do to adjust to existing conditions. The danger to Soviet rule results from the inability of the Communist leaders to obtain domestic support in the countries concerned. The only additional concession conceivable would be to collaborate in the Soviet repression of freedom by renouncing the *principle* of self-determination.

The case is different in Germany, however. Here a Communist regime has been established in only a portion of the country, a portion that has no historical, ethnic or cultural tradition distinct from Germany as a whole. The problem in East Germany is not only that a puppet government has been forced on a hostile population; a separate state there—even were it non-Communist—runs counter to German national feeling. Khrushchev himself has found it necessary to reiterate that unification is the ultimate goal of Soviet policy, though not until West Germany is ready to accept the Communist system.

Moreover, as long as Germany remains divided both governments, if they are to survive, must press for unification. The position of the East German regime is perforce precarious, as long as there exists a free and prosperous West Germany which is the symbol of an alternative—a condition which has not existed in any other satellite area. By the same token, no West German government can accept as permanent the forcible partition of German territory without undermining its domestic support. An alliance which demanded such a price from the German people would lose its meaning in German eyes. And whatever the self-restraint of either the Federal Republic or the Western Allies, the history of Europe in the nineteenth century and of the anti-colonial struggles of the twentieth demonstrates that the desire for national independence cannot be ignored by governments. Or are we to assume that the desire for self-determination and national dignity is less strong in the continent of its origin than in Asia or Africa?

The Federal Republic would suffer a perhaps irreparable blow if its allies accepted its present frontiers as final even if they *seemed* to accept them by not advocating unification. The division of Germany may be unavoidable, but for the West a great deal depends on demonstrating what makes it so. An excess of "realism" about accepting the division of Germany will enable the Soviet Union to shift the responsibility for thwarting unification on us. This has already been foreshadowed by Khrushchev's statement to a group of West German editors that the West preferred a divided Germany for economic as well as military reasons,[14] and by the acts of the East German delegation at the Geneva foreign ministers' meeting in 1959 in seeking to project itself as the defender of German nationalism. If the Federal Republic is persuaded that it cannot achieve reunification through ties to the West, it may attempt separate dealings with the East. Unification could then be used by the Soviets as a lure to ending, step by step, the achievements of European integration and to encouraging a race for Moscow's favor. Alternatively, there may be a resurgence of virulent nationalism. The argument will gain credence that close ties with the West having failed, Germany must pursue a policy of pressure and nationalistic advantage.

A country which was ruled by Hitler, experienced the shock of defeat, and has already lost a quarter of its pre-war territory is subject to sudden and perhaps violent fluctuations of mood. This is not to say that West Germany would turn Communist. But a resurgence of virulent nationalism would be bad enough. An attempt by Germany to play off the West against the East would prove disastrous for the peace of the world—as has been demonstrated twice within a generation.

It is sometimes argued that, whatever its frustrations, the Federal Republic would soon discover that its scope for separate dealings was severely limited. But this line of reasoning overlooks the history of German-Soviet negotiations on nationalist grounds as well as the question of timing. By the time the Federal Republic would have realized how circumscribed its area of maneuver really is, Western cohesion would have been wrecked and European integration might have been replaced by squabbling, distrustful national rivalries. Retaining Germany as a willing member of the Western community is important not only for the future of Germany. It is even more vital for the peace of the world. The Soviet leaders are demanding recognition of their East German satellite so insistently because they know very well that acceptance by the West of the *status quo* is the best means for undermining the *status quo*.

To be sure, the Soviet Union almost certainly does not have a detailed master plan to communize all of Germany immediately. It

---

[14] *New York Times,* May 16, 1959.

would settle for separating Germany from its Western ties, because it would then have the opportunity of playing off Germany against its neighbors. It could appeal to German nationalism with the lure of unification and to the other European countries through their fear of Germany. The experience of the Middle East can serve as an example of the fate of regions which fail to achieve either unity or purpose. The U.S.S.R. first backed Israel in order to stimulate Arab nationalism. It then supported Nasser, who used this nationalism to expel the West. Next it shifted its favor to Iraq, which gave promise of putting nationalism into the service of Communism. The Soviet moves were obviously not planned in detail, for they depended on many factors outside of Soviet control. The Kremlin did strive to bring about a situation which gave it maximum opportunity for creating chaos. Even if chaos is not the deliberate objective of Soviet policy in Western Germany, it will be its practical consequence.

Soviet and East German Communist declarations make clear that the acceptance by the West of the East German satellite is conceived as a first step in bringing *all* of Germany into the Soviet orbit. Khrushchev said in Leipzig on March 7, 1959:

On what foundation should Germany be reunited? I think the question of reunification should be approached primarily from class positions. Can we agree when the capitalist world proposed to achieve the reunification of Germany at the expense of the German Democratic Republic *and thus narrow down the front of socialism*? [italics supplied] We have not and we do not live to yield to capitalism. . . . The question can also be put thus: Why not reunite Germany by abolishing the capitalist system in West Germany and establishing there the power of the working class? *But it would be unrealistic today* [italics supplied] . . . I repeat we are for German unity and the German people will be reunited. Therefore, do not hurry, the wind does not blow in your faces. . . . If you want your children and grandchildren to remember you with gratitude, you should fight for the conclusion of a German peace treaty which would be an important step towards the unification of Germany.[15]

The attempt to demoralize West Germany and to separate it from its allies has come to expression also in the draft peace treaty urged by the Soviet Union since January, 1959. This treaty, to begin with,

---

[15] Quoted from *Foreign Radio Broadcasts: Daily Report,* No. 62, 1959, BB2 ff.

is to be signed by both German regimes, thus bringing about the immediate recognition of East Germany. Its provisions would force the Federal Republic to give up all its ties to the West, even in the economic field. It also contains clauses which would permit the Soviet Union to interfere constantly in West German affairs, ostensibly in order to protect the "democratic" character of the Federal Republic. Finally, it requires that the question of unification be settled through negotiations between the two German regimes.

Obviously, the draft treaty is conceived to be the beginning, not the end of a process. Recognition of the East German regime would bring about a situation where in the future any change in Germany would have to be to the disadvantage of the West. It would foreclose unification on a democratic, but not on a Communist basis. The minimum result would be a severe disillusionment in the Federal Republic. The Communists could then attempt to cajole or threaten West Germany into a "neutralist" course. If this failed, they could withdraw recognition from the Federal Republic as "fascist" or as betraying the interests of the German people and deal with the East German regime as the representative of *all* of Germany. If the West had previously recognized the East German satellite, it could hardly retaliate by withdrawing its recognition without exposing itself to the charge of cynical power politics and of using the principle of self-determination for tactical ends only. Having given up a position which was morally and politically unassailable, we would become hostages of future Soviet moves. We would be forced to contest the issue of Germany on ever more unfavorable ground.

This sequence of events may seem farfetched today. But it would merely repeat Communist tactics already used in Eastern Europe and China, of first demoralizing the intended victim, then isolating and finally destroying him. It is already foreshadowed by the vicious Soviet attacks on West Germany. It cannot be supposed that the Soviet Union will indefinitely continue relations with a regime which it describes as the direct descendant of Hitler. The first step in applying these tactics can be found in Khrushchev's Leipzig speech: "The German Democratic Republic is a republic of the working class. It is a republic of workers and peasants, the homeland of *all* German workers"[16] (italics supplied). A similar point was made by a leader of the East German Communist party in March, 1959:

Socialism will triumph in the German Democratic Republic in the next few years. When we will place this question before the entire German people and in what manner depends on necessary real, objective conditions. *Under present circumstances* the main task in West Germany and West Berlin is to bring about a change in the balance of forces in favor of peace and democracy, *without as yet posing the demand for a transformation of the social order.* Everything depends on taking a stand not as a party of opposition but as the leading and the largest party in all of Germany, a party which has a program for the solution of the cardinal concerns of the *entire* German nation. [italics supplied][17]

But what about the Soviet demand that the future of Germany be settled by negotiation between the two Germanys? The cynicism of this proposal is matched only by the readiness of too many in the West to take it seriously. It is hardly to be supposed that the subservient satellite whose government would be eliminated as a result of German unification will prove any more tractable on the issue of resolving the division of Germany than its patron in the Kremlin. Even if the two German governments were to negotiate with each other in "good faith"—whatever is the significance of that phrase in this particular context—the result would undoubtedly be an increase rather than a decrease of tension. Negotiations can succeed only through persuasion or through pressures which make agreement seem preferable to intransigence. Persuasion presupposes agreement on some standard of reasonableness. But the statements of the two German governments indicate a schism even deeper than that which has rent East and West because it is compounded by thwarted national aspirations. Each German government is therefore under nearly irresistible pressure to subvert the other. And given the interest of the East European satellites in the division of Germany, they are likely to use their influence to exacerbate all tensions. Confederation is thus a euphemism for recognizing East Germany. It is not a means of unifying Germany but a device by which the West accepts the division of Germany.

[16] *Ibid.*
[17] *Berliner Zeitung,* March 5, 1959.

Confederation would also enable the East German satellite to gain a voice in the national affairs of the Federal Republic. In a confederation, domestic and foreign affairs are very difficult to distinguish—even assuming good will on both sides, which is not likely to be present. The East German regime, by adding its weight to the opposition of any existing government, could demoralize political life in the Federal Republic or, at the least, force it into a rigid mold dangerous to democracy. It could press for weakening West Germany's European ties by insisting that they conflicted with unification. If the Federal Republic refused to give up its West European relationships, East Germany, having obtained international recognition of its sovereignty by the very fact of confederation, could withdraw from it as the advocate of German nationalism. If the Federal Republic accepted the Eastern overtures for weakening its Western ties, fuel would be added to Western suspicions and bring about a cycle of still further estrangement.

It can be objected that the confederation principle works both ways. Would not the establishment of an all-German institution enable the Federal Republic to influence events in the East? The symmetry is more apparent than real. The apparatus of a police state makes the East German regime relatively immune to domestic pressure, especially if Soviet troops remain in Eastern Germany. But even in their absence, not too much should be expected in the way of liberalization of the East German regime. The experience of Poland, so often invoked as a model for a possible evolution, is a poor guide. In Poland national and religious feeling combined to support a relatively liberal Communist regime as the best possible solution from the point of view of the Polish nation. There was no outside focus of national loyalties. In Eastern Germany the situation is quite different. The Communist regime is considered the chief obstacle to national aspirations. Freedom is not identified with the liberalization of the East German regime but with the West German alternative. Any loosening of control by the East German regime is likely to lead to its overthrow.

Moreover, even if liberalization should occur, progress towards German unification will not necessarily follow. Poland, during its most liberal phase—long since reversed—achieved a measure of freedom in its domestic affairs only at the price of rigid adherence to the Kremlin line in international affairs. Unification, however, on any basis consistent with free popular expression would mean that East Germany would leave the Soviet orbit and that its regime would be changed.

For all these reasons, a wise Western policy will see to it that the Soviet Union is forced to accept the onus for the division of Germany. We should seek to make clear not only that the Soviet Union rejects our optimum program, but that it opposes *any* scheme for unification that recognizes the principle of free popular choice, at whatever stage. Our failure to pursue this course during the period of greatest Soviet confusion in 1953-1957, and our seeming reluctance to negotiate when we should have forced the Soviet leaders to come to grips with the issue of Germany are among the causes of our present difficulty.

Any negotiation on Germany faces two seemingly contradictory dangers, then: that we accept the division of Germany, or that in bargaining for unification we agree to solutions which lay the basis for the Soviet domination of all of Germany. It is important for the West not only to advocate German unification but to take its stand on issues that do not lend themselves to obfuscation. Though we can offer formulas designed to save Soviet face—such as an interim period before free elections—we cannot surrender the right of the German people to determine its own fate at a time not too far distant.

Once the principles of free popular expression and a specific timetable for unification were accepted, we could be extremely flexible about method and the sequence of steps leading towards unity. There could be an initial period in which free movement of peoples within Germany and the right of free political activity were reestablished. This could be followed by free local elections to permit a gradual change. When the issue of unification was finally put to the nation as a whole, the voting could be carried out by states— a system which would weight the vote in favor of the less densely populated Eastern Germany. Even a confederation of the two areas now containing the Federal Republic and the East German puppet could be considered, provided that the East German government emerged from a UN-supervised free election. The key question remains, however, whether the Soviet Union is prepared to consider *any* formula consistent with even the most flexible interpretation of Western notions of freedom. If the answer were in the affirmative, a variety of face-saving formula could be worked out. On the other hand, there is no substitute for such a decision.

If we leave the firm ground of the principle of national self-determination, we will be in the realm of technical expedients where the Soviet Union will have endless opportunities for delay, confusion and obstruction. We will then find it next to impossible to make the Soviets assume the onus for the continued division of Germany. No voting formula, however subtle, can replace Soviet willingness to permit free popular expression. The Soviet leaders will not give up East Germany through an oversight. We can concede a great deal regarding the mode and timing of elections, but to give the East German regime a veto of unification, directly or indirectly, is either to legitimize the continued division of Germany, with dire consequences for the political stability of West Germany and Western Europe, or to prepare the way for a Soviet Germany.

It is said by some that nobody really *wants* German unification, including the Germans. It has been argued that the West German people will submerge their thwarted national aspirations in the general prosperity. Nobody, so it is claimed, would wish to run any risks on behalf of the compatriots under Communist rule. And the recent history of Western Europe, so the argument goes, provides a powerful motive for keeping Germany divided. Both France and Great Britain, it is said, prefer a divided Germany to a unified, free one.[18]

As for the attitudes of the Germans towards a united Germany, it is striking that even the Soviet leaders have found it wise to appear as advocates of unification. It is no less remarkable that all West German political leaders, regardless of party, vie with each other in expressing concern for unification. They would hardly do so were they not convinced of a deep popular demand. And even should the issue of unification remain dormant for a while, it

[18] See Walter Lippmann, *New York Herald Tribune*, May 7, 1960.

could, if coupled with any other grievance, shake democracy in West Germany.

The psychological situation in Western Europe is more ambiguous. The anguish and suffering inflicted by Germany provide every cause for distrust—a fact well understood and subtly exploited by the Soviet leaders. Yet the countries of Western Europe and the United States must wrench themselves loose from their memories. If the West understands its interests, it *must* advocate German unification despite the experiences of two World Wars and despite the understandable fear of a revival of German truculence. The West may have to acquiesce in the division of Germany but it cannot agree to it. The division of Germany may be unavoidable but the cohesion of the West and the future of the North Atlantic Community depends on our ability to demonstrate what makes it so. Any other course will in the end bring on what we should fear most: a militant, dissatisfied power in the center of the Continent.

These considerations bear importantly on the question of Berlin. For the issue in Berlin is not whether a city completely surrounded by Communist territory is "worth" a war—as is often asserted. Berlin has become the touchstone of the West's European policy. A defeat for the West—that is, a deterioration of Berlin's possibility of living in freedom—could not help but demoralize the Federal Republic. It would mark the end to any hope for reunification. The scrupulously followed Western-oriented policy would be seen as a fiasco. This would become a warning to all other states in Europe of the folly of resisting Communist pressure. Berlin would illustrate the irresistible nature of the Communist advance to the rest of the world. Whatever their view of the merits of the issue, the uncommitted would come to believe that the protection of the West is illusory, that wisdom, if not ideological sympathy, counsels adjustment to Communist standards. And even in the relations of some of these states to each other, a Western defeat in Berlin would serve to increase tensions. The precarious peace which is being maintained between the Arab states and Israel in part by the fear of Western intervention against aggressive acts might not long survive a demonstration of Western impotence in Europe.

Though the people of Berlin have become involved in a contest which transcends them, not least at stake are the two million people who have chosen freedom and who have maintained this way of life in a city entirely surrounded by a Communist sea. If they are deserted, the claims of the West to stand for self-determination and human dignity will become a mockery. If it is not possible to rally public opinion in the West, indeed in the world, on this issue, it will be hard to avoid the conclusion that the West defends its principles only when no risks are involved. The blandness and lack of urgency in much of the West's reaction to the crisis raises doubt as to whether the capacity for indignation of too many in the West is not confined to the free world's shortcomings.

Of course, there have been repeated statements that we would defend Berlin against military attack. Unfortunately the threat is more subtle than a military one. The real danger to Berlin resides in a slow whittling away of the Western position through a series of steps each of which is so small that it does not seem to justify a major risk and in a pattern of negotiations about the status of Berlin by which the West purchases a series of respites at the price of jeopardizing the future.

Both of these dangers have become magnified since Mr. Khrushchev opened the crisis over Berlin with his ultimatum of November 27, 1958. The Communists have engaged in a series of harassing moves aimed at cutting off Berlin from Western Germany. And the West's response has been confused and divided. At every stage of the crisis, a Western position has emerged only after prolonged and painful public wrangling. And even then it has represented an uneasy compromise which has rarely withstood Soviet pressure. Whatever else Mr. Khrushchev may have obtained as the result of his threat to Berlin, its effect as a source of discord within the alliance surely has been a major gain.

A symptom of this confusion is the way in which the alternatives have been stated. Some have argued that there is no point whatever in negotiating about Berlin. Our legal position is clear; to give it up would merely invite new Soviet demands. Opponents of this point of view urge that we ought to "improve" the status of Berlin. Why not remove irritants, they maintain, and thereby improve the safety as well as the freedom of the people of Berlin?

But the West can at least strive to avoid disingenuousness in facing this dilemma. There is of course nothing sacrosanct about any particular arrangement for Berlin. There is no magic in the *status quo* for its own sake. Naturally, we should strive to "improve" the position of that city. But it is surely preposterous to imply that Mr. Khrushchev has kept the world in a state of crisis for two years in order to "improve" *our* position.

The West owes it to itself not to confuse its alternatives. The West *can* agree to any change which in fact ameliorates conditions. What the West cannot do is to make concessions which represent a worsening of Berlin's position, in other words a restraint on its existence as a democratic city. And because Berlin's position even now is highly precarious, the range of possible concessions is unfortunately limited. These facts have hardly been influential in the diplomacy that began with Mr. Khrushchev's threat to turn over the access routes to Berlin to its East German satellite.

Despite protestations to the contrary, the West has been in effect negotiating under duress. The deterioration of its psychological position is shown by the process of negotiations since November, 1958. Before the abortive summit conference at Paris, Mr. Khrushchev felt obliged to withdraw his threat of unilateral action—if somewhat ambiguously. That conference was to deal with the whole gamut of international problems. Just five months later, during the 1960 session of the General Assembly, Mr. Khrushchev reintroduced his demand for a summit conference and threatened to "solve" the Berlin problem unilaterally unless his demand was met. Moreover, he insisted that the agenda of the proposed meeting, in contrast to the previous one, was to be confined to the future of Germany— the issue on which there is a maximum possibility of disagreement among the Western allies. Nevertheless, his ultimatum was greeted, if anything, with relief. The West seemed more interested in the respite it had been offered than concerned with the fate which was waiting at the end of the period of grace. At any rate, pressures for another summit conference immediately started again.

Mr. Khrushchev has been able not only to dictate the pace of the negotiations; he has also imposed his pattern on their actual conduct. He started the Berlin crisis by calling the situation in

Berlin "abnormal" and asking the West to "solve" a "problem" which would not have existed but for his unprovoked threat. The practical consequence of this procedure is that every Western offer has the tendency to weaken the West's position. Every new proposal establishes not the principle that the status of Berlin should be ameliorated—which is unexceptionable—but that it should be changed. Each Western offer is in effect "banked" by the Soviet Union and becomes the minimum condition for the next round. The result of negotiating according to "rules" where the *quid pro quo* for a substantive Western concession is the withdrawal of a Soviet threat is that the West *must* lose. The only thing to be determined by negotiation in these conditions is the extent of the defeat.

The intensity of Soviet pressure has served to confuse the problem of just what rights *are* at issue. The impression has been created that we are negotiating about access to Berlin in general. In fact, the only access route to Berlin at issue is the one that supplies the Western garrison of ten thousand soldiers. Control over Western military traffic is what Mr. Khrushchev has threatened to turn over to the East German satellite. Control over civilian traffic to the Berlin population of two million was transferred to the East German satellite on September 20, 1955, without effective opposition from the West—an omission for which a heavy price will now have to be paid. Thus no matter what concessions were made to safeguard military traffic, these would not prevent the East Germans from fomenting another and even more serious crisis by interrupting civilian traffic.

With this background, perhaps the best point of departure for analyzing the nature of the negotiations over Berlin is the last Western offer at the Foreign Minister's Conference of 1959. Since this was to be the basis of the Western position at the Paris summit conference, and since it is not likely to be withdrawn, it may be used to illustrate the concern over the manner in which the issue of Berlin has been handled.

The West proposed a new interim agreement to guarantee its rights of access to Berlin. Though it first urged that the interim agreement apply until German reunification, the period finally proposed was five years. In return the West was to accept a limitation on the size of its military garrison in Berlin. It would forego stationing nuclear weapons in Berlin. No intelligence or "subversive" activities were to be conducted from West Berlin. Would this proposal, if accepted, in fact improve the position of Berlin?

Whatever aspect of the proposal is considered one must conclude that it goes to the very limits of safety and probably beyond them. To begin with, the offer transforms a permanent status into an interim one. Henceforth, the Soviet Union would have the final voice in the arrangements in West Berlin. When the interim agreement lapsed at the end of five years, the future of West Berlin would be subject to a Soviet veto. If the Soviet Union refused to agree to a new interim agreement or made conditions we could not accept, both our position in West Berlin and the freedom of the city would be in dire jeopardy. To be sure, the West has taken the position that the lapse of the agreement would reinstate its old rights. But it can hardly be maintained that the West would after a five-year interval defend rights for which it was not prepared to contend when they were first challenged and which were specifically altered by the interim agreement.

The substance of the proposal gives even greater cause for concern. The military clauses are innocuous. We have no nuclear weapons in Berlin, and no rational purpose would be served by stationing them there. As for the ceiling on the size of the garrison, there is no magic number which assures the safety of Berlin. The garrison should be sufficient to prevent the Communists from taking over the city by riots or by a sudden coup. Beyond that its size is subject to negotiation. Also, we do not need to conduct intelligence activities from Berlin.

The most serious problem is posed by the prohibition of "subversive" activities, unless this term is rigidly defined. There is, of course, no objection to a ban on subversive activities in the conventional sense. However, it is very likely that the Soviet Union would construe the very existence of freedom in the Western sense as a subversive activity. Any article in a free Berlin newspaper critical of the Communist regime might be taken as violating the agreement. All democratic parties in the Federal Republic have already been labeled "fascist" and therefore presumably subversive. The possibilities of interference would be endless. There would be many pretexts for abrogating the agreement and thus confronting the West with an even worse dilemma. The sense of insecurity of West Berlin would be magnified both by the interim nature of its status and the constant opportunities for Communist harassment. And all of these risks would be run for "rights" which are essentially meaningless, since, as has already been pointed out, the East Germans could interrupt civilian traffic any time and use this device to exact new concessions.

Can the status of Berlin be safeguarded in return for the recognition of East Germany? Such a result would be an enormous Communist victory. The Communists would gain international recognition for the partition of Germany and create a situation whereby they alone could emerge as the advocates of unification. The Federal Republic would be dealt a staggering blow for reasons already described. And for all of this the West would obtain a withdrawal of a unilateral, unprovoked threat. This is hardly a procedure calculated to discourage further Communist pressure.

Recognition might not even suffice to obtain a temporary guarantee for West Berlin. For the negotiating process is not symmetrical. Once we offered recognition, we would have given up the principle of self-determination. If the Communists then raised their demands, they would have transformed the question of recognition from a matter of principle into a question of negotiating expedients. Once we agreed that recognition was simply a problem of haggling over conditions, the Communists would have every reason to expect that they could exact it sooner or later, if not from us then from some of our allies.

Another scheme which has been suggested is to turn Berlin into a ward of the United Nations. But the Berlin "problem" is not amenable to such a solution. For one thing, if Berlin were made a United Nations city it would have to forego its special relationship to the Federal Republic. Germany henceforth would be divided into three parts. This would have disastrous psychological consequences in the Federal Republic, where it would be construed as the loss of yet another part of German territory. The impact on Berlin itself would be scarcely less unfortunate. The sense of isolation and helplessness would be magnified. The end of the special economic relationship with the Federal Republic would paralyze the economy of Berlin. Even apart from the economic problem, there would be many possibilities for Communist pressure against which a United Nations guarantee would not be effective. If each harassment were relatively minor, it is not likely that the new countries would run major risks—even the risk of Soviet displeasure —to spare the former imperial powers embarrassment. On the contrary, in any crisis the pressures of the uncommitted would almost certainly be in the direction of a kind of "compromise" which would grant part of the Communist demands. The inevitable result would be the attrition of Berlin's freedom.

What if the Soviet Union makes good its threat and signs a peace treaty with its East German satellite? The West should never have let itself be maneuvered into the position of seeming terrified of this legal fiction. The Soviet Union cannot abrogate its treaty obligations by a so-called peace treaty with a non-recognized government. Even from the strictly legal point of view, a contractual obligation cannot be transferred to a third party without the consent of the original partner. Signing a peace treaty with the East German satellite is simply a way of turning over access to Berlin, thereby precipitating a crisis unilaterally. The more important question is not whether we should strive to prevent this peace treaty but what we can do to prevent an interruption of traffic to Berlin.

Clearly, we cannot keep the Soviet Union from turning over control of the access to Berlin to the East Germans, either by signing a peace treaty or in some other way. The immediate *practical* result of such a Soviet move is that East German soldiers would replace those of the Red Army at the check points controlling military traffic to Berlin. This would raise the question of whether the West should refuse to show its documents to East German sentries. It seems that the line should not be drawn on this issue. We could simply treat the peace treaty as invalid and the East German soldiers as agents of the Soviet Union and permit them to exercise any rights previously granted to the Soviet Union.

The real problem will arise not when the East Germans exercise already established rights but when they set new conditions. Should the West then negotiate with the East Germans? It seems that the West can always go as far in dealing with the East Germans as has the Federal Republic. And the Federal Republic has established a precedent of technical conferences, particularly with respect to access to Berlin. As long as the West maintains that the right of access is not negotiable and that it is dealing with the East Germans only as representatives of the Soviets, it can follow the same procedure. It need not exclude negotiations with respect to the technical implementation of existing agreements.

However, a discussion of conceivable concessions should not obscure the real challenge before the West. The issue in Berlin is not primarily one of finding negotiating expedients. The West will have to face the much more difficult problem of defining at what point Communist harassment becomes an intolerable threat to the freedom of Berlin. The attempt to avoid this problem has brought on the dangers which it sought to avoid. It has encouraged the Communists step by step to increase their pressure and to stake their prestige in a manner that makes any settlement safeguarding the freedom of Berlin extremely difficult. And the West should have no illusions. The end of the freedom of Berlin would be the beginning of the end of the freedom of Europe.

But while we have a responsibility to advocate German unification and to defend the freedom of Berlin, we have an obligation also to take account of the fact that a united Germany may disquiet its neighbors. This fear takes two forms: (1) the concern of Poland that a united Germany would bring pressure to change the Oder-Neisse line; (2) a general disquiet on the part of all of Germany's neighbors about a resurgence of German militarism.

With respect to the Oder-Neisse line, matters would seem to stand as follows: At the Potsdam Conference in 1945 it was decided to place under Polish administration all territories east of the Oder-Neisse line, as a compensation for German depredations in Poland and for roughly one quarter of pre-war eastern Poland annexed by the Soviet Union. Poland then proceeded to expel about 13 million Germans from these territories. Today, for all practical purposes, no Germans remain. The Federal Republic has refused to recognize the Oder-Neisse line, partly to retain a bargaining counter vis-à-vis Poland, partly as a result of the pressure of the East German refugees, most of whom are in the Federal Republic.

In retrospect, the wisdom, indeed the morality, of simply shifting a country 300 miles to the west and of expelling millions of human beings from their ancestral homes may be doubted. Unquestionably, one of the attractions of this scheme for the Soviet Union was that it almost guaranteed a continuation of German-Polish enmity. Yet the mistakes of the past should not be compounded by new errors. The Federal Republic must realize that unification is impossible without its acceptance of the Oder-Neisse line. Poland must be given to understand that unification would not be a prelude to a demand for the revision of the present demarcation line. The minimum price the Federal Republic must prepare itself to pay for unification is to recognize the Oder-Neisse line as final. To be sure, this will be painful. But it does not make sense to maintain the frontier of a divided Germany on the Elbe because of a refusal to accept the loss of territories which no longer contain a German population and which probably could not be resettled if regained.

It is of course extremely unlikely that unification could be achieved at this price—especially since the Soviet Union cannot be too interested in settling German-Polish differences. But the West could reduce Polish enthusiasm for Soviet adventures over Berlin by making clear that support of them is not required to maintain Poland's integrity. At the least, the national interests of Poland should be separated from the ideological ones of a Communist ruling group. The Western allies could make a formal declaration that they would oppose any attempt to change the Oder-Neisse line by force. They could in effect give a military guarantee of the existing dividing line pending the unification of Germany, at which time it would be understood that formal recognition would follow. Though such a step would have no dramatic consequences, it would serve to define the issue and to some extent separate the question of German unification from that of the Polish-German frontier.

There remains the need to show understanding for the legitimate security concerns of Germany's other victims in World War II. What, then, of the schemes for arms control in Europe?

5. Arms Control in Europe

One test of a responsible scheme for European security is that it be designed to increase the security of *all* parties. The Soviet claim of the requirements of its security cannot be the only factor. The experience of World War II and of a decade of cold war should give us some guide to understanding this problem. An agreement that takes into account the "legitimate" security interests of both sides must protect the Soviet Union against the danger of a resurgent German militarism and against an attack from NATO territory. But it must also safeguard the West against the risks of Soviet pressure and encroachment. It is true that the Soviet Union's experience in this century may make it unusually sensitive to German military strength. But it is also true that for over a century the Russian Empire in one form or another has been pressing on all peripheral areas, including Europe. The Soviet Union has a right to demand protection against military attack. Yet in a society of sovereign states, *absolute* security is obtainable only by reducing all other states to impotence. It is the road to empire.

The stability of an international system depends on the degree to which it combines the need for security with the obligation of self-restraint. To rely entirely on the continued good will of another sovereign state is an abdication of statesmanship and self-respect. But to seek security entirely through physical domination is to menace all other countries. For absolute security for one country must mean absolute insecurity for all others. Where to strike this balance cannot be determined in the abstract; it is what makes diplomacy an art and not a science. But the balance must be established if the international order is to be stable.

In this sense the revolutionary quality of the Soviet Union has resided not in the fact that it has felt threatened—a measure of threat is inherent in the relations of sovereign states—but that nothing has been able to reassure it. Since the end of World War II, the Communist bloc has grown by the addition of Eastern Europe and Communist China; North Korea and North Vietnam have become Communist states; the Middle East has been penetrated; a nuclear arsenal has been created and with it the capability of menacing the territorial United States; economically the U.S.S.R. is rapidly gaining ground. Yet the claim of being threatened has never abated. It is therefore futile to debate whether the Soviet Union is "really" interested in world domination. For the problem may be that the Soviet conception of security results in undermining all other states. Soviet policy will have reached a turning point when Soviet leaders become willing to rest their policy at least in part on agreement and not simply on preponderant strength.

What, then, should be the general goal of such an agreement? Arms control negotiations must not become a device for the unilateral weakening of the West.[19] A scheme for European security, therefore, must take care not to wreck NATO, for without NATO each European country would face the preponderant Soviet might alone. It must not eliminate the possibility of local defense, lest our allies become demoralized by the threat of Soviet conventional and tactical nuclear strength. But while protecting our European allies against nuclear blackmail or conventional aggression, it must also give assurances to the Soviet Union against attack from NATO territory. The question then becomes whether it is possible to conceive of two military establishments on the Continent capable of defensive action but deprived through appropriate control measures of offensive power. Can these objectives be reconciled?

Arms control in Europe can be considered in relation to two hypotheses: (1) the assumption of a continued division of the Continent and (2) the assumption of a reunified Germany.

Turning first to arms control schemes along the present political dividing lines in Europe, the most frequent suggestions have been grouped under the general term "disengagement." Few concepts so vaguely defined have produced so much controversy. It is applied now to a freeze on forces in Central Europe, now to a reduction of troops. Sometimes it refers to the withdrawal of American, British and Soviet forces from Germany, Poland, Czechoslovakia and Hungary, sometimes to a demilitarized zone in Central Europe. It has been advocated as a step to be undertaken side by side with

---

[19] For a fuller discussion of general principles of arms control, see Chap. VI, "The Problems of Arms Control."

unification, as a step towards unification, and as a device to bring about relaxation of tensions in its own right. But the crowning confusion is that disengagement, no matter how it is defined, cannot be properly evaluated by the NATO countries because they lack common political and strategic goals and therefore yardsticks against which to measure their policy alternatives.

The arguments on behalf of disengagement can be summed up as follows: NATO has prevented a Soviet attack without ever meeting the force levels planned for it. Since Soviet ground strength has been preponderant throughout the existence of NATO, peace must have been maintained for one of two reasons or a combination of them: either because the Soviet Union had no intention of making a military attack on Europe in the first place or because it was deterred from such an attack by the threat of a general war with the United States. As a result, so the advocates of disengagement claim, a withdrawal of all foreign forces from Germany would merely shift the starting line for a Soviet advance 100 or 550 miles to the east without reducing the sanction against such a move. To be sure, the Soviet Union might decide to reoccupy the territories it had vacated. But it could do so, in Mr. Kennan's words, "only once and only for the highest stakes: in the contingency, that is, of general war."[20] Massive retaliation would furnish the deterrent against Soviet aggression whether on the Elbe, the Oder or the Bug.

The case for disengagement is further strengthened by the actual performance of the NATO allies. Since no ally, so the argument goes, is prepared to make the sacrifices required to achieve an adequate local defense, NATO might as well gain some political benefit from offering to perpetuate its weakness. Moreover, according to this line of reasoning, the growth of the German army will permit the withdrawal of American and British and French forces from the center of the Continent without any diminution of NATO strength. In short, many thoughtful people have seen the military establishment on the Continent as a bargaining counter: since it is not expected to play a significant military role, it can be reduced in order to achieve a *political* advantage. And its symbolic function

[20] George Kennan, "Disengagement Revisited," *Foreign Affairs,* January, 1959.

:ould be replaced by a more solemn promise by the United States
o defend Europe.[21]

An assessment of these arguments is made difficult because many
of them contradict one another. It is said, for example, that disengagement would contribute to a relaxation of tensions because it
would enhance Soviet security. But it is also urged that disengagement does not involve any risk because NATO forces in Central
Europe are in any case too weak to resist a Soviet onslaught. It is
maintained that German troops could replace those of the Western
allies without any diminution of Western security. But it is not
explained why, if the Soviet Union does feel threatened by the
present NATO strength, it should be reassured by a German military establishment of the same size. In other words, many of the
proponents of disengagement oscillate between arguing that it will
contribute to peace because it will reassure the Soviet Union and
maintaining that disengagement is wise because it enables the West
to obtain a political gain in return for agreeing to perpetuate the
present imbalance in local power.

So many different schemes have been advanced that they are
best analyzed in terms of two basic groups of justifications: (1) those
which are urged for largely political reasons and (2) those which are
based on essentially military considerations. The political argument
proceeds from the premise that the withdrawal of foreign forces
from Germany and from some of the East European satellites would
represent a step towards German unification. It is thought by some
that since the East German regime is maintained by Soviet troops,
a mutual withdrawal would bring about the collapse or at least
the liberalization of the East German satellite. The establishment
of a zone of controlled armaments, followed by the withdrawal of
American, British and Soviet forces, should be accompanied, it is
said, by "some form of negotiation" between the Federal Republic
and the East German satellite. This would, in an undefined manner,
bring the two regimes closer together and lead to reunification on

---

[21] See speech by Adlai Stevenson, *New York Times*, March 6, 1959; also a series
of articles by Denis Healey, "The Case for Disengagement," *New Republic*,
March 17, 24, 31, 1958.

the basis of some kind of free elections at an unspecified future
date.[22]

It would seem incumbent on anyone advocating this course to
give some indication of the nature of the contact between the two
parts of Germany and the manner in which it is supposed to reduce
the gap between the two systems. It is often argued that, at the
very least, disengagement would reduce the danger of an East German rebellion, leading to an intervention by the Federal Republic.
However, disengagement in a divided Germany would seem to
magnify this risk. The Federal Republic and East Germany, left
to their own devices, would find themselves under nearly irresistible
pressure to subvert each other. Neither government is secure as
long as the other exists. A withdrawal of foreign forces would not
only make an upheaval in East Germany more likely; it would also
remove many inhibitions against intervention by the Federal Republic.

At the same time, the Kremlin has made clear innumerable times
that it would not tolerate the overthrow of a Communist regime.
To be sure, Khrushchev has qualified this by saying that Soviet
troops would intervene only if requested by local leaders or if the up-
rising were inspired from abroad. But some Communist functionary
will always be found to ask for assistance on the model of Kadar in
Hungary or the Panchen Lama in Tibet. As the cases of Hungary
and Tibet have proved, uprisings against Communist rule are considered to be inspired from the outside by definition. Finally, were
the Soviets to hesitate, the satellites would press for intervention,
since the overthrow of one Communist regime would undermine
Communist rule throughout Eastern Europe and because a divided
Germany would seem to them the best guarantee of their security
on nationalist grounds. In short, disengagement which does not
address itself to the problem of German unification invites the very
dangers it seeks to avoid.

The political benefits of less ambitious schemes such as "thinning
out" of forces are even more problematical. Such a measure, whatever its significance for purposes of arms control, affords no possi-

[22] See Denis Healey, "Disengagement and German Reunification," *New Leader*,
March 20, 1959.

bility of lessening Soviet political control in the satellites or in East Germany. For purposes of political control two Soviet divisions are as effective as twenty: they symbolize Soviet power and they establish the possibility, if not the right, of intervention. There are very few Soviet troops in Poland, none in Rumania, Bulgaria and Czechoslovakia. This suggests that even without the presence of Soviet troops the evolution of the Communist satellites in a more liberal direction is far from certain. And as long as *any* troops remain, they could be quickly reinforced in case of trouble, as happened in Hungary. Their very presence would serve to forestall internal change.

On the military side, many of the proposals for arms control in Central Europe are designed to prevent any change in the military *status quo*. For example, a freeze on the level of forces in Central Europe or a "thinning out under appropriate inspection" has been proposed. Apart from the fact that the importance of inspection is vastly overrated in this context—existing intelligence in Central Europe being quite good—most of these schemes fail to come to grips with the real security problem. They do not affect significantly the capability of the United States or the Soviet Union, or even of Western Europe, to launch a sudden all-out attack. At the same time, since present or planned NATO forces are already inadequate for offensive ground operations, most schemes for troop reduction would merely weaken the capability for local defense of the West without providing an additional reassurance to the Soviet Union. They would improve the *offensive,* but not the *defensive,* position of the U.S.S.R. Even a troop freeze could keep NATO from adapting itself to changed strategic relationships. Unless coupled with a major reduction of Soviet forces or a build-up of conventional strength in the part of the Continent outside the controlled zone and probably through a combination of both, it will perpetuate an inequality which will represent a growing invitation to Soviet adventures as Soviet long-range missiles multiply.

Though the omissions of the first ten years of NATO have not yet led to the dire consequences so often predicted, it would be rash to assume that this will be true when the Soviet nuclear and missile arsenal is fully developed. In the age of invulnerable missile forces—if we succeed in reaching it—it simply will no longer do to rest the security of Europe on the result of heretofore successful gambles. It is sometimes said that, since Finland and Austria have survived without the presence of American troops, the same situation might obtain for Europe after the withdrawal of American forces.[23] To begin with, Finland is not the most comforting example, since it has had to grant the Soviet Union what amounts to a veto on the composition of its cabinet. But, in any case, Finland and Austria have maintained their independence *because* of the existence of NATO. Crushing their independence has not been "worth" the price of a redoubled military effort by NATO, which would be its consequence. The lesson from the experience of Finland is not that a military establishment on the Continent is dispensable, but rather quite the opposite. If it is present, nations which otherwise might long since have been swept into the Communist sphere can yet maintain their identities.

If NATO is prepared to create the forces of which it is capable, it would be able to negotiate with conviction about arms control in Europe. But to rest the argument for control schemes on the proposition that NATO, being unwilling to remedy its vulnerability, might as well offer to perpetuate its weakness for some political gain, is self-defeating. For an impotent NATO provides no incentive for the Soviet leaders to agree to any meaningful control scheme.

Similarly, it is a dangerous illusion to believe that we can substitute a verbal guarantee for an actual commitment of forces. It is little comfort for our allies to hear that they should take heart from the example of Korea, where an aggressor paid a heavy penalty for mistaking an American withdrawal for lack of determination.[24] To our European allies the significant feature is that the North Korean invasion *did* occur. And they have reason to doubt that our response would have been quite as prompt had it entailed the certainty of all-out war—which would be the inevitable consequence if NATO were to fail to bring into being a capability for local defense in Europe or if the present military establishment on the

[23] Emmet Hughes, *America the Vincible* (New York, 1959), p. 269.
[24] Denis Healey, "A Reply to My Critics," *New Republic*, June 2, 1958.

Continent were to be dismantled as a result of schemes for disengagement.

Many of these objectives can be achieved by the Soviet Union simply by *negotiating* about disengagement. It is frequently argued that we should at least offer disengagement "to test Soviet good faith" or as a propaganda move to demonstrate our peaceful intentions. It is not clear how Soviet good faith is tested by our making proposals which are undesirable from our point of view. Moreover, the West cannot offer a program without gearing its expectations to it. To offer disengagement would mean that all future NATO planning would have to take place in the shadow of the expectation of an American and British withdrawal from Central Europe. Disengagement negotiations in all likelihood would have the minimum consequence of "freezing" the present strategic relationship with its increasing perils.

What about the schemes which seek to limit not the level of forces but their range of equipment, specifically nuclear weapons? Following the initiative of the Polish Foreign Minister Rapacki, a number of plans have been advanced for zones in Central Europe from which nuclear weapons are to be excluded. Given the range of modern weapons, a denuclearized zone in Central Europe would not in itself affect the military situation decisively, so long as nuclear weapons could be stationed in the Low Countries and France. It *would* create a psychological and political imbalance, for the aggressor would retain his full nuclear arsenal while the area most menaced would be without the ability to retaliate. In these circumstances the Soviet Union might be encouraged to threaten Central Europe and to attempt to split the Western alliance by appealing to the countries controlling nuclear weapons that the issue was not "worth" a nuclear war. And, once a denuclearized zone was established, it would be difficult to deal with Soviet pressures to expand it to include eventually the entire Continent.

Moreover, it is difficult to imagine what denuclearization means concretely. It would be nearly impossible technically to determine whether secret caches existed—particularly in the case of United States and Soviet forces. Thus denuclearization, to be meaningful, would have to involve the withdrawal of the United States and

Soviet forces from the denuclearized zone and the Rapacki Plan should really be analyzed from that aspect. The establishment of a denuclearized zone, moreover, would require a kind of inspection which might serve as a pretext for constant Soviet interference.

This is not to say that a denuclearized zone in Central Europe can never be considered. It does mean that this would be extremely risky unless there were greater unity within the Western alliance. The different approaches within the Western alliance to the Soviet pressure over Berlin should cause us to have sympathy for the reluctance of countries directly exposed to violent Soviet pressure to depend solely on weapons based far away, and over which they have no control. A prelude to any denuclearization must therefore be a determined effort to bring about more political and military cohesion—in fact, and not simply in formal declarations. To the degree that each member of the alliance can have confidence that an attack on one part automatically involves every other, NATO can afford flexibility in the deployment of its atomic weapons. If NATO adopts greater integration of its nuclear components—either in the form of NATO control or in that of a European Atomic Force, described earlier—it could negotiate with considerable flexibility about the stationing of its common arms in return for a sharp reduction of Soviet conventional power in Eastern Europe. The areas in Europe without nuclear weapons might then feel protected by their ability to participate in the control of *common* weapons. Even then serious thought should be given to establishing a denuclearized zone by unilateral declaration rather than by formal agreement—lest the Soviet Union, in order to "reassure" itself about compliance with the treaty, gradually establishes its domination over the denuclearized area.

Similar principles could be applied to other arms control schemes. For example, a ceiling could be placed on NATO forces between the Rhine and the eastern frontiers of the Federal Republic and on Warsaw Pact forces in the East German satellite, so that the two military establishments would be substantially equal in number—provided NATO maintains adequate forces west of the Rhine to counterbalance Soviet forces east of the Oder. A control system could be established between the Rhine and the Oder to reduce the danger of surprise attack. Overlapping radar screens could offer a measure of protection against an attack by air. But we must be frank enough to admit that many of the acceptable schemes along the present dividing lines are such primarily because they are irrelevant to the real security problem of Europe. They are negotiable only because they do not mean very much.

Two conclusions follow:

First, the inadequacies of the current NATO effort may cause the Soviets to believe that they can gain no additional security from arms control schemes or that they can achieve the objectives of arms control through unilateral Western actions. They may not take Western proposals seriously because they believe themselves already protected by their local preponderance. Thus, effective negotiations may be prevented, not by the strength of NATO but by its weakness and irresolution.

Second, schemes for arms control in Europe cannot by themselves eliminate the problems which are caused by the Soviet suppression of freedom in Eastern Europe and particularly in East Germany. As long as Germany remains divided, the danger of an explosion exists, whatever the wishes of the chief protagonists. Measures to control armaments in Central Europe, to be effective, should therefore accompany a political settlement. The natural dividing line for arms control schemes is the Oder, not the Elbe. The two problems of German unity and arms control in Europe are thus closely related. Unification without a scheme for arms control will frighten all the states surrounding Germany. A European security system without German unification is either a palliative or it will magnify conflicts in Central Europe.

It is argued by some that the Soviet Union cannot permit German unification under present circumstances because such a step would place the frontier of NATO on the Oder. But to place the frontier of NATO on the Oder need not mean that NATO *forces* must advance to the Polish frontier. The Western proposal at the Geneva Foreign Ministers' Conference of 1959 specifically excluded that possibility. It might have gone further and offered the complete demilitarization of East Germany under international control. Such a control system would prevent a ground attack from NATO territory. For other forms of attack East Germany is unnecessary and the political situation there does not affect them. They must be dealt with by different types of arms control, to be discussed later.

A more comprehensive plan would be to take the eastern borders of a unified Germany as the dividing line for a European control system. For example, non-German forces could be required to withdraw the same distance from the Oder-Neisse line as non-Polish forces. The size of German forces on one side and Polish and Czech forces on the other could then be fixed so that they were roughly equal both in numbers and in equipment. United States, British and French forces on one side would withdraw to the line of the Weser while Soviet forces would withdraw to the Vistula. The German forces between the Weser and the Oder would be restricted to defensive armaments, as would the Polish forces between the Oder and the Vistula. To decrease the danger of an attack from German territory, NATO would agree not to station weapons of more than 700-mile range on German territory. An inspection system could be established to control these measures. Obviously, there are many variations of such a scheme, which could be the subject of negotiation both as to the width of the zone separating Western and Soviet forces and as to types of arms to be stationed in the area.

From a military point of view such a solution would make a major contribution to European stability. Offensive ground operations would become difficult, because the German and satellite forces would be approximately equal and they would separate the Soviet and Western military establishments. At the same time, there would remain sufficient Western strength on the Continent and within Germany not to tempt aggression and to resist it should it take place. Continued membership in NATO would help protect Germany against pressure from the east while the deployment of NATO forces would demonstrate their defensive purpose. By unifying Germany, such a program would remove the chief source of political tension in Europe. And it would create a zone of arms control which, if successful, should bring about a climate of confidence leading to further measures.

To be sure, short of a major policy reversal, the Soviet Union

would derisively reject any such proposals. But the reason is not
that they would fail to contribute to stability. Rather it is that
the Soviet Union is reluctant to give up its East German puppet,
its springboard for wrecking NATO and for the eventual domination of all of Germany. The melancholy fact may be that in their
present state of mind the Soviet leaders are interested only in those
agreements in Europe which contribute to instabilty.

6. A NEUTRAL GERMANY

IF, THEN, the reunification of Germany is of such central importance,
should it be purchased at the price of the neutralization of Germany? Should the West give up its demand that a unified Germany
be free to determine its own relationship to NATO and propose
instead that Germany be forbidden to enter military alliances?

Many in the West advocate the neutralization of Germany because they believe that once Germany supplies the preponderance
of the shield forces of NATO it will be strong enough to make its
own arrangement with the Soviet Union. According to this line of
reasoning, it would be wiser to anticipate this eventuality by offering the withdrawal which may soon be expected from us. For, if the
Western alliance ever appears as the obstacle to German unification,
it will lose its attractiveness for Germany.[25] Others argue that the
Soviet Union will never tolerate the liberalization of satellite regimes as long as there is a danger that the new government may
join NATO.[26] The neutralization of Germany could be a major
step in allaying these fears.

Of course, the fact that German troops will soon comprise the
largest element of a force which is itself too small is not an argument for weakening it even further by the withdrawal of Western
forces. And if the Soviet intervention in Hungary was in fact caused
by the fear that the former satellite might join NATO, it is not
clear why this danger would be removed by the neutralization of
Germany. Nothing short of the disbanding of the Atlantic alliance

---

[25] See, for example, Fritz Erler, "The Reunification of Germany and Security
for Europe," *World Politics*, April, 1958.
[26] Kennan, "Disengagement Revisited," *op. cit.*

would seem to offer a sufficient guarantee. The best means for dealing with this particular problem would have been to propose not the neutralization of Germany but the neutralization of Hungary or of any other satellite desirous of leaving the Soviet orbit.

Nevertheless, a proposal to neutralize Germany in return for unification has tempting aspects. Unification would remove one of the major causes of tensions in Europe. If we made an offer to neutralize Germany and it was rejected, this would demonstrate once and for all that German membership in the Atlantic alliance is not an obstacle to unification but rather a response to Soviet intransigence. The temptation to propose the neutralization of Germany is all the greater when it is considered that were Moscow ever to offer unification in return for military neutrality it would be next to impossible for a German government to refuse.

It is important to be clear, however, as to what is meant by neutralization. It could mean that Germany would leave NATO and that Western troops would withdraw from the Federal Republic, while Poland, Czechoslovakia and Hungary would leave the Warsaw Pact and Soviet forces would retire from these countries. Or it could mean the departure of foreign troops only from Germany. It could involve a limitation of German forces so severe as to render Germany defenseless. It could apply to limitations only in certain categories of forces. Or it could permit Germany to maintain its defense by whatever forces it considered necessary, provided it was not part of a military alliance.

If Soviet troops retire only to Poland and if German forces were limited to the types of weapons stipulated by the Soviets in its draft peace treaty, the U.S.S.R. would be able to exert an enormous pressure on an independent Germany. With self-defense against Soviet attack impossible, Soviet influence would be likely to grow relative to that of the West even if NATO could be satisfactorily based in the Low Countries and France—a possibility which, in the absence of careful study, cannot be taken for granted. It may be argued, of course, that even a neutral Germany would continue to enjoy the protection of NATO. The sanction against Soviet pressure or re-entry would be about the same as today: the fear of all-out war with the United States. But it is difficult to see wherein resides the sup-

posed attraction for the U.S.S.R. of a scheme which gives Germany
all the advantages of unification plus all the benefits of protection
by NATO. If, as is said, it must make *some* difference whether the
Soviet troops are on the Elbe or 100 miles to the east, it must also
make *some* difference what the sanction is against re-entry or
whether United States troops would be encountered on the way.
Otherwise, Soviet pressure for the withdrawal of American forces
would make no sense.

If Soviet troops withdrew only to the Oder and Germany should
be permitted forces adequate to defend itself, the result could
well be an increase in tension. German forces, to be effective, would
then have to be increased considerably beyond levels now planned.
But if NATO allegedly disquiets the Soviet Union, a German force
of similar strength under independent control would seem to be
an even greater cause for concern. Moreover, a militarily strong
Germany without the restraint of NATO would surely drive the
Soviet satellites closer to the U.S.S.R. A withdrawal of Soviet forces
only into Poland therefore involves the risk of constant tensions:
either an armaments race in Central Europe or, if German forces
were severely limited, a military vacuum hazarding Western
security.

The most persuasive scheme has therefore coupled the neutralization of Germany with that of Poland, Czechoslovakia and Hungary—the original Gaitskell Plan. No doubt such a scheme involves
a diminution of Western military security. At the same time, ending
the division of Germany would be an undoubted political gain.
Everything would depend on the ability of NATO to maintain a
substantial military establishment in Western Europe to back up
Germany. If forces capable of conducting a substantial local defense
are stationed in France and the Low Countries, the strategic balance
could be maintained, and it is possible to conceive of the development of a stable political life. If this should prove impossible, the
defense of the Continent would rest entirely on American retaliatory
power. And it simply does not make sense to assume that a deterrent which is losing its credibility under present circumstances
would serve to protect areas that never were a part of the Western
defense system or from which U.S. troops have been withdrawn.

Europe's impotence would then reduce the Continent to at least the status of Finland vis-à-vis the U.S.S.R.

At the same time, a neutral belt would present difficulties transcending the purely military aspect. The notion that Germany, Poland, Czechoslovakia and Hungary would constitute a single bloc under the common guarantee of the Western powers and the Soviet Union hides great complexities. Many of the arguments for a neutral belt proceed from the premise that the countries comprising it would conduct joint policies designed to safeguard their neutrality and that they would resist outside pressures as a unit. Quite the reverse is likely to be the case. The memory of World War II and its aftermath would seem to ensure that these countries, even when neutralized, would be unlikely to think of themselves as a unit. Distrust, if not animosity, rather than co-operation is likely to characterize the relations between Germany on the one hand and Poland, Czechoslovakia and Hungary on the other. Moreover, since the neutrality would have to be guaranteed by the Big Four, endless opportunities for interference would exist, particularly if each guaranteeing power is to be given a unilateral right of intervention —as Mr. Erler and some other advocates of a neutral belt suggest.

Soviet pressure on Germany to "safeguard its neutrality" could be prevented only by a tacit understanding which placed Germany under the protection of NATO and the East European satellites under that of the Warsaw Pact. The practical result of the neutral belt then would be either Soviet domination of Central Europe or the situation envisaged in the scheme outlined earlier: the Oder as the dividing line between NATO and the Warsaw Pact with a zone of controlled armaments on both sides to reduce the danger of surprise attack. An explicit arrangement to that effect would accomplish all the security objectives of neutralization without the political dangers of legitimizing Soviet pressure on a reunited Germany.

Moreover, the West ought to understand clearly the political hazards of negotiating about the military neutralization of a unified Germany. It may create a precedent by which, under the guise of expanding the neutral belt, the United States will be gradually pushed out of Europe. It may lay the basis for destroying all the achievements of European integration. One of the most constructive developments of the post-war period has been the progress towards European unity. The Coal and Steel Community and the Common Market have raised hopes that Europe will submerge its traditional rivalries in working for the common good and that Germany may become a helpful partner in the European community. These trends would be hazarded by the creation of a neutral belt. The Soviet Union, with its belief in the predominance of "objective" social forces, is unlikely to be content with military neutralization. The Kremlin, which attacked both the Marshall Plan and the Common Market as "aggressive imperialism," has already proposed in its draft peace treaty that Germany should not be permitted to be part of any arrangement not also signed by the U.S.S.R.—a clause which spells the doom of European integration.

From the Soviet point of view, this is even understandable. A Germany which is part of the European community in all respects except the military could not be neutral in any political sense. And if a substantial military establishment were retained in the Low Countries and France, and if Germany were permitted its own forces, the net result would not be very different from the present situation. However, if Germany were to be "really" neutral, if it were permitted no ties with any of the guaranteeing powers not granted to any other—as the Soviet Union has proposed—the result would be the end of European integration with dire consequences for the political stability of Europe.

For Germany is the last country that should be encouraged to "go it alone." Germany's attempt to pursue an isolated policy in the center of the Continent has brought disaster to Europe twice within a generation. It is often said that the future depends on the course taken by the neutral third of the world. And it is true that the past decade has been characterized by a contest for their favor. It seems inevitable that a neutral belt in Europe would transfer the contest to the center of the Continent. The advantage of deliberately bringing about a situation where one will be forced to compete for the allegiance of a region now committed to the West is not self-evident.

It may be argued that these dangers can be avoided by a "self-denying ordinance" by which the Big Four would agree not to intervene in Central Europe. But an area of such vital importance and comprising 200 million inhabitants cannot be isolated from world affairs. Its own inner dynamics would affect events, whatever the intentions of the guaranteeing powers. To force Germany to chart its own course separately from the rest of the Atlantic community would inevitably disrupt international order. This indeed may be the attraction of such a scheme for the Soviet Union. Thus, while military neutralization of Germany in return for unification is a possibility, and should indeed be offered under appropriate conditions, Western policy must, as one of its primary goals, seek to retain Germany as a willing member of European political and economic institutions, whatever the ultimate security arrangements.

A neutral belt in Europe, then, is tolerable only if *all* of the following five conditions are met: (1) If it is made part of a plan for German unification acceptable to the Federal Republic; for if Germany considers such a plan desertion by the West, its policy as part of the neutral zone might undermine all stability. (2) If a careful study shows that substantial United States and British forces can be stationed in the Low Countries and France; for otherwise the "neutral belt" would stand in danger of becoming a political appendage of the Soviet Union. (3) If a time limit is placed on the negotiations; for otherwise the Soviet Union would be able to achieve the paralysis of NATO and the end of European integration merely by engaging in endless conferences. (4) If there is firm agreement among the Western allies that neutralization applies only to military relationships and that German economic and political ties to the other European countries cannot be sacrificed and may be extended. For if German unity is purchased at the price of European integration, the West would have thrown away the fruits of the most helpful and constructive policy it has conducted since World War II. (5) If the remaining countries of NATO are confident that they can resist Soviet and domestic pressures against expanding the neutral zone to include all of Europe.

To state these conditions is to recognize the extremely hazardous nature of the proposals for a neutral belt. Such a course might be adopted by a cohesive, self-confident alliance, but not by one divided by doubts and lack of purpose. If it is nevertheless embarked upon, it should be without illusions and without begging all the principal questions. We should have understanding for statesmen reluctant to leave the familiar *status quo* for uncharted positions, if we recall the many instances where the "new course" of one year was decried as unimaginative and rigid a few years later. Thus a fear exists that concession may merely establish a precedent for a step-by-step retreat. The history of the proposals for a neutral belt in Central Europe—advanced first as a means for ending the intolerable division of Germany and now advocated by some as a device to make the division bearable—goes far to explain the rigidity of some of those with most at stake in a drastic change of course.

A neutral belt in Europe is too serious a matter to be advanced simply as a propaganda device. Before it is proposed, the West must ask itself how it can safely base its entire military establishment on France and the Low Countries; how cohesive its policy is likely to be in the face of Soviet procrastination; how purposeful its measures will be in the creative tasks that await it. If the West can answer these questions affirmatively with confidence, the neutralization of Germany can be proposed provided it is coupled with an acceptable plan for unification. If not, such an offer will simply speed up the erosion of the Western alliance.

7. Conclusion: Towards a North Atlantic Community

WHATEVER aspect of the Atlantic alliance is considered, the goal of Western policy must be to develop greater cohesion and a new sense of purpose. We are living in a period which, in retrospect, will undoubtedly appear to be one of the great revolutions in history. The self-sufficient nation-state is breaking down. No nation—not even the largest—can survive in isolation or realize its potentialities, material, political, or spiritual, on its own.

Nowhere is this more evident than in the Atlantic community. None of the major problems with which the nations surrounding the North Atlantic are confronted can be finally resolved on a national basis. On the contrary, policies of petty nationalist advantage will prove equally disastrous to everyone. The security problem is insoluble on a national basis. The attempt to achieve security by unilateral efforts will produce impotence. In the economic field, the nations of the Continent have already realized that their former quest for autarchy was self-defeating and that a united effort is essential for the common good. In the diplomatic field, separate policies will in time prove disadvantageous to every ally. The gains to be achieved will prove illusory. The respites afforded by separate approaches to the Soviet Union have already been proven both brief and a contributory cause of international tensions.

The diplomacy preceding the abortive summit conference of 1960 must ultimately be destructive to the alliance. Separate conversations imply the possibility of separate settlements or there would be no point in them. That such a style of diplomacy inherently creates distrust is shown by the fact that President Eisenhower, to demonstrate his good faith, found it necessary to tour Europe before receiving the Soviet Premier, and that each other head of state visited his colleagues to report on his conversations following his meeting with Mr. Khrushchev. Even more worrisome is the degree to which negotiations with the Soviet Union have become involved in the domestic politics of the Allies. In several countries of the alliance, political leaders have found it wise to run on a platform stating that they are peculiarly able to bring peace. This not only has created additional pressures for unilateral approaches; it has also contributed to an atmosphere where the alliance is often made to appear as an obstacle to a settlement, or at least where political leaders ask for support because of their special skill in dealing with "recalcitrant" or "bellicose" partners.

If the alliance is to regain its cohesion it must realize that it is impossible to combine all the advantages of partnership with all the benefits of independent action. Without a truly common position Western rivalries will either paralyze negotiations or enable the Soviet Union to use them to demoralize the West.

For these reasons, it seems time to examine carefully the possibility of creating some federal institutions embracing the entire North Atlantic community, however attenuated these may be at first. A conference of North Atlantic heads of state or foreign ministers should address itself to the following tasks:

(a) A recasting of the military effort along the lines described earlier.

(b) A definition of goals in the political and economic fields for a ten-year period.

(c) The definition of precise commitments to give effect to these goals.

(d) The development of a joint plan for economic assistance to the new nations and the devising of common institutions to give it effect.

(e) The creation of a North Atlantic Council composed of senior and respected citizens and charged with reporting to each government about the fulfillment of agreed goals and defining new needs or necessary adaptations.

The need for greater cohesion is apparent in every field. In negotiations with the Soviet Union, for example, it seems essential that the bargaining be carried out by a single negotiating team for the alliance as a whole. It is time to stop deluding ourselves that we can maintain unity while negotiating as separate national units. The effort to do so will necessarily create constant divisions. The Soviet Union gains opportunities for playing off the Allies against each other. If protestations of unity are not to be formalistic, an agreed Western position should be negotiated by a single delegation.

Similarly, in their relations with the newly independent nations, the countries of the North Atlantic community deprive themselves of the diversity of skills and resources they possess by proceeding each on its separate way. There are undoubtedly strong reasons why it would not be wise to identify ourselves completely with the former colonial powers in their erstwhile dependencies. But the problem could be avoided by an offer to match any European contribution and to pledge a certain minimum sum in order to develop a common North Atlantic program. Thus, the nations of the North Atlantic community—preferably outside the NATO framework—could form a Development Institution designed to deal with certain specified tasks in the newly independent countries, to which each member country would commit itself with a given amount for a specified number of years. The officers of that institution would be international and its program would be conducted on behalf of the North Atlantic community and not of any member nation.

There are many other areas in which greater cohesion depends largely on our purposefulness and our imagination. The North Atlantic Parliamentarians' conferences could be strengthened so that the recommendations to member parliaments would have greater weight. The United States could do much to bridge the gap opened between the rival economic groupings in Europe by pursuing liberal and enlightened trade policies of its own. The immediate task is a decision to break out of the mode of thinking that has imprisoned us for a decade and a willingness to embark again on ventures as bold and constructive as was the Marshall Plan a decade ago.

In the past, the Soviet threat has often produced Atlantic unity. It may again. But ultimately the unity of the West depends on what we affirm, not on what we reject. We of the West, who bequeathed the concept of nationalism to others, must summon the initiative and imagination to show the way to a new international order. Nothing is more crucial than for the West to develop policies which make of it a true community.

V

ON NEGOTIATIONS

1. THE INTRACTABILITY OF DIPLOMACY

AS ARMAMENTS have multiplied and the risks of conflict have become increasingly catastrophic, the demands for a "new approach" to end tensions have grown ever more insistent. No country, it is said, has any alternative except to seek to attain its aims by negotiations. The Cold War must be ended in order to spare mankind the horrors of a hot war: "The stark and inescapable fact is that today we cannot defend our society by war since total war is total destruction and if war is used as an instrument of policy eventually we will have total war," wrote Lester Pearson. "We prepare for war like precocious giants and for peace like retarded pigmies."[1]

There is no doubt that the avoidance of war must be a primary goal of all responsible statesmen. The desirability of maintaining peace cannot be the subject of either intellectual or partisan political controversy in the free world. The only reasonable issue is how best to achieve this objective.

And here there is reason for serious concern. A welter of slogans fills the air. "Relaxation of tensions," "flexibility," "new approaches," "negotiable proposals," are variously put forth, as remedies to the impasse of the Cold War. But the programs to give these phrases meaning have proved much more difficult to define. The impression has been created that the missing ingredient has been a "willingness to negotiate." While this criticism is correct for some periods, particularly John Foster Dulles' incumbency as Secretary of State, it is not a just comment when applied to the entire

[1] Lester Pearson, Speech at Oslo, Dec. 11, 1957, quoted in the *New York Times,* Dec. 12, 1957.

post-war era. Hardly a year has passed without at least some negotiation with the Communist countries. There have been six Foreign Ministers' Conferences and three summit meetings. Periods of intransigence have alternated with spasmodic efforts to settle all problems at one fell swoop. The abortive summit meeting of 1960 proved that tensions have sometimes been increased as much by the manner in which diplomacy has been conducted as by the refusal to negotiate. The Cold War has been perpetuated not only by the abdication of diplomacy but also by its emptiness and sterility.

What, then, has made the conduct of diplomacy so difficult? Why have tensions continued whether we negotiated or failed to negotiate? There are four basic causes: (1) the destructiveness of modern weapons, (2) the polarization of power in the contemporary period, (3) the nature of the conflict, (4) national attitudes peculiar to the West and particularly to the United States.

It is not an accident that the diplomatic stalemate has become more intractable as weapons have grown more destructive. Rather than facilitating settlement, the increasing horror of war has made the process of negotiation more difficult. Historically, negotiators have rarely relied exclusively on the persuasiveness of the argument. A country's bargaining position has traditionally depended not only on the logic of its proposals but also on the penalties it could exact for the other side's failure to agree. An abortive conference rarely returned matters to the starting point. Rather, diplomacy having failed, other pressures were brought into play. Even at the Congress of Vienna, long considered the model diplomatic conference, the settlement which maintained the peace of Europe for a century was not achieved without the threat of war.

As the risks of war have become more cataclysmic, the result has not been a universal reconciliation but a perpetuation of all disputes. Much as we may deplore it, most major historical changes have been brought about to a greater or lesser degree by the threat or the use of force. Our age faces the paradoxical problem that because the violence of war has grown out of all proportion to the objectives to be achieved, no issue has been resolved. We cannot have war. But we have had to learn painfully that peace is something more than the absence of war. Solving the problem of peaceful change is essential; but we must be careful not to deny its complexity.

The intractability of diplomacy has been magnified by the polarization of power in the post-war period. As long as the international system was composed of many states of approximately equal strength, subtlety of maneuver could to some extent substitute for physical strength. As long as no nation was strong enough to eliminate all the others, shifting coalitions could be used for exerting pressure or marshaling support. They served in a sense as substitutes for physical conflict. In the classical periods of cabinet diplomacy in the eighteenth and nineteenth centuries, a country's diplomatic flexibility and bargaining position depended on its availability as a partner to as many other countries as possible. As a result, no relationship was considered permanent and no conflict was pushed to its ultimate conclusion. Disputes were limited by the tacit agreement that the maintenance of the existing system was more important than any particular disagreement. Wars occurred, but they did not involve risking the national survival and were settled in relation to specific, limited issues.

Whenever the number of sovereign states was reduced, diplomacy became more rigid. When a unified Germany and Italy emerged in the nineteenth century, they replaced a host of smaller principalities. This reflected the dominant currents of nationalism. But from the point of view of diplomatic flexibility, some of the "play" was taken out of the conduct of foreign policy. To the extent that the available diplomatic options diminished, the temptation to achieve security by mobilizing a country's physical strength increased. The armaments race prior to World War I was as much the result as the cause of the inflexibility of diplomacy. France and Germany were in fundamental conflict. And neither state could organize an overwhelming coalition. As a result, power had to substitute for diplomatic dexterity and the period prior to World War I witnessed a continuous increase of the standing armies.

World War I accelerated the polarization of power. By the end of World War II only two major countries remained—major in the sense of having some prospect of assuring their security by their own resources. But a two-power world is inherently unstable. Any relative weakening of one side is tantamount to an absolute strengthening of the other. Every issue seems to involve life and death. Diplomacy turns rigid, for no state can negotiate about what it considers to be the requirements of its survival. In a two-power world these requirements are likely to appear mutually incompatible. The area where diplomacy is most necessary will then appear most "unnegotiable."

The inherent tensions of a two-power world are compounded by the clash of opposing ideologies. For over a generation now the Communist leaders have proclaimed their devotion to the overthrow of the capitalist world. They have insisted that the economic system of their opponents was based on exploitation and war. They have never wavered from asserting the inevitability or the crucial importance of their triumph. To be sure, periods of peaceful coexistence have alternated with belligerence, particularly since the advent of Mr. Khrushchev. But one of the principal Communist justifications for a *détente* can hardly prove very reassuring to the free world; peace is advocated not for its own sake but because the West is said to have grown so weak that it will go to perdition without a last convulsive upheaval. At the height of the spirit of Camp David, Khrushchev said: "The capitalist world is shaking under the blows of the Socialist camp. What shakes it even more than the rockets is the attitude of our workers towards their work. . . . We have the will to win."[2]

Negotiations with Communist leaders are complicated by one of the key aspects of Leninist theory: the belief in the predominance of "objective" factors. One of the proudest claims of the Communist leaders is that in Marxist-Leninist theory they possess a tool enabling them to distinguish appearance from reality. "True" reality consists not of what statesmen say but of the productive processes—the social and economic structure—of their country. Statesmen, particularly capitalist statesmen, are powerless to alter the main outlines of the policy their system imposes on them. Since everything depends on a correct understanding of these "objective factors" and the relation of forces they imply, "good will" and "good faith" are meaningless abstractions. One of the

[2] *New York Times*, Dec. 3, 1959.

chief functions of traditional diplomacy—to persuade the opposite party of one's view point—becomes extremely difficult when verbal declarations are discounted from the outset. Khrushchev said in 1959: "History teaches us that conferences reflect in their decisions an established balance of forces resulting from victory or capitulation in war or similar circumstances."[3]

Much of the diplomatic stalemate has therefore little to do with lack of good will or ingenuity on the part of the statesmen. Without an agreement on general principles, negotiations become extremely difficult. What will seem most obvious to one party will appear most elusive to the other. When there is no penalty for failing to agree and when at the same time the balance of power is so tenuous, it is no accident that the existing dividing lines are so rigidly maintained. For the *status quo* has at least the advantage of familiarity while any change involves the possibility of catastrophe. At the same time, since these dividing lines are contested, protracted tension is nearly inevitable.

This impasse has led either to long periods in which diplomacy has for all practical purposes abdicated its role; or else it has produced a form of negotiations which has almost seemed to revel in *not* coming to grips with the issues dividing the world. The reference which is often made to the coexistence achieved by Mohammedanism and Christianity or by Protestantism and Catholicism is not fully relevant to the contemporary problem. In both cases, coexistence was the result of protracted, often ruinous, warfare—the very contingency diplomacy is now asked to prevent. We must be aware that the factors that intensify the desire to resolve the impasse of the Cold War may also make a creative response more difficult.

These obstacles to serious negotiations are magnified by Western, and in particular American, attitudes towards negotiating with the Communists. A *status quo* power always has difficulty in coming to grips with a revolutionary period. Since everything it considers "normal" is tied up with the existing order, it usually recognizes too late that another state means to overthrow the international system. This is a problem especially if a revolutionary state presents

[3] Speech at Leipzig, March 7, 1959, quoted in *Foreign Radio Broadcasts: Daily Report*, No. 62, 1959, BB 16.

each demand as a specific, limited objective which in itself may seem quite reasonable. If it alternates pressure with campaigns for peaceful coexistence, it may give rise to the belief that only one more concession stands in the way of the era of good feeling which is so passionately desired. All the instincts of a *status quo* power tempt it to gear its policy to the expectation of a fundamental change of heart of its opponent—in the direction of what seems obviously "natural" to it.

Were it not for this difficulty of understanding, no revolution would ever have succeeded. A revolutionary movement always starts from a position of inferior strength. It owes its survival to the reluctance of its declared victims to accept its professions at face value. It owes its success to the psychological advantage which singleminded purpose confers over opponents who refuse to believe that some states or groups may prefer victory to peace. The ambiguity of the Soviet challenge results in part from the skill of the Soviet leadership. But it is magnified by the tendency of the free world to choose the interpretation of Soviet motivations which best fits its own preconceptions. Neither Lenin's writings, nor Stalin's utterances, nor Mao's published works, nor Khrushchev's declarations has availed against the conviction of the West that a basic change in Communist society and aims was imminent and that a problem deferred was a problem solved.

It is only to posterity that revolutionary movements appear unambiguous. However weak it may be at the beginning, a revolutionary state is often able to substitute psychological strength for physical power. It can use the very enormity of its goals to defeat an opponent who cannot come to grips with a policy of unlimited objectives.

The United States has had particular difficulty in this respect. From the moment in our national history when we focused our attention primarily on domestic development, we met very few obstacles that were really insuperable. We were almost uniquely blessed with the kind of environment in which the problems that were presented—those at least that we really wanted to solve—were difficult but manageable. Almost from our colonial infancy we have been trained to measure a man, a government, or an era by the degree of energy with which contemporary problems have been attacked—and hence by the success in finding a final, definite solution. If problems were not solved, this was because not enough energy or enough resolution had been applied. The leadership or the government was clearly at fault. A better government or a better man would have mastered the situation. Better men and a better government, when we provide them, *will* solve all issues *in our time*.

As a result, we are not comfortable with seemingly insoluble problems. There must be *some* way to achieve peace if only the correct method is utilized. Many of the erratic tendencies in American policy are traceable to our impatience. The lack of persistence, the oscillation between rigid adherence to the *status quo* and desire for novelty for its own sake show our discomfort when faced with protracted deadlock. We grow restless when good will goes unrewarded and when proposals have to be maintained over a long period of time.

When reality clashes with its anticipated form, frustration is the inevitable consequence. We have, therefore, been torn between adopting a pose of indignation and seeking to solve all problems at one fell swoop. We have been at times reluctant, indeed seemingly afraid, to negotiate. We have also acted as if all our difficulties could be removed by personal rapport among the statesmen. Periods of overconcern with military security have alternated with periods when we saw in a changed Soviet tone an approach to an end of tensions.

The quest for good will in the abstract has been as demoralizing and as fruitless as the insistence that negotiations are inherently useless. The abortive summit meeting in Paris is as certain a symptom of the perils of a purely formal conciliatoriness as Secretary Dulles' rigidity was a symptom of a largely mechanical intransigence. It is, therefore, necessary to examine Western, and particularly American, attitudes towards negotiations in more detail.

2. The Notion of War and Peace as Successive Phases of Policy

Perhaps the basic difficulty has been that our historical experience is very much at variance with the world in which we live. What had come to seem to us as the "normal" pattern of international relations has clashed at every turn with the realities of the post-war period. For over a century and a half, America asked little of the rest of the world except to be let alone. For over a century following the War of 1812 we never confronted the danger of foreign attack. Safe behind two oceans, we came to consider our invulnerability natural. The efforts of less favored nations to protect themselves against potential dangers seemed to us shortsighted and petty, indeed a contribution to international distrust. We believed that the measure of our invulnerability was that many nations would be involved long before we could be directly threatened. It is easy to forget that if the safety of the world of 1914 or of 1939 had depended on America's willingness to commit itself, the aggressor would have prevailed without opposition. Neither the invasion of Belgium nor the attack on Poland seemed to Americans of the time to impair our security to the extent that we should run the risks of war.

Because of our distance from the scene and our invulnerability we developed notions of war and peace both mechanical and absolutist. Peace seemed to us the "normal" relation among states. This is another way of saying that we were satisfied with the international order as it was and wished to enjoy its benefits undisturbed. The instrument for settling disputes during periods of peace was diplomacy, which we conceived as being analogous to commercial negotiations, attaching a disproportionate emphasis to bargaining technique. Because the advantages of peace seemed self-evident, we necessarily had to ascribe the cause of war to the machinations of wicked men. Our military actions were thereby transformed into crusades to punish the aggressor. Once this was accomplished, the "normal" pattern of international relations would reassert itself. Since we were satisfied with the existing international system—it seemed so natural to us that we never thought of it as a system—we rarely addressed ourselves to the problem of the nature of a stable international order.

The notion that war and peace were separate and successive phases of policy has been at the root of much of our post-war policy. It came to expression in the dominant Western policy of the post-war period: the policy of containment. This was based on the assumption that a substantial effort to rebuild Western strength had to *precede* any serious negotiation with the Soviet Union. Conferences would be futile until the Communist countries found themselves confronted by preponderant strength all around their periphery. "What we must do," said Secretary Acheson, "is to create situations of strength; we must build strength; and if we create that strength then I think the whole situation in the world begins to change. . . . With that change there comes a difference in the negotiating position of the various parties and out of that I should hope that there would be a willingness on the part of the Kremlin to recognize the facts . . . and to begin to solve at least some of the difficulties between East and West."[4]

In the context of 1951, these statements were highly plausible. After three years of Communist provocation, after the Berlin blockade and the invasion of Korea, it was understandable that we should have given priority to achieving security against Soviet invasion. How the strength we were building was to be conveyed to the Communist leaders, and how precisely one went about negotiating from strength seemed then questions not worth considering. Expansionism was believed inherent in Stalinist Communism. Thwarted in the possibility of foreign adventures, Communism would have to transform itself. At that point fruitful negotiations would be possible.

Given the atmosphere of disillusionment after the wartime hopes of a reconciled humanity, this view of the nature of negotiations was inevitable when it was first formulated. But as the containment theory came to be applied under Secretary Dulles, what had originally been considered the condition of policy—security against aggression—seemed to become its only goal. The Baghdad Pact, SEATO, the Eisenhower Doctrine marked steps of a policy which seemed unable to articulate any purpose save that of preventing an expansion of the Soviet sphere.

In the process, many of the difficulties which earlier had been obscured by the fear of imminent Soviet aggression became appar-

---

[4] Hearings before the Committee on Armed Services and Committee on Foreign Relations, U.S. Senate, 82nd Congress, "Military Situation in the Far East," p. 2083.

ent. As Soviet pressure grew more subtle, the preoccupation with the military aspect of containment made it increasingly difficult to rally the people of the West for the effort needed to ensure their security. The longer we deferred negotiations, the easier it became for the Soviet leaders to maneuver us into the position of being the intransigent party. The closer we approached the theoretical point at which, according to the containment theory, fruitful negotiations should have been possible, the more elusive they seemed.

Our literal view of containment caused us to be mesmerized by the vast Soviet ground strength. Though the Soviet Union could have overrun Europe at any time, it was in a very inferior position for a showdown until 1956 at least. Because of our obsession with building strength, we overlooked the fact that our relative military position would never be better than it was at the very beginning of the containment policy. We were so aware of the vulnerability of our allies that we underestimated the bargaining power inherent in our industrial potential and our nuclear superiority. By deferring negotiations until we had mobilized more of our military potential, we in fact gave the Soviet Union time—the most precious commodity considering its losses in World War II, its inferiority in the nuclear field, and its need to consolidate its conquests.

The Western statesman who understood this problem best was Sir Winston Churchill. His repeated calls for a diplomatic confrontation in 1948 and 1949 were based on the realization that a failure to negotiate would mortgage the future. In a major, much-neglected speech, he said in 1948:

The question is asked: What will happen when they get the atomic bomb themselves and have accumulated a large store? You can judge yourselves what will happen then by what is happening now. If these things are done in the green wood, what will be done in the dry? If they can continue month after month disturbing and tormenting the world, trusting to our Christian and altruistic inhibitions against using this strange new power against them, what will they do when they themselves have large quantities of atomic bombs? . . . No one in his senses can believe that we have a limitless period of time before us. We ought to bring matters to a head and make a final settlement. We ought not to go jogging along improvident, incompetent, waiting for something to turn up, by which I mean waiting for something bad for us to turn up. The Western

Nations will be far more likely to reach a lasting settlement, without blood-shed, if they formulate their just demands while they have the atomic power and before the Russian Communists have got it too.[5]

Particularly after the death of Stalin, the rigid persistence in the patterns appropriate to an earlier period afforded the new Soviet leadership the breathing spell it required to establish itself without making any concessions on the issues which had produced the Cold War. During the period of maximum confusion in the Kremlin, the West seemed afraid of diplomatic contact. When the possibility was greatest that the new Soviet leadership might break with its past, if only to consolidate itself, we proscrastinated. The longer we deferred negotiations, the more committed the new Soviet leadership became to the empire it had inherited and the more it was tempted into adventures by the upheavals associated with the rise of the new nations. The more uncertain our performance, the more confident the successors of Stalin became.

During this period, it became increasingly apparent that the guiding notion of our strategic planning—the concept of deterrence—could not support the key assumption of the containment theory that strength would more or less automatically lead to negotiation. Deterrence is tested negatively by actions which do *not* happen. But, unless there is aggression, our strength is not demonstrated and can supply no incentive to negotiate. Since Secretary Dulles was unwilling to assume the diplomatic initiative, a stalemate was the inevitable consequence.

As ever more destructive weapons entered the weapons arsenals and as the notion that war was unthinkable began to gain currency, many of the benefits we had once expected to realize from a position of strength failed to materialize. At the precise moment when, according to the theory of containment, positions of strength should have led to fruitful negotiations, the peoples of the Western world began to waver. Because strength proved so elusive and because the Cold War persisted, many drew the conclusion that the containment policy had been wrong altogether. Containment was not criticized for being too one-sided. Rather, the preposterous argument

[5] Winston Churchill, Speech at Llandudno, Oct. 9, 1948, quoted by *New York Times*, Oct. 10, 1948.

was advanced in many quarters that, since the quest for strength had produced a stalemate, weakness, by reassuring the Soviet Union, might lead to a settlement. The assumption of an automatic connection between a position of strength and an effective diplomacy was countered by arguments which implied that power was irrelevant, if not an obstacle to the conduct of negotiations.

The gulf between strategy and diplomacy reduced the effectiveness of both. While we were in the phase of building strength, this separation caused us to delay defining for ourselves the kind of world for which we were striving. When we did address ourselves to the problem of negotiations, there was a great deal of talk about peace as the ultimate goal. But too frequently we seemed to have in mind a kind of terminal point at which the need for further effort would disappear. The slogan of peace was rarely coupled with an effort to give it content, thus reflecting the typical American nostalgia: since peace is the "natural condition," it need only be wanted; its nature being self-evident, it requires no definition.

3. The Reliance on Personalities: The Problem of Summit Meetings

When the Paris summit meetings collapsed, a sudden reversal took place in the West. What for years had been advocated as the magic solvent for all tensions came to be considered as a parody of diplomacy. Within the span of weeks, all the arguments in behalf of summit diplomacy which had seemed so persuasive while the conference was being planned were replaced by their precise opposite. Personal diplomacy, which had been thought capable of ending the Cold War, was now held responsible for perpetuating it. As Mr. Khrushchev's mood changed, the West seemed as much in danger of being mesmerized by his frown as it had earlier been beguiled by his smile.

Yet the panicky reaction to a crisis obscured what should have been the major focus of the debate. After all, if the risks of summit diplomacy were so obvious, why in the months preceding the fiasco at Paris had no one pointed out these perils? Why was it that there had been practically no discussion of the vagueness and superficiality which had attached so much importance to the fact of a meeting and which had paid so little attention to its purpose or content? Even without our inept handling of the U-2 incident it was not clear what a summit conference assembled in this particular manner and with this particular preparation should be able to accomplish. In the years to come Soviet insistence on summit conferences can be expected to be renewed. Indeed, Mr. Khrushchev has already indicated that he will demand a meeting of heads of state in 1961. A great deal depends, therefore, on our ability to clarify the advantages and disadvantages of this kind of diplomacy. Above all, we must give up the illusions which have caused the fiascos of the previous summit meetings.

The temptation to conduct personal diplomacy derives from the notion of peace prevalent in both the United States and Great Britain. If peace is the "normal" relation among states, it follows that tensions must be caused by shortsightedness or misunderstanding and that they can be removed by a change of heart of the leading statesmen. President Eisenhower, before embarking on an unprecedented round of visits to foreign capitals, was at pains to insist that his purpose was to "clear" the atmosphere rather than to negotiate. If peace ultimately depends on personalities, abstract good will may well seem more important than a concrete program. Indeed, the attempt to achieve specific settlements can appear as an obstacle rather than as an aid to peace. "Our many post-war conferences," said President Eisenhower in 1955, prior to the Geneva summit conference, "have been characterized too much by attention to detail, by an effort apparently to work on specific problems rather than to establish the spirit and the attitude in which we shall approach them."[6]

Within two years of assuming office, President Eisenhower, whose party had charged its opponents with being soft towards Communism, found himself engaged in a summit meeting which called forth a flood of self-congratulatory comment, both in America and abroad. After a decade of Soviet intransigence, the press was almost

[6] *New York Times*, July 16, 1955.

unanimous in its assertion that Soviet policy had been mellowed by the personal charm of one man. "No one would want to underestimate the change in the Russian attitude," said the *New York Herald Tribune.* "Without that, nothing would have been possible. . . . But it remains President Eisenhower's achievement that he comprehended the change, that he seized the opening and turned it to the advantage of world peace."[7] "Mr. Eisenhower had done even better than defeat an enemy in battle as had been his assignment a decade ago," read an editorial in the *New York Times.* "He had done something to prevent battles from happening. . . . The occasion was, in fact, made for Mr. Eisenhower. Other men might have played strength against strength. It was Mr. Eisenhower's gift to draw others into the circle of his good will and to modify the attitudes if not the policies of the little band of visitors from the other side of the Elbe."[8]

The conviction was widespread on both sides of the Atlantic that the Cold War had been due largely to personal distrust. Since this had been removed at Geneva, an era of peace was beginning: "It is indeed an intense sense of relief which unites President Eisenhower with President [sic] Bulganin. Neither ever conceived that his own country would launch war. But each giant was quite convinced that the other giant was capable of doing so. It was this conviction which created the climate of cold war and precipitated the rearmament race. *The cold war was suddenly called off at Geneva because both sides recognized that these suspicions were entirely unfounded.*"[9] [Emphasis added].

Both in the United States and in Great Britain it was implied without significant opposition that good will supplied its own rationale, that to intrude specific proposals into the atmosphere of *détente* could only disturb the prevailing harmony. Diplomacy was seen as a public debate between us and the Soviet Union with other nations occupying the moderator's chair and awarding the winner's prize: "The chief result of the Geneva conference is so simple and

[7] *New York Herald Tribune,* Editorial, July 21, 1955.

[8] *New York Times,* Editorial, July 25, 1955.

[9] "Problems of the Garden-Party Peace," *New Statesman and Nation,* Aug. 13, 1955.

breath-taking that cynics and comma-chasers still question it and Americans, for other reasons, find it a little difficult to grasp. *The championship of peace has changed hands. In the mind of Europe, which judges this unofficial title,* it has passed from Moscow to Washington."[10] [Emphasis added.]

Perhaps the most moving, if also fatuous, statement of the philosophy of personal diplomacy was made by the then Foreign Minister Macmillan. At the end of the Foreign Ministers' Conference in 1955, in a statement which goes far to explain his later policy as Prime Minister, he said of the Geneva summit meeting:

Why did this meeting send a thrill of hope and expectation round the world? It wasn't that the discussions were specially remarkable . . . it wasn't that they reached any very sensational agreement. It wasn't really what they did or said. What struck the imagination of the world was the fact of the friendly meeting between the Heads of the two great groups into which the world is divided. *These men, carrying their immense burdens, met and talked and joked together like ordinary mortals* . . . The Geneva spirit was really *a return to normal human relations* . . . It meant seeing the other man's point of view. It meant, above all, the human note . . . I cannot help thinking that last summer's *Geneva idyll* was not a vague or sham affair.[11] [Emphasis added.]

It is easy to sympathize with Mr. Macmillan's call for a return to normal human relations. One wonders, however, whether the democracies' notion of normality is not their Achilles' heel. An atmosphere of confidence is undoubtedly helpful. It is less certain, however, whether the free countries render themselves or the cause of peace a service by making a settlement seem so simple and by evading all difficult issues. Had the Cold War really resulted from personal distrust or were the causes deeper? Was the tension caused by the intransigence of the Soviet tone or the intransigence of Soviet acts? Is it not possible that the yearning for agreement revealed in statements such as Mr. Macmillan's and the identification of a settlement with good personal relations are themselves obstacles to serious negotiation? What conceivable incentive could be

[10] *Life,* Editorial, Aug. 1, 1955.
[11] Closing statement at Geneva Foreign Ministers' Conference, Nov. 16, 1955, quoted on pp. 73-77, *Documents on International Affairs* 1955, Royal Institute of International Affairs (Oxford, 1958).

left for the Soviet leaders to negotiate responsibly at a summit when the mere fact of its being assembled plays so large a role in Western thinking?

Hardly a year after the Hungarian rebellion of 1956, many in the West again insisted on a summit conference and dismissed all attempts to define an agenda as transparent attempts to sabotage a conference. At the time of the execution of Premier Nagy in 1958, a thoughtful observer wrote: "His [Khrushchev's] chances of ever being invited again to Windsor or of reaching the White House ended decisively with these murders. No man with such blood on his hands can hope to be received in such quarters."[12] Yet before another year had passed an invitation had been issued and was greeted as inaugurating a new era in Soviet-American relations.

In retrospect it may be doubted whether the protestations of our peaceful intent which were generally regarded as one of the main achievements of the Geneva summit conference were so unmixed a blessing, indeed whether it was not a misconception to believe that after a decade of Soviet intransigence it was *our* task to reassure the Communist leaders. Since we were unwilling or unable to relate the protestations of our wish for peace to a concrete program, the Soviet leaders may have become convinced that they could have a *détente* without solving any of the problems that had been thought to have caused the tensions before Geneva. If this is true, Geneva, rather than bringing about a spirit of compromise, may have removed any incentive for it. To the degree that we convinced the Communist leaders of our horror of war, they may have drawn the conclusion that they could greatly improve their bargaining position by seeming more willing to face a showdown than the West. On the way back from Geneva, Mr. Khrushchev stopped in East Berlin and committed himself to the sovereignty of East Germany, laying the basis for the crisis over Berlin three years later. And within a month the world learned of the Soviet sale of arms to Egypt, a transaction which produced two years of upheavals and brought the world on several occasions to the very edge of the abyss.

Since the Geneva summit meeting made no progress towards set-

[12] Joseph C. Harsch, *Christian Science Monitor*, June 27, 1958.

tling any of the issues that divided the world, it was no accident that a little more than a year later the concurrent crises of Suez and Hungary marked a renewal of the tensions of the Cold War. Nor is it surprising that the result was not a closing of ranks by the West, but an increasing chorus for another summit conference whose agenda was no more specific than that of the previous one, and which was advocated once more as a means for removing distrust, establishing good will, relaxing tensions, and contributing to the transformation of Soviet Society—although no one was able to say precisely how all this was to be done.

When the summit conference of 1960 collapsed before it had even started, a shudder of apprehension went through the world. A chance for peace seemed to have been lost. But what really imperiled peace was our self-righteousness and evasion of responsibility. After all, the prelude to the Paris summit conference had given little cause for the hopes attached to it. At first, we found ourselves maneuvered into the position of seeming to fear meeting the Soviet leaders face-to-face. By insisting on "progress" at a lower level before he would agree to a conference of heads of state, President Eisenhower only brought about the preposterous situation where he finally claimed that Mr. Khrushchev's ambiguous postponement of an unprovoked threat and his willingness to go to the summit were in themselves an indication of progress. These vacillations were hardly calculated to motivate the Soviet leaders to approach the summit conference with responsibility.

Moreover, many of the arguments advanced on behalf of summit diplomacy were fatuous in the extreme. It was urged that only the heads of state could settle the really intractable disputes. No subordinate, it was said, would dare to abandon the rigid positions of the Cold War. In the Soviet Union, in particular, only Mr. Khrushchev was in a position to make really fundamental decisions. And the mere fact that a summit meeting was in prospect was thought to place constraints on Soviet intransigence. A series of summit meetings, according to this line of argument, could not fail to relieve tensions.

Many of these contentions were open to serious doubt even before the collapse of the Paris Conference. It is trivial to pretend that problems of the complexity of those which have rent the world for a decade and a half can be solved in a few days by harassed men meeting in the full light of publicity. It cannot be in the interest of the democracies to adopt a style of diplomacy which places such a premium on the authority of a few leaders. Mr. Khrushchev may be the supreme ruler in the Soviet Union and the only one with sufficient power to make binding agreements. It does not follow that the democracies can coexist with a dictatorship only by imitating its method of operation.

The notion that a series of summit meetings might induce Mr. Khrushchev to forget his demands on Berlin did not do justice to the intelligence of the Soviet dictator. Surely it bordered on the frivolous to suggest that Mr. Khrushchev could be induced to table his demands without noticing it, as it were. This view, moreover, took no account of Mr. Khrushchev's domestic position. Even assuming that he is the most "conciliatory" Soviet leader, he could hardly be expected to tell his colleagues in the Kremlin that the privilege of meeting Western leaders periodically seemed to him more important than specific gains. Indeed, personal diplomacy of the type preceding the Paris summit meeting may force a Soviet leader either to press for some tangible gain or into outbursts of intransigence to prove his ideological toughness to his colleagues. Far from being the most moderate policy, it is the most risky one.

In any case, it soon became apparent that whatever the benefits of high-level meetings for the Soviet Union, these could be realized without any concrete concessions and indeed without a summit conference. The "preparatory" meeting between Mr. Khrushchev and the Western heads of state individually still further reduced the already slight chances of the summit meeting. They gave Mr. Khrushchev all the symbolic gains he might have expected from a summit conference and without the need of confronting the Western alliance as a unit. They ensured that nothing of consequence could possibly happen at the summit. If concessions were to be forthcoming, it was certain that Mr. Khrushchev would prefer to make them to the Allies individually than at a summit conference— where they might appear as a response to Western unity.

At the same time, one crucial function of high-level meetings—to inform the heads of state of each other's point of view—had already been accomplished in individual conferences and with a greatly heightened possibility of misunderstanding. It has been argued that Mr. Khrushchev interpreted President Eisenhower's behavior at Camp David as indicating a readiness to make major concessions on Berlin and that part of his rage during the abortive summit conference was due to disappointment in this respect. Whether or not this was in fact the case, the diplomacy leading up to the summit was made to order for this kind of misapprehension. Moreover, since each side had staked a great deal on a presumed expertise in assessing the domestic situation of the other, they were forced into repeated public declarations designed to reassure their own public opinion and—in Khrushchev's case—their own die-hards. This in turn guaranteed that statements of extreme intransigence would alternate with intimations of normality through a year and a half of ambulatory diplomacy which was unable to settle any of the issues or even define them.

Finally, the idea that the imminence of a summit meeting places a constraint upon intransigence is not borne out by the record. In the period preceding the summit, both sides restated their positions in the sharpest possible forms. Mr. Khrushchev in particular delivered a series of extremely menacing speeches. The West, if it wanted to proceed with the summit, thus found itself in the humiliating position of having to explain that no threat had been uttered. These maneuvers were inherent in the nature of personal diplomacy. When heads of state are the principal negotiators, their most effective bargaining device—in some circumstances the only available one—is to stake their prestige in a manner which makes any concession appear as an intolerable loss of face.

The evasion of concreteness, the reliance on personalities, the implication that all problems can be settled with one grand gesture, all these tempt the Soviet leaders to use negotiations to demoralize the West. It is in the Soviet interest to turn all disputes into clashes of personalities. The peoples of the free world cannot be expected to run risks or to make exertions because of a personal dispute. If the only obstacle to peace is the absence of personal rapport among leading statesmen, then all tensions and exertions of a decade and a half have been a frivolous imposition. Whenever the Soviet leaders succeed in giving the impression that all tensions are due to an unfortunate misunderstanding or else to the evil machinations of individuals, they make it that much more difficult for the West to raise later the need for concrete settlements. This is why whenever the Communist leaders have pressed for a relaxation of tensions they have tied the success of it to personalities. Then, whenever the underlying causes of the tension reassert themselves—as they inevitably must if not resolved—the charge can be made that the breakdown is due to the operation of the capitalist system or to the predominant influence of hostile personalities—as is shown by Mr. Khrushchev's vicious attacks on President Eisenhower after the abortive summit conference at Paris. By contrast, it should be the responsibility of our statesmen to make clear that, while we are always ready to negotiate, the negotiation must be serious, detailed and specific.

This is not to say that summit conferences are always to be avoided. It does suggest that we must learn to distinguish form and substance. In assessing the utility of summit meetings, it is essential to weigh the pros and cons without sentimentality.

The advantage of a summit meeting is that the participants possess the authority to settle disputes. The disadvantage is that they cannot be disavowed. A summit conference can make binding decisions more rapidly than any other diplomatic forum. By the same token, the disagreements are liable to be more intractable and the decisions more irrevocable. The possibility of using summit conferences to mark a new departure in the relations of states should not be underestimated. At the same time, it would be foolish to deny the perils of having as principal negotiators the men who make the final decision about the use of hydrogen bombs. Frustration or humiliation may cause them to embark on an irrevocable course. A summit conference may contribute to clarification of the opposing points of view. But this is helpful only if the original tension was caused by misunderstanding. Otherwise, clarifying the opposing points of view may only deepen the schism. In short, the same factors which make for speed of decision also increase the risks of disagreement.

Moreover, when heads of state become the principal negotiators, they may soon find themselves so preoccupied with the process of bargaining that they have little time or energy available for formulating policy.[13] In the ambulatory diplomacy preceding the Paris summit conference, it was an oddity when all heads of state were at home simultaneously. During his last two years in office President Eisenhower was at conferences, preparing for or recuperating from good will visits almost constantly. Such a diplomacy may suit a dictatorship or a state which wishes to demoralize its opponents by confusing all issues. It is not conducive to developing constructive long-range policies. It is a useful device to buy time, though at a price which makes it unlikely that the time will be well used.

In such an atmosphere, agreement all too often becomes an end in itself. However unimportant the settlement, no matter how irrelevant, it is said to contribute to a climate of confidence which will "improve" the situation. In 1958, Mr. Bevan urged as follows:

> I know that the Prime Minister has said and it has been said by others, "Why is it that we should accept only the Russian proposals for the summit conference and not put forward proposals of our own" . . . But is this a conference aimed at agreement or is it a conference aimed at disarmament. . . . It is on the American side that there is an apparent attempt at disarmament because President Eisenhower has put forward as his alternative agenda the liberation of Eastern European states. I know very well that in present circumstances that is impracticable. Really no one is arguing here for a moment or defending Russian policy in Eastern Europe. We are seeking to find ways of reaching agreement which will make further agreement easier.[14]

The inevitable consequence of such a conviction is that more ingenuity is expended in findings things to agree on, no matter how trivial, than in coming to grips with the issues that have caused the tensions. In the process, a curious distortion takes place. The difficulties which are "ironed out" are often soluble only because they are inconsequential. But the mere fact that they are settled is taken as a proof of the possibility of "progress." Agreements, rather than

[13] For a brilliant discussion of the problem posed by summit diplomacy for the American presidency see Dean Rusk, "The President," *Foreign Affairs,* April, 1960, pp. 353-369.

[14] *Hansard* 582, p. 1417, Feb. 20, 1958.

contributing to a solution of the real issues, become a means of postponing coming to grips with them. They do not end the Cold War; they perpetuate it.

This is illustrated by the topics which were slated to be discussed at the Paris summit conference: exchange of persons, nuclear testing, arms control, and Berlin. These are either so unimportant that they can be solved fairly easily, but would hardly require the attention of heads of state, or they are so complicated that a summit conference can at best serve as a means of deferring a decision.

Exchange of persons is hardly a subject that requires the attention of heads of state. (This is quite apart from the fact that the significance of cultural exchange in reducing immediate political tensions is vastly overrated.) The nuclear test ban negotiations depend on technical considerations to which a meeting of heads of state can add little. And indeed they have continued essentially as before despite the collapse of the summit conference. Arms control, as will be seen below, is so complicated that the contribution of the summit could at best have been a general statement leading to a detailed examination later. This leaves the issue of Berlin. Here, the Soviet Union could have made a greater contribution to peace by never provoking the Berlin crisis than by insisting on holding a summit meeting about it.

Whether or not to resort to summit meetings is essentially a practical and not a moral issue. They should be held only when there is some clear, substantive advantage in prospect. It is sometimes easier for heads of state to break a deadlock and to chart a new course than it is for their subordinates, who are inevitably committed to existing policies. High-level meetings can ratify agreements and give general guidelines for further detailed negotiations. They should be used for these purposes with courage and conviction. But to see in them a magic solvent for all difficulties is to build policy on illusion. Such a course creates constant temptations for the Soviet leaders to use meetings of heads of state to demoralize the West. Phrases such as "relaxation of tensions" and "peaceful coexistence" become devices to press extreme demands. The West is invited to accept Soviet proposals or suffer the penalty of a return to the vilifications of the Cold War.

When the primary purpose of summit meetings is thought to be the fostering of abstract good will, they become not a forum for negotiations but a substitute for them; not an expression of a policy but a means of obscuring its absence. The constant international travels of heads of government without a clear program or purpose may be less an expression of statesmanship than a symptom of panic.

The real indictment of the diplomacy culminating in the fiasco at Paris, then, is the attitude of trying to get something for nothing, the effort to negotiate without goal or conception. This is what must be remedied. The problem is not to save summit diplomacy by leavening it with the presence of heads of state from the uncommitted areas—as has been suggested.[15] Rather, it is to clarify our program for whatever negotiations may take place at any level. We can negotiate with confidence if we know what we consider a just arrangement. If we lack a sense of direction, diplomacy at any level will be doomed.

4. THE TRANSFORMATION OF SOVIET SOCIETY

THE reverse side of the reliance on personalities has been the tendency to relate diplomacy to assumptions regarding Soviet domestic developments. The conviction that peace is "natural" has led to the belief that a settlement presupposes either a change of heart by the Soviet leaders or a basic transformation of Soviet society, or both. Once the Soviet system had altered, peace would follow nearly automatically. The rationale for the theory of containment was precisely that it would promote the emergence of a more liberal and humane domestic structure within the Soviet Union. The contrary argument was, of course, equally valid. Barring the evolution of the Soviet system negotiations were futile. Any diplomatic overture by the Communist leaders was likely to be designed to subvert the free world. In its extreme formulation, this view implied that we were obliged to oppose anything favored by Communist leaders regardless of the merit of the particular proposal. Indeed, carried to absurd lengths, this school of thought urged the rejection even of Soviet agreement to our own proposals. An editorial in the *Wall Street Journal* can

[15] Denis Healey, "The View from London," *New Leader*, June 13, 1960.

serve as an example: "If, despite all this, the Soviets should suddenly agree to sign today the West's proposed disarmament pact in toto, that would be reason for serious concern. The supposition would be strong that the Soviets saw in the pact an opportunity to harm the West."[16]

Our official policy never went this far. But for long periods of time negotiations were considered hopeless. In particular, Secretary Dulles' view of negotiations was wary. Diplomatic contact with the Communists was a necessary evil— but essentially meaningless until Soviet society had been transformed. General declarations of good will were likely to undermine the willingness of the West to make the sacrifices necessary to conduct the Cold War.[17] In a sense, a state of tension was desirable. It would save the West from its proneness to illusion. It would prevent Mr. Khrushchev from luring the free world into a state of complacency.

Mr. Dulles' view of negotiations was influenced not only by his distrust of general protestations of good will. He also had serious doubts about the validity and enforceability of specific settlements: "What is an agreement? An agreement is a meeting of minds. And so far I do not know of any agreement that the Soviet Union has made which has reflected a real meeting of minds. We may have agreed on the same forms of words, but there has not been a meeting of minds. . . . What's the meaning, the real significance of an agreement not to interfere in internal affairs if the Soviets mean that they can do anywhere what they did in Hungary and that this is not interference in internal affairs?"[18]

It was characteristic of Mr. Dulles' legalistic approach to diplomacy that he saw the cause for this state of affairs in the separation between the Communist party and the Soviet government: "The power behind the Soviet government is the Soviet Communist Party. It operates as a sort of superstate, not subject to any of the rules and regulations that apply to the conduct between states. And

[16] *Wall Street Journal*, Aug. 15, 1957.

[17] See, for example, John Foster Dulles, speech of Jan. 16, 1958, quoted in *Department of State Bulletin*, Feb. 3, 1958, p. 161.

[18] News conference comments by the Secretary of State (Dulles), Oct. 16, 1957, quoted in Paul E. Zinner (ed.), *Documents on American Foreign Relations 1957* (New York, 1958), pp. 163-164.

you make an agreement with the Soviet government, for example, the Litvinov Agreement, which had tried to be a very tight agreement. It was violated right away. But it was violated, they say, not by the Soviet government, but by the Soviet Communist Party and you didn't make the agreement with the Soviet Communist Party."[19]

If general agreements were dangerous and specific settlements meaningless, the prime function of diplomacy was to hold the line, rally the free world, and wait for the inevitable transformation of Soviet society. For this reason, Mr. Dulles almost invariably replied to Soviet pressures for conferences with a demand that the Communist leaders first demonstrate their "good faith." Therefore, too, the initiative for negotiations always seemed to come from the Soviet side. On too few of the great issues dividing the world did the United States articulate a positive program. The impression was created that for us foreign policy was exhausted in the quest for military security or in negating Soviet purposes. Because our diplomacy took Soviet bad faith for granted and failed to demonstrate it to the rest of the world, the United States was often considered the obstacle to a settlement. We were cast into the ridiculous position of seeming to fear diplomatic contact.

Mr. Dulles' policies thus had consequences precisely contrary to those intended. The very rigidity of his posture accelerated the demoralization which he strove so hard to prevent. Mr. Dulles failed to consider that the tension he thought so inescapable was supportable only if the people of the free world understood that every effort was being made to end it. If the Soviet leadership was really as intransigent as Mr. Dulles thought, negotiations were particularly essential if only to define the issues for which to contend.

A coalition of democracies cannot confine itself to a policy of negation. The free world requires an attitude of conciliation for its very cohesion. It cannot be asked to wait rigidly in the face of mounting tensions without making an effort to break the deadlock. Mr. Dulles was more often right than his critics is assessing Soviet intentions. And the course of events since his death has borne out his distrust of personal diplomacy. But he took for granted what it should have been his constant effort to demonstrate. He made a

[19] *Ibid.*

strong case for what to reject, but he was not equally convincing about what to affirm. The difficulty with Mr. Dulles' policy was not that he was wrong about Communism but that he was right about so little else.

The notion that the primary goal of Western policy had to be the transformation of Soviet society turned the debate over negotiations into an almost sociological argument about Soviet domestic developments. As the death of Stalin saw no change in the West's rigid distrust of negotiations, many thoughtful people, anguished by the prospects of infinitely prolonged tension, sought, almost desperately, to prove that the moment for a diplomatic confrontation had arrived at last. The idea that a Soviet change of heart had to precede effective negotiations was rarely questioned. The practical requirements of coexistence in the nuclear age did not seem to be sufficient justification for the need to negotiate. Instead, a great deal of ingenuity was expended in proving that a Soviet change had occurred. "It is surely evident that internal changes have taken place within the Soviet Union and that, partly as a result, there has been some change in the Soviet attitude to the outside world," wrote Hugh Gaitskell. "Admittedly this may be just a change of tactics, but it would be very surprising if, over the years, economic progress in Russia was not accompanied by social change and if these two things did not influence the attitude of the Government towards the outside world."[20]

The theory of the inherent bad faith of the Communists was thus countered by another theory which sought to demonstrate that Soviet society was in the midst of a basic transformation. The growing bureaucracy would impose legal restraints. Universal education would encourage a more skeptical attitude. The pressure for consumers' goods had already made the Soviet government more conciliatory. Mr. Khrushchev was said to be the apostle of this new course.[21] He was thought to be the most liberal of Soviet leaders and any reluctance by the West to negotiate would undermine his

[20] Hugh Gaitskell, "Disengagement: Why? How?" *Foreign Affairs*, July, 1958, p. 547.

[21] For a popular summary of these views, see Edward Crankshaw, *Khrushchev's Russia*, A Penguin Special, 1959.

domestic position: "The prospect that the survival of Nikita S. Khrushchev's liberal regime rests upon a meeting this year [1958] between the Soviet Premier and Western leaders is being discussed by Western diplomats."[22] And a year later, during the preliminaries to the Foreign Ministers' Conference, another dispatch quoted experts on the Soviet Union as saying that if Mr. Khrushchev failed to reach an understanding with the West he would have to adopt a neo-Stalinist policy and shift Soviet policy away from negotiation back to the rigid conflict of the early days of the Cold War.[23]

The heat of their argument sometimes obscured the fact that the advocates and the opponents of negotiation agreed in their fundamental assumptions. They were in accord that an effective settlement presupposed a change in the Soviet system. They were at one in thinking that Western diplomacy should seek to influence Soviet internal developments. Both groups gave the impression that the nature of a possible settlement with the Communist world was perfectly obvious. At least they debated more about the desirability or the form of negotiations than about their substance: whether, for example, to meet at the summit or at some lower level. They differed primarily about the issue of timing. The opponents of negotiation maintained that the Soviet change of heart was still in the future, while the advocates claimed that it had already taken place.

"If these [liberalizing] forces go on and continue to gather momentum," Mr. Dulles said, "then we can reasonably hope, I said within a decade or perhaps a generation, that we would have what is the great goal of our policy, that is a Russia which is governed by people who are responsive to the wishes of the Russian people, who had given up their world-wide ambitions to rule and who conform to the principles of civilized nations and such principles as are embodied in the United Nations charter."[24] "The Communists are actively digging their own graves," said Mr. Bevan in what he thought was a rebuttal of Mr. Dulles, "because the more they indus-

[22] Drew Middleton, *New York Times*, London Dispatch, May 5, 1958.
[23] Harrison Salisbury, *New York Times*, April 2, 1959.
[24] News conference statement, May 15, 1956, quoted from Zinner (ed.), *op. cit.*, p. 204.

trialize their community, the more their community is diversified; and the more technical skills are built, the more Soviet leaders will have to share power with the masses. That is why I cannot understand that our American friends are so blind to the situation."[25]

In the process, more attention was paid to whether we should negotiate than to what we should negotiate about. The dispute over Soviet domestic developments diverted energies from elaborating our own purposes. It caused us to make an issue of what should have been taken for granted: our willingness to negotiate. And it deflected us from elaborating a concrete program which alone would have made negotiations meaningful. The advocates of "positions of strength" as well as the proponents of negotiation were so preoccupied with the "automatic" transformation of Soviet society that they overlooked the more important task of defining for ourselves just what kind of settlement would be consistent with our values and relevant to our security—regardless of the domestic structure of the Soviet Union.

The tendency to base policy towards the U.S.S.R. on an assumed change in Soviet society should not be ascribed simply to a reaction to Mr. Dulles' rigidity. On the contrary, it has been a constant theme in our public discussion. Whenever a relaxation of tensions has been sought or advocated, it has been justified not by the practical requirements of coexistence but by the argument that the Soviet system is becoming more "liberal."

The notion that Soviet purposes had fundamentally altered was first advanced during the war. After Stalin disbanded the Comintern, Senator Connally said: "Russians for years have been changing their economy and approaching the abandonment of Communism, and the whole Western world will be gratified at the happy climax of their efforts."[26] And the *Times* of London commented editorially on the same occasion: "The decision announced from Moscow to dissolve the Communist International is a wise step and one of the most important political events of the war. . . . [It] refutes the insinuation that the spread of Communism in Europe is the Russian

[25] Address of Oct. 1, 1957, quoted in the *Times* (London), Oct. 2, 1957.
[26] *New York Times,* May 23, 1943.

peace aim and the natural sequel of a Russian victory."[27]

It is understandable that countries engaged in a life-and-death struggle could not face the prospect of renewed schism. What is significant for our present purposes is not the inevitable stress laid on the practical need for co-operation but the insistence on discovering a convergence of the two systems—a view resurrected fifteen years later. "The Russians cannot fight a war as drastic as the one they are engaged in without being changed by it," wrote Max Lerner. "We can as yet have little inkling of the character or extent of the change. But we can guess that the thoroughgoing organization of the war economy, the civilian resistance, the guerrilla warfare could only be achieved in a war that had become democratic in its inner nature."[28]

The liberalization of Soviet policy was thought also to reflect the predilections of the Soviet dictator. Though Marshal Stalin has lately been described as "paranoid" and the primary cause of the Cold War, it is worth remembering that this was not always the view. "Russia will prefer the peace of Europe to its communization," wrote *Fortune*. "The arguments in favor of this assumption are that Trotsky is dead and that Russia will be too weak for aggression in Europe, even ideological aggression, after the war. It is the essence of Stalinism to use communism as an instrument of Russian nationalist foreign policy; and as a nation Russia, though she has been gradually expanding for centuries, is not so much land-hungry as hungry for security on her borders. Given this security she is likely to fix her attention on the development of her enormous internal resources."[29]

In short, Marshal Stalin was contrasted with his chief rival in much the same terms as a decade later Khrushchev was to be compared with his predecessor. Sir Bernard Pares wrote: "What will Stalin do after victory? We have to wait for the victory, but perhaps this sketch will offer some answer. The normal thing for Stalin to do is to return to the vast program of home construction, so far only initiated, which has been the great task of his life. It is simple fantasy to imagine that the man who drove out Trotsky on the issue

---

[27] *Times* (London), Editorial, May 24, 1943.
[28] Max Lerner, "After the Comintern," *New Republic*, June 7, 1943.
[29] *Fortune* supplement, "The United States in a New World," April, 1943.

of world revolution will now desert to the program of his enemy."[30]

The fact that these assumptions were erroneous does not, of course, necessarily invalidate similar arguments made in a different context. It should, however, make us cautious about staking too much on the assessment of Soviet trends. To be sure, given the pressures of wartime, no other course was conceivable. The West could not have endured the tensions of the Cold War had it not striven so hard to come to terms with the Soviet leaders during the period of our alliance. But for our illusions we would never have known whether a more trusting approach might not have been effective. It is striking, however, that after seventeen years of further experience with the Soviet Union, the rationale for negotiations with it has remained essentially unchanged.

The reason for this attitude is not difficult to discern. A people to whom the advantages of peace seem self-evident will always be strongly tempted to consider intransigence a temporary aberration. They will see in every change of tone a change of heart. This tendency is powerfully reinforced by our separation for nearly a century and a half from the mainstream of international affairs and the priority we assigned to the development of an unsettled continent. With such a tradition, economic life came to appear as the most significant field of activity. It was easy to believe that any sensible nation would prefer economic development to foreign adventures.

This accounts for the persistence with which it has been claimed that the economic needs of the Soviet Union would impose a more conciliatory policy on it. Sooner or later, so the argument has run, the Communist countries would have to give the "proper" priority to economic matters. "The present Soviet government has made it clear that world revolution . . . has at least been temporarily abandoned," wrote Sumner Welles during the war. "Upon the conclusion of the present war, the Soviet government will undoubtedly have to dedicate its chief energies for years to the rehabilitation and reconstruction of its devastated cities and territories, to the problem of industrialization and to the achievement of a rise in the

---

[30] Sir Bernard Pares, "On the Fear of Russia," *New Republic*, April 19, 1943.

popular standard of living."[31] In 1948, Henry Wallace returned to this theme: "I believe Russia is committed by her history of centuries of Czarist tyranny to the use of repressive measures . . . until such time as an abundance of consumers' goods makes possible the freedoms which mean so much to us in the West."[32] At the time of the Geneva summit conference in 1955, it was reported that: "Foremost among the reasons why Russia could greatly profit from a relaxation of tension, these experts [on Russia] say, is its desire for access to supplies in the West of heavy machinery, consumer goods, rolling stock and other materials that would speed both Russia and its principal ally, China, towards their ambitious industrial goals."[33] And in 1959 Averell Harriman wrote: "I think Mr. Khrushchev is keenly anxious to improve Soviet living standards. I believe that he looks upon the current Seven Year Plan as the crowning success of the Communist revolution and a historic turning point in the lives of the Soviet people. He also considers it a monument to himself that will mark him in history as one of his country's great benefactors. However, as I have indicated elsewhere, he is finding it difficult to attain the ambitious goals set forth in the plan as long as armaments are making such heavy demands for scientific genius, technical skill and capital investment."[34]

Thus, whatever aspect of the Soviet system they have considered, many in the West have sought to solve our policy dilemma by making the most favorable assumptions about Soviet trends. At one time, we drew comfort from the fact that the Soviet leaders required peace in order to devote themselves to building up their economy. A decade and a half later, a more benign Soviet policy was predicted with exactly the opposite argument. Now the already accomplished industrialization was thought to give the Soviet leaders too much of a stake in their society for them to risk foreign adventures.

Our concern with the transformations of Soviet society causes us to be either too rigid or too accommodating. It makes us overlook

[31] Sumner Wells, *The Time for Decision* (New York, 1944), p. 405.
[32] *New York Times*, April 24, 1948.
[33] *New York Herald Tribune*, July 18, 1955.
[34] Averell Harriman, *Peace with Russia* (New York, 1959), p. 168.

that we have to deal in the first instance with Soviet foreign and not with its domestic policy. From the notion that a settlement depends on a change in Soviet society, it is not a big step to the view that liberalization of Soviet society is equivalent to a settlement. In such an atmosphere, it is not surprising that a controversy should have raged about the desirability of relaxing tensions but not about the conditions which would make such a relaxation meaningful, about the need for peace but not about the elements of stability, about the level at which we should talk but not what we should discuss once we get there.

By concentrating on the need for negotiation rather than on the program of negotiations, the West has deluded itself with a host of extraneous considerations. For example, it is said that effective negotiations are possible because "Mr. Khrushchev is himself above all a pragmatist. He prefers to adapt his doctrine to the facts rather than bend the facts to doctrine."[35] There may be cold comfort, however, in this assessment. Mr. Khrushchev's pragmatism may furnish as powerful an incentive for an aggressive policy as Stalin's dogmatism if he should become convinced that the Soviet Union is militarily superior and that the West is in disarray. Pragmatism is not an unmixed blessing if the opposition seems confused and the balance of power appears favorable.

The tendency to justify negotiations by changes in Soviet attitude makes us vulnerable to largely formal Soviet moves. It leads us to see concessions in the failure of Soviet leaders to press their most extreme demands. Thus, after the meeting at Camp David, it was generally explained that Mr. Khrushchev had "withdrawn his threat." Actually, as he was soon to reiterate in Budapest, he had only postponed it. Similarly, Gromyko's failure at the Geneva Foreign Ministers' Conference in 1959 to insist on his proposal to seat the East Germans at the conference table was greeted by the Western press as a "victory." In fact, the Soviets achieved their basic purpose: when East and West German delegations joined the conference as advisers an important step was taken towards giving the East German satellite the same international status as the Federal Republic, thus lending authority to the Soviet claim that unifica-

[35] Denis Healey, *The Observer*, Sept 13, 1959.

tion should be settled by the two German regimes directly.[36] And every time the Soviet delegation at the disarmament conference in 1960 used the word "control," it was treated as a concession, though the substance of the Soviet proposals almost invariably was to strip inspection of all meaning. The formalism of our approach to negotiations enables the Soviet leaders to obtain a dual advantage from intransigence. They can increase the uneasiness of the West by making an extreme statement and then gain a reputation for being conciliatory by retreating to a position still considerably in advance of their starting point.

To interpret every Soviet overture as a symptom of deep-seated change may indeed cause us to miss perhaps the most effective means of affecting Soviet internal development. Granting that there is an element in Soviet society which is interested in a more peaceful course, and assuming that it can translate its preferences into political pressure, a basic accommodation would seem extremely unlikely as long as daring gambles like the pressure on Berlin, the move into the Middle East, and the threat over Cuba bring such substantial returns. The possibility of evolution of Soviet policy in a more conciliatory direction may be jeopardized by the eagerness with which it is predicted. It may encourage a belief on the part of Soviet leaders that they can reverse any course, no matter how intransigent, by a diplomatic note and that the West can always be reconciled to a *fait accompli* by protestations of peaceful intentions. When, on the basis of past performance, the Soviet leaders have every reason to believe that, regardless of Mr. Khrushchev's incredible behavior at the summit and the brutal rupture of the disarmament talks, the mere willingness to return to the conference table is likely to be considered a change of heart, a continuation of alternate periods of vicious hostility and seeming relaxation is inevitable.

Indeed, the constant invocation of the approaching liberalization of the Soviet system may make spasms of Soviet intransigence inevitable. No Communist leader can afford to make a settlement on a personal basis. No member of the Soviet hierarchy—whatever his convictions—can advocate a program to his colleagues with the

[36] See p. 135.

argument that he is promoting good will in the abstract. The more we speculate about the liberal nature of individual Soviet leaders, the more we may force them into actions designed to demonstrate their ideological purity to their colleagues as well as to their allies.

These considerations apply also to the frequently voiced view that we should conduct our diplomacy so as to bring about a rift between Communist China and the U.S.S.R. Of course, the possibility of a rift must not be overlooked. And if it occurs, we should take advantage of it rather than force the erstwhile partners into a new alliance through intransigence. Yet this is a far cry from the proposition that we can promote a split. In 1948 no Western policy could have set itself the goal of encouraging Tito to break away from Stalin. The attempt to do so might have been the best way to prevent it. Similarly, our diplomacy cannot have as a goal what we can only treat as a fortunate event. We will be better advised to concentrate on our purposes than to chase the will-o'-the-wisp of Soviet domestic developments or a split in the Communist bloc.

It is not necessary to settle the question of the *real* intentions of the Communist leaders in the abstract. For we should be prepared to negotiate no matter what Communist motivations may be. Our responsibility is essentially the same whatever assessment we make of Communist purposes or trends. This becomes apparent if we ask ourselves whether we would offer concessions to a "liberal" Soviet leader which we would refuse to make to a Stalinist. An affirmative answer would be patently absurd, for it would mean that a liberal Communist could exact gains from us denied to a more intransigent one. Surely the liberalism of a Soviet leader is not tested by the concessions which *we* have to make to him—though Mr. Khrushchev has striven hard to create this impression.

A responsible approach to negotiations must be quite different. We should make no unjustified concessions to a Soviet leader simply because we consider him to be liberal. We should not refuse to make concessions, which are otherwise desirable, simply because we consider a Soviet leader Stalinist. The ultimate test in either case is whether a given measure enhances stability or detracts from it. Above all, our measures should not be so dependent on either the Kremlin's smiles or its frowns. Negotiations with the Soviet Union must be justified by our purposes, not theirs. If the Soviet Union really wants a settlement, negotiations will reveal this. If Soviet overtures to end the Cold War are a tactical maneuver, a purposeful diplomacy should be able to make Soviet bad faith evident.

5. BARGAINING TECHNIQUE AND PURPOSE

ANOTHER symptom of the formalistic nature of our view of negotiations has been the excessive concern with bargaining technique. Flexibility has been the insistent demand. But occasionally the impression has been left that the diplomatic deadlock is due at least in part to the inadequacy of the diplomatic method. It has been said that we have an obligation to make "acceptable" proposals. It has been urged that we must break diplomatic deadlocks with new offers. The frustration of the Cold War can be ended, so the argument goes, through willingness to compromise. When two sides take positions, each unacceptable to the other, it is said that the solution lies somewhere in between.

These maxims, unobjectionable in themselves, reflect the fact that the primary experience of our society with negotiations has been in the commercial field. In commercial negotiations, the rules of the game are known. Usually, there is an implicit understanding that an agreement will be reached. Restraints are imposed by the need for a continuing relationship. Both sides generally are in accord on what constitutes a "reasonable" argument. When each party believes that it has gained some advantage both will settle. The courts will interpret the agreement and enforce it.

Most of these factors are lacking to a greater or lesser degree in negotiations with Communist states. In contrast with most of our domestic experience, what has been at issue has been not the adjustment of disputes within a framework which could be taken for granted, but the framework itself.

In this situation, many "normal" bargaining rules of thumb become either irrelevant or dangerous. On the face of it, for example, the proposition that we should make "acceptable" proposals seems unexceptionable. However, if we can only offer what the Soviet leaders have indicated they will accept, the framework of every conference will be established by the other side and the terms of the settlement will be Soviet terms. Or else agreement will become an end in itself. Negotiations gravitate towards problems which seem "soluble"— often only because of their unimportance.

Pushed too far, such an approach implies the surrender of all judgment. It will cause us to fail in one of the major tasks of a revolutionary period: to make clear to the people of the free world the nature of the issues in dispute. While all possibilities of a settlement must be explored, it is equally necessary to develop conviction about the problems that are impossible to solve. It is important for us to be conciliatory if the Soviet leaders should be prepared to negotiate seriously. But it is no less crucial that we force them to bear the onus for their failure to accept responsible proposals.

Similar considerations apply to the proposition that we must always seek to break diplomatic deadlocks with new proposals. Such a "rule" deprives the Communist leaders of the incentive to accept *any* proposal. However moderate our offers, the Soviet leaders will be tempted to reject them in the hope that we will come up with even more favorable plans. The absurd lengths to which this method can be carried was demonstrated at the Geneva Foreign Ministers' Conference of 1959. Before the Western proposal had even been presented, a clamor arose in the British and American press for a fall-back position. It should have been obvious on purely pragmatic grounds that if a fall-back position is known to exist, any motive for accepting the first offer disappears. The only result can be to transform the fall-back position into the starting point of the negotiations and to raise the need for yet another fall-back position.

Implicit in the "principle" that we must break every deadlock with new proposals is the tentativeness of every position. In the long run, the conclusion will be inescapable that no issue is worth contending for and no Western proposal final. The people of the free world, or the Soviets for that matter, will never know whether a given offer is serious or simply a bargaining position. The result must be the confusion of all issues.

This becomes even more apparent when one considers another rule of thumb which is frequently heard: that the way to resolve disputes is to find a compromise somewhere between the initial positions. For the result of such a maxim again is likely to be the opposite of what is intended. If agreement is usually found between the two starting points, there is no point in making moderate offers. Good bargaining technique would suggest a point of departure far more extreme than what one is willing to accept. The more outrageous the initial proposition, the better is the prospect that what one "really" wants will be considered a compromise.

Such a method of negotiation is particularly difficult for a democracy. When the negotiators adhere to a maxim which makes compromise desirable in itself, effectiveness at the conference table depends on overstating one's demands. Yet extreme proposals make it difficult to muster public support. The dilemma is real. If we want to be perfectly flexible, we should start with a maximum program and offer "concessions" in the course of the conference. On the other hand, if we make proposals in which we really believe, we must inevitably be somewhat rigid about them. We cannot change our view about a just arrangement every year. At some point, our program must be settled or no American proposal will mean anything.

The emphasis on compromise for its own sake brings about an atmosphere of "damned if you do and damned if you don't." If the West develops a careful, serious program and maintains it over a period of years, it will be accused of inflexibility, no matter how moderate the original proposals. But if it starts with a bargaining program, it runs the risk of being accused of intransigence. And when it seeks to combine both approaches, it faces the dilemma that the program will not be precise enough to be maintained with conviction and yet will not have sufficient "play" in it to permit major concessions.

One result is that a double standard develops between our positions towards the uncommitted and the Communist worlds. It is often said that the uncommitted will judge us by the reasonableness and the moderation of our proposals. But towards the Communist world the recommended criteria are said to be "acceptability," "novelty," "compromise"—criteria which depend eventually on the Soviet willingness to settle. On the one side, the standard is substantive; on the other, largely formal. At the least, moderation and reasonableness come to be identified with accepting part of the Communist demands.

This confusion of bargaining technique with purpose causes the diplomatic debate to be confined to issues of maximum embarrassment to the West, issues, that is, which the Soviet Union has raised and on which the West feels obliged to negotiate because, as the saying goes, no avenue of settlement must be neglected and because the mere readiness of the Soviet to talk about *anything* is considered "encouraging." Conversely, the West is prevented from raising issues of possible embarrassment to the Soviet Union because, it is said, we must not destroy the climate of confidence by making "unacceptable" proposals. On some issues an aura of unintended cynicism therefore surrounds Western proposals. For years before the Soviet ultimatum over Berlin there had been no Western initiative on German unification. Under the pressure of the Soviet menace a proposal was hastily put together. As soon as Soviet pressure relaxed somewhat, no more was heard of this plan.

Diplomacy thereby becomes a form of Soviet political warfare. For if we can negotiate only on issues that the Soviet leaders have declared soluble, it is not surprising that the attention of the world is focused on the symptoms rather than the causes of the difficulties: on NATO, but not the Soviet hostility which produced it; on the all-too-inadequate Western defense effort, but not on the preponderant Soviet strength which called it forth; on the dangers to peace in case of another satellite upheaval, but not on the Soviet repression without which the danger of upheaval would not exist; on the Soviet scheme for total disarmament, but not on more meaningful proposals which might have some prospect of slowing down the arms race; on the Congo or Cuba, but not on Hungary, Tibet or East Germany. The illusion is created that the Cold War can be ended by proclamation.

The formalism of the Western approach to negotiations raises the question whether the real obstacle to a flexible and purposeful Western diplomacy is not the absence of moral assurance. The impression is sometimes strong that too many in the West consider conviction incompatible with negotiation. Too often the laudable tendency to see the other point of view is carried to the extreme of refusing to make any moral distinctions. In 1948 Henry Wallace professed to be able to discern no difference between the policies of the West and those of the U.S.S.R.—if anything, he was much more charitable towards the latter. And this attitude survives to our day. The preposterous argument has been advanced that the brutalities of Stalin were due to the refusal to admit Russia into the League of Nations in 1923 and the current hostility of Khrushchev to the failure to accept the Soviet disarmament package of May 10, 1955.[37] NATO is equated with the Warsaw Pact; the British landing in Egypt with the Soviet repression of Hungary; our overseas bases with the establishment by the Soviet Union of a satellite orbit in Eastern Europe. In some pronouncements Chancellor Adenauer is dealt with more harshly than Mr. Khrushchev and accused of wanting German unification only as an issue for domestic German politics.[38]

Some of these reactions express the understandable fear that to admit claims to superior moral values would lead to the demand for a crusade and this to nuclear war—an attitude not dissimilar to that of many serious people towards Hitler in the 1930's. "I also agree in welcoming so far as Europe is concerned the attempt of the Government to establish contact with the rulers of Germany," a British Labour leader said in 1937. "Any attempt to separate the sheep from the goats and to have the world divided in two or more camps based upon ideological grounds would be absolutely fatal to the future welfare of mankind."[39] After German troops reoccupied the Rhineland in 1936 Arthur Henderson said:

Herr Hitler's statement [offering to negotiate] ought to be taken at face value. Herr Hitler made a statement sinning with one hand but holding out the olive branch with the other, which ought to be taken at face value.

[37] See broadcast by Philip Noel-Baker, the Norwegian Broadcasting Co., reprinted by the New England Regional Offices, American Friends Service Committee.

[38] See, for example, an appeal by Norman Thomas signed by a number of eminent Americans, *New York Times,* May 8, 1959.

[39] *Hansard* 330, p. 1841, Dec. 21, 1937.

They may prove to be the most important gestures yet made. . . . It is idle to say these statements were insincere. . . . The issue is peace and not defence.[40]

Others are reacting against the popular tendency to see complicated political problems in absolute terms of black or white and to identify policy with the amassing of military force. But in attacking such oversimplification, many critics run the risk of reducing all issues to a single shade of gray.

Self-examination is of the essence in a democracy. But it is impossible to base policy on the deep distrust of the American people revealed by many current expositions. Some critics seem to feel that unless the United States is deprived of all conviction it is likely to prevent a settlement through belligerence or self-righteousness. Of course, there are many causes for concern in contemporary America. But our test will be whether we treat our shortcomings as a challenge or as an excuse to withdraw from the scene. If we are moderate only when confused, if conciliatoriness requires us to abdicate our moral judgment, the future of freedom is dim indeed. The tendency to equate our moral shortcomings with those of the Soviet bloc deprives the West of the inward assurance to negotiate effectively. It leads to a policy of the guilty conscience.

Controversy about diplomatic method must remain barren as long as we are unable to define the reality to which slogans such as rigidity and flexibility refer. If we cannot give our desire for peace concrete content, the danger is real that negotiations, rather than leading to a settlement, will be used by the Soviet leaders to demoralize the free world and to wreck its cohesion. Mr. Khrushchev is well aware of this opportunity:

Why is it that the imperialist circles do not wish to hold talks and conclude agreements with us? They fear that agreements with us and with other countries of the socialist camp will undermine the very basis of imperialist propaganda. . . . And then the entire system of aggressive pacts created by the imperialists—all the NATO's, SEATO's, Baghdad Pacts and so forth—will begin to crumble. The fable of the Communist danger is the main thread which holds together that system of military pacts. Figuratively, it looks like a knitted article: Pull out one thread and the

[40] *Hansard* 309, pp. 1976-1977, March 10, 1936.

whole article will fall apart and become no more than a shapeless heap of threads.[41]

A lasting settlement is possible only if the Soviet leaders become convinced that they will not be able to use the West's desire for peace to demoralize it. If they are serious about their desire to avoid war, they must realize that negotiations can be used for purely tactical purposes only so often and that, measured against the dangers of such a course, the gains they may score are paltry. We in turn should strive to demonstrate to the Soviet leaders that they have a real policy decision to make which we will do everything possible to ease. They must face the fact that the policy of applying relentless pressures on the West creates untold perils for all the peoples of the world. On the other hand, they must be convinced that they can increase their security through negotiation. Should they seriously seek a settlement, they would find us flexible and conciliatory.

Negotiations are important. But it is essential to conduct them without illusions. We do not need to postulate a basic Soviet transformation in order to believe in the possibility of a settlement. Nor is it a prerequisite to successful negotiation to pretend that a relaxation of tensions is primarily within Western control. The West must have much more positive goals than to divine Soviet intent. We do ourselves an injustice if we make an issue of the desirability of relaxing tensions or of ending the Cold War. The test of conciliatoriness does not reside in interpreting Soviet trends in the most favorable manner. Nor does it consist of proving the desirability of peace—which should be taken for granted. Rather, the challenge which confronts the West is to determine what are the possibilities of a settlement which does not hazard our security and is consistent with our values. Only in the purposeful is flexibility a virtue.

---

[41] Speech at Soviet-Czech Friendship Meeting, July 12, 1958, *Foreign Radio Broadcasts.*

VI

THE PROBLEMS OF
ARMS CONTROL

1. THE PROBLEM

IF SERIOUS negotiations are possible between the free world and the
Communist states, arms control would seem the obvious subject.
In the past, a nation's security was guaranteed essentially by its
military power. Though proposals for disarmament were made
from time to time, particularly after World War I, there was an air
of unreality about them. In the era of what we now call conventional weapons, the force-in-being was not nearly so significant as
the industrial potential and the mobilization base. A country
planning to attack had to engage in extended preparations which
were very difficult to hide. Technology was relatively stable. Travel
was unrestricted. Since surprise was not so crucial, and since victory
could generally be achieved only through a prolonged mobilization
of resources *after* a war had started, the contribution which arms
control might make to stability seemed marginal. Armaments, it
was then correctly said, were the symptom and not the cause of
tension. The best method of achieving a stable peace was to remove
the causes of political conflict.

Although this remains true today, conditions have basically
altered. Technology is extremely volatile. The advantage of surprise
can be overwhelming. The forces-in-being are almost surely decisive
—at least in all-out war. A major cause of instability is the very
rate of technological change. Every country lives with the nightmare
that even if it puts forth its best efforts its survival may be jeopardized by a technological breakthrough on the part of its opponent.
It knows also that every invention opens up the prospect of many

others. No country can protect itself against *all* the technological possibilities increasingly open to its opponents. Conversely, an advantage once achieved will produce a powerful incentive to exploit it, for the scientific revolution which made it possible also ensures that it will be transitory.

The fear of a momentary weakness is compounded by the dangers of being surprised. As long as the retaliatory forces are composed primarily of liquid-fuel missiles and airplanes—as they will be until the middle sixties—the side which strikes first will have a perhaps decisive advantage unless the defender's retaliatory force is in a state of high readiness. But when two retaliatory forces so constituted confront each other, their very structure may contribute to instability. Even if the intentions of the opponents are peaceful, each side must seek to protect itself against catastrophe by increasing the readiness and security of its retaliatory force. Yet such measures, taken in what is conceived to be self-defense, may be indistinguishable from a decision to launch a surprise attack. For a force which requires no extended preparation before retaliating is also capable of striking without warning. There will consequently always exist a powerful incentive to anticipate this eventuality by launching a pre-emptive attack, or at least to obtain the greatest degree of warning possible by any means available. Since the penalty for being surprised can be national catastrophe, the need to protect the retaliatory force may override all other considerations.

After mobile, solid-fuel missiles become operational in the 1960's, vulnerability will be substantially reduced and the need for extreme readiness correspondingly lessened. Nevertheless, invulnerability is a relative term which depends on numbers, accuracy and defensive capabilities. In a volatile technology it will always be precarious.

Both sides should therefore have an interest in stabilizing the arms race as much as possible. All countries should be concerned with preventing a war which might break out simply because of the automatism of the retaliatory forces. At the very least, they should strive to make certain that war, if it does start, is the result of a deliberate decision and is not produced because the opponents, in taking measures which they deem to be defensive, push each other into an attack in self-defense. In short, with modern technology, arms—at least certain types of them—are themselves a factor of tension. As a result arms control acquires a new significance.

No single aspect of the arms race contributes more to insecurity than the fear of surprise attack. The power of modern weapons and the speed of their delivery make it possible for a country to be destroyed in a matter of hours. The measures it takes in what it conceives to be self-defense may increase instability—for they may be interpreted by the opponent as a prelude to attack. Where the advantages of a first blow are so great—and perhaps even decisive— the temptation to launch a pre-emptive war may be overwhelming. Any consideration of arms control almost inevitably returns to the problem of surprise attack.

Almost equally serious is the problem posed by the many trouble spots out of the direct control of the major powers. The emergence of so many new states and their integration into the international system would produce difficulties even if the Communist countries did not actively promote chaos. There is always the possibility that disputes such as between Arab states and Israel or upheavals such as that of the Congo can flare up into hostilities. Similarly, the events triggered by the revolution in Iraq underscore the possibility of the embroilment of the nuclear powers regardless of their intentions. In such a situation, it may be to their interest to reduce the likelihood of the outbreak of war, or, if that should prove impossible, to provide safeguards so that it does not spread automatically into a general conflagration.

Then there is the problem of the diffusion of nuclear weapons to still more countries. The greater the number of countries capable of launching nuclear war, the greater is the risk of accident. Though some of the consequences of nuclear diffusion have been exaggerated and though not all of them are inevitably destabilizing, there is no doubt that here is an issue requiring the most urgent attention. A serious effort to think through the implications of what has been called the "Nth country problem" is all the more essential because the early 1960's represent perhaps the last moment when it can still be dealt with.

The importance of arms control measures is therefore beyond dispute. Effective schemes may well arrest a slide towards a cataclysm. They could reduce the risks of accidental war. They may prevent, or at least slow down, the spread of nuclear weapons. If the two sides cannot give expression to this community of interests by proposing concrete, serious programs, little hope exists for negotiations on other subjects.

At the same time, the factors which make negotiations on arms control so important also set its limits. While schemes for arms control could prove highly useful in reducing the tensions caused by weapons themselves, they should not be considered a substitute for dealing with the political causes of the Cold War. Until progress is made towards solving these more fundamental problems, measures for arms control can ameliorate but not remove the existing climate of distrust.

Also, arms control to be meaningful must be devised in relation to the technological factors which produce the need for it. It cannot be conceived in a fit of moral indignation. Effective schemes require careful, detailed, dispassionate studies and the willingness to engage in patient, highly technical negotiations. Otherwise arms control may increase rather than diminish insecurity. Much as arms control may be desired, it must not be approached with the attitude that without it all is lost. The consequence of such a conviction must be to encourage the Communists to seek to use arms control negotiations primarily for psychological warfare in order to demoralize the West. The belief may grow that if negotiated agreements prove impossible, unilateral disarmament must be attempted. Arms control, in short, should be a device to enhance stability, not a prelude to surrender.

2. The Prevention of Surprise Attack

A. Unilateral Measures and the Problem of Numbers

Though negotiations to "safeguard against surprise attack" have been taking place off and on for nearly five years, the danger which they were supposed to alleviate has never been adequately defined. There are at least three types of control schemes which can be said to deal with the problem of "surprise attack." These are: (1) measures to reduce the incentive for deliberate attack; (2) measures designed to reduce the incentive to pre-emptive attack; (3) measures designed to reduce the likelihood of pre-emptive attack based on misinformation; in other words, the problem of accidental war.

The incentive for launching a deliberate attack is, of course, closely related to the incentive to launch a pre-emptive blow. To the degree that deliberate attack is made more difficult, the incentive for pre-emptive war is reduced as well. Deliberate surprise attack can be inhibited by two broad types of measures: (a) through a reduction in the physical capability to win by a surprise attack and (b) through a reduction of the possibility of achieving surprise—generally by means of systems of inspection.

Turning first to the problem of reducing the physical capacity for launching a deliberate attack, the most obvious solution is to eliminate retaliatory forces and nuclear weapons altogether. But the seeming simplicity of such a proposal is deceptive. To be effective, an arms control scheme must have a built-in incentive for observation. A participant must not be able to achieve a decisive advantage through evasion or feel that he will put himself at the mercy of the opponent if he observes the agreement but the other side cheats.

Complete elimination of stockpiles of weapons and of retaliatory forces would have a built-in incentive for evasion. In case of complete nuclear disarmament, even fifty hidden weapons could confer a perhaps overwhelming superiority. And no conceivable control system could possibly account for such a number. Whatever the possibilities of controlling fissionable materials when the Baruch-Lilienthal Plan was first formulated in 1946, so much has been produced in the interval that there is no way to discover caches of hidden weapons of the numbers which could be decisive in case of complete nuclear disarmament.

Why not ban all means of conveying nuclear weapons? Without these, hidden stories of weapons would lose their significance. But banning the means of delivery is no simpler than controlling stockpiles of weapons. An effective prohibition of means of delivery would have to proscribe *all* missiles, even those ostensibly defensive, for there is no way of telling the range of a given rocket by inspecting it. As solid-fuel missiles develop and the weight of nuclear warheads diminishes, many missiles now considered defensive or short-range may become useful for strategic purposes. The same applies to airplanes. With minor adjustments even fighter planes can approach intercontinental ranges. And if all military planes should be banned, Piper cubs on merchant ships or ordinary civilian transport planes could be used to make an attack which could be overwhelming under conditions of complete disarmament.

In short, since inspection could not, in these circumstances, guarantee against catastrophe, each side would be almost forced from the very beginning to hold back a part of its arsenal for fear that the opponent might do so. To observe the agreement might magnify a country's sense of insecurity. To evade it would be demoralizing and undermine the confidence necessary for further progress in the field of arms control.

After a decade and a half of the growth of nuclear stockpiles and nearly a decade of the development of missiles, simple remedies can no longer work. The goal of responsible arms control measures must be to determine, free from sentimentality, not how to eliminate retaliatory forces but how to maintain an equilibrium between them. It is more worthwhile—at least for the immediate future—to seek to reduce the incentive to attack rather than the capability for it.

What measures can reduce the incentive to make a surprise attack? An all-out nuclear attack is liable to result from one of two sets of conditions. An aggressor may feel sufficiently confident that a sudden attack could reduce the counterblow to acceptable proportions. Or a threatened country may feel so vulnerable that it seeks to eliminate the danger through a pre-emptive attack. Thus a control system will add to stability if it complicates the calculations of the attacker and facilitates those of the defender. Or, put another way, the objective should be to increase the uncertainty about the possibility of success in the mind of the aggressor and to diminish the vulnerability of the defender. To the degree that the aggressor feels uncertain either about the chances of success or, what amounts to the same thing, the likelihood of escaping unacceptable damage in retaliation, deterrence will be increased. Stability will be enhanced if the defender does not feel so vulnerable that he becomes obliged to launch his retaliatory force at the first ambiguous warning.

It follows that both sides can take unilateral measures designed to reduce vulnerability and thereby increase stability. It is essential to recognize, however, that unilateral actions, whatever their intent, may be interpreted as threatening by the opponent. Thus, whenever a choice exists, it is desirable to choose a measure whose defensive characteristics are easily identified. For example, the invulnerability of the retaliatory force is undoubtedly increased by multipling the number of missiles and dispersing them. Even if each individual weapon is highly vulnerable, an aggressor now requires a more substantial force for success. This, coupled with the difficulty of co-ordinating a larger attack, complicates his calculations and thus adds to deterrence. At the same time, as the defending retaliatory force grows, it becomes not only more invulnerable but more threatening as well. The response of the other side may be to launch a pre-emptive blow. Or, more likely, the result would be a spiraling arms race. In either case, the result is to increase instability.

On the other hand, if invulnerability is sought not through numbers but through "mobility" or "hardening" of the retaliatory force, deterrence will be improved without adding to the offensive threat. Such a step can be considered a unilateral contribution to arms control. It enhances the ability to strike back; it does not add to the capacity for surprise attack. The opponent loses only in the ability to launch a deliberate attack; no additional threat is posed to its security. Here, then, is a unilateral measure which meets the two requirements for arms control outlined earlier: it complicates the calculations of the aggressor and it eases those of the defender. It magnifies the uncertainty of success of the attacker while increasing the security of the side which concedes the first blow.

While a secure retaliatory force is basic to any arms control scheme, invulnerability is a relative term. It depends on numbers, dispersal, mobility, hardening and similar factors. These relationships are so complicated that to seek to protect the retaliatory force solely through unilateral measures is very likely to produce an arms race. If the goal is stability, negotiated arms control schemes must therefore accompany unilateral efforts to enhance invulnerability. Their objective should be to define a stable equilibrium between the opposing retaliatory forces and then to devise a control system which protects both sides against violations. This raises the question of the significance of numerical limitation.

The discussion about nuclear disarmament has revealed the paradoxical fact that there is a certain safety in numbers. And this is true even if both sides scrupulously observe an agreement to limit nuclear weapons or the means of delivery. Instability is greater if each side possesses 10 missiles than if the equilibrium is stabilized at, say, 500. For an attack which is 90 per cent successful when the defender has 10 missiles leaves him one—or a number hardly likely to inflict unacceptable damage. An attack of similar effectiveness when the defender possesses 500 missiles leaves 50—perhaps sufficient to pose an unacceptable risk in retaliation. And of course it is technically more complicated to destroy such a large number. Reduction of numbers is thus not an infallible remedy. A very small and vulnerable retaliatory force may increase the danger of war by encouraging the opponent to risk surprise attack.

It follows that stability is greatest when numbers are sufficiently large to complicate the calculations of the aggressor and to provide a minimum incentive for evasion but not so substantial that they defeat control. The efficacy of a control scheme to limit numbers thus depends on the answers to two queries: What advantage will the side violating the agreement gain through its first violation? How difficult is the system to inspect for violations?

If the permissible number of long-range delivery vehicles is set at zero—if, in other words, both sides agreed to destroy all ICBM's and nuclear weapons—even a small evasion, say ten hidden missiles or airplanes, will confer a decisive advantage. And such an evasion is almost impossible to discover. If the number is set very low, say at 10, an additional 15 may make a surprise attack possible. In such circumstances, there would be a dual incentive for evasion: fear of the opponent's evasion and the temptation to deal with the security problem once and for all by launching a surprise attack.

On the other hand, if the number is set relatively high, say at 500, even a fairly substantial violation would not confer a decisive advantage.[1] In that case, 50 additional long-range missiles or airplanes would not enable the violator to launch a surprise attack. A decisive advantage can be obtained only by so many weapons that the risk of detection is likely to appear excessive.

These considerations can be summed up as follows:

(a) The primary goal of any arms control scheme must be to remove the incentive for deliberate attack. A precondition is that both sides should strive to develop invulnerable retaliatory forces.

(b) Since invulnerability is a relative term, a major purpose of arms control measures must be to strengthen so far as possible the relative position of the defender, either by enhancing the security of his force or by complicating the calculations of the aggressor.

(c) The equilibrium should be established at a level at which a strategic advantage can be gained only by such a substantial violation that the likelihood of its going undetected is very small. The goal should be a balance of forces stable enough to ensure that deterrence will not fail even if the agreement is upset. A violation, in short, should start an arms race and not a war.

(d) In addition to negotiated schemes, or even in their absence, both sides can take unilateral steps which promote stability. Wherever possible they should seek to assure the invulnerability of their retaliatory force by measures which are manifestly defensive.

B. Inspection and Tactical Warning

As originally conceived, inspection against surprise attack was intended to provide tactical warning—i.e., an indication of an impending attack. It was believed that a sudden blow required such extensive preparations that they could not be hidden. Planes would have to be serviced and perhaps moved to forward bases. Warning radar would be placed on increased alert. A control system on the ground coupled with periodic aerial inspection could not fail to detect these efforts. The defending country would then be able to protect its retaliatory force by making it airborne or increasing its

---

[1] The number 500 should not be taken as the author's idea of a tolerable balance. It is used for illustrative purposes only. The optimum number from the point of view of stability would require a technical study.

readiness by other measures. Once the advantage of surprise was removed and the possibility of destroying the retaliatory forces eliminated, no incentive for aggression would remain.

Whatever might have been the significance of obtaining tactical warning when airplanes were the backbone of the retaliatory force, the quest for it is extremely dubious in the missile age. The greater the readiness of the retaliatory force, the more difficult it is to determine whether there is an intention to use it. And instant readiness will soon be a special characteristic of missile forces. Even the present generation of liquid-fuel missiles is reported to require a countdown of less than an hour. When solid-fuel missiles become operational, around 1964, the interval between the command and the actual firing will be a matter of minutes. Then, perfect inspection perfectly communicated could add only about ten minutes to the warning time already available.

If the security of a retaliatory force depends on a warning of ten minutes, the situation will be unstable regardless of the effectiveness of the inspection system. Its narrow margin of safety will make the retaliatory force prey to all kinds of ambiguous alarms and increase the risk of its becoming the catalyst of accidental war. Indeed, a properly designed missile force should not have to rely on tactical warning at all. Though it is safe to launch airplanes on the basis of an unconfirmed warning (they can be recalled), missiles are irrevocable when launched. Hence, they must be designed to ride out an attack.[2]

Inspection in order to obtain tactical warning may also prove inconsistent with the security of the retaliatory forces. Because of the special characteristics of missiles, the only sure method for obtaining tactical warning against a missile attack is to establish continuous surveillance of the launching sites. But such surveillance may help a potential aggressor more than the defender, thus violating one of the cardinal principles of arms control. The defender learns only what he already knows: the instant readiness of the aggressor's force. At best he gains an additional warning time which is so short that his retaliatory force cannot possibly be designed to make use of it.

[2] See p. 21.

The aggressor, on the other hand, gains vital strategic information. He learns the exact location of every missile at every moment —thus nullifying to a considerable extent whatever advantage his opponent may have achieved through mobility. He will know precisely the pattern of operation of the retaliatory force he is planning to destroy. The conclusion is inescapable that inspection to obtain tactical warning may detract from stability rather than add to it.

The Soviet Union's adamant refusal to permit inspection of its striking forces is understandable. The Kremlin undoubtedly has a reasonably accurate notion of where our retaliatory forces are based. We, on the other hand, probably do not know the precise location of many Soviet bases. In these circumstances, a system of constant surveillance may appear to the Soviet leaders as a form of unilateral disarmament, which would improve our capacity for surprise attack without increasing their security.

But even from our point of view there is a serious question whether constant surveillance of the retaliatory forces is desirable. The practical difficulties of inspection are complicated by the sheer mass of information that must be reported and the speed with which it must be transmitted and analyzed. Since the countdown and the time in transit of missiles is so short, each inspection station would probably have to report to the control organization on the average of once a minute. An automatic system would have to analyze the data and inform the policymakers. This alone is likely to use up the additional warning time provided by on-site inspection. Moreover, the moment when surveillance is most needed is also the time when the opponent has most incentive to interrupt it.

The problem of devising adequate sanctions is more difficult still. If the penalty for suspected evasion is very rapid and drastic, the inspection system may contribute to the tenseness of relationships. Its instabilities will in effect be added to those inherent in the existence of retaliatory forces. On the other hand, if the reaction is slow or weak, no benefit has been derived from the additional warning time.

A country which becomes aware of what it believes to be an imminent attack has four broad choices:

1. It can await the blow and gear its retaliation to the scale of

attack. This can be done only if its retaliatory force is invulnerable.

2. It can increase the readiness of its own retaliatory force in the hope that, having lost the element of surprise, the aggressor will desist from his course.

3. It can give the opponent an ultimatum demanding an end to his preparations and a return to a more peaceful posture—perhaps feeding information into the inspection system on its side to reinforce the threat.

4. It can launch a pre-emptive blow.

Of these options the safest course is the one which is least dependent on tactical warning: that of developing a retaliatory force so well protected that it can await the blow. All other measures are likely to make the situation more tense. Increasing one's readiness—whatever the significance of this phrase may be in the age of solid-fuel missiles—may deter. But it may also cause the opponent to accelerate his preparations and even to transform what may have been merely a threat of surprise attack into a pre-emptive blow. In the missile age, an ultimatum is almost bound to bring on what it seeks to avoid. The recipient—unless his forces are highly invulnerable—cannot possibly run the risk of waiting to see whether the threat is serious. And if his forces are invulnerable, an ultimatum is pointless. This raises the question whether a country would not have a powerful incentive *not* to recognize hostile preparations. In certain circumstances, indeed, the best contribution to stability may be to seem not to notice the information supplied by the inspection system.

Even if war is avoided, a pattern of diplomacy may well develop which uses the inspection system for purposes of blackmail. When missile forces are in a high state of readiness, it is difficult to support a verbal threat with concrete actions that are convincing. But with an inspection system, overt preparations could be demonstrated to the opponent. Though the margin by which the readiness of solid-fuel missiles can be increased is relatively small, constant surveillance would detect it where other means would not. Inspection can then become a device for blackmail. The blackmailer can take steps he is certain will be detected in order to bring pressure on his opponents, particularly on those which are known to be most reluctant to risk all-out war.

Even if the threatened country does not succumb to the menace, the potential aggressor can use the inspection system to obtain vital strategic information. Whether the threatened country ignores his blackmail or makes counterpreparations, the aggressor will learn the likely pattern of its response. In short, inspection in order to obtain tactical warning is either illusory or dangerous.

These considerations go beyond the problem of surprise attack. They suggest that the whole question of inspection is in need of reconsideration. In our previous approach to arms control, the notion that inspection is desirable in itself has rarely been challenged. However, there are kinds of inspection which may add to the tenseness of relationships. There are others which can become a device for pressure. A country can, after all, demand the right to reassure itself to an extent which amounts to physical control over its opponent. It is well to remember that our goal is stability and that inspection is a means, not an end.

C. Preserving the Equilibrium: Negative and Inventory Inspection

Though inspection for the purpose of providing tactical warning does not seem promising in reducing the capability for deliberate attack and may be dangerous, surveillance could be of great significance in stabilizing the opposing retaliatory forces. This raises two questions: How can inspection reveal the size of a weapons system which is mobile? How can it be reconciled with the unilateral measures to promote invulnerability which were described earlier?

The answer is that inspection to determine numbers can and should be different from inspection designed to obtain tactical warning. The difficulty with *constant* surveillance is that it reveals not only the number of missiles but their locations. It contributes to stability by supplying information to each party about the size of the opponent's striking force. But it increases vulnerability by revealing the location of the opponent's most sensitive targets. Yet, if the problem is not solved, arms control negotiations will become increasingly sterile. The danger is real that they will be reduced to a largely symbolic effort, devoted to ritualistic incantations of general goals and producing agreement only on measures that are meaningless.

One difficulty is that the problem of inspection may have been conceived too rigidly. Most arms control negotiations heretofore have addressed themselves to the problem of inspection in situations in which the opponent is assumed to be interested in hiding something. But a control scheme designed to produce what may be called "negative evidence"—the absence of violation—suffers from a built-in factor of uncertainty. In the nature of things it can never be clear whether the absence of a violation is due to the integrity of the signatories or their skill in evasion. The greater the distrust which has produced the demand for inspection in the first place, the less reassured the parties may be by a control scheme. Lack of evidence of evasion may not seem proof of compliance so much as a symptom of the inadequacy of the inspection system.

In order to develop criteria for an effective inspection system, it is necessary to consider again the objectives of an effective scheme to control surprise attacks:

1. The opposing strategic striking forces should be stabilized at a level which reduces to a minimum the incentive to attack.

2. The inspection system should be reliable enough to prevent evasions which can upset the strategic balance, yet not so pervasive as to destroy the security of the retaliatory force. How can these objectives be reconciled?

In a subject of such technical complexity, it would be rash to offer any proposal as a final solution. But if a scheme does no more than indicate the complexity of the problem, it will have served its purpose. In arms control, simple answers are almost surely wrong and the quest for them is an obstacle to real progress. If we really want to deal with the problem of surprise attack, we must be prepared to face complicated situations.

Thus, it may be useful to consider a combination of "negative evidence" inspection with what may be termed "inventory" inspection, the purpose of which is to determine not so much evasions as the actual strength of the opposing forces.

Under this system, each country possessing nuclear weapons would designate regions where it would agree to station no retaliatory weapons and another group of areas in which retaliatory weapons up to a certain number would be permitted. The areas stripped of retaliatory weapons would be open to unlimited inspection designed to find out the *absence* of retaliatory weapons. For purposes of this scheme, it would be best to treat the NATO area as a unit in establishing a ceiling and to include the British and French retaliatory force with ours.

In the regions where retaliatory weapons are stationed, only inventory inspection would be permitted. Inventory inspection would mean that at some agreed interval, perhaps twice a year, inspectors would have free access to determine the strength of available forces. But they would be barred at other times. During the period of inventory, the retaliatory force would have to be stationary, a fact which could probably be monitored through an adequate combination of ground and aerial inspection. But it could be mobile at other times.

It may be objected that such a system would increase vulnerability during the period of inventory inspection when the precise location of the opposing force would be known. This danger can be overcome by placing the land-based retaliatory force in several different areas separated by territories in which uncontrolled inspection would be permitted. The inventory in various areas could then be taken at different times. Thus, the retaliatory force would continue to be mobile in some regions even while it is being counted in others. Uncontrolled inspection in the territory separating these areas could monitor the shifting of weapons from one region to another.

Such a system should be effective in preserving the equilibrium or at least in keeping evasions within limits that prevent either side from obtaining a decisive advantage. Uncontrolled inspection in the "disarmed" regions would provide also a measure of control over the production of retaliatory weapons, particularly if the "armed" areas were located so that they contained a minimum of industry—as they should be. The system could be further strengthened by stationing inspectors at all access points to armed areas. In these circumstances it would seem unlikely that either side would be able to increase its retaliatory force beyond agreed levels on a scale sufficient to be worth the risk of detection, either by means of uncontrolled surveillance or through the system of inventory control. Inventory inspection would be adequate to determine the strength of the retaliatory force within acceptable limits of error. It would not be sufficient to determine its location and thereby compromise its security.

The scheme described here may be a means also of giving effect to another common interest of the two sides: to protect as much of the civilian population as possible should deterrence fail by accident or miscalculation. The first objective of a surprise attack must be to destroy the opposing retaliatory force. Even the maddest aggressor would know that an attack on cities which failed to eliminate the defender's capacity for retaliation would merely guarantee a devastating counterblow. Moreover, once the retaliatory force of the opponent is destroyed, the aggressor may have a positive interest in sparing the civilian population. For blackmail purposes, the opponent's civilian population is more useful alive than dead. Thus surprise attack against centers of population is likely only if they are thought to shelter retaliatory weapons. If major population centers are in the "disarmed" areas, the consequences of a failure of deterrence would be much mitigated.

This raises the problem that including all major population centers in the disarmed areas may defeat the possibility of land-based mobility. Cities are usually also the hub of the road and rail network. Another objection may be that a system which opened all cities to uncontrolled inspection would be bound to be unacceptable to the Soviet Union. One solution is of course to design land-based retaliatory systems so that they can be moved cross-country without using roads or railways. If this is deemed impractical, each signatory of the agreement suggested here could be given two choices. It could "disarm" its centers of population even if they were located in "armed" areas. In that case, it would have to admit permanent inspection teams whose task would be to verify that the city sheltered retaliatory weapons only when in transit—and this term would have to be very rigidly defined. Or else a country could refuse to admit inspectors into the population centers in "armed areas" except for inventory, in which case it would have to take its chances in case of war. This would place the population of the cities concerned in the position of inhabitants of fortified towns in conventional warfare.

As in any arms control scheme, a number of loopholes suggest themselves. One concerns the part of the retaliatory force based at sea. Here the system of inventory control would obviously be impossible and constant surveillance, even if it could be designed, might defeat one of the chief advantages of a sea-based retaliatory force: the uncertainty about its location. One solution that occurs to the author—though more intensive study would undoubtedly reveal others—is to include all port cities and harbors in the regions of unlimited inspection. This would provide a check on new construction—a useful form of surveillance if the system came into being before sea-based forces became too large. And since ships, whatever their endurance, have to return to port from time to time, an inventory of the total force could probably be obtained in this manner.

A lesser difficulty is posed by airplanes. An inventory by region is not possible here because airplanes can be moved so easily and are not subject to control while in transit. Thus, if each area were inspected in turn, the count could be falsified by shifting planes out of the region being inspected. The solution is to begin the inventory with a count of all airplanes in *all* armed regions. At the beginning of the inventory all planes would be grounded and inspection teams would move into the airfields. After the airplanes have been counted, the inventory of missiles would proceed region by region. To prevent the airlifting of missiles out of areas where inventory is about to take place, the inspection teams would remain at the airfields until the inventory in all regions was completed.

This schematic outline leaves open several problems which would require technical analysis, for example, the definition of what constitutes a retaliatory weapon, how the range of delivery vehicles is determined, and similar matters. However, the risks of a mistake are much smaller when the equilibrium is established at reasonably high numbers than in the case of complete abolition of delivery vehicles. Nevertheless, it may be best to begin installing the system of inventory inspection in a few limited areas in order to gain experience with it.

It would be idle to pretend that such a system—if it could be negotiated—would guarantee stability for the indefinite future. The problem of a technological breakthrough will always remain with us. Stability in numbers of offensive weapons—which is essentially the purpose of the scheme outlined here—could be made irrelevant by a major advance in defensive weapons and systems. If one side developed a defense against ballistic missiles which it considered highly effective, it could use even its controlled retaliatory force for blackmail since it might feel safe from a counterblow.

The difficulty of devising a method to obtain a count of weapons already produced suggests the complexity of controlling scientific research and development. An effort of this nature would have to wait until the two sides gain competence through the operation of simpler control schemes. In the meantime, no alternative exists except to keep up in the technological race and to seek to maintain stability through coupling arms control schemes with an unremitting effort in research and development.

It must be stressed that the system described here can work only if the major nuclear powers are very few in number. If many countries come to possess substantial retaliatory forces, the problem of defining an equilibrium would become extremely complex. Then it would be necessary to group possible opponents in order to establish a meaningful limitation. In these circumstances arms control would have the strange result of contributing to the polarization of international relations. And alignments once made would have to be rigid, for under these conditions a shift in the balance could come about only through a country's shifting sides. To be meaningful over any length of time an agreement to deal with surprise attack will have to be coupled with measures to control the Nth country problem.[3]

D. Accidental War and Positive Evidence Inspection

The concept of "inventory" inspection can be expanded to include "positive evidence inspection"—designed to produce information—not of what each side may want to hide but what it is eager for its opponent to know. In certain circumstances both sides may desperately wish to make certain that the opponent understands they are *not* preparing an all-out blow. If accidental war is to be avoided,

[3] See pp. 240 ff.

there must be means by which the nuclear powers are able to inform each other rapidly and convincingly that an ambiguous action was not intended to be the prelude to a surprise attack. In the extremely unlikely event that one of our bombers crashed on a training mission and its hydrogen bomb exploded, it would be vital to have some means to convince the Soviet leaders rapidly that a genuine accident had occurred. The same would be true if a nuclear-powered rocket designed to place a satellite into orbit should malfunction and land on the opponent's territory. Similarly, limited wars—even those not sought by any of the major powers—may threaten suddenly to boil over into a final showdown. In these situations, everything may depend on the ability to reassure the opponent clearly and convincingly.[4]

In the contemporary turmoil, many situations are conceivable which could flare up into hostilities not sought by any of the major powers and yet threatening to embroil them—as, for example, the revolution in Iraq. It becomes important to provide safeguards to prevent a spread of local incidents into a general conflagration. All-out war must not occur simply because the nuclear powers have not considered how to back away from the precipice.

This suggests that the West and the Communist countries may have a common interest in setting up a control system which will enable them to exchange and verify information, particularly in periods of crisis. A minimum requirement is for a joint Soviet-Western technical study to examine the types of accident and miscalculation that can now be imagined. This study should seek to devise means for avoiding them—and, if they should occur nevertheless, to keep them from spreading into a cataclysm.

A scheme which merits attention is the establishment of a communications system to enable the leaders of both groups to communicate instantaneously. Joint Western-Soviet offices might be established in Moscow and Washington with their own communications equipment. In addition, special surveillance teams could be set up either under United Nations or joint Western-Soviet control. These teams should be trained to move quickly to trouble spots to

---

[4] Thomas C. Schelling has discussed this problem brilliantly in *The Strategy of Conflict* (Cambridge: Harvard University Press, 1960), pp. 246-254.

verify information which one side wishes to convey rapidly to its opponents. Both the communications and the special surveillance teams should run frequent exercises designed to guard against the dangers of accidental war and miscalculation revealed by the technical study. The notion of establishing a control system especially designed for critical periods admittedly sounds strange. But its strangeness is due to the fact that we still have not yet comprehended the revolutionary nature of our present world. The new technology can be mastered only by political innovations as dramatic as those in the field of science.[5]

To be sure, in their present state of mind the Soviet leaders are likely to dismiss such a scheme out of hand. And probably it will be ridiculed in the West by those persons who are so horrified by the prospect of nuclear war that they refuse even to consider the possibility that deterrence may fail despite our best efforts. But it is necessary to provide some means for preventing the automatic spread of every conflict into a holocaust. "Positive evidence" inspection can reduce the danger of a war brought about because one side is afraid that its opponent is afraid. One test of the sincerity of the Soviet leaders with respect to arms control would be their willingness to participate at least in the technical discussions proposed here. If no meaningful scheme involving inspection is acceptable, the melancholy conclusion may be that the requirements of the Soviet domestic system are incompatible with serious arms control measures.

3. ARMS CONTROL AND LOCAL AGGRESSION

A. Surprise Attack and Local Aggression

Whatever the utility of any particular scheme, it is essential to understand that a price may have to be paid for each step towards arms control. To the degree that the risk of surprise attack is reduced, the threat of local aggression may be increased. To the extent that the "positive evidence" concept of inspection makes accidental war less likely, it may encourage probing action and new

[5] For further discussion see Thomas C. Schelling, "Arms Control: Proposal for a Special Surveillance Force," *World Politics,* October, 1960.

forms of blackmail. We should be willing to pay the price of the increase of these dangers; but we should not deny that there is a price.

One of the key sanctions against local aggression is the fear that whatever the intentions of the side which initiates it, neither side may know how to limit its scope. The control measures outlined above would remove much of this fear. One of the chief purposes of the "positive evidence" type of inspection is, after all, to control the scope of any conflict which may break out and to reassure the opponents in tense situations. Similarly, if inspection of the size of the retaliatory forces is effective, the result must be—indeed is intended to be—the total incredibility of the threat of all-out war. Massive retaliation will thereby lose its last vestige of significance.

Effective control against surprise attack not only may make limited wars more likely, it may also cause them to increase in intensity. If communication between the protagonists is assured and if a mechanism exists for verifying that a given act is *not* a prelude to surprise attack, an aggressor may become confident that no matter what the scale of aggression he will always be able to keep matters under control. When both sides have accepted the notion that accidents must not lead to a showdown and when they have examined means of containing a conflict even in the face of very substantial provocation, an aggressor may be tempted to step up pressure, at least within the limits of the confidence he has in the inspection system. It would be ironic indeed if the violence of conflicts increased because statesmen seemed *too much* in control of events.

Nevertheless, the benefits of a scheme to prevent surprise attack outweigh the dangers. The perils can be met if we are willing to admit their reality and if we do not treat an agreement on surprise attack as an excuse for relaxing our efforts. As arms control reduces the possibility of surprise attack, forces for local defense must be increased. The contribution of the system of inspection outlined above is not that it ends the possibility of Communist pressure but that it channels it into an arena of conflict where the alternatives are less stark and the risks less dreadful.

Moreover, it would be a mistake to look at the problem only

from the point of view of strategy. A control system against surprise attack as comprehensive as the one described above could not fail to have profound political and psychological consequences. A system requiring the degree of co-operation described above could not fail to produce an atmosphere which would facilitate negotiations on other problems.

B. The Problem of Complete Disarmament

As in the case of surprise attack, it is important to guard against simplified answers to the problem of local aggression. What could be simpler than to seek to escape the difficulty of comparing different weapons systems by abolishing weapons altogether? Since war requires arms, why is it not self-evident that total disarmament would guarantee universal peace?

The attraction of such panaceas has been considerable and it has been skillfully exploited by Soviet diplomacy. Ever since its origin the U.S.S.R. has periodically proposed total disarmament, usually in circumstances when it was bound to be a propaganda gesture. Yet, when Mr. Khrushchev proposed it again before the General Assembly of the United Nations in 1959, his words—despite the Soviet Union's far from pacific record in the interval—were greeted in many quarters as a significant contribution to the debate about arms controls. It was felt that whatever Mr. Khrushchev's motives, the West could simply not afford to fail to associate itself with the goal of total disarmament.[6]

But the issue posed by total disarmament is, after all, whether striving to cut the Gordian knot with one blow helps the cause of peace or detracts from it. The implications of total disarmament are far too little understood for us to announce it as an immediate end. The prospects of arms control can be endangered as much—and more lastingly—by the proclamation of vague goals as by the rigid insistence on achieving security entirely through military means. Mr. Khrushchev's proposal may be a subtle maneuver to prevent the adoption of *any* meaningful control scheme or at least to turn negotiations into a propaganda duel. By stating a sweeping

[6] See, for example, the statement by the Democratic Advisory Council, *New York Times*, September 24, 1959.

goal which is clearly unattainable in the immediate future attention can be diverted from the more complicated measures required to discipline the arms race *now*. If it took us two years of negotiations to define minimum—and risky—control requirements for a nuclear test ban, a decade may be consumed in devising an inspection system for total disarmament. In the interval the arms race would continue—perhaps out of control.

Our responsibility is not to outdo Mr. Khrushchev in propaganda slogans but to seek to conduct negotiations seriously and concretely in keeping with the gravity of the situation we confront. Whether Mr. Khrushchev is sincere or not, the prospects are equally disquieting. If he is sincere, he is ignorant about the nature of the problem; if he is insincere, he is presumably turning the gravest challenge before mankind into a tool of Soviet political warfare.

Total disarmament generally is taken to mean the reduction of military forces to a level sufficient to maintain internal security but inadequate for offensive operations. Accordingly, inspection would have to be able to account not only for existing weapons systems but also for possible new technological developments. And a technological breakthrough would become especially significant at very low levels of armament. At the same time, certain weapons made obsolete by the rapid rate of technological change would again become significant if their successors were drastically reduced in number. A control scheme for total disarmament will therefore have to include six broad types of inspection: (1) of stockpiles of weapons permitted by the control plan for internal security functions; (2) of military installations; (3) of technological progress, particularly in the missile and nuclear fields; (4) of nuclear and missile tests; (5) of production facilities; (6) of fiscal, budgetary and procurement documents of the governments concerned.

This is a staggering task. Such an inspection system as applied to the United States has been conservatively estimated as requiring at least 30,000 highly trained specialists, exclusive of clerical personnel.[7] The stationing of so many inspectors in foreign countries

---

[7] *Inspection for Disarmament*, edited by Seymour Melman (New York, 1958), p. 49. The figure is arrived at by adding the inspections Melman considers necessary for each category.

and the surrender of control over what have traditionally been considered key attributes of sovereignty would in itself present problems on which analysis has barely begun. The problems of dealing with evasions, or even of defining the nature of an evasion, would be formidable. In each category where inspection is required it would be necessary to determine what constitutes a military application and then to devise means for controlling it. The impossibility of accounting for all nuclear stockpiles and the difficulty of establishing criteria for comparing military manpower have already been touched on.[8] The distinction between reserve and ready forces, territorial and standing armies, between paramilitary organizations (like the Chinese communes) and organized armed forces will prove even more elusive.

Complete disarmament—even if inspected—might have the ironical consequence of placing a premium on the militarization of a society. Under conditions of total disarmament and in the face of the threat of evasion by the opponent, security could best be maintained by the militarization of what has been traditionally considered the civilian aspects of national life. If the civilian aspects of life were difficult to distinguish from the military, inspection would be complicated or meaningless and the ability to react to an evasion by the opponent would be at a premium.

Similar problems would exist with respect to determining the size of standing forces. Obviously there are differences in geographic location, domestic stability, and vulnerability that have to be taken into account. But the criteria for measuring the security requirements of an island power against those of a continental state are not likely to be simpler to determine at low levels of armament than in an arms race. And how is one to measure the need for security forces to assure domestic tranquility? Another ironical result of a total disarmament scheme might be that countries would have an incentive to exaggerate their domestic instability in order to justify the largest level of military force.

It is not necessary to apply these considerations in detail to other fields of inspection, many of which are even more intractable. To cite only one more example: how would one determine whether a

[8] See p. 214.

given industrial product is designed for military or for civilian use? It is well known that the chassis of Soviet tractors before World War II was identical with that of Soviet weapons carriers and anti-tank guns. Is inspection going to be so detailed as to proscribe all products that could have military applications?

In short, total disarmament has all the difficulties of a deterrent equation stabilized at very low levels. A relatively minor violation would confer a substantial, perhaps a decisive, advantage. Total disarmament would require a control system so complex and the criteria of determining evasions would be so elusive that it might well compound the feeling of insecurity. In the hands of a ruthless power such a control system may even become a means to establish political domination.

The reply is often made that total disarmament is feasible if it has the sanction of an international police force. Superior to any national military establishment or any combination of them, it could enforce the orders of a central organ and in time even furnish the mechanism for peaceful change.[9]

In assessing the contribution of an international police force to stability, two situations must be distinguished: (1) a conflict among smaller countries in which the major nuclear powers are not directly involved; (2) conflicts which engage the major nuclear powers directly or indirectly.

In the first case—conflict among smaller countries—an international police force can be highly useful. There are potential trouble spots, such as the Middle East, where the major nuclear powers would prefer to avoid a conflict but where direct intervention is impossible for political or psychological reasons. Or else actual crises can occur where the intervention of the major powers would exacerbate tensions and increase the dangers of a holocaust. In such situations an international police force can make a major contribution, precisely because the major powers agree—at least to the extent of seeking a mechanism to avoid a showdown. Indeed, the creation of

[9] For the most thoughtful study of the possibilities of such a scheme, see G. Clark and L. B. Sohn, *World Peace through World Law* (Cambridge, Mass., 1958).

a stand-by international police force for these purposes would be highly desirable.

The situation is quite different with respect to conflict among the major nuclear powers. Here the notion that an international police force could overcome tensions confuses the expression of law with its formulation. An enforcement agency can contribute to bringing about peaceful change only in a society where legal norms are generally accepted and where their observance is unchallenged by an organized minority. In such circumstances, violations will generally appear clear and unambiguous. Enforcement becomes a technical problem of detecting the wrongdoer and of assembling overwhelming power against him. In less stable societies, the police force is not considered nearly so benevolent. In the absence of agreed values, those who control the tools of power are in a position to impose their will almost arbitrarily.

This would be a special problem with an international police organization. To be effective, such a force would have to be decisively superior to any potential violator. It would have to be capable of recognizing violations quickly. It would have to be in a position to move decisively and overwhelmingly. It would have to function in an environment where the criteria for action were clearly understood. Each of these conditions is extremely difficult to fulfill.

The international police force would have to be strong enough to defeat an aggressor even when he has secreted a perhaps fairly substantial number of nuclear weapons. This would involve the creation of a retaliatory force under international control with its own nuclear stockpile and its own warning net. To state the problem is to define its complexity. What areas would be considered sufficiently disinterested to serve as bases for the international force? Who would man it? How could it be commanded so that it would react quickly if attacked without at the same time becoming a menace for the world?

Even assuming good will, the composition, basing and protection of such a force would present difficulties exceeding those of any scheme discussed in this chapter. Obviously these forces cannot be stationed in the territory of the major contenders, for that would make them susceptible to pressure, perhaps to capture, during periods of tension. But to station them elsewhere might easily reduce their responsiveness to control and it would place a premium on the actions of regions whose understanding of the issues at stake might not be commensurate with their new-found power.

The control of this force would become even more a subject of contention than its composition. Few countries will be willing to subject their survival to majority votes in the General Assembly or even two-thirds majorities. But, unless there were some system of majority vote, the countries which are most likely to disturb the peace would have a veto over the international police force. Indeed, countries sufficiently concerned about their survival to demand a veto—and this would probably include all major powers—are unlikely to be satisfied with procedural safeguards. As long as physical control over the international force lies elsewhere, they know that it could be used against them in an extremity regardless of voting arrangements. They could protect themselves against this contingency only by exercising a measure of physical control—at least sufficient to prevent the international force from being used against their will. This alone would tend to reduce its effectiveness to situations where the major powers agree—the situations, in short, which are most amenable to settlement now. It would be least useful in dealing with disputes that threaten the world with cataclysm and have produced the arms race.

Even if the technical and procedural problems and command arrangements could be solved, the problem of defining or recognizing aggression would likely prove intractable. Whatever the strength of the international force, its composition and the safeguards against arbitrary use would make it much less responsive to crises than national military establishments or coalitions of countries with similar interests. Under some circumstances this might be an asset. It would at least reduce the danger of a war that breaks out by accident or because countries seek to protect their retaliatory forces. However, the same qualities might encourage pressure and blackmail. Asian and African countries would be hardly as sensitive to pressure against Europe as NATO and by the maxims of disinterestedness, or even of majority rule, they would have the decisive vote. An international police force would be not the cause but the result of an end of tensions.

C. Stabilizing a Balance of Local Power

Whatever the long-term prospects of total disarmament or of an international police force, there is an immediate problem of reducing the danger of local aggression. A possible solution may be to apply the principles dealing with surprise attack, as described earlier in this chapter. The equilibrium of forces suitable for local conflict should be stabilized at a level where the demands made on the inspection system are not so severe as to magnify insecurity. The evasion required to upset the equilibrium should be sufficiently large so that it could not fail to be detected. And even then a violation should not confer a decisive superiority. As in the case of the balance for all-out war, a violation should start an arms race, not a war.

However, it is necessary to recognize the paradoxical fact that forces suitable for local conflict are less amenable to control than the retaliatory forces. For one thing, tactical warning may be even less significant in local aggression than in the case of an all-out attack. Before the attack on Belgium and Holland in May, 1940, the Low Countries were well aware that a German blow was imminent. Indeed, six months previously a German courier plane landed by error in Belgium with the plans for the attack. (Though the Belgians believed this to be a feint, they could hardly have doubted that *some* aggression was being planned). Nevertheless, the German attack was completely successful. The reason was not lack of information but inadequate strength and doctrine. Similarly, the successful Soviet offensives against Germany in World War II were preceded by weeks if not months of preparation which could not be hidden. And the weakness of NATO is not due to ignorance about Soviet power. Even the most perfect inspection system cannot protect a decisively inferior force; indeed, it may only reveal to it the extent of its peril.

This is why the Soviet proposal of fixed inspection posts at major rail and communications centers would ameliorate the danger of local aggression only if the balance of local forces were redressed.

The reason is not, as is frequently maintained, that the information obtained from fixed inspection stations would be insufficient. The Soviet leaders are probably correct in pointing out that such inspection posts could not fail to reveal significant troop movements. The difficulty is that, given the present relation of forces, the inspection system proposed by the Soviets safeguards the West only against surprise, not against local preponderance. But protection against surprise attack is helpful only if surprise is itself a decisive factor. It is useless if the aggressor is so much stronger that he will prevail regardless of what information the defender possesses.

To be sure, an equilibrium can be brought about in part through negotiated agreements. But when the disparity in local strength is as large as it is now, a build-up of Western local power should be coupled with a reduction of Communist conventional strength and the whole arrangement should be monitored by an inspection system. Even then we must recognize the great difficulty of inspecting the size of a standing army or of stores of conventional weapons. At the end of World War I, Germany agreed to limit its forces and was subjected to a rigorous system of inspection. Nevertheless, even before its open abrogation of the restrictions of the Treaty of Versailles, Germany had succeeded in evading the inspection system and in building forces far in excess of permissible levels.

It will be difficult in the extreme to establish a stable balance of local power, even more complex to devise adequate controls. Even if the Soviet Union were to reduce its forces to the levels described in Mr. Khrushchev's speech of January 14, 1960, the pressure of the vast, speedily mobilizable Soviet reserve strength would remain. This problem is complicated further, because whenever the Soviet leaders have reduced their forces they have declared that military training would now have to be furnished outside the regular military establishment. In his speech announcing a cut in the standing army Mr. Khrushchev declared: "Looking ahead, we can visualize military units being formed on the territorial principle. Their effectives will get their military training outside their working hours and, wherever necessary, the required means of transportation, such as aircraft and other military technique [sic], will enable the forces to be massed whenever required."[10] Mr. Khrushchev did not make clear whether he considered these territorial units part of the standing army or an extension of it.

Even greater difficulties are presented by Communist China. Every member of a commune is known to receive military training. Are the communes, then, an organization of farmers who also are trained as soldiers? Or are they soldiers, part of whose duties includes farming? Threatened countries may consider the distinction academic. Given the present social organization of Communist China, dramatically announced troop reductions would be almost meaningless. Thus paramilitary organizations and mobilizable reserves will have to be included in any control scheme against local aggression.

A scheme for dealing with local aggression must therefore meet these requirements: (a) It must establish an equilibrium of forces suitable for local war through a combination of build-up in the West, reduction in the Communist countries, and inspected ceilings on manpower. Though this appears to be one-sided, it is the condition of stability. The less desirable alternative is a unilateral Western build-up to be followed by a control scheme. (b) It must be coupled with an inspection system adequate to monitor the level of forces within acceptable limits of error. (c) It must provide for zonal limitations, because local aggression depends not only on the size of the forces but on their deployment.

Thus a control scheme against local aggression could be combined with the system to deal with surprise attack described earlier. The zones of unlimited inspection should be located to adjoin troubled or disputed areas. Fixed inspection points as proposed by the Soviet Union could control access into other zones where only inventory inspection would take place. At some agreed interval, say once a year, a census of forces in the "restricted" areas would be carried out to determine that they do not exceed agreed levels. This scheme should establish not only an over-all ceiling on forces, but also a ceiling on forces to be maintained in particular zones in accordance with the principles laid down in the discussion on arms control in Europe.[11]

[10] *New York Herald Tribune*, Feb. 29, 1960.
[11] See "The United States and Europe," Chapter IV, pp. 148 ff.

But we must not delude ourselves. Any significant arms control scheme presupposes a willingness on the part of the Soviet Union to allow meaningful inspection. If neither negative evidence nor positive evidence nor inventory inspection proves negotiable, Mr. Khrushchev's pressure for complete disarmament will stand revealed as a cynical propaganda hoax.

4. THE Nth COUNTRY PROBLEM

A. *The Nature of the Nth Country Problem*

One of the foremost concerns of arms control negotiations must be what has been called the Nth country problem—the spread of nuclear weapons to more and more nations. A report of a committee of the American Academy of Arts and Sciences has come to the conclusion that eleven countries could produce nuclear weapons of their own within five years of making the decision to do so.[12] Eight others could follow shortly. Of these nineteen nations, six are members of NATO (Belgium, Canada, Denmark, Italy, the Netherlands and West Germany). Four are members of the Warsaw Pact (Czechoslovakia, East Germany, Hungary and Poland). There are five European countries not part of NATO (Austria, Finland, Sweden, Switzerland and Yugoslavia). Three are located in Asia (China, India and Japan). Australia completes the list of countries capable of producing nuclear weapons in the near future. At least six others should be able to do so within a decade. In short, there is no longer any atomic "secret." The only obstacle is lack of technical competence, particularly in engineering. Given a certain level of industrial development, any country will be able to produce nuclear weapons.

If the diffusion of nuclear weapons continues unchecked, the structure of international relations will be profoundly altered. With many countries possessing nuclear weapons, the possibility of nuclear war obviously increases. A country allied with a major nuclear power may force the latter into an all-out conflict by launching an attack on another major nuclear power. This is why, in the opinion

[12] *The Nth Country Problem and Arms Control*, National Planning Association, Planning Pamphlet No. 108 (1959).

of many, the Soviet Union cannot look with equanimity on the emergence of a powerful China armed with nuclear weapons. The unchecked diffusion of nuclear weapons is said also to raise the specter of what has been called "catalytic" war—a conflict started by an irresponsible smaller country with a nuclear attack on a major nuclear power. Since in the missile age the direction from which the blow comes may be difficult to determine, the attacked nation may react by an all-out blow against its chief opponent. All these factors must almost inevitably add another element of instability to an already very volatile situation.

In assessing the nature of the danger posed by the spread of nuclear weapons, we must distinguish two sets of relationships: that of Nth countries to the major powers and that of the Nth countries towards each other. The danger of increased instability can mean a greater readiness to go to war with a big power, a greater capacity to blackmail a big power, or a greater willingness of the Nth countries to go to war with each other. These dangers have to be seen in relation to the motives for possessing an independent nuclear establishment. Four are suggested: (1) fear of one of the larger powers; (2) a desire to be independent of the established nuclear powers; (3) rivalry with, or fear of, other Nth countries; (4) national prestige.

As for the relationship of a minor to a major nuclear power, the situation would seem to be as follows: For present purposes a major nuclear power is one which is able to protect enough of its retaliatory force against an attack so that it can inflict unacceptable damage in retaliation. None of the countries listed in the report of the American Academy of Arts and Sciences can become a major nuclear power in this sense within the next decade. Even Great Britain, a member of the nuclear club for nearly a decade, possesses only a retaliatory force which is rather small and ineffective compared with those of the United States and the U.S.S.R. France, if she proceeds on her own, is expected to possess only fifty planes capable of reaching the Soviet Union by 1966. This would not enable her to reduce Soviet retaliatory power significantly, much less eliminate it. Since these weapons could not be decisive against a major nuclear power, it would be folly to initiate hostilities.

While nuclear weapons would give the Nth country a greatly in-creased capacity to inflict damage, they would probably not improve the strategic position of the minor vis-à-vis the major nuclear powers. No foreseeable Nth country with the possible exception of China would be able to withstand a pre-emptive attack by a major power. A surprise attack by any foreseeable Nth country—again with the possible exception of China—on a major nuclear power would not significantly reduce the latter's power of retaliation. For that matter, foreseeable Nth countries would be almost totally vulnerable even to a second strike. The disparity in stockpiles, training and sophisti-cation in the use of weapons would seal their fate if they initiated hostilities and even more decisively if they were attacked first—China again perhaps excepted.

Thus, of itself, the possession of nuclear weapons should not in-crease the willingness of a minor nuclear power to go to war against a major opponent. Indeed, Nth countries would have to be ex-tremely cautious about even threatening nuclear war against a major power. For if they are taken seriously—which can be the only purpose of such a threat—they may trigger a pre-emptive strike which could not fail to be decisive and devastating. A country reasonably tolerant of harassment by conventional weapons may—indeed it almost must—react sharply to even an implied menace of a nuclear attack.

Nor is a nuclear arsenal under national control a means for be-coming independent of big power tutelage. A major nuclear power, confronted by an Nth country not backed by another major nuclear power, could always strike pre-emptively. Thus Nth countries would continue to be dependent on the support of a major nuclear power. By the same token, the danger in the proliferation of national nu-clear establishments is that it may enable some Nth countries—and particularly Communist China—to commit their more power-ful allies to nuclear war.

It is important, however, not to press this argument too far. The difference is one of degree, not of kind. Even non-nuclear countries can start a war to commit their nuclear allies. Communist China may not require nuclear weapons to obtain Soviet support in case of a major conflict in the Pacific. Conversely, the major nuclear powers have every interest not to be forced into a showdown against their will. If they are not looking for a pretext for all-out war, they are likely to go to great lengths to dissociate themselves from the irresponsible actions of their allies—witness the Suez episode.

Moreover, the operation of an alliance system should be distinguished from the problem of catalytic war, which is often invoked as an argument against nuclear diffusion. As described in *On the Beach,* a catalytic war starts with a nuclear attack by one of the Nth countries on a major power which, unable to discover the origin of the blow, retaliates against its chief opponent. The possibility cannot be completely excluded. But it does appear far more remote than is generally asserted. Catalytic war is likely only if the retaliatory forces of the major nuclear powers are highly vulnerable, if the source of an attack is in fact quite obscure, and if the major powers find themselves in a state of tension. If all these factors are combined, it is conceivable that a relatively moderate blow by a third party would evoke a violent reaction and against the source of the chief peril: the major nuclear opponent.

On the other hand, when two vulnerable retaliatory forces confront each other, innumerable accidents more likely than an attack by an Nth power may trigger a showdown. A condition of mutual vulnerability must be avoided regardless of the Nth country problem. By 1965—the earliest date at which any Nth country can develop any kind of nuclear stockpile—the major nuclear powers should have succeeded in protecting their retaliatory forces through a combination of mobility, hardening, and the short reaction time inherent in solid-fuel missiles. By that time, too, the major nuclear powers should have perfected systems for determining with high accuracy the point of origin of an attacking missile. When the opposing retaliatory forces have become invulnerable, the risk of catalytic war would seem to be negligible—all the more so as neither side can have an interest in being forced into a conflict against its will. An invulnerable retaliatory force can afford to ride out an attack; it has time to determine the extent of the blow and the direction from which it came before undertaking retaliation. And both sides would seem to have a powerful incentive to place themselves in such a position regardless of the existence of Nth countries.

In these circumstances it is difficult to imagine the reasoning which would impel any Nth country to launch a nuclear attack on a major nuclear power for the purpose of catalyzing a showdown. If its aim is to elicit retaliation against a major nuclear power, it will have to mask the origin of the attack. It therefore cannot launch a blow during a dispute with a major nuclear power because it would immediately reveal itself and be destroyed. But to launch a nuclear attack in a quiescent period on the off-chance that the victim would direct its retaliation elsewhere would seem the height of foolhardiness. The hope of inheriting the world after the major powers have destroyed each other seems too vague. The probability that the country launching the blow would be discovered and subjected to overwhelming retaliation seems too high; the gains to be achieved too problematical; the risks out of proportion to any objective—particularly if one considers that even if successful in starting an all-out exchange, the country launching the war might become the victim of heavy fall-out. And if the major nuclear powers were aware of the risk of catalytic war—as they would have to be—and were not looking for a pretext to launch an all-out attack on each other, they might even unite to destroy or at least to disarm the country which had brought them so close to the abyss.

The major instability produced by the spread of nuclear weapons is not so much in the increase of the risk of general war as in the relations of Nth countries to each other. This is particularly the case where tension already exists, as between the Arab states and Israel. If the spread of nuclear weapons is not symmetrical, the country acquiring them first may have a very strong incentive to exploit its advantage, which it knows to be transitory. If the spread *is* symmetrical, if the chief opponents acquire nuclear weapons more or less simultaneously, the situation will be unstable for a somewhat different reason, namely, the destructiveness of nuclear weapons. None of the smaller countries will have the resources to create much more than a rudimentary first-strike force. The elaborate combination of warning, hardening and mobility needed to survive a surprise attack seems beyond their capability. Therefore a symmetrical spread of nuclear weapons, if it miraculously occurred, would be unlikely to produce a nuclear stand-off among the Nth countries.

On the contrary, in order to safeguard their hard-won nuclear capabilities, Nth countries will find themselves under nearly irresistible pressures to launch a surprise attack. This may not be apparent when, blinded by the vision of enormously increased offensive power or impelled by the fear that their enemy may acquire nuclear weapons, smaller countries enter the nuclear race. But the effort to achieve security in this manner is an illusion which will make a series of small nuclear wars highly likely. And these conflicts may involve the major powers.

There are, then, considerable dangers in the unchecked diffusion of nuclear weapons—but how shall the diffusion be checked? Any attempt to deal with the Nth country problem must take into account the two means by which nuclear weapons can spread: Nth countries can obtain nuclear weapons through developing them on their own or else they can acquire them from an established nuclear power. To control either method of diffusion is far from simple.

Because production of nuclear weapons is primarily an engineering problem, inspection becomes extremely complicated. Within a decade many countries will possess nuclear reactors, some of them furnished by the established nuclear powers. The end product of most nuclear reactors is plutonium, the basic component of the cruder versions of nuclear weapons. Any country possessing a nuclear reactor will be able to produce some nuclear weapons if it wishes to make the effort and if suitable controls are not imposed. Only the strictest accounting of fissionable material can control local production of weapons and then only before a substantial stockpile of plutonium comes into being.

Production by the Nth countries of their own nuclear weapons is a slow process, however. No Nth country, with the possible exception of China, can develop an arsenal capable of menacing a major nuclear power unless it has the support of another major nuclear power in the acquisition of weapons. Moreover, diffusion of weapons from existing stockpiles is extremely difficult to control. The prospect is, then, that the major source of diffusion may well prove to be the existing stockpiles of the major powers.

There are, then, three approaches to the so-called "Nth country problem": (1) An agreement by the present non-nuclear countries not to produce or acquire any nuclear weapons—with an adequate control scheme. (2) An agreement by the major nuclear powers, particularly the United States and the Soviet Union, to abstain from the diffusion of weapons from their stockpiles and from assisting the Nth countries with technology, and again with suitable controls. (3) A combination of these two measures.

B. *The Non-nuclear Club*

On the surface the simplest solution is the plan of a non-nuclear club. All nations, save the United States and the U.S.S.R., would adopt a self-denying ordinance not to produce nuclear weapons or to accept them from others. When this plan was first offered by the British Labour party in June, 1959, it included a proposal that in return for the formation of the non-nuclear club Britain should renounce its own nuclear arsenal.[13]

Though hailed as a major advance in dealing with the Nth country problem, the non-nuclear club hides great complexities. To be effective, an arms control scheme must have built-in incentives against evasion and meaningful sanctions. Both are very difficult to conceive. A non-nuclear club would require a complicated inspection system capable of accounting for all fissionable materials either produced locally or brought in from the outside. It would have to be able to prevent the diversion of fissionable materials from peaceful to military purposes. In the case of countries like Great Britain and France, which would join the non-nuclear club *after* having developed their own weapons, the system would have to be able to find secreted fissionable material. The control scheme would have to be applied on a world-wide basis and by the Nth powers themselves. Countries with the least knowledge of nuclear affairs and the smallest material resources would thus be obliged to operate a highly complex and expensive inspection system. Even if evasion would not enable an Nth country to threaten a major nuclear power, it might be sufficient to upset the strategic balance between rival Nth countries. And their awareness of this possibility might supply the precise incentive for evasions.

At the same time, while some members of the non-nuclear club would feel mortally threatened by evasions, others would not be

[13] See *Times* (London), June 24, 25, 26, 29, 1959.

particularly concerned. Secretion of a few nuclear weapons in an Arab country may be a matter of life and death for Israel; it is of much less significance for, say, France. Thus an elaborate machinery would be set up for what may seem to at least some members of the non-nuclear club a marginal gain.

The differential in incentive for maintaining the non-nuclear club would be matched by an inequality in the ability to pose meaningful sanctions against violations. All the members of the non-nuclear club combined could probably not bring effective pressure on Communist China. Not only would Communist China be difficult to control, but any country evading the agreement and supported by Communist China would find itself immune from penalties. Or else the inspection system of the non-nuclear club could become a device to establish Communist Chinese tutelage over at least the contiguous areas of South-East Asia. The non-nuclear club, in short, cannot be self-enforcing. In the absence of effective sanctions, the temptation may be irresistible to be less scrupulous about inspection. Ultimately the result could be a clandestine spread of nuclear weapons.

Finally, a non-nuclear club requires the co-operation of the established nuclear powers. The progress of potential Nth countries, if they rely on their own resources, is likely to be slow. But the major powers could defeat the purpose of the non-nuclear club by giving or bootlegging weapons to client states and they could prevent sanctions from being applied against countries violating the agreement.

At the same time, in so far as the non-nuclear club is supposed to increase the security of the major powers, the latter would have to participate in the control arrangements. The inspection system would have to be so designed that they could reassure themselves against the danger of surprise attack. They would have to be able to check on the diversion of fissionable material from peacetime uses. This might provide constant opportunities for interference and pressure. On the other hand, a non-nuclear club without the participation of the established nuclear powers would be an anomaly, incapable of enforcing its restraints and irrelevant to some of the major security problems.

To be sure, a non-nuclear club even with these inadequacies

would have the advantage that the possession of nuclear weapons by the Nth countries would have to be clandestine. They could therefore not be used for diplomatic pressure. An overt threat might end the non-nuclear club. But this benefit does not outweigh the disadvantages. A non-nuclear club cannot reassure the major powers and even less so other Nth countries, for an evasion which a major power would consider trifling could upset the strategic balance with respect to other Nth countries. In the long run such a system does not contribute to stability.

C. The Nth Country Problem and the Major Nuclear Powers

What about dealing with the Nth country problem through agreement among the established nuclear powers? Could the United States and the Soviet Union undertake not to sell or give away nuclear weapons to the Nth countries? Such a course would formalize the situation which already exists by tacit agreement. Paradoxical as it may seem, however, a formal agreement would not improve the situation; indeed, it might make it worse. It would expose both countries to severe criticism by some of their allies for placing them in a second-class status. And it would be very difficult to inspect. To be effective, such an agreement presupposes a world-wide inspection system with respect to both weapons stockpiles and fissionable materials from the peaceful uses of nuclear energy. This could easily lead to a form of tutelage by the United States and the Soviet Union over the rest of the world. The mere suspicion that this could be a result would not only separate us from our allies; it could also spur local production of nuclear weapons all over the world in order to achieve independence from the two colossi.

There are four other difficulties with an effort to solve the Nth country problem solely through agreement among the established nuclear powers. These are: (1) it would not deal with the problem of local production of nuclear weapons; (2) it would not significantly reduce the danger that an Nth country allied to a major nuclear one would trigger a nuclear war, either with weapons from its own production or with weapons obtained in a clandestine manner from its ally; (3) it would not significantly reduce the fear of Nth countries that a rival might develop a nuclear arsenal—particularly if the Nth countries are not part of the control system; (4) it would not even eliminate the possibility of the diplomatic use of nuclear weapons for purposes of blackmail since weapons from local production would be adequate to this end.

If the diffusion of nuclear weapons is to be stopped at this point, the third solution listed above seems necessary: (a) an agreement between the present nuclear powers (or preferably the new and unified NATO structure advocated in Chapter IV) not to give or sell nuclear weapons to any other country; (b) an agreement among the non-nuclear countries (including China) that they would not produce or acquire nuclear weapons. The two agreements would require a world-wide inspection system—preferably under United Nations control. International auspices would be important so that the inspection system did not become a device for Communist pressure on weaker countries. Since for the foreseeable future the chief source of plutonium in most Nth countries will be from the peaceful uses of nuclear energy, the International Atomic Energy Agency should be strengthened so that it can effectively account for all fissionable materials. It should be given the exclusive responsibility for all nuclear reactor development in all Nth countries. The established nuclear powers would agree to channel assistance for peaceful uses of nuclear energy through this agency—the United States has in fact already done so. The agency would remain accountable and set up appropriate controls.

What, then, of our relations with Europe? It is essential to realize that Nth country negotiations will pose particular problems for NATO, both psychological and military. On the one hand, the uncontrolled diffusion of nuclear weapons creates the illusion of security while in the long run undermining the alliance. On the other hand, we must take care not to give our closest allies the feeling that they have become bargaining objects. We cannot be placed in the position of co-operating with the source of the menace to control our closest friends. Countries which for years have been subject to Soviet blackmail should not be declared less reliable than the blackmailer.[14] Important as it is to arrest the spread of nuclear

---

[14] For an elaboration of the problem of NATO and nuclear weapons, see Chap. IV, p. 110.

weapons, the effort to do so must not jeopardize the possibility of establishing a North Atlantic community. Arms control negotiations must not become a means to separate us from Europe. The result of seeking to pursue an isolated policy may in any case have the paradoxical consequence of speeding the diffusion of nuclear weapons. As has already been pointed out, if our allies should become convinced that we are capable of neglecting their vital interests, they may have an added incentive for developing their own nuclear capability in order to become independent of us.

The strategic problem is equally compelling. As the retaliatory forces grow more awesome and invulnerable, increased reliance must, as we have seen, be placed on local defense. But even a conventional defense is impossible unless Europe is protected to some extent against nuclear blackmail. This does not mean, of course, that nuclear weapons must be placed under national control. But attempts to control the Nth country problem must not stand in the way of a NATO nuclear military establishment merging the British and French retaliatory forces together with part of the U.S. Strategic Air Command as described earlier.[15]

Once this establishment exists and provided we have taken at least initial steps towards greater political integration, NATO can negotiate as a unit about the Nth country problem. The NATO allies should negotiate with a single negotiating team and a single position. For purposes of Nth country negotiations, NATO should be treated as an entity. NATO's contribution to the solution of the Nth country problem would be an agreement that nuclear weapons stationed in Europe would remain not under national but under NATO control and that they would not be sold or given away to countries outside the NATO area.

Admittedly such an arrangement would be difficult to control. No system of inspection would be able to guarantee that in crisis periods the nuclear weapons would not revert to national control after all. But this is true even today. The "double veto" system offers no assurance that if Soviet pressure becomes too great nuclear weapons may not be turned over to the threatened country. The possibility could be eliminated only by the denuclearization of all

[15] See Chap. IV, p. 122.

of Europe and the withdrawal of all American forces, since their equipment is so obviously nuclear—an impossible price to pay for an Nth country agreement.

The question then arises whether these command arrangements are so vague as to deprive the scheme to deal with the Nth country problem of any significance. If the Soviet Union is concerned about offensive measures by individual European nations, the system described here would seem to offer a considerable guarantee. A NATO or European atomic force could not conceivably be used in the pursuit of a single nation's quarrel with the U.S.S.R. No component of NATO would be in a position to initiate nuclear war against the U.S.S.R.—unless the vital interests of *all* members including the United States were involved. The arrangement of NATO control thus would pose no *additional* threat to the U.S.S.R. It would remove the temptation for blackmail inherent in a situation in which we retained sole control over nuclear weapons and the Soviet Union as well as our allies came to believe that we might take the interests of our allies less seriously than our own.

If a NATO nuclear establishment proves unfeasible, the established nuclear powers will have to negotiate individually. In that case, unless we insist on a special status for the NATO area, the pressures for the denuclearization of the European Nth countries and the withdrawal of American forces from their territory will become very great.

It can be argued that this line of reasoning, if pushed sufficiently far, would counsel the formation of at least regional nuclear establishments. If no area can defend itself by *any* means without possessing a sanction against Communist nuclear blackmail, the unchecked diffusion of nuclear weapons around the Soviet periphery, for all its perils, would turn into the lesser of two evils. There is no doubt that the denuclearization of any area exposes it to blackmail by a nuclear opponent. At the same time, we can afford to run a calculated risk with respect to every area except Western Europe. As long as NATO remains strong and capable of resisting Soviet nuclear blackmail, a Soviet nuclear attack on the so-called "gray areas" is extremely unlikely. For one thing, the disparity in conventional power between the U.S.S.R. and, say, Iran is so enormous that there would be little military purpose in nuclear aggression. More important, such an action probably would not be worth the political cost. It would lead almost certainly to the rapid diffusion of nuclear weapons all over the world. It would cause the Soviet Union to suffer enormously in the eyes of the uncommitted nations. It would evoke a mobilization of the Western alliance. Only Europe is "worth" the risk of nuclear blackmail to the Soviet Union.

If a nuclear establishment remains in Europe, how can Communist China be prevented from acquiring nuclear weapons? Of course, a NATO nuclear system does not materially affect China's strategic position. Such a nuclear establishment in Europe may be used as an excuse for a Chinese nuclear effort; it does not provide a motive for it. By the same token, the denuclearization of China does not alleviate Europe's major security problem, which is posed by the U.S.S.R. In fact, the denuclearization of Europe and of China would not be a symmetrical process. Europe denuclearized might turn into an impotent appendage of the U.S.S.R. Communist China denuclearized has proved willing to engage in military adventures around its periphery. A sense of impotence is the least of the problems of Communist China.

Of course, we should encourage China to enter any Nth country arrangement. If it showed its willingness to become a responsible member of the international community by accepting restrictions with respect to nuclear production, we could withdraw our objections to Chinese membership in the United Nations. And we might explore the idea of restrictions on stationing nuclear weapons in the Pacific, particularly in Japan, Korea and Taiwan.

What if Communist China insists on becoming a nuclear power nevertheless? Probably China cannot be prevented from becoming a nuclear power—even by the U.S.S.R. The hopes attached to the possibility that the U.S.S.R. would bring pressure on Communist China to keep it from becoming a nuclear power seem altogether excessive. It is probable that the U.S.S.R. has misgivings about the nuclearization of China. It is likely that it will not easily make available its own nuclear weapons. But this is a far cry from taking active steps to prevent China from developing its own nuclear weapons. By the time any Nth country negotiation is far advanced, it is probable that Communist China will have exploded a nuclear device.

The minimum consequence will be that the pressures for the expansion of the nuclear club would multiply. All the countries which have been or may be threatened by a powerful Communist China would have to consider acquiring nuclear weapons. Whatever their present views, India and Japan at least would over a period of time be pushed in the direction of developing a nuclear arsenal.

The impact on the United States would be equally serious. The prospect that China by 1975 might have the nuclear capability of the Soviet Union in 1960 is terrifying. Many of the notions of mutual deterrence may not apply with respect to a country which has shown so callous a disregard of human life.

What has come to be called the balance of terror may seem less frightful to fanatics leading a country with a population of 600 millions. Even a war directed explicitly against centers of population may seem to it tolerable and perhaps the best means of dominating the world. Chou En-lai is reported to have told a Yugoslav diplomat that an all-out nuclear war would leave 10 million Americans, 20 million Russians, and 350 million Chinese. The question then becomes whether we can stand idly by while this peril develops, simply trusting that a more humane group of leaders will replace the incumbents. Can we afford to permit China to develop the capability to destroy humanity without control?

The plan outlined here will not obviate major efforts to maintain the security of the free world. It will not eliminate the danger of nuclear war among the major powers—the scheme against surprise attack is designed for that. Its major utility will be in keeping the conflicts among the smaller countries from becoming nuclear. Even if some evasions occur, they will not upset the equilibrium unless they are substantial. A country possessing clandestine nuclear weapons will not be able to use them for diplomatic pressure or for blackmail. To do so would be to admit the evasion and invite sanctions from all signatories of the control scheme. Clandestine weapons are therefore largely useless as a diplomatic tool.

D. *Some Consequences: A Cut-off on Nuclear Production and Re-duction of Stockpiles*

As with every arms control scheme, it is essential to understand the political implications. We cannot insist at one and the same time that the diffusion of nuclear weapons should be stopped and that the defense of the free world depends on these weapons. A corollary of arms control schemes which place a stigma on nuclear weapons must be a willingness to step up the conventional defense forces throughout the free world. Otherwise the military policies of the nuclear areas will furnish an incentive for the nuclear arma-ment of *all regions*. Or else they will produce paralysis in the face of nuclear blackmail. To undertake a major program of controlling nuclear weapons without restoring the balance of conventional forces is sheer irresponsibility.

Moreover, if the nuclear stockpiles of the major powers continue to grow, control of the Nth power problem may soon become il-lusory. The claim on the weapons in the stockpiles of the major nuclear powers will grow. The demand of the non-nuclear areas to possess nuclear weapons of their own will become ever more in-sistent. Every increase in the disparity of power between the nuclear and non-nuclear countries will furnish an incentive for the diffusion of nuclear weapons.

The established nuclear countries should therefore seek ways to demonstrate their seriousness in reducing their own reliance on nuclear weapons. Provided that they can provide appropriate con-trols, they should accept restrictions on the production of nuclear weapons and on the size of their stockpiles. Concurrent with the agreement not to give away or sell nuclear weapons to Nth coun-tries, the nuclear powers (for these purposes the North Atlantic community of states as a unit and the U.S.S.R.) should consider the following control scheme: (a) a cut-off of nuclear production—if it can be inspected; (b) a reduction of nuclear stockpiles by turning over a substantial part of their stockpile to the International Atomic Energy Agency. This reduction should be made on an over-all basis by the North Atlantic community as a whole and not by individual countries.

A cut-off on nuclear production—if it can be inspected—would freeze stockpiles. This alone would furnish a constraint against giving nuclear weapons to Nth countries. It would also complicate the elaboration of weapons which could upset the deterrent equation. For example, in case of a cut-off on nuclear weapons production a country would have the problem of dividing the allocation of its stockpiles among retaliatory weapons, air defense and tactical weapons. Though such allocations could be made and though they need not remain fixed once decided upon, a freeze on the size of stockpiles would make it most difficult to achieve an overwhelming advantage in a new strategic category. Assuming that the existing stockpiles would enable both sides to protect their retaliatory forces —the prerequisite to any arms control scheme—a cut-off on nuclear production would at least reduce the possibility and therefore the fear that the security of a country could be suddenly jeopardized by a dramatic technological breakthrough.

These tendencies would be powerfully reinforced if both sides made a substantial reduction of their nuclear stockpiles, turning over the fissionable material to the International Atomic Energy Agency for peaceful uses. While it is impossible to outline the size of the reduction without a careful technical study, some general observations may be pertinent: The reduction, while substantial, should not upset the equilibrium between the retaliatory forces, which should themselves be limited by agreement as described earlier. The reduction should stabilize stockpiles at a level where the allocation between various uses can be maintained (albeit with difficulty) but where a sudden shift from one category to another would create a basic weakness somewhere. Such a reduction of nuclear stockpiles would diminish the incentive to share nuclear weapons, for no country could give up part of its nuclear capability without weakening itself.

A reduction of nuclear stockpiles is reasonably easy to establish with respect to the amount of fissionable material actually turned over to an international agency. The difficulty will arise in estimating the size of the stockpile and therefore in fixing the amount of material each side should relinquish. It would therefore be necessary to establish a control system at least as rigorous as that for dealing with surprise attack described earlier—indeed, a cut-off on nuclear production could well be joined to such a control scheme. In that case, all nuclear production plants could be required to be located in the areas open to unlimited inspection. Inventory inspection in the rest of the country, if useful in discovering missile sites, should also be able to detect nuclear production facilities. Once the nuclear production plants were known, a fairly good estimate of existing stockpiles could be made. The amount of fissionable materials to be turned over to the International Atomic Energy Agency could then be determined.

The details would have to await a technical study regarding the feasibility of monitoring a cut-off on production and of fixing the amount of nuclear material to be turned in. Though the two steps can be taken separately, a cut-off on production could be fatal if there is not an almost foolproof inspection system. For the side continuing production could overwhelm its opponent not only by numbers but by refinements in technology.

Everything would depend therefore on the ability to devise an airtight system to monitor a cut-off on nuclear production. Before any proposal of this nature is made we *must* be sure in our minds on this point: The effectiveness of an inspection system would have to be far superior to that devised, for example, for the nuclear test ban. Nothing short of the opening up of Soviet society by the inspection system as described earlier would seem to offer an adequate guarantee.

The Nth power problem can therefore be summed up as follows:

1. The risks of catalytic war are often exaggerated. The likelihood of an attack by a smaller country on a major nuclear power is probably not substantially increased by the spread of nuclear weapons.

2. There are two dangers, however, in the diffusion of nuclear weapons: (a) It may exacerbate the relations of Nth countries with each other because of the difficulty of protecting a small nuclear establishment against surprise attack. (b) It may tempt an Nth country allied to a major nuclear power to attack another major power in order to force a showdown. This would seem to apply almost exclusively to Communist China.

3. An agreement among the present non-nuclear powers to forego the possession of nuclear weapons is likely to be ineffective because

of the inequality in motive, power and possibility of enforcement among the members of the non-nuclear club.

4. An agreement among the present nuclear powers to arrest the diffusion of nuclear weapons might lead either to a form of tutelage over the rest of the world or else it could serve to spur local production.

5. For this reason the two approaches should be combined: (a) the nuclear countries (with NATO being treated as a unit) would agree not to sell or give nuclear weapons to any presently non-nuclear area; (b) the non-nuclear countries would agree not to manufacture nuclear weapons of their own.

6. All development for peaceful uses of nuclear energy in the non-nuclear areas would be placed in the hands of the International Atomic Energy Agency, which would be accountable for all fissionable material. The nuclear countries would extend no aid to non-nuclear countries in this field except through the IAEA as provided in its charter.

7. To show their good faith, to reduce the pressures for the spread of nuclear weapons, and to arrest the nuclear race, the nuclear powers would negotiate a cut-off on nuclear production and a reduction of their stockpiles—provided that suitable controls can be devised.

5. NUCLEAR TESTING

THE emotions kindled by the nuclear test ban controversy have been so strong that a dispassionate analysis is next to impossible to find. The impression is unavoidable that this particular measure is sought or rejected as a symbol rather than for its substantive merit. When a nuclear test ban was proposed by Adlai Stevenson in 1956, it was ridiculed by the Eisenhower Administration as jeopardizing national security. It was described as undesirable. It was rejected as impossible to inspect.

Within less than two years, the Eisenhower Administration decided that a monitoring system could be set up after all. This decision was based on a single experiment—the so-called "Mount Rainier" underground shot. Having relied on the technical argument that inspection was impossible, the Eisenhower Administration found itself obliged to undertake a step whose full political and strategic implications had not been fully considered. An East-West conference of scientists was called to determine the feasibility of a monitoring system. Though the conference was supposed to furnish technical data for a *subsequent* political decision, we felt impelled to announce a moratorium on all testing—including underground testing—even before the political conference was assembled. This moratorium has remained in effect for over two years.

In the interval most of the conclusions of the technical conference have been proved either overoptimistic or simply wrong. Yet the basic positions have been oddly unaffected by the new knowledge. Different arguments to defend well-entrenched positions have emerged to replace the old. The near certainty that, regardless of the ultimate fate of the test ban with respect to underground testing, no country will resume the kind of atmospheric testing which produces fall-out has not lessened the ardor of many groups originally organized to seek a test ban to combat the genetic danger. The unreliability of the inspection system devised at the technical conference at Geneva has not reduced the pressures for an agreement originally advocated because it was inspectable. Indeed, a test ban is now urged for a reason contrary to the one employed two years ago. The fact of an inspection system is now considered more important than its adequacy. The gains to be achieved by evasion are said to be so marginal that we can well afford to run a "calculated risk." And in any case, it is said, the Soviet Union has no intention of cheating. Many well-meaning people have therefore drawn the conclusion that if the United States and the Soviet Union fail to agree on a test ban all hope for arms control is ended. The attitude towards nuclear testing has become a test of sincerity with respect to arms control in general.

Those urging an end to nuclear testing begin from the premise that arms control, if it is ever to be achieved, will require an initial step, however small. A nuclear test ban seems to them to offer such an opportunity. From the military point of view, it does not affect the power of our weapons arsenal since the most destructive weapons have already been tested. Freezing weapons technology at present levels may, it is said, even add to deterrence because it places the

Soviet leaders on notice that retaliation must inevitably take the most cataclysmic form. At the same time, a test ban is believed to be a means for strengthening the more responsible elements in the Kremlin who may be seriously trying to bring about a relaxation of tensions.

Proponents of a test ban grant that the course they urge will prevent the elaboration of new types of nuclear weapons: the so-called "clean" weapons, whose radioactivity is reduced or eliminated; air-defense weapons, particularly for use against ballistic missiles; and tactical nuclear weapons which can discriminate between civilian and military targets. They reply that the significance of these advances is vastly overrated. They contend that it will be no consolation to an attacked city to know that the weapon which destroyed it was "clean." Moreover, what is the sense of using "clean" weapons against an opponent who uses "dirty" weapons in retaliation? Nuclear war will be horrible, whatever its form. Any attempt to mitigate it, proponents of a test ban argue, is an illusion. By destroying these fantasies, a test ban will restore responsibility to our military thinking.

As for air-defense weapons, it is admitted that they will be very difficult to develop in the face of a test ban. But, so the advocates of a test ban insist, an anti-ballistic missile defense is probably an impossible undertaking in any case. Countermeasures against an anti-ballistic defense are easier to develop and less costly than the defensive weapon itself. A freeze on defensive developments may, according to this line of reasoning, stabilize mutual deterrence, for it would protect both sides against the kind of technological breakthrough which tempts a surprise attack.

The same considerations are applied to the refinement of tactical nuclear weapons. For one thing, it is held, no amount of "discrimination" between civilian and military targets on our part will ensure that an opponent will observe similar restraints. Since a "limited" nuclear war is likely to become all-out, anything which increases the inhibitions against it, so the argument goes, will contribute to a saner military policy.

Indeed a test ban is considered by many an important first step towards banning nuclear weapons altogether. The argument runs as follows: A prolonged test ban would mean that a generation of military men would grow up unfamiliar, except theoretically, with the capabilities of nuclear weapons. At the same time, the nuclear stockpiles would consist of weapons of which none has been proof-tested, i.e., the random testing of weapons to determine their operational adequacy. Many advocates of a test ban hold that in these circumstances military men, inherently conservative, will lack the confidence ever to resort to their nuclear arsenal. A nuclear test ban, if maintained over a long period of time, is believed tantamount to nuclear disarmament.

The strategic gains are said to be complemented by perhaps even more important political benefits. An end of nuclear testing would be an effective step in dealing with the Nth country problem. Since nuclear weapons development is impossible without extensive experimentation, a nuclear test ban would prevent the growth of further national atomic armaments at least from indigenous production. Even the diffusion from existing stockpiles would be inhibited to some extent because the military leaders of any Nth country might be reluctant to rely on weapons with which their own army had not had a chance to train. Though a nuclear test ban among the major powers would not bind countries like France and China, it would mobilize world opinion against any further efforts to develop nuclear weapons on a national basis. A test ban among the nuclear Big Three, it is argued, would soon become world-wide.

Advocates of a test ban see a major political breakthrough in the establishment of the inspection system required for it. A big step towards the evolution of the Soviet system would be taken if inspectors could gain access to it even on the restricted basis of the proposal of a quota system of inspections not subject to veto. These advantages are believed to outweigh any loopholes in the inspection system. To begin with, the advocates of a test ban maintain, there is no such thing as a "foolproof" control scheme. Evasions are prevented not by the certainty of detection but by a sufficient degree of uncertainty that the risk could be run. No country would shoulder the opprobrium of having violated the test ban if the likelihood of detection were as high as 50 per cent. Above all, the mere fact of co-operation with the Soviet Union on a nuclear test ban would bring about a climate of confidence which might lead to other, more fundamental, agreements. In fact the proponents of a ban on nuclear testing see in this measure a model which may well make or break the future of all other arms control negotiations. These, in brief, are the main arguments made in behalf of the test ban as now conceived.[16]

The desire to make a start on arms control is understandable. Yet the idea that a nuclear test ban can be a model for other agreements cuts both ways. It is not clear why an inadequate control scheme should be a model for anything except another inadequate control scheme. Precisely because it is so important to make a start towards arresting or slowing down the arms race, we should be doubly careful about the direction in which such a start will take us. And there is serious reason for concern about both the efficacy of the inspection system and the political implications of a test ban.

As for inspection, it is generally agreed that surface nuclear explosions can be detected at considerable distances by equipment which measures radioactivity and shock waves.[17] The difficulty arises with underground testing, high-altitude testing, and oceanic testing. And the problem of sanctions for violations has not been adequately studied. Moreover, despite the bitterness of the debate, the essential facts are not in dispute. The controversy concerns the interpretation of their significance.

With respect to underground testing, the first Geneva conference of technical experts agreed in 1958 that a world-wide system of 180 inspection stations would be able to detect underground explosions above the one-kiloton (1,000-ton) level—with a "gray" zone of uncertain detection in the area between one-half and one kiloton. Of these stations 21 were to be in the territory of the U.S.S.R. Since explosions of below half a kiloton were thought not to be useful for weapons research, the system devised by the experts was believed adequate to police an effective ban on nuclear weapons. This inspection system has since been proved inadequate.

[16] For a fuller statement of the arguments on behalf of a nuclear test ban, see Hans A. Bethe, "The Case for Ending Nuclear Tests," *The Atlantic*, August, 1960.

[17] For a very good account of methods of detecting nuclear weapons testing, see "The Detection of Nuclear Weapons Testing," by Jay Orear, in Melman, *op. cit.*, pp. 85 ff.

Any discussion of the control problem immediately involves a never-never land of figures based on extrapolations and educated guesses, or on unproven hypotheses. For example, the conclusions of the Geneva technical conference were based on a single experiment: the "Mount Rainer shot"—detected at a distance of some 1,200 miles. The figures which establish energy equivalents for earthquakes and underground tests are based upon the characteristics of nuclear explosives in one type of earth, namely tufa. Granite or other surrounding materials might give quite different energy equivalents. Similarly, we know very little about the world-wide incidence of earthquakes. The figures on which the inspection system is based represent extrapolations of an *average* incidence in limited areas of Europe and the Western Hemisphere. No extensive survey of the incidence of earthquakes in the U.S.S.R. exists. The extrapolation may therefore be wrong by a factor of two or three in either direction. Moreover, the figures are averages, and they may vary in any given year by another factor of two. Similarly, the figures for the smaller earthquakes—those with energy equivalents of five kilotons and below—are guesses based on the *probability* that frequency increases as size goes down. This rate of increase cannot be proved since the appropriate seismic equipment has not yet been developed. But even if the figures on which the Geneva control scheme is based are accepted as precise rather than as the best guess, major difficulties remain.

The difficulties are due to three factors: (1) the problem of distinguishing underground explosions from earthquakes with similar characteristics; (2) the nature of the inspection required to determine a violation; (3) the unforeseen possibilities of "decoupling" underground explosions, i.e., reducing the shock wave so that the seismic reading will be much less than the actual force of the explosion.

There are about 100 earthquakes a year with characteristics similar to a 20-kiloton explosion and above in the territory of the Soviet Union. If the detection system were installed only in the Soviet Union, about 70 of these would remain "unidentified" within the meaning of the Geneva control system; i.e., the shock waves could not be distinguished from an explosion. If the control system were world-wide—and it must be remembered that negotiations with other countries have not even been started—the number of unidentified earthquakes in Soviet territory with characteristics similar to a 20-kiloton and above explosion would be reduced to 35. This is because a world-wide system of control stations would permit greater accuracy of detection. There would be some 1,000 earthquakes with characteristics similar to underground explosions in the range of one to twenty kilotons. Of these 800 would remain unidentified if the control system were world-wide; 900 if it were confined to the U.S.S.R. And underground explosions of less than 500 tons would not even be detected.[18]

Even if every "unidentified" event could be inspected, the control problem would be formidable. There would be hundreds of incidents where conclusive proof could be obtained only by finding the location of the suspicious occurrence and then boring for radioactive samples. This is a considerable task. Existing seismic equipment can narrow down the location of an unidentified earth tremor only to an area which, according to the estimate of the specialists at Geneva, may vary from a minimum of 78 square miles (the Soviet figure) to a maximum of 195 square miles (the United States figure).[19] Even if the Soviet figure is accepted the probability of

---

[18] For an excellent summary of the detection problem, see "Technical Aspects of Detection and Inspection," Joint Committee on Atomic Energy, 86th Congress, 2nd Session. The breakdown of the Geneva inspection system by area is as follows:

North America	24
Europe	6
Asia	37
Australia	7
South America	16
Africa	16
Antarctica	4
Islands (sic)	60
Ships	10

Of course, the problem of inspection should not be viewed in terms of a sharp cut-off on detection. At 1 kiloton the probability of detection by the Geneva system is about 2 per cent. The probability decreases in almost geometric ratio with the force of the explosion. In order to favor the control system the subsequent extension of decoupling has therefore taken 500 tons as a cut-off point.

[19] *New York Times,* March 8, 1960.

finding radioactive debris underground in such a vast area is not too high.

Moreover, the Soviet Union at first refused to accept what would have amounted to hundreds of highly detailed investigations on its territory and insisted on a veto over every inspection. In order to break the deadlock and to overcome the technical impossibility of investigating every suspicious occurrence, Prime Minister Macmillan developed the concept of a quota of "free," i.e., veto-proof inspections. According to it, a given number of events registering on the seismic apparatus could be inspected without Soviet veto. For the remainder, Soviet concurrence would be required. The argument on behalf of the quota system is that evasion would be too risky as long as the Soviet Union could not be certain when the West would exercise its right of inspection. And it is said to be the only practical method of inspection, since an impossibly large staff would be required to investigate *every* suspicious occurrence.

The theory of a quota of free inspections has considerable merit. Nevertheless, the numbers now being discussed seem extremely low. The Soviet Union has offered three veto-free inspections. The West has asked for twenty. Considering the problem of finding conclusive proof and the hundreds of unidentified, hence "suspicious," occurrences, the Western proposal appears to go to the absolute limit of what can still be considered statistically safe—all the more so as the problem of how the quota is to be used has barely been studied. Thus the inspection system planned for a test ban has serious shortcomings, even with respect to underground explosions in the range of 1 to 20 kilotons when there is no major effort to hide them.

To complicate the situation further, studies of "decoupling" explosions have demonstrated that if a country is willing to devote sufficient resources to concealment, it will be able to test without furnishing *any* evidence to the inspection system. Methods of buffering explosions, recently discovered, are capable of reducing the seismic signal to as much as 1/300 of its original force. The usual method of decoupling is to conduct the test in an underground cavity. Thus, if a 20-kiloton explosion were to take place in a cavity of sufficient size, it would have the same characteristics as an ordinary, i.e., undecoupled, explosion of 67 tons. A decoupled 100-kiloton (100,000-ton) explosion would have the same characteristics as an explosion of 333 tons without any attempt to hide. Since the planned control system cannot even *detect* explosions much below 1,000 tons and since inspection could take place only on the basis of seismic signals, the quota system does not apply to any decoupled explosion up to 150 kilotons and perhaps even higher. A country seeking to evade the inspection could decouple its explosions so as to be below the threshold of detection. The fact that the quota of free inspections would reveal no violations would prove exactly nothing. Experiments can be carried out without exceeding the threshold at which the right to inspect a suspicious occurrence becomes operative.

To be sure, a cavity able to decouple a 100-kiloton explosion by a factor of 300 would be enormous—as large as the largest natural cavities now existing. It would take some time to construct. It may cost as much as $10 million. But measured against a nuclear development program such a figure is almost trifling. The real cost would depend on the importance attached to the test. If a fundamental technological breakthrough seemed possible, the expense of underground testing would hardly be an obstacle.

Moreover, an evasion to be successful does not necessarily have to be decoupled by a factor of 300. If decoupling were to be by a factor of 20, a much smaller cavity would be required. In that case 10 kilotons could be tested without fear of detection. It is sometimes argued that to construct underground holes for decoupling would require an effort which could not be hidden.[20] But considering the fact that the seismic belt of the Soviet Union—the area of most-frequent earthquakes and therefore the logical site for secret testing—is located in the most inaccessible regions, this seems hardly warranted. Efforts much more substantial than this have been kept secret in Communist countries. Even if we learned of the construction of a cavity, we could do nothing about it. The free inspections can be used only on the basis of a seismic signal—the very contingency which is prevented by decoupling. Whatever we "knew" or thought we knew, the evidence of the control system would point

[20] Bethe, *op. cit.*

the other way. In short, the chief significance of the control system seems to be that it would increase the cost of testing, though not prohibitively, if a country believes real progress is possible.

There are other methods of evasion almost equally beyond the capacity of the control system. No provision yet exists to control testing in outer space. Besides, some evasions may succeed not through the difficulty of detection but through the difficulty of identifying the violator. A test conducted in the ocean would be easily discovered, but could not be so easily traced to the testing country.

The shortcomings of the control system now being negotiated can be summed up as follows: (a) Ordinary underground explosions below 1 kiloton cannot be detected (i.e., the probability of detecting them is less than 1 per cent and decreases rapidly). (b) To control "undecoupled" explosions above 1 kiloton some hundreds of unidentified occurrences would have to be investigated by means of a maximum of twenty "free" inspections. (c) Decoupling would make possible evasions up to perhaps 150 kilotons without detection. Most significant tests can be conducted in this range. (d) Other methods of evasion exist. Some, such as high-altitude testing, are not yet adequately understood. Others, such as testing in the oceans, are easy to detect but difficult to identify.

The negotiations about a nuclear test ban have followed a strange process, then. There has been much haggling over an inspection system known to be incapable of discovering many of the evasions it is supposed to monitor. And yet so much effort and devotion have gone into devising this system that there has been an enormous reluctance to admit failure or even to propose an adequate system of inspection lest the Soviets accuse us of sabotaging the conference.

The confusion and indeed demoralization is illustrated by the reaction to the evidence with respect to decoupling. The Soviet Union, after denying for months that the inspection system devised by the experts was inadequate, suddenly admitted that certain underground explosions could indeed not be detected. It proposed to install the present system to monitor detectable explosions and to declare a five-year moratorium on all other tests. This was hailed by the West as a major concession, though it is not clear why agreeing to a scientific fact should be so described. In return for admitting that the test ban is uninspectable, the Soviet Union urged an uninspectable test ban.

The principle of a moratorium on undetectable explosions has been accepted by the West. This action has been justified by the argument that the period of the moratorium might see a refinement of detection techniques. It has been maintained that a determined scientific effort of the magnitude heretofore devoted to some military programs could not fail to improve seismic equipment.

No doubt improvements in the art of detection are likely. But these must be weighed against the refinements in the skill of evasion, an area in which, after all, research has also started only recently. It seems an odd procedure to accept a control system known to be inadequate, in the hope that it may be made adequate by refinements which no one has yet described. Indeed, the methods now available to improve the control system are so clearly unacceptable to the Soviet Union as to raise serious doubt about the prospect of obtaining Soviet agreement to any drastic modification of the Geneva system once it is in operation.

For example, in order to deal with the problem of decoupling there would have to be installed on Soviet territory 600 stations if the whole Soviet territory were to be covered and 200 if the rigorous system were confined to the seismic belt. In addition, several hundred would be required for Communist China. They would take over three years to install at a cost of $3 billion. Though most of these stations could be unmanned robots serviced at regular intervals, there is little doubt that the Soviet Union would not even consider increasing the original 20 control stations by a factor of 300. Indeed, we have never formally proposed the new figure for fear of demonstrating the inadequacy of the "Geneva system" and wrecking the conference.

Even were the Soviet Union to accept a revised control scheme we would then come up against the problem that the quota of free inspections would have to be renegotiated. For there are between 5,000 and 10,000 earthquakes in the Soviet Union with characteristics similar to a 67-ton underground explosion (i.e., 20 kilotons decoupled) and 4,000 to 7,000 in Communist China. Even if the revised detection apparatus could identify 90 per cent of these as earthquakes—a highly optimistic assumption—this would leave in the neighborhood of 1,000 additional unidentified events to be accounted for. If these refinements of the present system seem so unacceptable that we have not even proposed them, little hope exists for the implementation of whatever may be revealed by a technical study during the period of the moratorium.[21]

Moreover, we should not delude ourselves. Once a control system is installed, there will be little incentive for the Soviet Union to change it. This is not necessarily because of an intention to evade; the motive may be simply to reduce inspection to a minimum. Whatever the Soviet purposes are, the moratorium comes very close to being a permanent ban. Once a treaty is signed, the political and psychological pressures against the resumption of testing will be enormous. At the expiration of the moratorium it will be argued —and not without justice—that if we could rely on Soviet good faith for three years, the risks of evasion cannot justify abrogating this step towards arms control. After all, it has already been claimed that, regardless of the outcome of the Geneva negotiations, world opinion will keep us from resuming testing.

Of course, there is no such thing as a foolproof control system. No conceivable method of inspection can protect against *all* violations. In any arms control agreement we must be prepared to run a calculated risk. The problem with the Geneva inspection system is not that it is imperfect but that probably it is useless as applied to decoupled explosions. The calculated risk we are invited to run refers not to the possibility of evasion but to the chance that the limit of the strategically significant has already been reached in nuclear weapons development so that the Soviets have no incentive to evade. If, however, the Soviet Union considers it worthwhile to evade, the "Geneva" system will be only a minor obstacle. It is suitable for discovering only the clumsiest evasions—the kind a country prepared to violate a solemn agree-

---

[21] These figures are extrapolations and subject to the qualifications discussed above. However, even if they are changed by a factor of two in either direction the argument would remain valid.

ment almost certainly would avoid. Indeed, in the light of the inadequacy of the original control scheme, the Soviet charge that we are less concerned with the danger of evasion than with penetrating Soviet society becomes understandable.

To be sure, we will possess sources of information other than the control system. Intelligence activities may give us some indication of suspicious activity. At the same time, this is also the kind of knowledge least useful for political purposes—as is conclusively demonstrated by the U-2 incident. We may be reluctant to reveal the source of our information and we may find it impossible to furnish conclusive proof. This problem becomes all the more intractable because the evader could invoke the fact that the control system had failed to show any violation. One can easily imagine the reaction of world opinion if we announced that we would resume testing because we knew of Soviet violations even though the inspection system had failed to reveal any. Thus in some ways the control system might actually facilitate evasions by furnishing "proof" of compliance even when secret testing was taking place.

It can be argued that the Soviet Union might be inhibited from secret testing if it knew that we knew testing was taking place—even if we were unable to capitalize on our knowledge before world opinion. The fact remains that the inhibition supplied by ordinary intelligence activities has nothing to do with the control system being negotiated.

The complexity of inspection is matched by the difficulty of devising sanctions. The mere danger of detection does not of itself deter evasions unless it is coupled with a penalty the evader is unwilling to pay. But these sanctions are far from obvious—indeed the treaty as it now stands contains no provision for sanctions. A violation of the nuclear test ban clearly is not a *casus belli*. It may not even be a sufficient cause for the injured party to start testing again— particularly if the violation appears ambiguous or is disputed, as it surely will be. Once nuclear tests have been banned, the free world will not abrogate its agreement easily—its hesitations are revealed by its reluctance to end an uninspected moratorium. It may even seek to escape the need for making difficult decisions by fudging the interpretation of the results of the control system.

And should it decide to test again after a prolonged ban, years might be consumed before it could do so. A nation which had observed the ban might by then have nothing to test. A ban extended over a period of years would almost certainly lead to the attrition of our weapons laboratories, whose ablest scientists would be increasingly tempted to concentrate on fields where scientific progress was more promising. The U.S.S.R., by contrast, is in a position to keep its research staffs together much more easily. Even a strong indication of Soviet violation might therefore leave the United States at a serious disadvantage or at least without adequate recourse.

It is often maintained that a violation of the test ban would have a catastrophic impact on world opinion. But this assumes a degree of certainty about Soviet behavior which is belied both by the nature of the control system and by all past experience. The Soviet Union has always been skillful in masking its own actions by charging its opponents with similar transgressions. Were the Kremlin intent on evasion, it would surely accuse us of the same violations it was contemplating. In the resulting atmosphere of recrimination, it would be difficult to separate sincere charges from the customary exchanges of the Cold War.

It is possible, of course, that the Soviet Union has no intention of evading. But, if so, it is not because the control system offers a significant obstacle. The reason would be, as is often maintained by advocates of a test ban, that no motive for evasion exists since a point has been reached in nuclear weapons development where further experiments cannot yield a strategic advantage. If this is true, however, it is difficult to understand why so much significance is attached to a nuclear test ban. It simply does not make sense to say that a complete ban on nuclear testing is an essential first step towards arms control and to excuse the inadequacy of its inspection system with the argument that what it purports to control is of no substantive significance. If the chance of Soviet violation is low, then much of the concern with refining the inspection system is beside the point, and the collateral benefits of a control system would be the chief purpose of our insisting on it.

On the other hand, if decisive advances are still possible, the present control scheme is highly dangerous. It is impossible for a non-scientist to be certain as to what constitutes basic progress in the nuclear field. Yet if secret testing made possible, for example, the development of an anti-ballistic missile defense, deterrence could easily fail. It is not necessary, however, to describe the progress which evasions may make possible. It is, after all, in the nature of technological breakthroughs that they are often beyond what is now conceivable. The fact remains, in any case, that either no progress is possible, in which case the test ban is of marginal significance as an arms control measure, or else progress *is* possible, in which case the present inspection system would allow many evasions with impunity.

Moreover, whatever were Soviet intentions at the beginning of the negotiations, it is difficult to see how the Kremlin could in the interval have avoided considering the problem of evasion. Two technical conferences have addressed themselves to this topic. The Soviet leaders have had the benefit of our studies regarding the possibilities of secret testing. This is not to say, of course, that the Soviet leaders would sign the agreement, having already decided to cheat. That decision will depend on many factors, including how promising the prospects for a real breakthrough are. However, whenever evasions seem profitable to them, the Geneva control system can be circumvented without excessive risk.

If, then, we continue on our present course we must do so in full awareness of three propositions: (1) that the test ban as now conceived is not so much imperfect as uninspectable with respect to decoupled explosions or tests in space; (2) that we are prepared to run this risk because we believe that no further strategically significant progress is possible; (3) that we agree to a test ban above all because of its collateral advantages.

What then of the collateral benefits often ascribed to a test ban, such as its utility in preventing the spread of nuclear weapons and the advantage of installing an inspection system on Soviet territories?

With respect to the Nth country problem, it is often argued that, once the established nuclear powers agree to a test ban, world opinion will force all other countries to follow suit. Without testing, no other country will be able to develop its own arsenal of nuclear weapons. For all its surface attractiveness, this argument is open to serious doubt. It is true that without the inclusion of other countries, particularly of Communist China, the nuclear test ban will be deprived of one of its chief purposes. But it is important to remember that no Nth country so far has indicated any willingness to join the agreement. France, indeed, has explicitly refused. It will be no easy matter to negotiate an elaborate inspection system for Communist China—especially since it is hard to see what Communist China would gain in return for such an agreement when we have already stopped testing.

If no other countries join the test ban agreement, the opportunities for evasion by the established nuclear powers will multiply, to the disadvantage of the West. The possibility that the Soviet Union could test in China would not be matched by Western experiments in French territories. It is exceedingly doubtful whether we would be permitted to use the French proving ground or would desire to do so. In any case, it would be an ironic turn of events if the major consequence of a test ban were to shift the testing sites from the territory of the major nuclear powers into that of their allies.

On the other hand, if the signatories to the test ban bring pressure on their allies to adhere, these may demand the sharing of weapons in order to make testing unnecessary. In that case, the result of the test ban would be to speed the diffusion of nuclear weapons from existing stockpiles.

If these obstacles are overcome—if all other countries join a nuclear test ban without making new conditions—the problem of the inadequacy of the inspection system will re-emerge perhaps in even sharper form. To the established nuclear powers, the progress to be achieved by secret testing may be so marginal that it does not seem worthwhile to run even a small risk of being found out.

But the Nth powers would seem to have the maximum incentive to evade. For them, *any* secret test is likely to produce progress. And the problem of sanctions is much more difficult. A violation by an established nuclear power may be inhibited by the danger that such a step might abrogate the test ban. It would not make too much sense, however, to end a world-wide test ban because an Nth country was found to be cheating.

It can be argued, of course, that Nth powers do not have the resources for the elaborate installations required for effective evasion. But this surely does not apply to Communist China or France or West Germany. Where it does apply, a ban on detectable explosions would serve the purpose equally well without many of the risks of the present system.

Even if the established nuclear powers do not share their weapons and even if the Nth countries do not test, this may not prevent the acquisition of a crude nuclear arsenal. Testing is most essential for sophisticated weapons systems: those which depend on discrimination for purposes of limited war, or on precise timing, as certain air-defense weapons. However, most Nth countries—particularly the smaller ones—are primarily interested in a rudimentary retaliatory force. Most scientists are of the opinion that even without testing it is possible to construct with a high degree of confidence weapons suitable for this purpose. Their explosive power may vary by as much as 30 per cent from that estimated. But if destructiveness is the primary purpose, this will not be a crucial obstacle. Thus, the major utility of a world-wide test ban would be not so much to prevent the acquisition of nuclear weapons as the ability to threaten with them, for to do so would be to admit violating the ban. Even that benefit depends on a concurrent agreement by the nuclear powers not to share their weapons.

The seriousness of the Nth country problem imposes on us an obligation not to seek to solve it by subterfuge. It should be dealt with directly and by the measures already described: an explicit agreement to stop the spread of nuclear weapons, to impose a cut-off on nuclear production, and to reduce nuclear stockpiles. As now conceived, however, a test ban may bring about the illusion of progress and the reality of a growing insecurity. In the field of nuclear arms control, half a loaf may well be worse than none.

What about the collateral advantages which are supposed to flow from a system of inspection in Communist territory? These, too, are vastly exaggerated. It is to be doubted that twenty-one control stations, confined to a maximum of twenty "free" inspections a year, will add significantly to the liberalization of the Soviet regime. There are, after all, increasing numbers of tourists. Foreign consulates exist in Communist cities. Scientific and cultural exchanges are taking place. It is not self-evident that the opening up of

Soviet society would be greatly accelerated by the kind of control system envisaged for the test ban. Moreover, it is one thing to agree to an inspection system in which one has confidence because it *also* has desirable collateral consequences. It is quite another to urge a demonstrably inadequate control scheme only, or even largely, because of its assumed collateral political advantages. Such a course can only strengthen Soviet suspicions that we are less interested in inspection than in penetrating Soviet society. Far from removing distrust, it may magnify it.

Similar considerations apply to the proposition that a complete ban on all weapons tests is imposed on us by world opinion. To be sure, we must be sensitive to world opinion. But we cannot stake our survival on it alone. It is worrisome that so much attention has focused on a ban on nuclear testing while the Soviet refusal even to consider control over nuclear weapons placed into orbit—or, what amounts to the same thing, their insistence on tying it to general disarmament—has gone almost unnoticed. A ban on such vehicles would be a more significant control measure; it is infinitely easier to enforce and more difficult to evade than a nuclear test ban. Why has so much attention focused on the Soviet proposals and why have we found it so difficult to mobilize world opinion on behalf of our schemes? One reason is surely that to many the test ban seems attractive largely because it appears attainable. And it appears attainable because the Soviet Union has indicated its interest in it. Such a pattern comes close to permitting the Soviet Union to determine the pace as well as the pattern of arms control negotiations.

For all these reasons, there is serious cause for concern about the course of the test ban negotiations. What was once advocated on the grounds that it permitted the establishment for the first time of an effective inspection system was later urged because however inadequate the control system the Soviet Union is said to have no intention to cheat. We have been jockeyed into a position in which we first maintained an uninspected moratorium for over two years and then agreed to a moratorium on undetectable explosions for another extended period. Every day that passes without the establishment of an inspection system in which we can have confidence must weaken our ability to insist on one. It is a curious bargaining method to seek an inspected test ban through maintaining an uninspected one. The result may be that the Soviet leaders will be encouraged to try to apply similar tactics in future arms control negotiations to wear down the West and to obtain a unilateral advantage. If the standards of adequacy for the inspection system for the test ban were applied to other fields, such as surprise attack and the Nth country problem—and we will now be under strong pressure to do so—they would pose an intolerable risk.

Equally worrisome are the passions which have been aroused by the test ban controversy. There can be little doubt that some of the opponents of the ban have invoked vistas of nuclear weapons development more significant for technical ingenuity than as a contribution to strategic thought. It is also clear that many of the advocates of the ban have been equally one-sided by presenting only the advantages of a cessation of tests and begging the principal question: whether the control system is adequate to achieve this end. The moral and political attitudes have deeply colored the interpretation of scientific facts—to an extent that many scientists have themselves become political partisans.

One of the principal movers of the test ban has written:

I had the doubtful honor of presenting the theory of the big hole [with respect to decoupling explosions] to the Russians in November, 1959. I felt deeply embarrassed in so doing, because it implied that we considered the Russians capable of cheating on a massive scale. I think that they would have been quite justified if they had considered this an insult and had walked out of the negotiations in disgust.

The Russians seemed stunned by the theory of the big hole. In private, they took the Americans to task for having spent the last year inventing methods to cheat on a nuclear test cessation agreement. Officially, they spent considerable effort in trying to disprove the theory of the big hole. This is not the reaction of a country that is bent on cheating.

Two of the Russian scientists presented to the Geneva Conference their supposed proof that the big hole would not work. A day or two later, Dr. Latter and I gave the counterproof and showed, with the help of the Russian theory itself, that the Russian proof was wrong and that the theory of the big hole and the achievable decoupling factor were correct. We have been commended in the American press for this feat in theoretical physics. I am not proud of it.[22]

[22] Bethe, *op. cit.*

It is not clear why denying the well-established theoretical possibility of decoupling demonstrates the absence of an intention to evade. And it is difficult to understand why the chief American negotiator should have been quite so defensive about presenting our case. After all, if arms control is to have any meaning, negotiations about inspection *must* assume the possibility that the other side may cheat. The absence of trust is precisely what makes arms control so important. When the survival of society is involved, it does not seem unreasonable to strive for safeguards other than the word of men who arrested the leaders of the Hungarian revolution while negotiating an armistice with them and who executed them despite a promise of safe-conduct.

This is not to say that the test ban negotiations have been entirely without benefit. If nothing else, they have caused our government to pay systematic attention to arms control. The relation between strategic doctrine and arms control has been more clearly understood. Progress has been made towards working out at least a procedure for future negotiations. These are not small gains. It remains to relate them to control schemes in which it is possible to have greater confidence.

A complete test ban has become such a symbol of *all* arms control that it is easy to forget that initially the choice was not between a complete ban or no agreement. Had we understood the problem, we could have split up the negotiations into two parts. We could have offered a ban on tests which were inspectable immediately along the lines of the United States proposal at Geneva of February 11, 1960. The remaining portion of a test ban should have been made conditional on wider arms control agreements, particularly a cut-off of nuclear production, a reduction of stockpiles, and perhaps an inspection system against surprise attack. Or else it should have awaited the development of an inspection system of greater reliability than present methods of detection afford.

Moreover, the United States could have unilaterally renounced any future testing capable of producing fall-out. It could have urged the creation of a United Nations committee to monitor world-wide fall-out, thus shifting to the Soviet Union the responsibility for any genetic damage from radiation resulting from continued testing. It is the measure of the distance we have come that a unilateral renunciation of fall-out testing which would have been considered a stunning initiative only two years ago would today undoubtedly be treated as an act of intransigence.

With respect to underground testing and testing in outer space, the United States could have offered to accede to any agreement within the limits of confidence inspired by technical studies. It could also have agreed to register all future tests not detectable by present methods with the United Nations and to use them to refine existing control measures, preferably in co-operation with the Soviets.

Finally, we could have proposed that we would be prepared to end all tests even with the present detection machinery, provided the Soviet Union accepted the wider control schemes described above, particularly the reduction of nuclear stockpiles, the cut-off of nuclear production and the scheme to safeguard against surprise attack. For if these schemes were in operation, it would be possible to control, if not secret testing, at least the uses to which it might be put.

The approach outlined here would have been responsive to many of the concerns of humanity without exposing the free world to the peril of the current approach. It would have been a "first step" which would have avoided most of the dangers of our present course and yet achieved many of its goals. If no further progress is likely in the nuclear field, the costs of underground testing would have made it appear unattractive in relation to the gains to be achieved. If major advances are possible, such an agreement would have kept the test ban from turning into a source of unilateral weakness for the West. If other countries had agreed to this version of the test ban, their development of nuclear weapons would have been inhibited almost as much as by the version now being devised.

Now that matters have reached the present point, it is essential that we face the situation squarely. A new Administration will have to decide whether the test ban negotiations can be continued much longer without result. If no terminal date is placed on them, the practical consequence will be the same as an uninspected moratorium on *all* testing. We face essentially two choices: we can sign the test ban agreement being negotiated at Geneva with all its inadequacies or we can adopt the program outlined above: a renunciation of fall-out testing (unilaterally if necessary), coupled with joint efforts to refine the detection methods for underground testing or testing in space. If we adopt the latter course— which is the more clear-cut and wiser—we will pay a heavy political price in the short run. There is little reason to doubt that the Soviet Union would succeed in mobilizing world opinion against us. In the long run, however, the situation could be quite the reverse. It must be ultimately demoralizing to sign an agreement known to be inadequate simply because we have maneuvered ourselves into a situation where we have only a choice among evils. The future of other arms control measures may well depend on the sense of responsibility with which we approach the test ban negotiations—though not in the sense usually claimed.

If, as seems likely, the present concept of a ban is adopted, its implications must be understood. Its risks can be reduced only in these conditions: (a) if we undertake a major program to improve methods of detection and are willing to face the results even if they should be different from what we might wish; (b) if we continue to spur research in the nuclear field in order to understand the kind of breakthrough which might be achieved by evasions. Research in detection methods must not be conducted with the attitude that every flaw is fatal nor with a debater's approach of seeking to disprove every difficulty. If we do not make progress in improving the detection apparatus or if startling breakthroughs in the nuclear field appear possible, the proposed moratorium should be ended at its expiration.

Another conclusion must be a substantial build-up of our conventional forces. A test ban would inevitably increase the psychological inhibitions against the use of nuclear weapons in resisting local aggression. Already powerful inhibitions will be reinforced by the argument that the strategic benefit of using nuclear weapons is outweighed by the political consequences of a step which is almost certain to end the test ban.

It is even more important to define the next step in arms control negotiations. A determined effort should be made to use the period of the moratorium to make progress on the other schemes described in this chapter and to be prepared to end the moratorium should it become clear that the Soviet Union seeks to use the negotiations to weaken the West rather than to increase stability. If a nuclear test ban is to be a first step, everything depends on our ability to take other steps with confidence, precision and responsibility. If the test ban should lead to other control measures, more conducive to disciplining the arms race, it may yet prove worthwhile. But if over any length of time it should prove to be the only attainable agreement, its perils will become magnified. Whatever one's attitude towards a test ban, both opponents and proponents should be able to unite in treating it as a challenge to devise more significant and less dangerous accords.

6. Conclusion—The Nature of the Debate

NO ASPECT of American policy has received less systematic attention than arms control. Substantial intellectual as well as material resources have been devoted to the study of strategy. Yet arms control, which is its reverse side, has lacked a focus of attention. As a result, our government has found it difficult to achieve agreement about desirable goals and, even more, to develop a dynamic program. Before there can be successful negotiation on arms control we must get our intellectual house in order.

The need is all the greater because the rate of technological change has continually outstripped the pace of negotiations. Whatever may have been the possibilities of controlling nuclear weapons when the Baruch-Lilienthal Plan was first formulated, the number of weapons produced in the interval and the size of the stockpiles have made complete abolition impossible to inspect. Similarly, in the early stages of the missile age it might have been possible to arrest the proliferation of rockets, either by a ban on testing or through a severe limitation on production, or both. But neither side sufficiently understood the implications of missile technology for this proposal ever to be seriously advanced. Today, measures to control the missile race are infinitely more complicated. Three conclusions follow:

First, arms control schemes should be developed with a clear understanding that their rate of obsolescence is as rapid as the rate of technological change. The obsolescence of arms control schemes is likely to be no less great than that of strategies. They must therefore have a built-in mechanism for adaptation and review.

Second, there are few universal schemes of arms control. We must be prepared to face the fact that proposals which may be highly desirable given one state of technology may have to be replaced by a contrary policy when conditions change. For example, as long as only four countries possess nuclear weapons, it would be highly desirable to advance the schemes outlined earlier in the chapter to deal with the Nth country problem. Should nuclear weapons spread to a considerable number of countries, however, arms control—in the sense of striving for a maximum of stability—may have to set itself different goals. Then the danger to peace will reside in the vulnerability of the newly developed retaliatory forces and in the danger that nuclear weapons may not spread symmetrically between Nth countries which consider each other mortal enemies. Arms control properly conceived may then have to strive to help Nth countries *protect* their new-found nuclear arsenals and assure that the spread is symmetrical.

Third, there is a critical point in the development of any weapon after which arms control becomes impossible or at least extremely intricate. After this point is reached, it will seem to both sides—and probably correctly—that they will be more secure through unilateral efforts than through any control system that they are able to devise, agree on and inspect. This suggests the crucial importance of controlling new weapons in the very early stages of development. It means also that we have to come to grips with controlling arms when the implications of new developments are still least understood.

Unfortunately, the debate about arms control has often contributed more to passion than to understanding. The notion that a country can increase its security by sharing information with a potential enemy rather than by withholding it—central to many arms control schemes—is difficult for men who have spent a lifetime with the conviction that secrecy is a military weapon. Not every technological advance increases a society's safety and a certain equilibrium of destructive ability may prove more conducive to the prospects of peace than an unchecked arms race. But these notions require a fundamental readjustment of traditional categories of thought.

And this re-examination is made difficult by a number of factors, including the manner in which the alternatives are put. For one thing, it is becoming increasingly clear that no real progress is possible in the field of arms control until we achieve agreement within our military establishment and within the Western alliance about the elements of security. Without an agreed strategic doctrine we will possess no criteria to determine whether a given scheme would add to stability or detract from it. The view we develop about the significance of local defense will determine the conclusions about the feasibility of demilitarized zones. The strategic assessment of the role of nuclear weapons will shape the attitude towards such issues as the nuclear test ban or the Nth country problem. The interpretations of vulnerability influence the schemes for the prevention of surprise attack. Since we have resolved none of these issues in our own military establishment or within the Western alliance, it is not surprising that Western arms control proposals have been so weak and often beside the point.

The situation has not been helped by the attitudes of some of the most vocal and passionate advocates of arms control. Too often they have given the impression that simply because their goal is important it can be reached easily. Though they have argued correctly that a purely strategic approach may prove self-defeating, they have carried this proposition to the extreme of dismissing strategic considerations impatiently as representing the attitude of short-sighted or power-mad men.

Thus the absolutism that identifies safety with physical power all too often has been countered by another absolutism which pretends that arms control is an alternative to our security effort rather than a complement to it. Emphasizing the reduction of striking power or the exchange of military information, which is, after all, one of the purposes of arms control measures, many military experts have seen in them an inevitable weakening of our strategic position. Stressing the co-operative nature of a disarmament agreement, many proponents of arms control have considered the fact of an agreement more important than its substance. It is understandable that military men who have dedicated their lives to a study of strategic problems find it difficult to be sympathetic with programs of deliberate limitation of power or with an effort to exchange information. It is natural that many of those who had met incomprehension and ridicule when first suggesting the need for arms control now adopt essentially an advocate's position and seem more concerned with finding some argument to refute an objection than with examining it dispassionately. Nevertheless, their debate has paralyzed understanding because the unstated assumptions and the mutual distrust have been more significant than the arguments actually advanced.

A symptom of this confusion has been the manner in which most of our proposals have been developed. The general pattern has been that we have been under pressure to come up with some scheme simply because a conference was approaching, instead of entering arms control negotiations because we had a program which we were eager to see implemented. Our positions have generally reflected not so much strong conviction or clear understanding as the necessity for coming up with *something*. Both the negotiations on the prevention of surprise attack in November, 1958, and the disarmament conference of March, 1960, were prepared by *ad hoc* committees assembled when the conference was imminent. The Coolidge Committee, which was supposed to develop the U.S. position for the 1960 conference, was much maligned and its report was finally discarded. The real villain, however, was not the committee but the conception which called it into being. It was against all reason to expect an *ad hoc* committee, most of whose members were spending only part time on their assignment, to resolve in less than six months a subject of such technical complexity and on which opinion has been so divided.

Whatever the cause, when the Western diplomats assembled a month before the conference to prepare their program, an American position had not yet been developed, and a week before the talks the Western allies had not yet reached agreement on their proposals. Inevitably the Western program had an air of improvisation. The process by which it emerged was directly responsible for the lack of assurance with which it was maintained.

The failure to make progress towards arms control is not, of course, primarily the fault of the United States. Soviet proposals so far indicate that either the Soviet leaders have as much difficulty in understanding the problem as we do, or else that they are using the negotiations to demoralize the free world and to induce it to disarm unilaterally. It is discouraging that almost every Soviet proposal seems more designed to exploit the weariness of the West or to achieve a unilateral advantage than to slow down the arms race. Our recognition of the importance of the problem and our eagerness to find a solution must not blind us to the lack of seriousness of much of the Soviet performance.

But our judgment about the Soviet approach does not excuse the confusion of our response. Whatever the Soviet intentions, our task is essentially the same. Perhaps no serious negotiation is possible at all. But we will be able to determine this only by becoming clear in our own minds about the purpose of arms control and by devising serious, specific schemes for attaining it. If the Soviet Union rejects proposals which are designed to increase its security together with ours—which is the essence of any responsible program—it will have given clear proof that there is no alternative to the arms race.

Before we can advance serious proposals we have to clarify our purposes. It is said that we must engage in arms control to free resources for the *real* competition, which is in the field of economics. It is claimed that arms control may reduce the burden of taxation. Arms control is advocated as a means of speeding up the evolution of the Soviet system. Involved explanations are advanced that we can trust the Soviet Union to observe any agreement. Almost all these arguments are essentially irrelevant. The Soviet leaders can hardly be attracted by schemes whose primary purpose is announced to be the transformation of their system. Useful schemes ought not to depend on whether or not we can trust the Soviet leaders—indeed, if we could trust them, they might be less important. Arms control schemes will be effective if they contain their own incentive for observation and if there can be confidence, not in the other side but in the control arrangements.

The argument about freeing resources for economic competition begs the principal question, which is, after all, precisely whether it is possible to develop arms control measures which promote stability and achieve this end. To promise that savings from disarmament are to be applied to economic development programs confuses the issue in two ways: by implying that there will be savings and by creating the impression that two courses of action, each vital in its own right, are dependent on each other. It is not a big step from the assertion that resources saved from arms control will be applied to economic development to the proposition that expanded economic development must *await* disarmament. Or else the argument can be reversed in an equally misleading manner: arms control can be advocated in order to free resources for economic development. Because they have accepted this notion, many groups in America and many more abroad have felt impelled to establish an illusory priority between economic development and security. Such an attitude is equally disastrous to arms control and to economic development. Our economic programs do not have to await disarmament. The required resources are well within our capabilities even on the assumption of a substantial defense effort.

Then, again, it is not at all certain that arms control will in fact free resources, particularly in its early phases. Inspection is expensive. Additional funds for research are essential. A recasting of our military establishment will almost surely have to accompany arms control. To justify arms control as a device to save money may cause us to be attracted to the wrong schemes for the wrong reasons.

We must not confuse collateral with primary goals. The purpose of arms control is to enhance the security of *all* parties. Any attempt to achieve a unilateral advantage must doom arms control. Similarly, neither reduction of forces nor inspection can be an end in itself. The test of any agreement is whether it adds to or detracts from stability, whether it makes war less likely or more so. No collateral benefits will be able to compensate for badly conceived control measures.

In this examination, sentimentality is as dangerous as rigid persistence in the patterns of the arms race. The apparently simple remedies may be the most dangerous. Preventing accidental war is so important an objective in itself that we need not confuse it with sociological explanations of the impact of inspection on the Soviet system. Reducing the fear of surprise attack is a worthy enough task for us to engage in without making elaborate arguments about the freeing of economic resources. Dealing with the diffusion of nuclear weapons requires the best analysis of which we are capable rather than a strident debate between extreme positions.

At the same time, however dedicated we may be to arms control, it is important not to approach it with the attitude that a failure of negotiations will inevitably doom humanity. Such a conviction is bound to produce pressures for unilateral disarmament and therefore remove any incentive for serious negotiations on the part of the Communists. If the Soviet leaders are convinced that the fear of war overrides all other considerations, two consequences will follow. They will be encouraged to engage in the most violent threats in order to demoralize the free world further. And they will become convinced that arms control is unnecessary since they are already protected by the free world's fears. Paradoxical as it may seem, a measure of instability in the arms race is required to provide an impetus for arms control.

Moreover, a feeling of despair should arms control prove unattainable would also be factually wrong. Without arms control stability will be more difficult to achieve. But it probably can be achieved even then. In the equation of retaliatory forces, advances in mobility will probably promote a degree of invulnerability even without a negotiated agreement. And we could take unilateral measures of arms control along the lines described earlier in the chapter. In short, while arms control is *one* road to peace and a crucial one, it is not our sole chance to bring it about. For this reason, it is probably unwise to call the proposed new agency charged with the responsibility of coordinating and devising arms control proposals a National Peace Agency, as has been suggested. To be sure, arms control measures may, if properly devised, contribute to stability. Also, a focus for concern with this problem in our government is essential. It is regrettable, however, to leave the impression that there is only *one* road to peace or that only *one* organ of our government has this goal. In the nuclear age, all national policies must be directed towards peace, our diplomacy and our military program no less than our arms control effort. No agency should claim a monopoly on the quest for peace.

If we are to make progress in the field of arms control, the military establishment must come to understand that in the present state of technology an arms race is the most unstable of all forms of security, and that properly conceived arms control must increase the security of *all* countries. And many enthusiasts for arms control must realize that ardor is no substitute for precision. A great deal depends on the ability to be concrete. In the next few years we may have perhaps our last opportunity to stabilize the arms race by means of negotiation. Perhaps Communist obduracy will foil our most earnest efforts. But it would be unforgivable if we failed because we refused to face either the importance or the complexity of the challenge.

VII

OF POLITICAL EVOLUTION: THE WEST, COMMUNISM, AND THE NEW NATIONS

1. POLITICAL EVOLUTION AND COMMUNISM

PERHAPS even more worrisome than specific policy dilemmas—with which the previous chapters have dealt—has been our interpretation of the contemporary revolution. Sometimes pretending that peace, conceived simply as tranquility, was just around the corner, sometimes confusing rhetoric with policy, we have been unable to define the world that we wish to see emerge—much less the means for attaining it. All too frequently we have relied for the solution of our problems on an evolutionary theory in which the assumed forces of history have replaced purpose and action. The notion of an inevitable development towards a more desirable and enlightened political structure has been applied equally to the two great revolutions of our time: Communism and the emergence of new nations in formerly colonial areas.

With respect to Communism, the argument is frequently heard that the Soviet Union is in the midst of profound and inevitable transformations. As it produces more consumers' goods, it will become a less ideological and less militant society, increasingly concerned with material comforts. As the standard of living of Soviet citizens improves and they develop a greater stake in their society, so the argument goes, they will exert increasing pressure for the freedoms long familiar in the West. Industrialization requires technical skills and education fosters a questioning spirit.

The managerial class will not submit to the pressures of a police state. The methods appropriate to fostering economic development in a primitive society will no longer work in a highly elaborated one. Khrushchev's Russia, as distinguished from Stalin's, is a "going concern" and therefore less interested in aggressive policies to solidify its domestic hold.

According to this theory, a key goal of Western policy must be to promote this beneficial evolution. To the extent that there is a relaxation of external tension, the Soviet leaders will have no choice but to ameliorate their own political system. To the degree that we can encourage the Soviet Union to concentrate on the economic development of its vast territory, we will also foster all the elements inconsistent with dictatorial rule and an aggressive foreign policy.

Similar propositions are advanced with respect to the new nations. They are said to be in the phase of industrial development where the requirements of economic growth inevitably take precedence over those of political organization. The ability to promote industrialization and a rising standard of living is for them the chief test of political leadership, much more meaningful than terms like "freedom" and "human dignity." Means will necessarily be subordinated to ends. In the early stages of development some form of dictatorship is therefore extremely likely. The West, according to this school of thought, would make a great mistake were it to seek to promote in the new nations its own political forms or values, since these are either not understood at all or else interpreted as a newer and subtler form of foreign intervention.

The hope for the West in the underdeveloped areas, it is said, is to identify itself with the striving for economic growth. Competition with the Communists should take place above all in the realm of industrialization. Our task should be to prove our ability to raise the standard of living more efficiently than our Communist opponents without resorting to their methods of regimentation. In the long run the satisfaction of wants will promote a more liberal political system as well. In our approach both to the new nations and to Communism we should expect political results not from the impact of our ideas but from the indirect influence of a transformation of the economy.[1]

The interesting question then presents itself: are these interpretations, often hailed as alternatives to Marxism, not in fact a purer version of Marxism than that practiced in Communist countries? The notion that the economic structure inevitably has certain associated political forms is surely acceptable to Marxists. The proposition that values are altered by changing the economy is also one of the keystones of Marxism. Indeed, the Communist interpretation of history differs from many of the evolutionary theories of the West not so much in its assumptions as in the conclusions drawn from them. The dispute is not between two different philosophies but instead concerns the interpretation of a very similar orthodoxy: Communism maintains that industrialization inevitably produces the dictatorship of the proletariat. The evolutionary theories described above hold that economic development involves an automatic trend towards liberal institutions.

The difference between the two approaches is much less theoretical than psychological. Communism uses its philosophy of history as a *spur* to effort. Faith in evolution provides the conviction for major exertions. Too many in the West rely on history as a *substitute* for effort. As a result, survival becomes their primary goal. All will end well, if we live to see it. This is an attitude of resignation, destructive of purpose and values. The irony of our period is that the successes of Communism are due less to that ability to forecast events on which it prides itself than to its self-assurance in shaping them. History for Communism is an incentive for action, a guarantee of the meaningfulness of sacrifice. The West, on the other hand, has a tendency to use evolutionary theory as a bromide. Waiting for history to do its work for it, it stands in danger of being engulfed by the currents of our time.

It seems probable that the evolutionary theories so popular in the West are less a help in describing the future than a reflection

[1] For example, see *United States Foreign Policy: Economic, Social, and Political Change in the Underdeveloped Countries and Its Implications for United States Policy*, U. S. Senate Committee on Foreign Relations Study No. 12, especially Chap. 8, p. 50.

of our attitudes. There was a time when the West believed that an overwhelming economic superiority guaranteed its triumph over Communism—without ever being able to describe just how. Though this attitude was fatuous, it is no less fatuous to draw so much comfort from the hope that when the Soviet Union equals our economic performance it will become as consumer-oriented and as bland as we are. This is hardly a heroic attitude, nor one likely to appeal to a world where millions strive for a new sense of direction.

There is, moreover, serious doubt about the historical validity of these evolutionary theories. The record regarding the relationship between economic development and a moderate foreign policy, between industrialization and enlightened domestic institutions, between education and the questioning spirit is not nearly so hopeful as is so often suggested. Industrialization did not make Germany less militant; quite the contrary. A rate of economic development exceeding that of any contemporary new nation did not make Japan a peaceful country. The opposition to modern totalitarianism has rarely centered in the bureaucracies or in the universities. The educational system of Germany was one of the glories of the nation. Yet the evidence would indicate that its support of one of the most vicious dictatorships of modern times far outweighed its resistance to it. Nor is the situation very different in the Soviet Union. For many centuries and in many societies education has had the function of indoctrination. It has been conceived as a tool to strengthen state control. On the historical record this attempt has succeeded more frequently than it has failed, particularly if one judges events by the time scale relevant to the life of an individual and not by centuries.

Indeed, there is no country in which democratic institutions developed *after* industrialization and *as a result of* economic development. Where the rudiments of democratic institutions did not exist at the beginning of the industrial revolution, they did not receive impetus from industrial growth. Democracy may be firmly established in contemporary Germany and Japan, but it came about as the result not of evolution but of a catastrophic war. In all the traditional democratic societies, the essentials of the governmental system antedated the industrial revolution. The American Constitution was developed in a largely agricultural society and so were the fundamental institutions of the British system. These institutions were broadened and elaborated as the countries prospered—but their significant features preceded economic development and are not attributable to it.

On the contrary, in so far as there is a relationship between industrialization and the emergence of democracy, it is that in the nineteenth century political freedom was considered a means *to bring about* economic advance. Democracy was then considered the most "progressive" form of government, not only from the moral point of view but also because it was believed to be the most effective system for promoting material welfare. Feudal rule had excluded the most talented and enterprising members of the community from any share in governmental affairs. The mercantile system had hedged economic activity with governmental restrictions, all the more unbearable because those most affected had no voice either in promulgating or in administering them. In these circumstances, democratic theory expressed the desire of the most active members of society to participate in formulating the rules affecting their welfare.

As a result, the economic justification for democracy was little concerned with the moral significance of freedom. Its emphasis was utilitarian: the greatest good for the greatest number. The contribution of government was thought to be essentially negative: that government was best which governed least. The free play of economic forces would automatically assure the maximum benefit for the largest number of people. Liberty was identified with the absence of governmental restraint. Throughout the nineteenth century when democratic institutions were being elaborated, the notion was prevalent that government had few positive tasks to perform. It was asked to provide for law and order and to enforce contracts. But it was expected to stay out of the field which was thought to be of greatest importance: that of the operation of the ultimate economic laws which in turn would bring about economic development.

This suggests that industrialization, rather than producing

democracy, may remove the economic incentive for it. When the government does not impede economic development but systematically encourages it, the more enterprising members of society, far from opposing the existing system, will identify themselves with it. When the middle class is deliberately endowed by state action with considerable prestige, it may not value political liberty as highly as did its counterpart in the eighteenth and nineteenth centuries. Wherever the feudal classes did not oppose industrialization but fostered it, the pressure for democratic institutions was substantially reduced, if not eliminated. In these cases, the managerial group on the whole accepted the political order preferred by the feudal classes in return for a substantial degree of freedom in the economic sphere. In both Germany and Japan industrialization was achieved by an alliance of industrialists and the landed aristocracy. In both countries the managerial group proved more interested in nationalism than in liberalization. The success of economic development enhanced the prestige of the form of government promoting it.

This is no accident. Industry depends on predictability, efficiency, productivity. These may require a certain constitutionalism—the elaboration of a set of rules commonly understood and to which it is possible to adjust. They do not require democratic government as the term is understood in the West. As long as the economic sphere affords a reasonable degree of freedom—sufficient to permit a concentration on output and efficiency—the managerial group is not likely to insist on participation in political activity.

Moreover, the industrial process hardly promotes notions of political liberty. Industrial organization is based on a specialization of functions. There is little in the industrial ethos as such which would find repugnant the notion of a group of political specialists exercising absolute control. Again, industrial enterprise has a highly developed sense of hierarchy. Its dynamism derives from its ability to reduce its components—including the human beings involved—to manipulable quantities. To be sure, this does not exclude humane and enlightened measures. Indeed, the wisest industrialists pioneered high wages and sought to spur consumption. But the motive was less a recognition of human dignity than a conviction that an enlightened social policy was the best means to increase output. Industrialists *qua* industrialists would not, in their economic experience, find anything that is likely to produce rebellion against a paternalistic absolutism.

The industrial experience is in fact quite different from the commercial framework which animated the leaders of the democratic revolutions in the eighteenth century. Industrial enterprise involves manipulation, specialization, direction. Commerce is much more dependent on persuasion, consensus, agreement. Industry places great emphasis on maximizing the output of autonomous units. Its test is efficiency; its formal relation to other economic units is confined to relatively few specific needs. The essence of commerce is exchange. Its sensitivity to social trends is therefore considerably greater. Industry seeks above all autonomy. Commerce strives for an enlightened social environment. It is no accident that the businessmen most successful in government have represented banking, the quintessence of commercial exchange.

Finally, it must not be forgotten that the managerial group has the most to lose from instability. It is composed, after all, of the individuals with the "biggest stake" in society. All their instincts will impel them to work within the existing system. Most of them are primarily interested in concrete technical matters and not in political abstractions. Their pragmatism provides a powerful incentive to adjust to any system that does not become unduly arbitrary. Their emphasis on technique causes them to be generally uninterested in political ideas. Industrialists are unlikely material for revolutions or even for political struggle.

This is not to say, of course, that industrialists in the West are not interested in democracy. No doubt, they hold the values of their society as deeply as anyone else. But they are not brought to these convictions by the industrial process. Where the managerial group is devoted to democratic values, it proves the predominance of the social environment over the values of economic organization.

As a result, Communism in many respects represents a monstrous historical joke. When Marxism was formulated, it held that the abuses of nineteenth-century industrialism were due to private ownership. It is now obvious that the human problems of large-scale industry have much less to do with who possesses title to the plant than with the ethos and beliefs of those who administer it. The irony of Communism is that most of the evils it ascribed to capitalism—many of which were real enough—have become magnified and have grown more intractable under the Communist system.

The abuses of the nineteenth-century industrialism which spawned Marxism were due above all to the enthronement of efficiency and productivity as the primary goals. The real evil was that the values of the industrial process achieved primacy over those of human dignity. Economic development is, of course, always a painful process for the generation which must implement its early stages. Capital accumulation is achieved by deprivation in the present for the sake of the future. Industrialization requires social discipline and a system of values which justifies deprivation and makes it acceptable. In the West, these values were provided by the theory of laissez-faire economics combined with principles of limited government and they were buttressed by convictions of religious origin such as the Calvinist belief in the virtue of effort and perseverance. The result was a heretofore unimaginable degree of capital accumulation.

In time the abuses of this system were ameliorated for reasons which Marx did not foresee. Political democracy and the universal franchise were to prove inconsistent with excessive economic inequality. Popular participation in political life in time proved more significant than the belief that economic affairs were outside the scope of government. In all countries with universal suffrage economic conditions increasingly became a social concern. In no case, however, was the fight for political liberty and social reform led by the managerial group as such.

The separation between political and economic legitimacy which provided the impetus for political and social change in the West—partly by accident—does not exist under Communism. In Communist countries, the managerial group possesses not only an economic but a *political* sanction. The elimination of private ownership has not reduced but has enhanced the role of the industrialist. One reason why the process of industrialization has proceeded faster in the Communist world than in capitalist countries has been the availability of a political framework which has made possible exactions unthinkable by purely economic means. The irony of Communism is that it repeats most of the evils of nineteenth-century capitalism without supplying the means for ameliorating them through the political process. No political organization for expressing grievances exists. The very possibility is dismissed by definition—in a state owned by the workers no social injustice is possible. Any manifestation of dissatisfaction consequently is treated as treason. The fusion of politics and economics which made feudalism so persistent in agricultural societies has reappeared in the Communist states.

The Communist system is in many respects the feudalism of the industrial epoch. Its managers, like the feudal lords, combine political and economic power and their authority is as difficult to assail by those below them. The managers may insist on constitutional forms—on a Magna Carta of legal principles. But they are not likely to be more concerned about freedom in general than were the feudal lords who exacted the original Magna Carta. It is well to remember that it took five hundred years before the principles of the Magna Carta were thought to apply to the population at large and then the fight for democratic institutions was not led by the feudal class.

The experience of "liberal" Communist regimes such as Poland supports rather than contradicts this view. Pressure for liberalization came not from the groups produced by the industrial process, but rather from traditional segments of society: the church demanding autonomy, the intellectuals invoking Western values of freedom of thought, the peasantry insisting on private ownership of their land, and nationalists inspired by the traditional Polish yearning for independence.

But how about the collateral effects of industrialization, such as the spread of education? Will not education produce a questioning spirit incompatible with autocratic rule? Can an educated society continue to be regimented? There can be little doubt that compulsory, universal education has a profound impact. It is doubtful, however, whether it inevitably produces liberalization, first because the "questioning spirit" may not suffice to bring about liberalization, and second because education does not necessarily have to foster an attitude that is critical of political life.

Of course, respect for the critical faculty is of the essence in a free society. The question is, however, whether freedom can be won—as contrasted with being maintained—simply by its exercise. Basic transformations of a society can be achieved in one of two ways: through persuasion or through violence. In practice they have usually been unattainable without some measure of the latter. Even in Great Britain in the nineteenth century, where violence was avoided, the awareness that it might occur and the example of the French Revolution spurred the enactment of the early Reform Bills. Whether the emphasis is on persuasion or on struggle, however, it is not the questioning spirit as such but the affirmation of some absolute value that transforms societies.

When skepticism becomes an end in itself, it can easily lead to stagnation or resignation. Where nothing is certain, nothing will be strongly maintained. This may make for ease of relations in a stable society. It does not provide the motivation for running risks. And without a willingness to sacrifice no entrenched system can possibly be altered. The phrase "give me liberty or give me death" may be trite. But liberty may indeed require a readiness to face death on its behalf. The power of despotism can be confirmed as much by its subjects' lack of conviction as by its own inherent dynamism.

Be that as it may, education does not necessarily produce a critical attitude relevant to political action. Democratic theory of the eighteenth and nineteenth centuries was the product of many factors: the secularization of the concept of the uniqueness of the individual soul which originated in Christian theology, the scientific revolution, a rationalistic philosophy asserting the pre-eminence of reason. All these together led to the notion of the "universal man" capable by the exercise of his reason of judging all facets of human experience. The pre-eminent field of study was philosophy —the effort to give significance to life itself.

Such an education tended to produce independent political

judgment. It is much less clear, however, whether the same is true in the twentieth century. Education is or can be made largely vocational. It can be made to repeat the specialization of an industrial society. And specialization in day-to-day life is purchased at the price of considerable ignorance of most other fields.

Even in the field of science, the correlation between scientific and political freedom is far from absolute. Studying Hegel or Kant or Locke produces reflection and concern about the nature of authority and freedom. The study of physics and chemistry need not. It is true that the scientific spirit requires a willingness to accept whatever results research may reveal. But this presupposes an autonomy of the scientific sphere, not freedom as such. In science there is a certain manipulative element which in a different social context than ours may prove by no means inconsistent with "forcing men to be free."

In short, the values which are often described as the inevitable consequence of social evolution need not necessarily be reproduced in other societies with different traditions and different political structures. The notion that each citizen is entitled to an opinion in political matters or is capable of forming one is characteristic of Western political development. It is not nearly so self-evident as nineteenth-century thought assumed.

Throughout the medieval period, for example, it was held that justice and rationality were defined by a divine standard. Not having been established by man, this standard could not be changed by any political process, including majority rule. The interpretation of the prevailing doctrine was in the hands of the Church, and within the Church it was the responsibility of the hierarchy.

This was not thought inconsistent with fostering education; it was, after all, the Church which had salvaged the West's store of knowledge in the Dark Ages and maintained the system of education into the modern period. Yet it would never have occurred to a layman, no matter how well educated, that he had a voice in Church affairs. Rebellion occurred not in the name of freedom but as a different interpretation of the basic orthodoxy. Inevitably, it arose from within the ranks of those entitled to hold views on spiritual matters: the priesthood. It took the form of heresy, not of a struggle for liberty. The freedom demanded was not that of doctrinal independence but that of imposing a different doctrine. The pluralism of the West arose in the first instance because groups demanded freedom for themselves, not freedom in the abstract.

From the ideological point of view, the Communist regime resembles a monastic society much more closely than it does the modern democratic state. A priesthood—the Communist party—controls a doctrine of considerable complexity. It relies on a special liturgy with its own vocabulary. Those not part of this monastic order have no right to an opinion. Those within the Communist hierarchy conduct their disputes as a struggle over doctrine. Opposition, when it takes places, expresses itself as a reinterpretation of the existing orthodoxy. Almost invariably it is confined to the circle of those who are authorized to make a political judgment. The monastic nature of Soviet society is shown by the fact that in every struggle for pre-eminence those who were in charge of the doctrine defeated those who relied on the traditional levers of power. Stalin defeated Trotsky and Khrushchev ousted Malenkov, though Trotsky was head of the Red army and Malenkov was in control of the bureaucracy. In both cases, the guardianship of the doctrine proved more powerful than what in other societies had been considered the real elements of strength. Whatever schisms may develop in the Soviet Union are more likely to originate in the Communist party than in the intellectual community or among the industrialists. To the extent that these groups become vocal, they will act politically, not in the capacity of intellectuals or scientists or industrialists, but in their role as Communists.

A fundamental transformation is particularly difficult as long as the Communist ruling groups remain reasonably alert to the task of recruiting the ablest people into their ranks. A revolution always has two prerequisites: a grievance against the existing order and a group of people capable of leadership and willing to pay the price of opposition. The liberal revolutions of the eighteenth and nineteenth centuries were the result of the exclusion of the ablest and most energetic group—the bourgeoisie—from participation in the affairs they considered most significant. Since there was no way by which the most talented people could be integrated or achieve respect, they were a ready-made reservoir of leadership for all opposition. The same group also organized the Russian Revolution.

However, when a career is available to the talented within the existing structure, only the most dedicated will take the road of rebellion and accept the social ostracism which it might involve. The temptation is nearly overwhelming, even for those with serious reservations about the existing system, to seek to improve it from within rather than to overthrow it. The more educated they are and the greater their stake is in society, the more they may prefer a form of collaboration to risking everything on outright opposition. A major obstacle to a dramatic change in the Communist system is posed by the systematic Soviet attempt to integrate the ablest individuals into the existing order through preferment, indoctrination, propaganda, and if necessary, pressure. By constantly recruiting the most talented into its ranks, the Communist hierarchy deprives any opposition of its potential leadership.

Classical democratic theory assumed that the tyranny to be resisted was that of a minority conscious of serving its own ends. When the majority was explicitly excluded from government, both formally and in reality, and was conscious of it, an appeal to democratic values was bound sooner or later to topple the existing structure. However, this theory fitted primarily feudal governments or the crudest versions of one-man rule. The essence of modern totalitarianism is that it justifies itself, not as government by a minority but as the most direct expression of the popular will. Hitler's Germany, Castro's Cuba, Communist Russia and China all claim to represent the will of the people in a more direct way than Western democracy.

And probably they do have the support of the majority. That this support is obtained by propaganda, a rigging of incentives, and the suppression of all alternatives only underlines the fact that modern totalitarianism is an aberration, indeed a caricature, of democracy. Its evolution must take completely different forms from that which produced democratic governments in the feudal period. Change will be much less likely to occur as a result of an upheaval from below than from the weakness inherent in any doctrinaire

orthodoxy: the inability to settle disputes without treating opponents as heretics.

This is not to say that an evolution in Communist societies is
impossible. On the contrary, it is inevitable. No system of government is immune to change. No country has ever maintained an unaltered social structure. But the nature of the transformation is by
no means foreordained. It can move towards liberalization; but it
can also produce the gray nightmare of *1984*. It can lead to the en-
hancement of freedom; it may also refine the tools of slavery. Moreover, the mere fact of a transformation is not the only concern of our
generation. Equally important is the time scale by which it occurs. It
was, after all, no consolation for Carthage that 150 years after its
destruction Rome was transformed into a peaceful *status quo* power.

The process of evolution does not operate so smoothly or in so
clear a direction as it appears to posterity. The pluralism of the
West was the result of hundreds of choices, each of which, if taken
otherwise, could have led to an entirely different result. Though
in retrospect it seems that the tendencies were towards political
liberty, the conscious choices which led to it became concerned with
freedom in the abstract only at the end of a long development.
When the Reformers insisted on the primacy of the individual
conscience, they were not interested in encouraging pluralism.
Rather, they were convinced that all right-thinking people would
inevitably come to the same conclusion. The process by which
democracy emerged had many features peculiar to the West: a
church organization outside the control of the state and therefore
symbolizing the limitation of governmental power; the Greco-
Roman heritage insisting on justice and human dignity; an
emerging bourgeoisie; a stalemate in religious wars imposing
toleration as a practical necessity; a multiplicity of states. Industrialization was by no means the most significant of these factors.
Had any of the others been missing, the course of Western political
evolution could have been radically different.

In short, it is incorrect to think of political evolution as some
kind of fulfillment towards which all roads converge. And it is a
form of abdication to entrust the future to an assumed theory of
evolution. The mechanism of evolution is choice, which to the

actor seems to involve alternatives, though the choice necessarily vanishes once the act is performed. A great deal, therefore, depends on the starting point of the process of evolution and the criteria by which alternatives are resolved. It is necessary to consider the evolutionary process from this perspective.

2. THE PROCESS OF EVOLUTION RECONSIDERED

A HISTORIAN of evolution examines an array of forms which have lived and passed on. They are static and orderly and obviously connected. To such an observer the whole train of evolution has a foreordained appearance. Furthermore, the trend is almost invariably from simple to more complex forms, from "lower" to "higher" types, from lesser to greater elaborations of structure and behavior, from more primitive to more advanced skills. It is only too easy to draw the conclusion that evolution is a directed process, orderly, connected, and moving towards "progress."

But it is only to posterity that evolution appears inevitable. The historian of evolution deals only with successful elements, and the blatantly successful ones at that. He has no way of knowing what was most significant to the participants: the element of choice which determined success or failure. He is bound by the nature of his evidence to dismiss the fact that for every successful adaptation thousands may have tried the road and for a variety of reasons— not necessarily essential to their own nature—have failed. He cannot determine in retrospect whether a very slight change in circumstances might not have made recognized successes out of many failures or whether many brilliant innovations faded out simply because they could not be assimilated by the existing framework. In other words, many experiments may have failed not because they did not represent progress or history but because they anticipated it too much.

Historians fond of evolutionary interpretations tend to overlook the fact that what animated even the successful adaptations was not a theory of evolution but some purpose expressing their inner nature. By the same token, societies have collapsed not because their leaders did not understand what the environment demanded of them but because they understood it only too well. The Austro-Hungarian Empire failed to survive because to adapt to the forces of nationalism and liberalism seemed to its rulers inconsistent with the reason for its existence. It could have participated in the evolutionary process only by giving up its distinctive qualities—the qualities which made life seem worthwhile.

The evolutionary process goes on by means of two seemingly contradictory mechanisms. It is determined in the sense that the span of possible adaptations is delimited by the physical environment, the tradition, and the internal structure of the society concerned. This span may be large or small; it can in some instances even be widened by deliberate actions. But in its general scope it is fixed. At the same time, the process of evolution contains an element of choice.

Those who participate in the process of evolution appreciate through experience—as many current apostles of evolutionary theory do not—that evolution proceeds not in a straight line but through a series of complicated variations. At every step of the road there are turns and forks, which have to be taken for better or worse. The conditions governing the decision may be of the most delicate shading. The choice may appear in retrospect to be nearly random or else to be the only option possible under the prevailing circumstances. In either case, it is the result of the interaction of the whole sum of previous turnings—reflecting history or tradition or values—plus the immediate pressures of the need for survival. Moreover, however random the choice may appear at any given juncture, every successful turn affects the range of options of the next crucial decision.

As society becomes more elaborate and as its tradition is firmly established, the choices with respect to the internal organization grow more restricted. Units at the beginning of the evolutionary road are in a position to make radical shifts of course that are wholly impractical at a later stage. If a highly articulated unit—a society, a people, a complex biological organism—were to make radical shifts, this would do violence to its internal organization, to its history and values as embodied in its structure. At the same time, the more elaborate the structure, the greater in general will be the command over the environment. Then the society, though less adaptable to the environment, may gain an increased ability to shape it in the light of its values. And, if it cannot master the environment, it will become its victim.

The evolutionary movement towards greater internal elaboration and rigidity need not be inexorable. The more pluralistic a society, the longer can the trend towards petrification be deferred and perhaps even avoided. A pluralistic society contains many structures, all subject to more or less continuous change. In such a society parts of the intellectual, cultural and political framework are dying while others are being reborn. If the collapse of the old occurs without catastrophic consequences, and if the new is helped through its infancy, the over-all performance may show great vitality. As in the United States and Great Britain, the evolutionary process can accommodate changes which for other societies might have proved intolerable.

Yet it would be idle to deny the tendencies towards rigidity even in a pluralistic society. Only constant vigilance and a deliberate effort to foster creativity can prevent a decline which history indicates has been the lot of all societies—and often at the moment of their greatest success. Seen in evolutionary terms, there resides in every achievement the potentiality of tragedy. The temptation is often overwhelming to rest on one's accomplishments, all the more so when these have been considerable. Any society can reach a point in its development where it runs the risk of having exhausted all the possibilities of innovation inherent in its structure. Once that point is reached, the society will lose its adaptability. Sooner or later, no matter how great and powerful it appears to be, its environment will outstrip and eventually destroy it. The collapse of nations, then, is due to two factors: internal rigidity coupled with a decline in the ability, both moral and physical, to shape surrounding circumstances.

The inextricable aspect of the evolutionary process is this interplay between internal structure and environment. Close to the beginning of an evolution, the participant has a maximum number of choices and is in the best position to do something about them. But he also has the minimum knowledge by which to evaluate his actions and no tradition in which to set them. Later this framework of understanding expands, as does the possibility for wise decision. At the same time the *scope* of decision is progressively narrowed by the already elaborate structure and the increasing weight of tradition. Once a thoroughly elaborated framework has evolved, it will be to some degree irreversible. Generally, it can be drastically altered only by a revolutionary upheaval which destroys, rather than adapts, the old structure. Such a course almost inevitably has temporarily catastrophic consequences.

The problem of evolution then becomes one of "if youth but knew and age but could." The ideal situation, at least stated abstractly, is to combine the knowledge that comes from older and more sophisticated frameworks with the flexibility and naïveté which are the precious property of the newer and more loosely formed ones.

The problem of how the experience of the older societies can contribute a sense of direction to the flexibility of the new is subtle and complicated, particularly for democracies. It is characteristic of a developed society that it has achieved a certain degree of mastery over its environment. Though the span of its choices is actually smaller than that of a new society, its ability to choose is incomparably greater. To the more developed society, freedom of choice may therefore appear the quality most worthy of emulation. It will seem, moreover, a characteristic so "natural" that it need not be taught. The older society is likely to think of its contribution above all as removing impediments to the freedom of choice rather than infusing choice with purpose. The price the well-established society pays for the spontaneity of its institutions is that they seem self-evident beyond the need for being made explicit. This confers great inward security. It also produces a certain inarticulateness and lack of compassion.

For the new society, on the other hand, lacking well-understood criteria, choice may become most difficult and intractable. The appeal of Communism in many areas is precisely that it takes this burden from the shoulders of the new society. It sets in motion the process of evolution in *some* direction. By establishing criteria of judgment, it eases the problem of decision. And the same basic cause underlies the trend towards authoritarianism in so many new nations.

The vitality that can be imparted at the moment of maximum flexibility early in a society's evolution is well illustrated by the American experience. Few nations at the critical stage of their development have had as able and as sophisticated a group of leaders. The *Federalist Papers* have left a record of the choices made at the beginning of our history and of the deliberate task of political construction. Though many of the institutions have been modified, it is a measure of the original achievement that subsequent developments have been an evolutionary adaptation of the original framework.

And the same can be observed in many of the new countries. The difference of ability in mastering their problems resides not so much in the immediate economic performance as in the capacity to make effective choices. The per capita income of India is much lower than that of Indonesia or Ghana. But India has the benefit of a well-trained civil service and of an experienced leadership group. Of the new nations it is, therefore, in perhaps the best position to resolve its choices wisely and purposefully. It has a good opportunity to establish a framework permitting a rich evolutionary development.

The evolutionary process, then, depends on three factors: its starting point, the values animating the participant (expressed as criteria of choice), and the pressures of the environment. It is of course possible that the requirements of survival are so stark that they permit only one adaptation and only a very small degree of evolution. The Eskimo cultures are probably not conscious of any choice and may indeed possess only a very narrow range of viable alternatives. In the vast majority of cultures, however, the pressures of the environment have been less overwhelming. Various adaptations have proved possible and the initial choice has strongly influenced all subsequent ones.

The expectation of a more or less automatic transformation of societies in the direction of forms familiar to the West is therefore far too simple. In the early stages of evolution, the political framework may depend on seemingly random choices. There was certainly nothing foreordained about the Communist revolution in Russia in 1918. Had the liberal government of Kerensky possessed more dynamic leadership or the Communists a less ruthless one, Russia would probably have established a political structure very similar to that found in Western Europe. After nearly two generations of Communist rule, marked by a dramatic economic development, the possibilities of drastic change are much fewer. There may be a degree of liberalization—indeed there has been—but it will be a liberalization of a *Communist* regime, not an evolution towards a democratic one. The direction and nature of any transformation will be determined by the structure built up over forty years of Communist rule. We could make no worse mistake than to apply to it the criteria of our own evolution.

Indeed, the nature of evolution explains in part not only the persistence of Communism but also its failure. Contrary to its own expectations, Communism has been most successful in agricultural areas in the process of throwing off feudal rule and at the very beginning of the evolutionary development of industrialization. It has been least successful in the traditional democracies of the West where, by its own doctrine, it was expected to triumph. This is because Communism, both as a road towards economic development and as a type of political organization, is an alternative to Western democracy and not an evolutionary form of it. Where democracy existed in the early stages of industrialization, it was *strengthened* by the process of economic development. The very factors which Marx thought would lead to the collapse of democracy have tended to reinforce it.

Now that Communism has been established for over a generation, the evolutionary process, if anything, works in its favor. Too much should not be made of the loss of ideological fervor in the Soviet Union. For from the point of view of evolution the bureaucratic structures which have developed over a generation will generate their own momentum and may prove more intractable than the early fanaticism. In the early stages of a revolutionary movement, ideology is crucial. Then a great deal depends on the accident of personalities. If for some reason the leading figures disappear, the movement may collapse or alter beyond recognition. The Reign of Terror in France was ended by the elimination of a single man, Robespierre. But after a revolution succeeds in institutionalizing the early personal leadership, it develops structures with their own vested interests. The loss of ideological *élan* will be more than counterbalanced by the suppression of alternatives which were available earlier. The commitment to the existing system grows, moreover, in direct proportion to its successes. A Russian seeing the growth of the Communist empire over the past fifteen years would not naturally come to the conclusion that its system of political organization was basically wrong.

It is as idle to expect Communism, which has been expanding for over a quarter of a century, to transform itself into a democratic government, as was Lenin's opposite assumption that Communism was an evolutionary successor to democracy. To establish a democratic government of the Western type in the Soviet Union would require not evolution but a revolutionary upheaval. Though change is inevitable, the possibility of influencing it directly is rapidly diminishing. Whatever influence we have will depend less on what we say or even on specific acts of policy than on the creativity of our performance domestically and internationally. If we can be sufficiently vital, the leaders in Communist societies may in time seek to imitate what comes to be considered a more "progressive" system. But the key point is that after a certain stage of evolution the sources of the impetus for change from *within* the system are sharply restricted.

This is why the theories developed in both Great Britain and the United States that even a world-wide triumph of Communism would not prevent an eventual triumph of the values of liberty are so disingenuous. In the face of nuclear war, it is perhaps possible to understand an attitude which places survival above all else. However, it is unforgivable to seek to buttress this conviction with evolutionary theory. It is one thing to assert that war is suicidal. It is quite another to argue that it is possible to have all the benefits of surrender plus the advantage of an automatic evolutionary development which will safeguard our values. Relying on history to ameliorate a despotism is simply a way of deferring to another generation the sacrifices which are likely to become more difficult and perhaps meaningless as time goes on. What would have been Western history if the knights who defeated the Arabs at Tours had surrendered because they believed in the historic inevitability of the triumph of Christianity? Central Europe would today be Moslem. And while some sort of evolutionary development would undoubtedly have taken place, what we consider Western civilization would not have come into being. One can debate the historic significance of this. But there is no sense pretending that there are no turning points and only different roads towards a similar goal.

The prospects of political evolution are different in the new countries from those in the Soviet Union. Here real options are still available because the new countries are at the very beginning of the evolutionary process. Their difficulty is not the weight of a historical framework but the seeming multiplicity of options and the lack of criteria for choosing among them. It is to this problem that we must now turn.

3. EVOLUTION AND THE NEW COUNTRIES

A. The Problem

The problem of political development of the new nations is subtle and our relation to it is highly delicate. On the one hand, the greatest possibility for creativity exists at the very beginning of the evolutionary process, during the first decades of independence. At the same time, this is the period when the pressures of immediate problems are likely to be greatest. The technical task of setting up a going concern may absorb so much energy that little is left for reflection about its purpose. The new nations may hesitate to accept foreign advice and may interpret any attempt by the West to assist political development as simply another form of colonialism.

The inhibitions against offering political advice are almost equally strong on the part of the Western nations. Exporting democracy has become unfashionable. It is thought to constitute interference in the domestic affairs of other states. And many in the West believe that we must revitalize our own institutions before we can concern ourselves with their relevance to the emerging nations.

In these circumstances it has been natural for the West to concentrate on the problem with which it is most familiar and the solution of which has been so insistently demanded by the new nations: that of economic development. The incentive has been all the greater because of the conviction that raising the standard of living would eliminate the basic source of Communist appeal. As capital accumulates and a consumer economy develops, so the argument goes, some enlightened form of government is likely to emerge. The experience of the Marshall Plan in Europe seemed to confirm the existence of a causal relationship between economic progress and political stability.

Unfortunately, the problems of the new nations are infinitely more complicated than were those of Europe after World War II. In Europe the political framework had been elaborated over centuries. The administrative structure was well developed. The societies were cohesive. The threat to existing institutions arose because the war had shattered the industrial plant and because despair was threatening to produce a climate of extremism. By removing the causes of economic discontent, the Marshall Plan revitalized an *existing* political framework.

These conditions do not apply to any emergent nation with the possible exception of India. Economic development, to the extent that it succeeds, also tends to destroy the indigenous political structure, which usually is feudal. At the same time, sustained growth requires capital accumulation and this, in turn, presupposes a system capable of impelling savings. Even in the West, it was necessary to overthrow the feudal system before industrialization could take place. A new political framework preceded or at least accompanied economic development in the democratic countries.

The need for new political structures is even greater in the emerging countries because of their views of the role of the state in the process of development. Growth could, of course, be achieved by largely private measures—though this would not obviate the need for a different political system. In practice, however, all new countries are looking to the state to play the major role in industrialization. Laissez-faire economics is largely irrelevant not because it is unworkable—it works, in fact, best in relatively primitive economies—but because it is politically unacceptable. Indeed, one of the handicaps faced by Western-style democracy is its identification in the minds of many of the new countries with both colonialism and a form of individualism that seems to them largely self-serving. For better or worse, most of the people of the emergent nations judge a political system by the purpose with which it can infuse the social effort.

The problem of political organization thus confronts the new nations at the very beginning of the process of development in an even more acute form than it ever did the West. To rely on economic development to bring about enlightened political institutions is to reverse the real priorities. Whatever political system brings about industrialization may well be confirmed by it.

Here we face a great dilemma. Communism proclaims the unity of politics and economics. It insists on establishing a system of political order as a precondition to economic development. Its successes are due not to the excellence of its *economic* theory but to its *political* ability to mobilize national resources and organize the social effort. The West, on the other hand, has had a tendency to argue that its institutions are not relevant until a certain level of economic well-being has first been achieved. We are repelled by the ruthlessness of the Soviet system of control. Yet we are loath to offer any other, first because we fear that it may be resented and then because it seems to us that exporting democracy is a contradiction in terms.

This attitude is understandable. However, an excess of scruples may cause us to promote an industrialization which in the absence of humane political institutions may merely refine the tools of slavery. Obviously there is no question of imposing our system of government. Our precise institutional arrangements cannot be duplicated in the new nations and it would not be desirable to attempt to do so. The former colonial areas have to find political forms appropriate to their special conditions. Whatever our goals, there are clearly defined limitations to the impact we can have.

But the difficulty of the task does not absolve us from addressing ourselves to it. Unless we are able to make the concepts of freedom and respect for human dignity meaningful to the new nations, the much-vaunted economic competition between us and Communism in the uncommitted areas will be without meaning. If the issue is simply the relative capacity to promote economic development, the outcome is foreordained. In terms of physical capacity to improve output Communism has certainly proved its mettle. If we cannot demonstrate effectively the sacrifice of human dignity at which this increased output has been achieved, the clearer patterns of authority of the Soviet system may become increasingly attractive. If we rely on history to bring about automatically what we lack the conviction to affirm, much less to strive for, we may find that economic progress has been achieved at the cost of the quality of life that gives it meaning.

Of course, under the best of circumstances, a democracy would confront a difficult and delicate task in conveying its values to a new society. Its most cherished qualities are also the least tangible. By its very nature, democracy offers an attitude rather than a doctrine, a process and not a dogma. For societies confused by their problems and searching for definite answers, the democratic method may seem too elusive. The temptation is overwhelming to settle for some form of enlightened authoritarianism and to rely on evolution to ameliorate it.

But this is a delusion. The authoritarianism is likely to become more rather than less well established as times goes on. As it develops its own structure and its own values, the scope for affecting it will constantly diminish. To be sure, the new nations must find forms of democracy appropriate to their own special conditions. But we can hardly expect them to see the relevance of democratic principles and institutions to their circumstances if we do not affirm them ourselves.

It would be idle to deny that there is reason for serious concern about the future of freedom in the new countries. Democracy in the West grew out of a long tradition according to which the standards of justice were rooted either in the essential nature of man or in a divine dispensation, or both. The actions of governments were to be judged by criteria which, not being made by man, could not be abolished by government. When democracy developed, this conviction was embodied in specific institutions designed to safeguard individual rights. The postulate of the uniqueness of the individual and the belief that he was the repository of ultimate values had two consequences: they protected the individual against the exercise of arbitrary power and they produced the conviction that every citizen by the mere fact of being a citizen was entitled to make a political judgment and to participate in the political process. A certain constitutionalism—whether formal, as in the United States, or tacit, as in Great Britain—has been inseparable from democratic government.

A key test of democracy, then, is not the claim to justice—this can be made by any system—but the limits to which this claim is pressed. A free system, whatever its formal institutions, cannot function unless it is based on self-restraint. There must be some mechanism for dealing with dissent other than by destroying it. To be meaningful, self-restraint must set limits even to the exercise of righteous power.

This presupposes two seemingly contradictory conditions: On the part of the individual it presumes a measure of identification of his welfare with the welfare of society. On the part of society the fulfillment of the individual must be considered intrinsically valuable and indeed the chief reason for the social effort.

If the individual behaves purely selfishly, organized social effort becomes impossible. A truly free co-operative effort requires that a significant majority of the population should be convinced that in exercising self-restraint in matters of conduct and property and passion, it will not simply place itself at a disadvantage with respect to other less inhibited groups. Democratic government faces an almost insuperable dilemma as soon as a substantial minority does not accept its restraints. When this happens, the inevitable result is chaos or a dictatorship.

As for limitations on government, self-restraint must be expressed in some formal institutions. When the mere possession of the tools of power confers legitimacy, opposition will necessarily be treated as subversion or heresy. A vital element of any democratic system is the acceptance of limitation on the exercise of their power by those who are in control. And this limitation must be understood not simply as an act of grace—as an enlightened form of despotism—but as deriving from the nature of man and from the proper function of government. Constitutionalism or the limitation of governmental power is not in itself enough to bring about democracy. But democracy cannot be achieved without it.

Historically, limitations on governmental power have been produced by four factors:

1. *Technical Incompetence.* Limitations on the power of government have often resulted from lack of technical or administrative skill. Effective despotism depends on a ruling group of high morale and great cohesiveness which places the interests of the governing class above the self-interest of its members. In many countries despotism has been tempered by inefficiency and ameliorated by corruption. The governing group, however absolute its power, has been unable to define its goals or to make its policy prevail. Incompetence may have the same practical consequences as self-restraint or constitutionalism.

2. *Tradition.* Limited government can grow out of a set of tacit understandings. Actions are avoided not because they are "illegal" but because they are considered outside the pale of acceptable behavior. For example, there existed no institutions capable of thwarting the will of the kings by "divine right" of the eighteenth century. Still, their power was limited because certain measures were proscribed by tradition. None of the "absolute" monarchs of the eighteenth century could have levied direct taxes or conscripted his subjects into the army. It remained for the French Revolution and its notion of the general will—implying the irrelevance of traditional restraints—to expand governmental power into areas theretofore not even imagined.

The democracies which have been most successful have been those based on essentially aristocratic forms. Aristocracies by their very structure must oppose the pre-eminence of a single person and therefore oppose absolutist rule. Likewise, they are based on a concept of quality inconsistent with the excesses of egalitarian democracy. Without the self-restraint produced by such beliefs, democratic institutions can become the means for the most violent form of repression. The majority—by definition representing the people—may recognize no limits to the exercise of its rule and treat all dissent as sedition. At the same time, if democracy is to remain vital or even meaningful, the aristocratic concept cannot remain the province of a minority. The challenge to democracy—and not only in the new nations—is whether an entire society can live by values which in previous centuries were thought to be the virtue of small minorities. A democracy that does not set its sights this high is likely to fall prey either to conformity or to dictatorship.

3. *Legal Institutions.* In a few countries a written constitution serves as the final arbiter of the permissible sphere of governmental action. Though the limitation on authority is more formal than in the traditional societies, it is produced by similar factors. Formal constitutional restraints have been effective only in societies with a well-established tradition of respect for legal forms. Where this respect has been lacking, constitutions have turned into tools in the struggle for power. Far from being means to restrain political power, they have become an expression of it. Their standing is like that of any other law which can be altered by government. This has been the role of constitutions in many countries of Latin America. It has also been the function of the many French constitutions since the Revolution.

4. *A Conviction That Politics Does Not Matter.* Throughout the nineteenth century, the conviction was general that the primary function of government was to create a framework for the free play of the ultimately decisive economic forces. When government is viewed negatively, freedom comes to be seen as the absence of re-straint. Authority is thought to have a utilitarian and not an ethical function. Its task is considered regulatory, not directive. Society in a sense is then ruled extra-governmentally by social or economic pressures, by "things that are taken for granted."

These four factors are missing to a greater or lesser degree in the new countries. Economic growth requires an increase in technical and administrative competence. One of the chief goals of all development programs is to improve governmental efficiency. But as administrative skill increases, so will the technical ability to repress liberty. If the growth in technical competence is not matched by respect for human dignity and by institutions which express this, industrialization will make possible a degree of governmental pressure hitherto prevented or at least mitigated by administrative incompetence.

Nor can tradition provide a focus for self-restraint. Most of the new nations have developed in rebellion against their own past. They tend to blame it for the weakness which made colonialism possible. To the extent that they lose the cohesiveness afforded by custom they may have no alternative except to substitute force. It is the same with legal restraints. Formal constitutional prohibitions have proved empty in almost every new nation with the possible exception of India. There has been hardly any greater hesitation to alter the constitutions of the new countries than there has been to amend their laws. Many provisions of the constitution of Ghana can, for example, be changed by a simple majority.

Finally, the belief that the task of government is essentially regulatory—however useful in limiting the exercise of authority in the nineteenth century—is almost without relevance in major areas today. All the new nations see in the state a chief instrument for social and economic progress. Above all, it is the primary unifying force.

Constitutionalism depends to a considerable extent on a shared common purpose. But most of the new countries have great difficulty in precisely this respect. A revolution—and the anti-colonial struggle is no exception—is usually inspired by motives of negation. The desire to overthrow the *status quo* may unite the most diverse points of view. Inevitably positive programs are submerged in the immediate need for success. This is why in their hour of victory so many revolutions—including many of the newly independent countries—continue to manufacture enemies at home or abroad. The need for an enemy is directly proportional to the lack of a commonly felt purpose. It is a substitute for a sense of direction, a nostalgia for the unity of the revolutionary struggle.

The more successful the effort to sweep away the existing structure, the greater may be the difficulty of finding an adequate consensus for positive action. Revolutionaries are generally subject to the illusion that the new order for which they strive will have all the benefits of their ideals added to the advantages of the old structure. But victory reveals that every action has a price. New departures are obtainable only at the sacrifice of the stability and regularity that had been taken for granted.

Almost all the new countries find themselves in this position. The period of exaltation is over. Contrary to all expectation, the task of construction has emerged as less glamorous and more complex than the struggle for freedom. For a while resentment of the former colonial ruler can serve as a focus for unity. But sooner or later positive goals must replace the former resentment as a motive force. In most of the new nations this unifying function must be performed by the state.

Many of the new countries are the products neither of a common history nor of a common culture nor even of a common language —the unifying forces of European nationalism. The primary factor of cohesion very frequently is the common experience of colonial rule. Frontiers—particularly in Africa—reflect the administrative convenience of the former colonial powers or the outcome of imperial struggles. Most of the new states therefore are in quest not only of independence but of identity. They lack a social consciousness or they are split up into competing groups, each with a highly developed sense of identity.

When social cohesiveness is slight, the struggle for the control of authority becomes increasingly bitter. When government is the chief, sometimes the sole, expression of national identity, opposition tends to be considered treason. Many leaders of the new nations insist that political parties are unnecessary in their countries because the national purpose is generally shared. Quite the reverse is likely to be the case. So far as these statements do not reflect merely a desire to hold on to power—and it is well to remember that the notion that power might be relinquished voluntarily is both subtle and recent—they indicate an awareness of the centripetal forces of the new nation. It may be difficult to imagine intermediary points between total rule and chaos.

When social schisms are deep, the question as to which group rules can turn into a matter of life and death. The rule of the majority is bearable only if the minority can hope to transform itself at some point into a majority. The knowledge that any majority is temporary sets limits to the exercise of authority or to the violence of opposition. But where there exists a permanent majority, democracy has a hollow ring to all other groups—especially when these groups have a strongly developed sense of identity. Under those conditions the struggle for power takes on the characteristics of a civil war.

These difficulties are magnified by the economic conditions in the new countries and by the low level of education. When the most elementary wants are not met, liberty can easily appear as a useless abstraction. Though democracy survived the deprivations of nineteenth-century industrialism, expectations were not so high then and totalitarian alternatives were unavailable. The future of democracy requires that political freedom and economic progress do not appear antithetical.

Equally worrisome is the general educational level of most of the emerging nations. Democracy originally was based on the assumption of a citizenry capable of judging political issues and of being persuaded by rational appeals. These notions are altered radically when the electorate has an illiteracy rate of 90 per cent. At a moment when the government plays a very large role and the issues are much more complicated than in the early stages of Western democracy, the ability to define these issues is extremely circumscribed because of lack of sophistication on the part of both the leadership and the population. A premium is placed on propagandistic technique over substance. Demagoguery is encouraged. The rewards are for mobilizing mass emotions. Many pressures make for the emergence of the totalitarian form of democracy—a Caesarism which mocks the maxim of consent of the governed because it manufactures consent by pressure or blackmail.

The pressures in the direction of some form of totalitarianism derive also from psychological factors. The leaders of independence movements have sustained themselves through years of deprivation by visions of the transformations to be wrought after victory was achieved. To surrender power or to admit even the possibility of giving it up in their hour of triumph seems to many of them a negation of all their struggles. And having fought often while in a small minority and against heavy odds, they are not likely to be repelled by the notion that it is possible to "force men to be free."

It may be argued, of course, that this is an inevitable transitional phase. An authoritarian government can bring about the conditions of social, economic and educational advance without which democracy is empty. This, however, is an illusion. It is not only that industrialization has a tendency to strengthen the political system which brings it about. It is also that the leaders who achieve authority in these conditions do not normally conceive it to be their task to encourage democracy or know how to do so even if they profess it as a goal. Overwhelmed by the pressures of day-to-day problems, they are only too likely to be impatient about opposition or about even the possibility of dissent. They are placed in the office, after all, for their ability to get things done. Their strength is manipulation; their motive, to bring about personally inspired solutions. Ideally the authoritarian leader—if his emergence proves unavoidable—should be a teacher patiently bringing his people into the political dialogue without which democracy cannot function, encouraging respect for diversity and a sense of reverence for the human personality. It is rare, almost accidental, to find a leader who has the drive and sense of power to achieve authoritarian rule and yet is sufficiently self-effacing to work towards a limitation of his power.

All of this suggests that unless we address ourselves to the problem of encouraging institutions which protect human dignity, the future of freedom is dim indeed. To be sure, we may fail. But in such grave matters the unforgivable sin is not to have failed but never to have tried.

B. *The Opportunity*

There is no sense pretending that the problem of political development is very amenable to outside influence. The former imperial powers in particular—or those identified with them in the eyes of the new nations—have to behave with restraint, lest proffered assistance be construed as an attempt to establish a new and subtler form of control. Nevertheless, we delude ourselves if we believe that, as the leading nation in the free world, we do not affect other countries by acts either of omission or of commission. Economic assistance is a form of intervention and, by the claims of those who rely on the impact of economic evolution, a kind of political manipulation.

Moreover, while direct pressure would undoubtedly be resented, we do have many moral ties with the emerging nations. The values which we affirm and on which our society is based have also provided the impetus for most of the revolutions in the formerly colonial areas. The anti-colonial upheaval can even be considered one of the great conversions of history. When colonialism was first established it was not considered "foreign" by its subject peoples. The conquest of vast areas in Asia and Africa by very small numbers of Europeans was possible because the imperial powers replaced an existing ruling group according to patterns established for centuries. The mass of the population did not expect to participate in government and did not much care who ruled it if the exercise of authority was not too oppressive.

Had the imperial powers been content to rest their rule on the mere fact of being in power, colonialism might have continued for decades longer. Instead, they justified their imperialism on the grounds that it was designed to help the subject peoples towards self-government. However hypocritical this justification may have been, it proved in time inconsistent with the maintenance of imperial rule. The imperial powers imported into the colonial areas the twin doctrines of rational administration and popular participation in government which ultimately raised the very issue of their "foreignness." At the same time, they provided education in European universities for a small but able group of the indigenous populations which became committed to the values of human dignity, popular participation in government, and economic and social progress—and these very values were then invoked to overthrow colonialism.

The fact that almost all the leaders of the independence movements were educated in the countries against whose rule they later rebelled and that almost invariably they fought the imperial powers in the name of the principles learned from them accounts in part for the weakness of the resistance, especially in British territories.

It also explains why the anti-colonial upheaval has been most active where European rule was most enlightened and not where it was most oppressive. Where Europeans ruled by the mere fact of having seized power and where the tradition of the Enlightenment was weakest in the imperial center—as, for example, in the Portuguese territories—the independence movements have been least effective. When an effort was made to educate the local population in the doctrines of the West, opposition to imperial rule was most persistent. It was the *moral success* of the imperial powers which undermined their political rule.

Most of the new nations emerged into independence with constitutions in the Western mold and a political system drawn from the European example. The rights of man, the transcendent importance of human dignity, even the necessity of a party system, were unquestioningly accepted. Crises in many nations have arisen because it has not proved possible to transplant institutions and ideas quite so literally. It has become apparent that the seeming spontaneous development of Western institutions—in any case probably exaggerated in the eyes of the colonial peoples—was actually the product of a long historical process. As a result, values which seemed self-evident only a decade ago have become tarnished or have become mere incantations to justify the exercise of arbitrary power. The maxims of the origins of independence have been submerged in the expedients of day-to-day affairs or in the frustration of finding the gap between expectation and reality widening instead of narrowing.

While the principles of the Enlightenment are still being affirmed, doubt has arisen about the relevance to the conditions of the new nations. The problem has been made more difficult in Asia, at least, as the generation which struggled for independence is replaced by a leadership group less familiar with Western values and less committed to them. The easy conclusion is that the early enthusiasm for the values of liberty was a misunderstanding—that they have no relevance to the problems of the new nations.

But such a view is a counsel of despair. To be sure, in societies rent by social and cultural schisms, Western institutions are sometimes unworkable. For transitional periods, some form of authoritarian rule may be inevitable as a last resort. But where it is—and it is well to remember that this so-called inevitability is often a reflection of the lack of vitality of democratic ideas—a great deal depends on the attitude with which it is accepted, whether as a regrettable necessity or as desirable because efficient. At the least, every effort should be made to maintain the vitality of the principles of freedom which animated the struggle for independence. Just as colonialism was ultimately defeated by the values to which it paid lip service, so the affirmation of the values of human dignity and liberty may in time prove inconsistent with despotic rule. A cult of efficiency as the ultimate value, an obsession with economic progress as the primary standard, will mean the perpetuation and strengthening of all absolutism through the very process of industrialization.

It would be beyond the scope of this book to deal in detail with the problem of political development. The comments made here are offered not as a prelude to a master plan for "political aid." They are intended primarily as an appeal to recognize a problem which has been largely neglected or about which we have felt a tendency to throw up our hands in resignation. The challenge of the new nations is that they cannot live by bread alone; to offer nothing but bread is to leave the arena to those who are sufficiently dynamic to define their purpose.

Before we can deal with this problem we must admit its reality. Democracy is doomed if the leading democratic countries behave with diffidence about their fundamental values and do not make even the intellectual effort to explore their relevance to the new nations. In a crucial sense, then, the future of freedom abroad will depend importantly on the conviction with which we can confirm freedom at home. We cannot be convincing to others unless we convince ourselves. For too long our affirmations of human dignity have been mere incantations, our search for purpose a mechanical repetition of patterns of the past. The young men and women from the underdeveloped countries studying in our universities may learn many technically useful things. But it is questionable whether they sense the same vitality that inspired their grandfathers in European universities seventy-five years ago.

However self-righteous and hypocritical the Victorians and Edwardians may appear in retrospect, they left a more profound imprint on the rest of the world than their more skeptical, perhaps even insecure, grandchildren. Their belief in human dignity and freedom, however inadequately practiced, was deeply held. These principles spread across the world even in the face of imperialism and economic evils within the Western countries. It is doubtful that the West can give the same impetus while it argues that peace and domestic stability will result above all from an economic process whose chief feature is an obsession with consumption. If the West is serious about assisting the political evolution of the emerging countries, it should ask itself whether its own principles possess enough vitality to seem relevant to the concerns of these nations.

One of the difficulties we face in contributing to the political modernization of other countries is that we have not fully grasped the implications of our own modernization. It is not only in the new countries that democratic government is inhibited by illiteracy. In our own there is considerable illiteracy about many of the issues confronting us. We have rarely come to grips with questions such as these: What is the relevance of the democratic process to a subject as technical as the defense budget? What happens to democracy when Presidential candidates conduct research on the image they should project rather than on the substance of their program? What is the future of democracy when the propagandistic side of politics becomes more and more separated from the substantive side? We would have to deal with these questions even if the rest of the world did not exist. If our answers are vital, they may make a contribution also to other nations. If we do not admit even the validity of the questions, the democratic process will be doomed even in the countries of its origin.

Equally fundamental is our domestic performance. It is naïve to believe that the conversion of the colonial areas to the values of the Enlightenment was due entirely to the intrinsic merit of the ideas involved. Western technology and political theory triumphed not only because of their own inherent attractiveness. Their success was due also to the over-all performance of the countries advocating them. The imperial power might be disliked, perhaps even hated, but it was also respected. It seemed to represent power, purpose and progress. The economic and scientific pre-eminence of the West made it easy to see a causal connection between its political institutions and its achievements in other spheres. This is not to say that the values of political liberty and human dignity were not attractive in themselves; it only states that their wide and rapid acceptance in the colonial areas owed a considerable debt to the success of their proponents.

Many of these conditions have fundamentally altered. The rate of material progress of the Soviet system has been faster than ours in too many fields. Starting from a position of substantial inferiority in almost all areas, the Soviet Union has caught up with and surpassed us in more categories than is comforting. The new nations may see in this rate of advance an augury of what they too can attain, if they imitate the Soviet system. And the human cost may not seem so appalling in countries long subject to the ravages of famine and disease. The impact of Sputnik, after all, had little to do with its strategic significance. President Eisenhower's constant claim that space was militarily insignificant—even if correct—missed the crucial point. To many of the new nations Soviet supremacy in space may have the kind of attraction Western technological mastery had in the late nineteenth century.

For many in the emerging nations the Soviet rate of growth seems more significant than our historic achievement. For the foreseeable future, the level of our consumption is unattainable for any of the new countries. They are more interested in discovering a sense of direction than in the contemplation of an economic plateau, however high. An America seemingly fearful of its future, more aware of its risks than its opportunities, may become an object of envy. It cannot be a guide to the future. Nothing we can say will be so impressive as dynamic American performance, an aura of confidence, and a profound sense of purpose.

At the same time, important as is the impact of our performance on the future course of the uncommitted areas, we cannot derive the motive force for our actions from such considerations alone or even primarily. We are not putting on a play for the benefit of a foreign audience. The argument that we must solve the race problem in America because of the impact of segregation on the mind of Africa misstates our proper priority. We must overcome discrimination above all because of its impact on the mind and values of America.

Once we have injected more dynamism into our convictions and our performance, we can address ourselves with greater confidence to the problem of "political aid." This is not to say, of course, that our economic assistance programs will decline in significance. There is no doubt that our goal must be to help the new nations reach the point of self-sustaining economic growth. This requires economic assistance on a substantially larger scale than in the past decade. Indeed, assistance below the amount required to generate growth may do no more than to prevent catastrophe and in some conditions it may be a device for postponing the painful domestic reforms essential if real progress is to be made.

Little can be added here to the extensive economic literature on the subject.[2] It is important, however, to keep in mind the various levels of effort required: On the one hand, there is a need to help make the emergent nations going concerns. On the other hand, more and more nations are striving for the trappings of sovereignty at the precise moment that the nation-state is losing its significance. No country can live in isolation. The quest for autarchy is chimerical and disruptive of the well-being of all nations. Thus, while the United States should be sympathetic to immediate national needs, it should also encourage larger groupings, particularly on a regional basis.

As for the national aid programs, a greater concentration of resources seems indicated. The best method of having a major impact on many countries will be to make a going concern of *one* country. India in Asia, Brazil in Latin America, Nigeria in Africa could become magnets and examples for their regions if we acted with the

[2] See, for example: W. W. Rostow, *op. cit.*, and *The Process of Economic Growth* (New York, 1952); Rostow and M. R. Millikan, *A Proposal: Key to Effective Foreign Policy* (New York, 1957); Barbara Ward, *The Interplay of East and West: Points of Conflict and Cooperation* (New York, 1957). See also *United States Foreign Policy: Economic, Social and Political Change in the Underdeveloped Countries and Its Implications for United States Policy*, U.S. Senate Committee on Foreign Relations Study No. 12, especially Chap. 8, p. 50.

boldness and on the comparative scale of the Marshall Plan. More-over, the critical period for constructive action is before Soviet pressure makes our assistance appear to be a panicky reaction to danger. As late as 1958, a moderate program in Latin America could have become a symbol of United States initiative and of our commitment to a Western Hemisphere Association of free nations. The same program two years later appeared to be an effort to head off Castro. In some respects, it even gave our Latin-American neighbors a stake in the Cuban Revolution because they had every reason to believe that without Castro we would have been much less generous.

Still, for all its technical complexity, economic assistance is perhaps our simplest task in the new nations. Much more complicated is the degree to which we can support the development of democratic institutions. To some extent, of course, we can influence events by giving preferential assistance to countries which meet certain criteria for democratic institutions.

It may be objected that such an approach violates the principle of "aid without strings." And indeed, in the reaction to Mr. Dulles' tendency to use economic aid as an inducement to join military pacts, the phrase "aid without strings" has been elevated almost into dogma. As applied to using economic aid as a form of pressure to obtain military alliances, this is a proper doctrine. But if it leads to a notion—as it frequently does—of assistance without purpose and development without responsibility, it can produce hypocrisy on our side and irresponsibility on the part of the recipient country. No one can expect us to be without motive in giving aid. The new nations should judge us by the quality of our purposes, not by the absence of them. They have a right to object to specific goals we may have, and when they do they should find understanding and respect. They cannot require us to have *no* objectives. We should show restraint in the conclusions we draw from our preferences. But unless we wish to doom ourselves to blandness, we cannot avoid having preferences. If we are serious about promoting economic development in the new nations—as we must be—we have to be serious also about the political structure without which that development is impossible and which will shape the future of the country concerned.

Once we clarify our responsibility in this respect, we will have set a goal which might enlist not only the competence of technical experts but the latent idealism of America. Ideas have never spread automatically and rarely because of their inherent persuasiveness. There has generally been required a group "willing to bear witness." One of the dilemmas of democracy all over the world is that it has not succeeded nearly well enough in enlisting the idealism of the young generation. There are all too few willing to suffer or perhaps even sacrifice themselves on behalf of political liberty—except, ironically enough, in the countries of Eastern Europe where the deprivation of freedom has poignantly demonstrated its significance.

This will not be a simple task. For all the good will, there are in the American cultural mode major obstacles to understanding the revolution of our time and in contributing a sense of direction to it.

There are at least three reasons for this state of affairs. First, the psychological problem of understanding the nature of revolutionary leadership already mentioned is reinforced by a tendency to think of man as largely motivated by economic considerations. Nothing seems more natural than to "get ahead in the world," by which we generally mean material advancement. The "reasonable" course of action for a Castro or a Nasser to follow, it seems to us, is to concentrate on the economic development of his country. We fail to give enough attention to the fact that those who seek material advancement never enter revolutionary movements during their periods of struggle. What makes the deprivation and hazard of the early days of a revolutionary movement supportable is the prospect not of wealth but of power. The same qualities which cause a Castro or a Nasser to appear "wild men" by our standards also make them effective revolutionary leaders. It is therefore generally useless to appeal to this type of revolutionary to dedicate himself to running the domestic affairs of his country. Were Castro to place pre-eminent stress on Cuba's economic development, he would have to engage in detailed, to him no doubt boring, administrative measures. The best he could hope for would be to head a small, progressive country—perhaps a Switzerland of the Caribbean. Compared with leading a revolution throughout Latin America, this goal would appear to him trivial, indeed unreal.

The second factor is a corollary of the first. We consider an appeal to empirical reality a conclusive argument. We therefore find it difficult to follow the reasoning of many of the leaders of new countries who erect elaborate verbal structures on the basis of unproven assumptions or the Communist method of repeating slogans as if the mere act of repetition could make them come true. When Castro harangues crowds for four hours, we are prone to smile with an attitude of superiority. We tend to refute Communist charges by "proving" the lack of correspondence of their statements with empirical reality. But empirical reality is much less significant for individuals whose *raison d'être* is the desire to *change* reality. For them "true" reality consists not of what empirical study reveals but rather of the world they wish to bring about. To them, the vision of the changed world for which they are striving is much more "real" than the circumstances against which they are rebelling. It is much too easy to say that a Castro—or Nasser or Lumumba—is lying. It would be more nearly true to say that they have different standards of truth and reality than we.

The third cause for our lack of rapport with the contemporary revolution may be the most fundamental. Involved in the difficulty of communication between us and many of the new nations may be a clash between the separate lines of thought that since the Renaissance have distinguished the West from the part of the world now called underdeveloped (with Russia occupying an intermediary position). We are deeply committed—perhaps more deeply than we realize—to the notion that the real world, as we think of it, is external to the observer. Knowledge consists of recording and classifying it— the more accurately the better. Other cultures which escaped the early impact of Newtonian thinking have retained and expanded the essentially pre-Newtonian view that the real world is almost completely *internal* to the observer.

This attitude, which for so many centuries was a liability—for it prevented the countries holding it from developing the resources of technology and consumer goods which the West enjoyed—now becomes a tool of immense power, particularly if ruthlessly and deliberately used. It enables them to alter reality by distorting the perspective of the observer—a process which because of our cultural mode we are largely unequipped to handle or even to perceive.

And they can do this without even sacrificing technological progress. Technology comes as a gift; acquisition in its advanced form does not require the philosophical commitment that its development imposed on the West. Empirical reality has a much different significance for the new countries (with Russia again in a middle position) than for the West, for in an important sense they never went through the act of discovering it. At the same time, the difference in cultural modes causes us to appear selfish, cold, even supercilious, because the part of existence which is most meaningful to many outside the West is sometimes not even recognized as significant by us.

All of this suggests that the revolutionary leaders of our time fill above all a spiritual void. Even Communism has made many more converts through the theological quality of Marxism than through the materialistic aspect on which it prides itself. This explains the appeal of Communism among university students all over the world, despite the fact that this group has most opportunity to note its logical inconsistencies or the discrepancy between profession and reality. This makes comprehensible the acceptance in so many quarters of the sterile Communist justifications, that a Communist state being owned by the people is by definition just, however repressive, or that a socialist state, however bellicose, is really serving the cause of peace. The intellectual content of the Communist appeal may be shallow. But in the absence of a real alternative it has a clear field.

Of course, the United States cannot match the demagoguery of a Castro or the ruthless propagandistic manipulations of Communist leaders, nor should it seek to do so. We can compete only in terms of *our* values and *our* beliefs. But it is not inherent in our values to consider the contest for the minds of men as primarily a problem of salesmanship or to deal with the contemporary revolution, if at all, primarily as an economic phenomenon. Nothing we do can appeal ideologically to a Castro or to a dedicated Communist. But we *can* appeal to the millions on whose hopes and aspirations totalitarianism feeds. The crude interpretation of the Newtonian view of reality is already discarded in the West by its most sensitive thinkers. Domestically, many thoughtful observers are questioning the cult of productivity for its own sake. We therefore have come a long way towards the recognition of the importance of the intangible factors on which the future political relationships of the world may well depend. As we gain in compassion and understanding, there is every prospect that we can infuse the values of human dignity and freedom with enough vitality so that the younger generation all over the world will feel obliged to come to grips with them emotionally and intellectually. The argument that this kind of spiritual élan is beyond the capability of democracy is equivalent to saying that democracy is doomed.

4. The New Countries and International Relations

The problems of political and economic development would be difficult enough in their own right. They are complicated by the fact that the new nations find themselves drawn into international affairs to an unprecedented degree. While building a state and seeking to realize the most elementary aspirations of their people, they are being wooed, asked to form judgments or to assume international responsibilities. Whether they have joined political or military groupings or remained neutral, the contest for their favor has continued to rage. The result has been a diversion of the energies of the new states and a demoralization of international relations.

The United States approach to the new nations has not helped matters. As in most other fields of policy we have been going from one extreme to the other. For a time we acted as if the only political significance of the new nations was as potential military allies in the Cold War. The quest for neutrality was officially condemned. Great efforts were made to induce new nations to join security pacts. Within the space of a few years this policy has been replaced by its precise opposite. Instead of castigating neutrality we have been almost exalting it. Instead of seeking to create security pacts, we have conducted ourselves in a manner which may make allies, at least those outside the North Atlantic area, doubt the wisdom of close association with the United States. The oversimplification which could see no political role for the new nations outside the Cold War has been replaced by another oversimplification based on the premise that the "real" contest is for the allegiance of the uncommitted. We sometimes act as if we and the Communists were engaged in a debate in the Oxford Union, with the uncommitted nations acting as moderators and awarding a prize after hearing all arguments.

The questions arise, however, whether the exaltation of non-commitment is not as pernicious as the previous period of alliance-building and whether there is not an inconsistency between the desire of the new nations to be neutrals and their desire to be arbiters.

To begin with, there is a certain ambivalence, if not disingenu-ousness, in the sudden deference paid to neutrality. The impression is sometimes overwhelming that the difference between the approach to the new nations identified with Mr. Dulles and that which urges America "to respect neutrality" is primarily one of method as to how to win over the uncommitted areas. Both are designed to bring the new nations somehow to our side. Mr. Dulles thought the way to do so was to castigate their neutralism. Many of those who see in the new countries the arbiters of international relations imply that the way to win their friendship is to respect their desire for non-involvement. Both assumptions are based on an illusion.

For it is highly doubtful whether on a great variety of issues dividing the world *any* policy can win the support of the uncom-mitted. There is a tacit assumption in much of American discussion that the non-commitment of the new nations is due in large part to our failure to "present our case properly" or to the fact that the new nations have certain positive views which we have failed to take into account. But this line of reasoning fails to do justice to a com-plicated situation. On most issues, except those affecting them most directly, the new nations will take a position somewhere between the contenders regardless of their view of the intrinsic merit of a given dispute. Neutrality seems more important than any particular dis-pute because the new nations' image of themselves as well as their bargaining position depends on maintaining it: "Neither side has won us," said an African diplomat during the 1960 session of the General Assembly, "and we are determined that neither side will."[3]

[3] *New York Herald Tribune*, October 7, 1960.

America, of all countries, should be sympathetic to this state of mind. In the first 150 years of our existence no conceivable British policy could have led to an American alliance or even to American support on policies outside the Western Hemisphere. Our desire not to become involved was stronger than any views we may have had on international issues, save those affecting the Western Hemisphere most urgently. Nothing Britain could have said or done would have induced us formally to take sides. Throughout, we would have resented being asked to assume responsibilities and our predisposition would have been to invent reasons for not doing so. And if Britain had sought to meet our criticisms we would have invented new ones. The desire to remain aloof from world affairs was stronger than any views we might have had on the disputed issues.

There is no question, then, that we ought to respect the desire of the new nations to remain aloof from world affairs. The problem arises when the laudable view that we should *accept* their neutrality is transformed into an *exaltation* of non-commitment. Whatever the wisdom of such groupings as the South East Asia Treaty Organization (SEATO) when they were formed—and it would probably have been wiser to avoid them—it is surely going too far to seem to pay greater attention to neutrals than to allies. The correct attitude that we should not press the new nations to join alliances must not be carried to the extreme of discouraging those who have made a different choice. When non-commitment becomes a cult, slogans such as "appealing to world opinion" can easily turn into excuses for inaction or irresponsibility.

Again, our national experience can serve as a guide to understanding the problem. If Great Britain in 1914 or 1939 had made its resistance to German aggression dependent on American support (not to speak of that of other powers) the course of history would have been radically different. Neither the invasion of Belgium nor the attack on Poland seemed to Americans at the time to involve our interests sufficiently to justify giving up our neutrality. And no British policy, however respectful of our neutrality, could have induced us to forego this role.

It is no different with many of the new nations. They will take a stand against dangers which seem to them to affect their vital interests. They will not take a stand on problems which seem to them far away, or, if they do, it may make the situation worse rather than better, as will be seen below. The Chinese brutality in Tibet made an impression in India, whereas the equally brutal Soviet repression in Hungary did not. Despite all moralistic protestations to the contrary, the reason for the difference in attitude was practical and not theoretical. Chinese pressure on India's borders was a concrete danger and the events in Hungary simply were not. Though it is true that our policies with respect to the new nations have often been maladroit, it does not follow that different policies can change their non-alignment.

To be sure, the new nations sometimes create the opposite impression because their own attitude toward non-commitment is at least as ambivalent as ours. All too often, they couple insistence on respect for their neutrality with an attempt to play the arbiter's role in international affairs. But the arbiter's role implies that they will support one of the parties if they can be convinced of the correctness of its position. It is an invitation to a courtship. It encourages the pressure which is said to be resented.

Many of the leaders of the new states want the best of two worlds: of neutrality and of judging all disputes. They are flattered by the rewards that fall to the uncommitted in the competition of the major powers. For many of them, playing a role on the international scene seems more dramatic and simpler than the complex job of domestic construction. Many domestic problems are intractable. Almost all of them require patient, detailed efforts and their results are frequently long delayed. Domestically, each action has a price. But on the international scene, it is possible to be the center of attention simply by striking a pose. Here ambitious men can play the dramatic role so often denied to them at home and so consistent with their image of the role of a national leader.

Unfortunately, the same factors that make entry on the international arena so tempting—the possibility of being wooed, the chance of escaping from complicated domestic problems—also militate against the seriousness of the effort. It is the symbolic quality of international forums that is most attractive to many of the leaders of the new nations. They welcome an opportunity to declaim on the general maxims which never seem to apply quite so simply at home or to the foreign policy problems in which the uncommitted nation is directly concerned. But they are much less willing to assume substantive responsibilities, particularly in areas not directly related to their immediate interests.

If the new nations are encouraged to arbitrate all disputes, the impact on international relations will have to be demoralizing. Non-commitment will thereby defeat its own object. It will be merely another reason for occupying a place at the center of all disputes.

The utility of common action for carrying out tasks on which a real world opinion already exists is not at issue. For example, long ago we ought to have taken the lead in fostering a substantial economic assistance program through the United Nations. But it is essential to recognize that on many of the most difficult international problems there is no such thing as a meaningful world opinion. It is simply asking too much of the new nations which barely have achieved independence to help settle disputes of the technical complexity of disarmament.

The argument has often been heard that one of the obstacles to a wise United States policy on arms control is the absence of adequate technical studies. Yet our sophistication in this field is incomparably greater than that of any new nations, most of which do not have even one person studying the problem full-time. They have no modern weapons arsenal of their own to give them an understanding of strategic problems. They have no technical staffs to study the subject. What they do have is a volatile public opinion at home. In these circumstances, the new nations easily can fall prey to Soviet propaganda slogans which sound attractive but which in fact are disguised to disarm the West. The uncommitted are in no position to form a responsible judgment, much less to develop a serious program.

The result of gearing all policy to the presumed wishes of the uncommitted is that many issues are falsified and many problems are evaded. Abstract declarations substitute for concrete negotiations. Diplomacy is reduced to slogans. Pressure for confrontations of heads of state is not accompanied by any detailed program. There are many demands for peace in the abstract, but much less attention is given to defining the conditions which can alone make peace meaningful.

Far from aiding the diplomatic progress which is so insistently demanded, such a process tends to thwart it. Far from "strengthening the United Nations," it may ultimately undermine it. Soviet negotiators will lose any incentive for making responsible proposals, since they will be constantly tempted by opportunities for cheap propaganda victories. The West will grow increasingly frustrated when it finds itself incapable of enlisting the support of the new nations no matter how moderate or reasonable its program. And the new nations will be induced to take positions on issues on which the very act of non-commitment proclaims their disinterest and with respect to which their judgment is often highly erratic. It is not clear why nations said to be in need of assistance in almost all aspects of their national life, many of which have difficulty organizing their own countries, should be presumed to be able to act with more wisdom in relation to the whole gamut of international problems.

Indeed, when neutrality becomes an end in itself, it can lead the uncommitted unwittingly to add their pressure to that of the Communist bloc. The tendency to seek a position separate from the two big blocs can be used by skillful Communist diplomacy to drive back the West step by step.

When countries as varied as India, Yugoslavia, Indonesia, Ghana and the United Arab Republic form a "bloc," they are united above all by two motives: to stay aloof from the disputes of the major powers and to magnify their own influence. This desire is understandable. But it must not lead us to believe that they can be swayed by the logic of our argument or of our proposals. The internal requirements of a neutral bloc will prevent this, apart from domestic and Communist pressures. Individual neutralist nations will not easily separate themselves from their partners even should they disagree with them on specific measures. The tone of the whole neutral bloc can thus easily be set by the most irresponsible of its members. While we should have patience with these attitudes, we must understand also that on any given issue most of the new nations will seek a position somewhere between the two contenders regardless of the merits of the disputes.

As a result, a premium will be placed on Soviet intransigence. When Mr. Khrushchev spoke to the General Assembly in September, 1960, a considerable portion of the American press claimed that he "had overplayed his hand," that he had "alienated the uncommitted." His intemperance was contrasted with the sobriety and statesmanship of President Eisenhower. There is no doubt that Mr. Khrushchev was intemperate. It is less clear, however, whether in the long run his actions will not prove of considerable advantage to the U.S.S.R. The very violence of the attack on Mr. Hammarskjöld served as a warning to the new nations of the fate awaiting them should they displease the Communist countries too much. In any given crisis, therefore, the urgings of the new nations may be directed against us, not because they disagree with our position but because opposition to us carries few risks. Conversely, the virulence of Communist reaction to any criticism causes the uncommitted to behave with great circumspection in opposing Communist policies.

The speeches in the General Assembly of 1960 by such leaders as Nasser, Sukarno, Nkrumah or even Nehru illustrate this point. The attacks on the West were pointed and direct; those on the Communist bloc circumspect and highly ambiguous. Almost every speech by these leaders castigated Western imperialism. Not a single reference was made to the unprovoked Soviet threat against Berlin —not to speak of other Soviet policies in Eastern Europe. Nor did the uncommitted nations which were supposed to have been alienated by Mr. Khrushchev rush to the defense of the Secretary General.

Moreover, if one considers Soviet relations with the neutrals from the point of view of bargaining technique, Communist belligerence may not have been nearly as foolish as was often alleged. Since the new nations are not likely to support the position of either side completely, regardless of what arguments are presented, it may in fact be good negotiating tactics to start from extreme proposals. Then even if the new nations support Communist demands only partially, the Soviets can in effect add the pressure of the uncommitted to their own to realize at least part of their program. The requirements of maintaining formal neutrality force many leaders who have opposed the Soviet Union on one issue to support them on another. Thus at the 1960 session of the General Assembly, Mr. Nehru failed to support Mr. Khrushchev's proposal for change in the U.N. Charter with respect to the Secretary General. In return, he proposed organizational changes whose practical consequence came very close to meeting Mr. Khrushchev's aims. The danger then exists that Soviet brutality, coupled with the desire of the uncommitted to remain neutral above all else, can import into the United Nations the familiar Soviet diplomatic "rules," according to which the only changes of the *status quo* which prove acceptable are those which magnify the influence of Communism.

Conversely, by seeking to meet all the presumed wishes of the new nations we may force them to move away from us to demonstrate their independence. It would be ironical indeed if in seeking to approach them too closely we drove them in the direction of the Communist position.

World opinion is not something abstract which our diplomats must seek to discover and to which we then have to adjust. We have a duty not only to discover but to shape it. World opinion does not exist in a vacuum. It is compounded of many factors, including the imagination and decisiveness of our own policy. Many a leader from the uncommitted areas may well prefer a clear and firm United States position which gives him an opportunity to demonstrate his neutrality both internationally and at home to the almost desperate attempt to make him share responsibility for our actions.

This is not to say, of course, that independent action is desirable in itself. And like many dictators before him, Mr. Khrushchev may well overplay his hand. It does suggest, however, that when we are convinced of the correctness of our course we should pursue it, even if it does not gain the immediate approval of the uncommitted—particularly in fields such as disarmament and European policy, which are remote from the understanding or the concern of the new nations. If the uncommitted are to act as intermediaries there must be a position to mediate. Any other course throws on them or on the United Nations a responsibility which they will not be able to bear.

The crisis in the Congo illustrates this. Our objective of keeping the Cold War out of Central Africa was unexceptionable. But the measures adopted to achieve it were highly questionable. "Keeping the Cold War out of Africa" is an abstraction which must be given concrete application if it is to be meaningful. It could not possibly succeed without at least tacit agreement on some ground rules between us and the U.S.S.R. Instead of throwing all the responsibility on Mr. Hammarskjöld we should have come forward with a concrete charter of what we understood by the independence, the development and the neutrality of the Congo. This could then have been negotiated with the neutrals and the Communists. Instead we advanced vague resolutions which we left for the Secretary General to interpret, putting him into the position of assuming personal responsibility.

Though in this manner we achieved temporary tactical gains, we may well have mortgaged the future position of the Secretary General as well as that of the Congo. The motto of "Let Dag do it" became an evasion of a responsibility, at least part of which was ours. It may be argued, of course, that the Soviet Union was not interested in stability and would therefore not have accepted our charter. But quite apart from the fact that it would have been useful to make this evident, the course adopted forced the Secretary General to attempt to impose on the Communist countries a course of action highly distasteful to them. It was against all reason to expect them to accept from Mr. Hammarskjöld what we thought they would not even consider if made by us as a formal proposal.

Moreover, by not defining our position, we deprived the Secretary General of any real bargaining power. Rather than seeking to adjust conflicting views, he was forced to develop his own definition of stability. This had the practical consequence of bringing him into direct conflict with the Communist states and with some of the African countries as well. It is clear that the office of the Secretary General cannot survive the determined opposition of the Communist bloc together with its sympathizers among the neutrals, and it should therefore never be put into a position of seeming to be the sole originator of policy. This policy also encourages the African states to use the United Nations to extend their own influence—the Ghanese and Guinean troops in effect have taken advantage of the mantle of the United Nations to pursue their own national policies in the Congo.

In short, in a situation where a great deal depended on the ability to be concrete, our approach was uncertain, vague, and abstract. We proclaimed stability in circumstances where all criteria of judging it had evaporated, and we offered no others to take their place. The chief result was to sharpen the contest for Africa rather than to ameliorate it and to raise issues about the structure and operation of the United Nations which would have better remained muted. The slogan "strengthening the United Nations" can become a means for weakening the world organization.

In short, our role in relation to the new countries is much more complicated than engaging in a popularity contest for their favor. We must show sympathy and support for their efforts to realize their economic aspirations—to an extent considerably beyond our current contribution. We must respect their desire to stand aloof from many of the disputes which divide the world. On many issues we can work closely with the new nations and on all issues they are entitled to understanding and sympathy. But we must not build our policies on illusions. Neither economic assistance nor respect for neutrality should imply the expectation of short-term political support—nor the hidden motive that the way to win the new nations over to our side is to make a cult of their non-commitment. Painful as it may be, *some* situations are conceivable where we may have a duty to act without the support of the new nations, and perhaps even with some of them opposing us.

Though we of course prefer to be popular, we cannot gear all our policies to an attempt to curry the favor of the new nations. We cannot undermine our security for illusory propaganda victories, because the safety of even the uncommitted depends on our unimpaired strength—whether they realize it or not. As for the uncommitted, they cannot eat their cake and have it too. They cannot ask us to respect their neutrality unless they respect our commitment. They cannot remain uncommitted and seek to act as arbiters of all disputes at the same time.

We thus face two contradictory dangers: we can demoralize the new nations by drawing them into the political relationships of the Cold War. But we can demoralize them also by making a cult of their non-commitment and acting as if only incorrect United States policies kept them from taking sides. And the latter danger may be the more insidious because it is more subtle. We have to face the fact that in major areas of the world constructive programs as well as defense depend largely on us. Many tasks, if not accomplished by us, will not be carried out at all. Compassion, understanding and help for the new nations must not be confused with gearing all policy to their pace. A cult of non-commitment will doom freedom everywhere.

As the strongest and most cohesive nation in the free world we have an obligation to lead and not simply depend on the course of events. History will not hand us our deepest desires on a silver platter. A leader does not deserve the name unless he is willing occasionally to stand alone. He cannot content himself simply with registering prevailing attitudes. He must build consensus, not merely exploit it.

There is involved here a question of style as well as of substance. Moderation, generosity, self-restraint are all desirable qualities in our relations with the new nations. But if we seem forever on the defensive, frantically striving to stave off disaster, we will have great difficulty convincing others that our measures were motivated by these qualities. Generosity and moderation and self-restraint are meaningful, after all, only if it is believed that another choice is available. As long as our measures seem to be the consequence of our fears, our policy will seem to be the result of panic rather than of sober thought. Our constant defensiveness and our erratic behavior may merely convince the new nations that we are doomed regardless of what they may think of the individual measures. Even more important than a change in policy, then, is a change in attitude. We will finally be judged not so much by the cleverness of our arguments as by the purposefulness and conviction, indeed the majesty, of our conduct.

VIII

THE POLICYMAKER
AND THE INTELLECTUAL

1. Administrative Stagnation

It would be comforting to believe that our foreign policy difficulties are due to specific mistakes of policy which can be reversed more or less easily. Unfortunately, the problem is more deep-seated. It is remarkable that during a decade of crisis few fundamental criticisms of American policy have been offered. We have not reached an impasse because the wrong alternative has been chosen in a "Great Debate." The alternatives have rarely been properly defined. The stagnation of our policy is often ascribed to the fact that our best people are not in government service. But the more serious and pertinent question is how qualified our eminent men are for the task of policymaking in a revolutionary period.

One of the paradoxes of an increasingly specialized, bureaucratized society is that the qualities rewarded in the rise to eminence are less and less the qualities required once eminence is reached. Specialization encourages administrative and technical skills, which are not necessarily those needed for leadership. Good administration depends on the ability to co-ordinate the specialized functions of a bureaucracy. The task of the executive is to infuse and occasionally to transcend routine with purpose. Administration is concerned with execution. Policymaking must address itself also to developing a sense of direction.

Yet, while the head of an organization requires a different outlook from that of his administrative subordinates, he must generally be recruited from their ranks. Eminence thus is often reached for reasons and according to criteria which are irrelevant to the tasks which must be performed in the highest positions. Despite all personnel procedures, and perhaps because of them, superior performance at the apex of an organization is frequently in the deepest sense accidental.

This problem, which exists in all complex societies, is especially characteristic of the United States. In a society that has prided itself on its "business" character, it is inevitable that the qualities which are most esteemed in civilian pursuits should also be generally rewarded by high public office. As a result, the typical Cabinet or sub-Cabinet officer in America comes either from business or from the legal profession. But very little in the experience that forms these men produces the combination of political acumen, conceptual skill, persuasive power, and substantive knowledge required for the highest positions of government.

The American business executive (or the lawyer coming from a business background) who is placed in a high policymaking position is rarely familiar with the substance of the problems into which he finds himself projected largely because, in the rise through the administrative hierarchy, the executive is shaped by a style of life that inhibits reflectiveness. One of the characteristics of a society based on specialization is the enormous work load of its top personnel. More energies are absorbed in creating a smooth-functioning administrative apparatus than in defining the criteria on which decisions are to be based. Issues are reduced to their simplest terms. Decision-making is increasingly turned into a group effort. The executive's task is conceived as choosing among administrative proposals in the formulation of which he has no part and with the substance of which he is often unfamiliar. A premium is placed on "presentations" which take the least effort to grasp—in practice usually oral "briefing." (This accounts for the emergence of the specialist in "briefings" who prepares charts, one-page summaries, etc.) The result is that in our society the executive grows dependent to an increasing extent on his subordinates' conception of the essential elements of a problem.

In such an environment little opportunity exists for real creativity, or even for an understanding of it. Creativity is not consciously discouraged—indeed, lip service is always paid to it—but it often goes unrecognized. In the private sector of our society the debilitating tendency of this bureaucratization is not always apparent because most executives can substitute long experience in their line of endeavor for reflectiveness. The goals of the business effort are relatively limited; they involve less the creation of a policy framework than successful operation within one—in itself a conciliatory procedure. But when the same method is applied to national policymaking, its limitations become dramatically apparent. On entering government, the executive soon discovers that he must pay a price for his lack of familiarity with his new environment.

Many a high official has to start governmental service with extensive briefing on almost every aspect—and sometimes the most elementary aspects—of the subject matter for which he is responsible. He therefore can rarely benefit from the strong will which is often his outstanding trait. Great decisiveness in a familiar environment may become arbitrariness or at least erratic behavior when the criteria of judgment seem elusive. Consciously or not, our top policymakers often lack the assurance or the conceptual framework to impose a sense of direction on their administrative staffs. Their unfamiliarity with their subject matter reinforces the already powerful tendency to think that a compromise among administrative proposals is the same thing as a policy.

The bureaucratization of our society reflects not only a growing specialization but also deep-seated philosophical attitudes all the more pervasive for rarely being made explicit. Two generations of Americans have been shaped by the pragmatic conviction that inadequate performance is somehow the result of a failure to understand an "objective" environment properly and that group effort is valuable in itself. The interaction of several minds is supposed to broaden the range of "experience," and "experience" is believed to be the ultimate source of knowledge. Pragmatism, at least in its generally accepted forms, produces a tendency to identify a policy issue with the search for empirical data. It sees in consensus a test of validity. Pragmatism is more concerned with method than with judgment. Or, rather, it seeks to reduce judgment to methodology and value to knowledge.

The result is a greater concern with the collection of facts than with an interpretation of their significance. There occurs a multiplication of advisory staffs and a great reliance on study groups of all types, whose chief test is unanimity. Disagreement is considered a reflection on the objectivity or the judgment of the participants. Each difficulty calls into being new panels, which frequently act as if nothing had ever been done before, partly, at least, because the very existence of a problem is taken as an indication of the inadequacy of the previous advice.

The problem is magnified by the personal humility which is one of the most attractive American traits. Most Americans are convinced that no one is ever entirely "right," or, as the saying goes, that if there is disagreement each party is probably a little in error. The fear of dogmatism pervades the American scene. But the corollary of the tentativeness of most views is an incurable inner insecurity. Even very eminent people are reluctant to stand alone. Torn between the desire to be bold and the wish to be popular, they would like to see their boldness certified, as it were, by general approbation. Philosophical conviction and psychological bias thus combine to produce in and out of government a penchant for policymaking by committee. The obvious insurance against the possibility of error is to obtain as many opinions as possible. And unanimity is important, in that its absence is a standing reminder of the tentativeness of the course adopted. The committee approach to decision making is often less an organizational device than a spiritual necessity.

This is not to say, of course, that committees are inherently pernicious or that policy should be conducted on the basis of personal intuition. Most contemporary problems are so complex that the interaction of several minds is necessary for a full consideration. Any attempt to conduct policy on a personal basis inhibits creative approaches just as surely as does the purely administrative approach —witness the conduct of foreign policy by Secretary Dulles, whose technical virtuosity could not obscure the underlying stagnation.

The difficulty is not the existence of the committee system but the lengths to which reliance on it is pushed because of the lack of substantive mastery by the highest officials. When policy becomes identified with the consensus of a committee, it is fragmented into a series of *ad hoc* decisions which make it difficult to achieve a sense of direction or even to profit from experience. Substantive problems are transformed into adminstrative ones. Innovation is subjected to "objective" tests which deprive it of spontaneity. "Policy planning" becomes the projection of familiar problems into the future. Momentum is confused with purpose. There is greater concern with how things are than with which things matter. The illusion is created that we can avoid recourse to personal judgment and responsibility as the final determinant of policy.

The impact on national policy is pernicious. Even our highest policy bodies, such as the National Security Council, are less concerned with developing measures in terms of a well-understood national purpose than with adjusting the varying approaches of semi-autonomous departments. A policy dilemma indicates that the advantages and disadvantages of alternative measures appear fairly evenly balanced. (This leaves aside the question to what extent the committee procedure encourages a neutral personality to whom the pros and cons of almost any course of action always seem fairly even and who therefore creates artificial dilemmas.) But in assessing these alternatives the risks always seem more certain than the opportunities. No one can ever prove that an opportunity existed, but failure to foresee a danger involves swift retribution. As a result, much of the committee procedure is designed to permit each participant or agency to register objections, and the system stresses avoidance of risk rather than boldness of conception. The committee system is concerned more with co-ordination and adjustment than with purpose.

The elaborateness of the process is magnified by the tendency of advisors to advise. For silence may not imply a judgment on the idea under discussion; it may mean rather that the advisor is inadequate. Thus, the committee member is under pressure to speak whether he wishes to or not—indeed, whether he has anything to say or not.

The committee system not only has a tendency to ask the wrong questions, it also puts a premium on the wrong qualities. The committee process is geared to the pace of conversation. Even where the agenda is composed of memoranda, these are prepared primarily as a background for discussion, and they stand or fall on the skill with which they are presented. Hence, quickness of comprehension is more important than reflectiveness, fluency more useful than creativeness. The ideal "committee man" does not make his associates uncomfortable. He does not operate with ideas too far outside of what is generally accepted. Thus the thrust of committees is toward a standard of average performance. Since a complicated idea cannot be easily absorbed by ear—particularly when it is new —committees lean toward what fits in with the most familiar experience of their members. They therefore produce great pressure in favor of the *status quo*. Committees are consumers and sometimes sterilizers of ideas, rarely creators of them.

Unfortunately, not everything that sounds plausible is important. And many important ideas do not seem plausible—at least at first glance, the only glance permitted by most committees. Rapidity of comprehension is not always equivalent to responsible assessment; it may even be contrary to it.

The attitudes of our high officials and their method of arriving at decisions inevitably distort the essence of policy. Effective policy depends not only on the skill of individual moves, but even more importantly on their relationship to each other. It requires a sense of proportion and a sense of style. All these intangibles are negated when problems become isolated cases, each of which is disposed of on its merits by experts or agencies in the special difficulties it involves. It is as if, in commissioning a painting, a patron would ask one artist to draw the face, another the body, another the hands, and still another the feet, simply because each artist was particularly good in one category. Such a procedure of stressing the components would sacrifice the meaning of the whole.

The result is a paradox. The more intense the effort to substitute administration for conception, the greater is the inner insecurity of the participants. The more they seek "objectivity," the more diffuse their efforts become. The insecurity of many of our policymakers sometimes leads to almost compulsive traits. Because of the lack of criteria on which to base judgments, work almost becomes an end in itself. Officials—and other executives as well—tend to work to the point of exhaustion, as one indication that nothing has been left undone. The insecurity is also shown by the fact that almost in direct proportion as advisory staffs multiply they are distrusted by those at the top. Officials increasingly feel the need for "outside"—and therefore unbiased—advice. Memoranda that are produced within the bureaucracy are taken less seriously than similar papers that are available to the general public. Crucial policy advice is increasingly requested from *ad hoc* committees of outside experts, as, for example, the Gaither Committee on national defense or the Draper Committee on economic assistance or the Coolidge Committee on arms control.

These committees are often extraordinarily useful. They provide a fresh point of view. They can focus public discussion. They make possible the tapping of talent that would otherwise be unavailable, particularly in the scientific field. They may even galvanize the bureaucracy. Nevertheless, they rarely touch the core of the problem: to challenge the existing assumptions or to define a new sense of direction. This is because the assumption which calls the *ad hoc* committees into being is frequently mistaken. The assumption is that the obstacle to decisive policy has been the inability to resolve available facts into specific recommendations. But the lack of subtlety and comprehension of the top leadership is not much more amenable to outside committees than to the governmental variety because in the absence of criteria of judgment, advice often adds simply another element of confusion.

The result is a vicious circle: As long as our high officials lack a framework of purpose, each problem becomes a special case. But the more fragmented the approach to policy becomes, the more difficult it is to act consistently and purposefully. The typical pattern of our governmental process is therefore endless debate about whether a given set of circumstances is in fact a problem, until a crisis removes all doubts but also the possibility of effective action. The committee system, which is an attempt to reduce the inner insecurity of our top personnel, has the paradoxical consequence of institutionalizing it.

This explains to a considerable extent why American policy has displayed such a combination of abstractness and rigidity. The method of arriving at decisions places a greater premium on form than on substance. Thus, on any given issue some paper will be produced for almost any eventuality. But because policy results from what are in effect adversary proceedings, proposals by the various departments or agencies are often overstated to permit compromise or phrased vaguely to allow freedom of interpretation. In any case, what is considered policy is usually the embodiment of a consensus within a committee. The very qualities which make the consensus possible tend to inhibit sustained and subtle application. The statement is frequently so general that it must be renegotiated when the situation to which it is supposed to apply arises.

The rigidity of American policy is therefore often a symptom of the psychological burden placed on our policymakers. Policies developed with great inner doubt become almost sacrosanct as soon as they are finally officially adopted. The reason is psychological. The *status quo* has at least the advantage of familiarity. An attempt to change course involves the prospect that the whole searing process of arriving at a decision will have to be repeated. By the same token, most of our initiatives tend to occur during crisis periods. When frustration becomes too great or a crisis brooks no further evasion, there arises the demand for innovation almost for its own sake.

Yet innovation cannot be achieved by fiat. Crisis conditions do not encourage calm consideration. They rarely permit anything except defensive moves. Many ideas are first rejected in tranquil times because they are too far ahead of the thinking of the bureaucracy and then are accepted when a crisis produces the demand for a new approach, though it is now too late. Or else, they may be still relevant but rejected again because in the interim they have become "old hat."

The combination of unreflectiveness produced by the style of life of our most eminent people in and out of government, faith in administrative processes, and the conversational approach to policy has accounted for much of the uncertainty of our policy. It has led to an enormous waste of intellectual resources. The price we have paid for the absence of a sense of direction is that we have appeared to the rest of the world as vacillating, confused, and sometimes irrelevant.

It is sometimes argued that the characteristics described here are inseparable from the democratic process. But it surely is not inherent in a democracy that its most eminent people are formed by an experience which positively discourages political thinking and perhaps reflectivenes of any kind. In Great Britain, for example, the ablest young people have traditionally been drawn into political life. They have been exposed throughout their careers to a concern with problems very similiar to those faced when eminence is reached.

The balance between the private and public aspects of our life, which has been the subject of national debate with respect to our allocation of resources, may be even more important with regard to the conceptual priorities of our eminent men. If our ablest people cannot be brought to address themselves to problems of national policy throughout their lives, no organizational device will save them from mediocrity once they reach high office. Substantial policy cannot be improvised. A democracy cannot function without a leadership group which has assurance in relation to the issues confronting it. We face, in short, a test of attitudes even more than of policies.

2. THE POSITION OF INTELLECTUALS

How about the role of individuals who *have* addressed themselves to acquiring substantive knowledge—the intellectuals? Is our problem, as is so often alleged, the lack of respect shown to the intellectual by our society?

The problem is more complicated than our refusal or inability to utilize this source of talent. Many organizations, governmental or private, rely on panels of experts. Political leaders have intellectuals as advisors. Throughout our society, policy-planning bodies proliferate. Research organizations multiply. The need for talent is a theme of countless reports. What, then, is the difficulty?

One problem is the demand for expertise itself. Every problem which our society becomes concerned about—leaving aside the question of whether these are always the most significant—calls into being panels, committees, or study groups supported by either private or governmental funds. Many organizations constantly call on intellectuals for advice. As a result, intellectuals with a reputation soon find themselves so burdened that their pace of life hardly differs from that of the executives whom they counsel. They cannot supply perspective because they are as harassed as the policy makers. All pressures on them tend to keep them at the level of the performance which gained them their reputation. In his desire to be helpful, the intellectual is too frequently compelled to sacrifice what should be his greatest contribution to society—his creativity.

Moreover, the pressure is not produced only by the organizations that ask for advice; some of it is generated by the image the intellectual has of himself. In a pragmatic society, it is almost inevitable that the pursuit of knowledge for its own sake should not only be lightly regarded by the community but also that it should engender feelings of insecurity or even guilt among some of those who have dedicated themselves to it. There are many who believe that their ultimate contribution as intellectuals depends on the degree of their participation in what is considered the "active" life. It is not a long step from the willingness to give advice to having one's self-esteem gratified by a consulting relationship with a large organization. And since individuals who challenge the presuppositions of the bureaucracy, governmental or private, rarely can keep their positions as advisers, great pressures are created to elaborate on familiar themes rather than risk new departures.

The great value our society places on expertise may be even more inimical to innovation than indifference. Not only the executive suffers from overspecialization. The intellectual in this respect is often in the same situation. Panels of experts are deliberately assembled to contain representatives of particular approaches; a committee on military policy will have spokesmen for the "all-out war" as well as for the "limited war" concept. A committee on foreign policy will have spokesmen for the "uncommitted areas" as well as specialists on Europe. These are then expected to adjust their differences by analogy with the subcommittee procedure of the bureaucracy. Not surprisingly, the result is more often a common denominator than a well-rounded point of view.

This tendency is magnified by the conception of the intellectual held by the officials or organizations that call on him. The specialization of functions of a bureaucratized society delimits tasks and establishes categories of expectations. A person is considered suitable for assignments within certain classifications. But the classification of the intellectual is determined by the premium our society places on administrative skill. The intellectual is rarely found at the level where decisions are made. His role is commonly advisory. He is called in as a "specialist" in ideas whose advice is combined with that of others from different fields of endeavor on the assumption that the policymaker is able to choose intuitively the correct amalgam of "theoretical" and "practical" advice. And even in this capacity the intellectual is not a free agent. It is the executive who determines in the first place whether he needs advice. He and the bureaucracy frame the question to be answered. The policymaker determines the standard of relevance. He decides who is consulted and thereby the definition of "expertness."

The fact that the need for excellence is constantly invoked is no guarantee that its nature will be understood. Excellence is more often thought to consist of the ability to perform the familiar as well as possible than of pushing back the frontiers of knowledge or insight. The search for talent more frequently takes the form of seeking personnel for familiar tasks than of an effort to discover individuals capable of new and not yet imagined types of performance. The "expert" not uncommonly is the person who elaborates the existing framework most ably, rather than the individual charting new paths.

The contribution of the intellectual to policy is therefore in terms of criteria that he has played only a minor role in establishing. He is rarely given the opportunity to point out that a query limits a range of possible solutions or that an issue is posed in irrelevant terms. He is asked to solve problems, not to contribute to the definition of goals. Where decisions are arrived at by negotiation, the intellectual—particularly if he is not himself part of the bureaucracy —is a useful weight in the scale. He can serve as a means of filtering ideas to the top outside of organizational channels or as one who legitimizes the viewpoint of contending factions within and among departments. This is why many organizations build up batteries of outside experts or create semi-independent research groups, and why articles or books become tools in the bureaucratic struggle. In short, all too often what the policymaker wants from the intellectual is not ideas but endorsement.

This is not to say that the motivation of the policymaker toward the intellectual is cynical. The policymaker sincerely wants help. His problem is that he does not know the nature of the help he requires. And he generally does not become aware of the need until the problem is already critical. He is subject to the misconception that he can make an effective choice among conflicting advisors on the basis of administrative rules of thumb and without being fully familiar with the subject matter. Of necessity the bureaucracy gears the intellectual effort to its own requirements and its own pace; the deadlines are inevitably those of the policymaker, and all too often they demand a premature disclosure of ideas which are then dissected before they are fully developed. The administrative approach to intellectual effort tends to destroy the environment from which innovation grows. Its insistence on "results" discourages the intellectual climate that might produce important ideas whether or not the bureaucracy feels it needs them.

Thus, though the intellectual participates in policymaking to an almost unprecedented degree, the result has not necessarily been salutary for him or of full benefit to the officials calling on him. In fact, the two have sometimes compounded each other's weaknesses. Nor has the present manner of utilizing outside experts and research institutes done more than reduce somewhat the dilemma of the policymakers. The production of so much research often simply adds another burden to already overworked officials. It tends to divert attention from the act of judgment on which policy ultimately depends to the assembly of facts which is relatively the easiest step in policy formation. Few if any of the recent crises of U.S. policy have been caused by the unavailability of data. Our policymakers do not lack advice; they are in many respects overwhelmed by it. They do lack criteria on which to base judgments. And in the absence of commonly understood and meaningful standards, all advice tends to become equivalent.

In seeking to help the bureaucracy out of this maze, the intellectual too frequently becomes an extension of the administrative machine, accepting its criteria and elaborating its problems. While this, too, is a necessary task and sometimes even an important one, it does not touch the heart of the problem. The dilemma of our policy is not so much that it cannot act on what it has defined as useful—though this, too, happens occasionally—but that the standards of utility are in need of redefinition. Neither the intellectual nor the policymaker performs his full responsibility if he shies away from this essential task.

This does not mean that the intellectual should remain aloof from policymaking. Nor have intellectuals who have chosen withdrawal necessarily helped the situation. There are intellectuals outside the bureaucracy who are not part of the maelstrom of committees and study groups but who have, nevertheless, contributed to the existing stagnation through a perfectionism that paralyzes action by posing unreal alternatives. There are intellectuals within the bureaucracy who have avoided the administrative approach but who must share the responsibility for the prevailing confusion because they refuse to acknowledge that all of policy involves an inevitable element of conjecture. It is always possible to escape difficult choices by making only the most favorable assessment of the intentions of other states or of political trends. The intellectuals of other countries in the free world where the influence of pragmatism is less pronounced and the demands of the bureaucracies less insatiable have not made a more significant contribution. The spiritual malaise described here may have other symptoms elsewhere. The fact remains that the entire free world suffers not only from administrative myopia but also from self-righteousness and the lack of a sense of direction.

Thus, if the intellectual is to make a contribution to national policy, he faces a delicate task. He must steer between the Scylla of letting the bureaucracy prescribe what is relevant or useful and the Charybdis of defining these criteria too abstractly. If he inclines too much toward the former, he will turn into a promoter of technical remedies; if he chooses the latter, he will run the risks of confusing dogmatism with morality and of courting martyrdom—of becoming, in short, as wrapped up in a cult of rejection as the activist is in a cult of success.

Where to draw the line between excessive commitment to the bureaucracy and paralyzing aloofness depends on so many intangibles of circumstance and personality that it is difficult to generalize. Perhaps the matter can be stated as follows: one of the challenges of the contemporary situation is to demonstrate the overwhelming importance of purpose over technique. The intellectual should therefore not refuse to participate in policymaking, for to do so confirms the stagnation of societies whose leadership groups have little substantive knowledge. But in co-operating the intellectual has two loyalties: to the organization that employs him and to values which transcend the bureaucratic framework and provide his basic motivation. It is important for him to remember that one of his contributions to the administrative process is his independence, and that one of his tasks is to seek to prevent routine from becoming an end in itself.

The intellectual must therefore decide not only whether to participate in the administrative process but also in what capacity: whether as an intellectual or as an administrator. If he assumes the former role, it is essential for him to retain the freedom to deal with the policymaker from a position of independence, and to reserve the right to assess the policymaker's demands in terms of his own standards. Paradoxically, this also may turn out to be most helpful to the policymaker. For the greater the bureaucratization and the more eminent the policymaker, the more difficult it is to obtain advice in which substantive considerations are not submerged by or at least identified with organizational requirements.

Such an attitude requires an occasional separation from administration. The intellectual must guard his distinctive and, in this particular context, most crucial qualities: the pursuit of knowledge rather than of administrative ends and the perspective supplied by a non-bureaucratic vantage point. It is therefore essential for him to return from time to time to his library or his laboratory to "recharge his batteries." If he fails to do this, he will turn into an administrator, distinguished from some of his colleagues only by having been recruited from the intellectual community. Such a relationship does not preclude a major contribution. But it will then have to be in terms of the organization's criteria, which can be changed from within only by those in the most pre-eminent positions.

3. THE HIGHEST OF STAKES

ULTIMATELY the problem is not the intellectual's alone or even primarily. There is no substitute for greater insight on the part of our executives, in or out of government. Advice, however excellent, is not a substitute for knowledge. Neither Churchill, nor Lincoln, nor Roosevelt was the product of a staff. As long as our executives conceive their special skill to be a kind of intuitive ability to choose among conflicting advice on the basis of administrative or psychological criteria, our policy will be without a sense of proportion and a feeling for nuance. As long as our eminent men lack a substantive grasp of the issues, they will be unable to develop long-range policy or act with subtlety and assurance in the face of our challenges. In these circumstances, the policymaker's relation with the intellectual will produce frustration as often as mutual support. The executive, while making a ritual of consulting the intellectual, will consider him hopelessly abstract or judge him by his ability to achieve short-term ends. And the intellectual, while participating in the policymaking process, will always have the feeling that he never had a chance to present the most important considerations. The executives' lack of understanding of the nature of reflection and the administrative approach to policy cause them to place a premium on qualities in intellectuals which they can most easily duplicate in their own organization. It leads them to apply administrative criteria to the problems of creativity, thereby making it difficult to transcend the standards of the moment. The intellectuals' unfamiliarity with the management of men makes them overlook the fact that policymaking involves not only the clear conception of ideas but also their implementation.

The result is often a tendency on both sides to confuse policymaking with analysis—on the part of the policymaker as a means to defer difficult choices, on the part of the intellectual to acquire greater knowledge. However, policymaking, while based on knowledge, is not equivalent to analysis. Effective policy fits its measures to circumstances. Analysis strives to eliminate the accidental; it seeks principles of general validity. The policymaker is faced with situations where at some point discussion will be overtaken by events, where to delay for the sake of refinement of thought may invite disaster. Analysis, by contrast, can and must always sacrifice time to clarity; it is not completed until all avenues of research have been explored. The difference between the mode of policy and the mode of analysis is therefore one of perspective. Policy looks toward the future; its pace is dictated by the need for decision in a finite time. Analysis assumes an accomplished act or a given set of factors. Its pace is the pace of reflection.

The difficulty arises not from the analytic method but from the failure to relate it to the problems of the policymaker. The quest for certainty, essential for analysis, may be paralyzing when pushed to extremes with respect to policy. The search for universality, which has produced so much of the greatest intellectual effort, may lead to something close to dogmatism in national affairs. The result can be a tendency to recoil before the act of choosing among alternatives, which is inseparable from policymaking, and to ignore the tragic aspect of policymaking, which lies precisely in its unavoidable component of conjecture. There can come about a temptation to seek to combine the advantage of every course of action: to delay commitment until "all the facts are in," until, that is, the future has been reduced to an aspect of the past.

The solution is not to turn philosophers into kings or kings into philosophers. But it is essential that our most eminent men in all fields overcome the approach to national issues as an extra-curricular activity that does not touch the core of their concerns. The future course of our society is not a matter to be charted administratively. The specialization of functions turns into a caricature when decision making and the pursuit of knowledge on which it is based are treated as completely separate activities, by either executives or intellectuals. A way must be found to enable our ablest people to deal with problems of policy and to perform national service in their formative years. This is a challenge to our educational system, to the big administrative hierarchies, as well as to national policy.

In a revolutionary period, it is precisely the "practical" man who is most apt to become a prisoner of events. For what seems most natural to him is most in need of being overcome. It is most frequently the administrator who is unable to transcend the routine which has produced an impasse. For bureaucracies are designed to execute, not to conceive—at least not to conceive radical departures. They operate by a standard of average performance. Their effectiveness depends on the existence of some predictable norms. This confers great impetus when the task is technical or when the direction is known. In an age of upheaval, however, the routine which usually confers momentum generates insecurity. The standard operating procedure will clash with the requirements of creativity.

If a bureaucracy is to support and not to paralyze policy, it must have a leadership group conscious of two responsibilities: (1) to be vigilant that what is defined as routine applies in fact to the most frequent occurrences; (2) to take the responsibility for innovation. The specialization of functions on which a bureaucracy is based is meaningful only if the tasks assigned in fact correspond to the most usual challenges. Then the "ordinary" event can be dealt with by routine—a procedure established in advance of a given eventuality. Energies are freed for dealing with the unexpected or for creative acts. However, when the area of the unexpected becomes very large, the bureaucratic routine seems irrelevant to the tasks which eventually have to be mastered. Every problem becomes a special case. More energy is expended on adjusting the pattern of administration to reality than in developing a sense of direction. In a rapidly changing world, once successful patterns of action can become obstacles to effective policy.

The top leadership faces no more urgent responsibility than to combat the trends inherent in any highly elaborated society towards substituting routine for conception. The greater the seeming achievement, the heavier this duty. For the tragic aspect of history is that creativity is constantly in danger of being destroyed by success. The more effectively the environment is mastered, the greater is the temptation to rest on one's oars. The more an organization is elaborated, the easier it becomes to act by rote. Stagnation can then appear as well-being and blandness as wisdom. This is why creativity is usually at its height when society is sufficiently elaborate to keep choices from being random but the structure is not yet so over-whelming that the response verges on the mechanical. A society, if it is to remain vital, must be forever alert lest it confuse creativity with projecting the familiar into the future.

The United States is at a point in its historical development where it has mastered much of its physical environment. We can, there-fore, easily lose our adaptability in our satiety. The price we will pay for this will be all the higher for not having to be paid for a while. Earlier in our history, circumstances imposed the need for innovation. We must now work on treasuring our creativity de-liberately. Any society faces a point in its development where it must ask itself if it has exhausted all the possibilities of innovation inherent in its structure. When this point is reached, it has passed its zenith. From then on, it must decline, rapidly or slowly, but nonetheless inevitably. Only a heroic and deliberate effort can arrest narcissism and the collapse which starts at the moment of seemingly greatest achievement.

America is now at such a critical juncture. For a while longer we may be able to hold on to what we have and perhaps even extend our achievement by proceeding along familiar routes. None-theless, a turning point can prove decisive even though it is not easily recognizable. In the past some disaster—a depression or a war—usually made the need for innovation manifest. Our generation cannot afford a disaster, particularly in the international field. The question before America is whether it can muster the dedication and creativity *before* the worst has happened.

The issue may therefore turn on a philosophical problem de-scribed earlier. The overemphasis on "realism" and the definition of "reality" as being entirely outside the observer may produce a certain passivity and a tendency to adapt to circumstance rather than to master it. It may also produce a gross underestimation of the ability to change, indeed to create, reality. To recapture the ability and the willingness to build our own reality is perhaps our ultimate challenge.

The stakes could hardly be higher. The deepest cause of the inhumanity of our time is probably the pedantic application of administrative norms. Its symbol is the "commissar," the ideal type of bureaucrat, who condemns thousands without love and without hatred, simply in pursuance of an abstract duty. But we would do ourselves an injustice if we ignored that the commissar is not just a Soviet but a universal phenomenon—the Communists have simply encouraged its most extreme form. He is the leader whose goals are defined by his presumed understanding of historic processes outside of his control, the administrator whose world is defined by regulations in whose making he has had no part.

Our challenge is to overcome an atmosphere in which all sense of reverence for the unique and therefore the capacity for real innovation stands in danger of being lost. The obsession with safety and predictability must produce an attitude fearful of risk and striving to reduce everything, including man himself, to manipulable quantities. The way we face this challenge will determine the spontaneity of our national life, and the future of the concept of the dignity of the individual.

INDEX

"absolute" security, 148
accidental war, 24-25, 43, 46, 81; arms control and, 213, 285; blackmail and, 229-230; inspection system and, 227-229
accidents, types of, 228
Acheson, Dean, 177
Adenauer, Konrad, 207
administration, policymaking and, 340-348
aerial inspection, arms control and, 218
Africa, Cold War in, 337
aggression, deterrence against, 11-13; limited, see limited war; local, see local aggression; massive retaliation doctrine of, 14; mobile deterrent system and, 23-25; "price tag" for, 54; senselessness of, 59; technological change and, 13; vs. "uncertainty effect," 52; U.S. diplomacy and, 177-178
Air Force, U.S., "limited nuclear war" concept and, 82; vs. Navy on nature of targets, 28-29
airplanes, as retaliatory force, 18-19
air superiority, in missile age, 83-84
Alaska, defense of, as NATO analogy, 115
alliances and coalitions, deterrence and, 49-50; as security against attack, 45; stockpile "freeze" and, 254-255
allies, absence of retaliation threat among, 50-51
all-out war, after "first blow" by aggressor, 27-28; "catalytic" type, 241-243; Communist China's "residual manpower" following, 253; conceding of first blow in, 36-37; credibility of

threat in, 49, 67 (see also credibility); effect of in allies' defense contribution, 101-102; Europe's security vs., 102, 104, 107, 115; fear of in missile gap, 32; finite deterrence and, 36; futility of, 42, 104; graduated retaliation mistaken for, 68; initiative for shifted to Soviet Union, 107; inspection system and, 230; military policy leading to, 64; mutual invulnerability and, 41; as mutual suicide, 34; NATO strategy and, 105, 117, 124; negotiation as preventive of, 65; Nth country problem and, 240-244; outbreak of, 16, 42; as preferable to U.S. defeat, 68; senselessness of, 87; with Soviet Union or Communist China, 95-96; surprise attack and, 210; surrender preferred to resistance in, 64; tactical warning in, 237; technology and, 210-211 (see also technological change); threat of, 16, 26, 32, 55; uncertainty as deterrent in, 51-56; West's unpreparedness for, 98
American Academy of Arts and Sciences, 240, 242
analysis, vs. policymaking, 354-355
annihilation, risk of in surprise attack, 16
anti-ballistic missile, 271
anti-colonialism, 316, 319-320
anti-missile defense, 19, 259
Arab-Israel tension, 139, 212, 244
armament, see arms control
armed services, U.S., disagreement among over nature of targets, 28-29
arms balance, precariousness of, 25
arms control, 279-286; accidental war

Books written under the auspices of

THE CENTER FOR INTERNATIONAL AFFAIRS, HARVARD UNIVERSITY:

The Soviet Bloc: Unity and Conflict by Zbigniew K. Brzezinski
  (Harvard University Press, February, 1960)

The Necessity for Choice by Henry A. Kissinger
  (Harper & Brothers, January, 1961)

About the Author

HENRY A. KISSINGER attended George Washington High School in New York and then went to Harvard, where he received his Ph.D. From 1943 to 1946 he served in Europe with the United States Army and has been a consultant to various government boards and agencies.

During 1956 and 1957 Mr. Kissinger was director of the Special Studies Project, Rockefeller Brothers Fund, Inc., organizing the studies and writing several of the reports.

At Harvard, he is Associate Professor of Government, a faculty member of the Center for International Affairs, and Director of the Defense Studies Program. He is also Executive Director of the Harvard International Seminar, which began in 1951 and which is attended by leaders from many countries.

Mr. Kissinger's widely read book, *Nuclear Weapons and Foreign Policy,* grew out of a series of conferences held under the auspices of the Council on Foreign Relations. The volume was one of two books to receive the 1958 Woodrow Wilson Award, given annually to honor outstanding books in the fields of government and international politics.

Mr. Kissinger has written for many publications. He is also the author of *A World Restored: Castlereagh, Metternich and the Restoration of Peace, 1812-1822,* published in 1957.